The
A to Z of Victorian London

The
A to Z of Victorian London

Introductory Notes by
Ralph Hyde

LONDON TOPOGRAPHICAL SOCIETY
Publication No. 136
1987

ISBN 0 902087 24 X

Published for the London Topographical Society, 3 Meadway Gate, London NW11 7LA by Harry Margary, London in association with Guildhall Library, London

Printed in Great Britain by Headley Brothers Ltd The Invicta Press Ashford Kent and London

CONTENTS

NEW LARGE-SCALE

ORDNANCE ATLAS

OF

LONDON & SUBURBS

WITH

SUPPLEMENTARY MAPS,

COPIOUS LETTERPRESS DESCRIPTIONS,

AND

ALPHABETICAL INDEXES.

London:

Edited and Published by GEORGE W. BACON, F.R.G.S., 127, STRAND.

1888.

Title page for Bacon's *New Large-Scale Ordnance Atlas of London & Suburbs,* 1888. It is from this source that the maps and index for the present volume have been taken and adapted.

G. W. BACON AND HIS ATLASES OF LONDON

To speak of London as the capital of England merely would be an inadequate expression. London is something more even than the metropolis of an empire on which the sun never sets—it is the largest, most populous, and wealthy city in the world; it is the financial centre of the world.

With these words G. W. Bacon, FRGS, opened the introduction to his *New Large-Scale Ordnance Atlas of London & Suburbs* published in 1888. Bacon was proud of the London he lived in, proud too of the London atlas he was publishing. He celebrated the superiority of London over all other cities with a torrent of statistics. At the last census the population had totalled 3,816,483. Living within its bounds were more Scots than in Edinburgh, more Irish than in Dublin, and—a bit surprising this one—more Roman Catholics than in Rome. The streets of London were lit by 54,000 gas lamps fed by 5,000 miles of gas mains. The roads were being added to at a rate of thirty miles per year. London had 1,600 omnibuses and 8,000 cabs. The underground railways carried 110,000,000 passengers per year. Within seven miles of Charing Cross there were 250 miles of suburban railways. The Port of London attracted 20,000 vessels with a total tonnage of 6,500,000 each year. The *Post Office London Directory* was able to list 2,000 doctors, 6,000 barristers and solicitors, 1,000 architects, 2,000 beerhouse keepers, 1,700 dairymen, 1,300 butchers, 800 fishmongers, and 300 photographers. The London School Board—a body for which Bacon had special sympathy—was responsible for 5,500 teachers and had 300,000 children. One senses no anxiety in Bacon's recitation of statistics, no trace of fear of the 'infernal wen' or the city out of control. (Charles Booth's maps showing the extent of grinding poverty in London would begin to appear in the following year). In Bacon's description there is only pride and optimism. It is this which makes the maps in Bacon's atlas—the atlas we have utilised for this *A to Z of Victorian London*—invaluable. For Bacon's maps convey a quantity of useful information which is truly astonishing, and it is the volume of detail that makes them useful to the historian and fascinating for today's Londoners.

George Washington Bacon was born in 1830. At the age of thirty-two he established his firm at 48 Paternoster Row, a street of printers and publishers behind the Chapter House of St. Paul's Cathedral. The heading on the firm's early notepaper tells us that besides selling maps and atlases he sold sewing machines. At first Bacon & Co. described themselves as 'American Map Publishers and Importers. Bacon, with his very American name, had close American connections and interests. He acted as London agent for the American map publishers, J. H. Colton; his publications included a *Guide to America for the Capitalist, Tourist, or Emigrant; Bacon's Guide to American Politics; The Life and Administration of Abraham Lincoln;* and several maps showing the progress of the American Civil War. In 1866 Bacon was considered sufficiently respectable to be accepted into London's geographical establishment; in May of that year he was elected a Fellow of the Royal Geographical Society, Edward Stanford, London's principal mapmaker and Bacon's rival magnanimously acting as one of his sponsors. In the summer of 1867, however, the firm suffered a serious setback when Bacon and his partner, Francis Apperson, were declared bankrupt. An auction of Bacon's stock was held at Hodgson's Rooms in Chancery Lane on 5 September. The sale included seventy-six copies of a circular 'Pocket Map of London and Visitor's Guide', a large number of Colton atlases, and 270 stereo- and electro-types.

Bacon's bankruptcy did not bring about his permanent ruin. Two years later he is listed again in the *Post Office London Directory* at 337 Strand, opposite Somerset House, sharing premises with the National Temperance League and the mapmaker William Tweedie. (The site was cleared in 1900 for the building of Aldwych). By 1870 he had moved to 127 Strand, described in his advertisements as 'twenty doors west of Somerset House'. Number 127 stood on the south side of the street between Lancaster Place (then called Wellington Street) leading to Waterloo Bridge, and Savoy Street a few yards to the west of it. A branch of Horne's Mensware in Wellington House now stands on the spot. Bacon traded at this address until 1919 and then moved to Norwich Street, east out of Fetter Lane.

Mapmaking was never Bacon's sole interest. His sewing machines and guides to the American scene have been mentioned. The shopping sections of the guides that accompany his London maps give hints of other interests. Not only is Bacon listed under 'Maps and Atlases' but also under 'Domestic Machinery'. Whilst buying maps at 127 Strand one could also buy Bacon's Patent Domestic Gymnasium, patented by its inventor in October 1865. This equipment cultivated your strength, developed your muscles, and ensured perfect health. 'No home should be without one', warned Bacon. On 8

January 1868 he patented an improved version of the contraption—Bacon's Portable Gymnasium—which came in a box with one hundred illustrations, priced at one guinea. A trapeze bar with thirty-two coloured cuts and a swing adjustment were available as optional extras.

Didactic books and booklets flowed from 127 Strand—*Our Colds: How Caught, Prevented, and Cured; Breathing and Ventilation: Our Lungs and How to Preserve them; Keeping Young and Well;* and *A Practical Guide to Health and Longevity*—all written personally by Bacon. (Bacon lived to the age of ninety-two, incidentally). A National Temperance League spot map, 'The Modern Plague of London', used a Bacon publication to show the great rash of public houses in the capital.

Besides health and perhaps temperance Bacon was also involved in education. The Education Act of 1870 had made school attendance obligatory for all children between the ages of five and thirteen and many new schools were opened. Bacon published a variety of teaching aids—fraction diagrams, fruit cards for teaching numbers, bird charts, and botany charts. In 1894 he wrote to the London School Board offering to award £20 in prizes to those boys in the upper classes of the Board schools who produced the most perfect examples of map-drawing. In addition to receiving prize money the award winners would be offered employment at 127 Strand.

Now that we have looked at Bacon's life in skeletal outline and noted some of his marketing interests let us look at his London atlases, particularly at his *New Large-Scale Ordnance Atlas of London & Suburbs* of 1888 which we have adapted for the present atlas.

The first pocket street atlas of London was H. G. Collins' *Illustrated London with 7,000 References* published in 1844. This was made up of thirty-six maps, inconsistently orientated, and an excellent index. It was republished later in the same year as *London at a Glance* by Thomas Hodgson, who published an updated version in 1860. Darton & Hodge produced yet another edition of this atlas in 1862 for visitors to the International Exhibition. *London at a Glance* in due course had competition. Letts, Son & Co. brought out an atlas entitled *Hirschhorn's Business Map of London and Suburbs* in which business streets were distinguished by heavy lines. Alfred Boot in the 1880s published atlases based on 'The District Railway Map of London'.

Atlases of a larger format for the home or the office had a lineage reaching back to Ogilby and Morgan's survey of the City of London, 1676, which was published with a separate index volume. John Rocque's map of 1746 and Richard Horwood's of 1792-99 both had title pages and indexes and can be considered as atlases. So too can be James Wyld's eight-sheet 'London and its Environs', published with a title page in *c.*1849.

The basic requirement for a good London atlas in the nineteenth century was a good London map. G. W. Bacon had two that were suitable and these were utilised both for his pocket atlases and for his home and office atlases from the 1870s through to the early years of the twentieth century. In order to appreciate the maps in Bacon's *New Large-Scale Ordnance Atlas of London* one needs to know more about each of them.

The central area of London in Bacon's *New Large-Scale Ordnance Atlas of London & Suburbs* consists of thirty-four maps drawn on a scale of $9\frac{3}{8}$ inches to the mile. (Bacon always referred to these as his 'Nine Inch' maps). Though they do not carry the name of the original compiler and engraver the man in charge of compiling the maps and engraving them was Edward Weller, FRGS, a prolific and eminent cartographer who died four years before the atlas's publication. Originally the map was published by the *Weekly Dispatch* newspaper being issued between 6 January 1861 and 11 May 1862 in parts to its subscribers. The *Weekly Dispatch* map was well received by the public and in 1863 it featured with other *Weekly Dispatch* give-away maps in the *Dispatch Atlas*. In that year the plates were acquired by Cassell, Petter & Galpin of Belle Sauvage Yard, north out of Ludgate Hill. In September and October Cassell's issued it in parts with their *Illustrated Family Paper*.

The new owners of the 'Nine Inch' map put it to good use. 'Cassell's large map of London', they boasted, 'as well as being the largest is universally admitted to be the best map of London ever produced'. Cassell's were then canvassing publishers; their books were sold by representatives who went from door to door. The 1866 edition of their 'Immense Map of London', as they called it, was issued to subscribers either in weekly sheets or in monthly parts. In due course the maps built up into *Cassell's British Atlas*. For this edition of the map over 2,000 improvements and alterations were made to the plates; these included 900 new street names. Large areas of central London at this moment were being subjected to radical change. The Victoria Embankment, a new Blackfriars Bridge, Queen Victoria Street, and a new Smithfield Market were simultaneously being constructed, and preparations were under way for the building of the Holborn Viaduct and the new Law Courts in the Strand. The revision and correction of the map plates was carried out by John Dower, FRGS.

Between 1866 and 1871 the plates for the 'Nine Inch' maps were taken over by G. W. Bacon. Bacon extended the area covered by the map and used portions of it for maps of several London districts. The 'Nine Inch' map was also used to create a rival to Edward Stanford's 'Library Map of London and its Suburbs', unoriginally entitled 'Bacon's Library Map of London and Suburbs'. Only one copy of this has been located by the author; it clearly did not enjoy the popularity of Stanford's 'Library Map' which passed through at least twenty-one editions. But Bacon made full use of the map for his London atlases. The map updated features in his *Illustrated Complete Atlas*, 1871, and *Bacon's Large-Scale Map of London and Suburbs . . . with a Map of Twelve Miles Round London, and a Map of London in the Reign of Queen Elizabeth*, *c.*1877. (The Elizabethan map was a copy of the so-called 'Agas Map'). In 1879 he used the 'Nine Inch' map for *Bacon's New Ordnance Atlas of London & Suburbs*, and in 1888, of course, he used it for the *New Large-Scale Ordnance Atlas of London & Suburbs*. In both of the latter volumes four inch to the mile maps were used to extend the area covered way out into the environs.

Mercifully Bacon's 'Four Inch' map had a less complex history. In its most complete form it measured seven feet by six feet. It was marketed varnished, backed on cloth, and mounted on a roller. Extensions to Epsom and Croydon were available. In the *Catalogue of Bacon's Maps, Atlases, and Globes*, published in 1912, Bacon recommends his 'Four Inch' map to large business houses 'whose travellers cover the whole of London . . . It can be made', he explains, 'to embrace any desired area, and coloured to suit any particular requirement'. Areas of the map were used as plates in Kelly's local directories, and for 'Bacon's New Map of North London and Suburbs' and 'Bacon's New Map of South London and Suburbs'. The various 'Four Inch' Bacon maps for central London were given the common title, 'Bacon's New Map of London Divided into Half Mile Squares and Circles'. The map was also used in putting together a number of portable and quarto atlases, either by itself or, as in the case of the *New Large-Scale Ordnance Map of London & Suburbs*, with the 'Nine Inch' maps.

The London shown in the 'Nine Inch' maps in Bacon's atlas is no longer the town undergoing major redevelopment and upheaval. Nevertheless improvements of some significance were taking place. Victoria Tower Gardens immediately south of the Houses of Parliament, laid out between 1881 and 1882, are shown, and so is the Brompton Oratory built in 1884 and the entire Inner Circle Underground completed in the same year. An important feature of the Dublin Exhibition of 1872 had been the Albert Palace. This was re-erected just south of Battersea Park in 1885 to provide a venue for concerts and exhibitions. The venture was a flop, and the building was demolished in 1894. It is clearly shown in Bacon's atlas. So too are two important new streets—Shaftesbury Avenue built in 1886, and Charing Cross Road built in 1877. There is also a new goods station—Somers Town—built adjacent to St. Pancras Station and opened in 1887. The gardens of the Royal Horticultural Society, just south of the Royal Albert Hall, were dismantled in 1882 but are still shown. There is thus no sign yet of the Imperial Institute constructed on the site in 1887. Cold Bath Fields House of Correction in Farringdon Road, demolished in 1887 to make way for the Mount Pleasant Sorting Office, is also still shown. On the other hand the site of the Westminster Bridewell behind Victoria Street has been cleared for the building of Westminster Cathedral. Old Battersea Bridge is still shown in position. Putney Bridge is represented by both the old wooden bridge and its replacement.

The quantity of detail shown on the 'Nine Inch' maps is remarkable. It includes county courts, hospitals, workhouses, wash houses, theatres, chapels, temperance halls, hotels, livery halls, commodity exchanges, taverns, working men's institutes, railway workshops, banks, newspaper offices, insurance societies, statues, and floating baths. A large proportion of these buildings are labelled. Some of the terraces are named. Very little of this information is to be found even on the largest-scaled Ordnance Survey plans of London in this period. The ground plan of the Palace of Westminster is provided. In York Street by the Wellington Barracks is a building marked 'Panorama'. This was the Niagara Hall which housed Philippoteaux's panorama of the Niagara Falls. Burford's Panorama north of Leicester Square was converted into a Catholic church in 1863. It is labelled 'Burford's Panorama' still but also 'R.C. Chapel'. There are rifle ranges on Wormwood Scrubs, and cricket grounds at Highgate, Finsbury Park, Victoria Park, St. John's Wood (Lord's), Battersea Park, West Brompton, and Deptford. Curiously the Oval Cricket Ground is not represented. The offices of the *Weekly Dispatch* and Cassell's are very distinctly labelled. So too is Bacon's shop—127 Strand.

The 'Four Inch' maps are especially useful in showing the villages around London as they were shortly before being engulfed by the metropolis. Many of the suburban branch railways that triggered off this drastic development are already shown in position. The 'Four Inch' maps are slightly more updated than their 'Nine Inch' companions. The position of Tower Bridge, opened 1894, is indicated, and so is the route of the City and South London Railway from Stockwell to King William Street which was opened in 1891. The Imperial Institute begun in 1887 and completed in 1893 is shown. The site of Cold Bath Fields House of Correction has been cleared, Old Battersea Bridge has been replaced by a new, wider bridge, and Old Putney Bridge has been removed leaving just the new bridge which would open in 1890.

G. W. Bacon died in 1922. In 1944 his firm was bought out by the Edinburgh mapmakers, W. & A. K. Johnston, the merged firm becoming Johnston & Bacon. Johnston & Bacon in 1969 were taken over by Geoffrey Chapman Ltd., a subsidiary of Crowell Collier & Macmillan of New York. One of the last publications to use the Johnston & Bacon imprint was a map entitled 'The City of London Through Five Centuries', published in 1972.

Bacon's output was prodigious. The British Library's map catalogue lists just under four hundred of the firm's maps and atlases. Many of these publications today are of marginal interest: they differ little from the publications of Bacon's rivals. Bacon's *New Large-Scale Ordnance Map of London & Suburbs,* 1888, with its 'Nine Inch' and 'Four Inch' maps, however, is in a class of its own. No other Victorian atlas of London matches it either for the quantity of detail shown or for the extent of the London area covered. Fifteen years ago Bacon's London atlases were common; today they appear only rarely on the second-hand market. The present publication now makes the most useful material in Bacon's 1888 atlas available to all.

FURTHER READING

GLANVILLE, Philippa, *London in Maps* (London: 'Connoisseur', 1972).

HOWGEGO, James, *Printed Maps of London, circa 1553-1850.* 2nd edition (Folkestone: Dawson, 1979).

HYDE, Ralph, *Printed Maps of Victorian London, 1851-1900* (Folkestone: Dawson, 1975).—The sources for the essay on G. W. Bacon in the present volume are to be found in this work.

PUBLISHERS' NOTE

The indexes in *The A to Z of Victorian London* reproduce in facsimile the indexes to the 'Nine Inch' and 'Four Inch' maps of Bacon's *New Large-Scale Ordnance Atlas of London & Suburbs*. Though extensive and therefore invaluable they do not carry all the place-names that feature on the maps. This applies particularly to named yards, courts, and alleys.

The maps in this volume have been photographically reduced in scale from Bacon's originals by a 5:4 ratio. For convenience we have continued to refer to them (as Bacon did) as the 'Nine Inch' and 'Four Inch' maps. Users will find it useful to know that the 'Nine Inch' maps are divided into half mile squares, and the 'Four Inch' maps into half mile squares and circles.

The original Bacon atlas used for this publication is the copy in the Guildhall Library. The key maps have been drafted by Mr. Rodney Fry.

READER'S NOTES

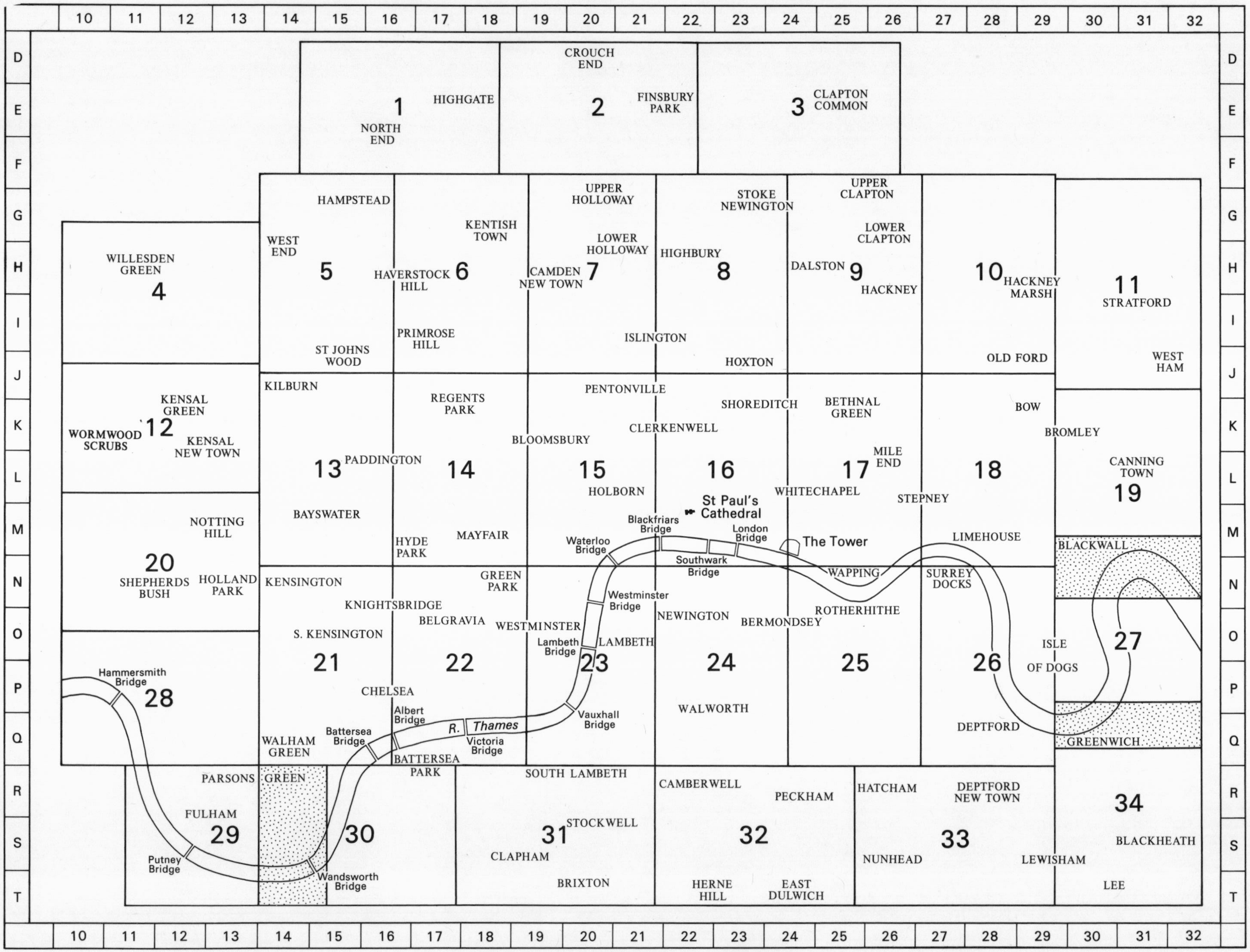
1 HIGHGATE NORTH END
2 CROUCH END FINSBURY PARK
3 CLAPTON COMMON
4 WILLESDEN GREEN
5 HAMPSTEAD WEST END ST JOHNS WOOD
6 KENTISH TOWN HAVERSTOCK HILL PRIMROSE HILL
7 UPPER HOLLOWAY LOWER HOLLOWAY CAMDEN NEW TOWN
8 STOKE NEWINGTON HIGHBURY ISLINGTON HOXTON
9 UPPER CLAPTON LOWER CLAPTON DALSTON HACKNEY
10 HACKNEY MARSH OLD FORD
11 STRATFORD WEST HAM
12 KENSAL GREEN WORMWOOD SCRUBS KENSAL NEW TOWN
13 KILBURN PADDINGTON BAYSWATER
14 REGENTS PARK HYDE PARK MAYFAIR
15 PENTONVILLE BLOOMSBURY HOLBORN
16 CLERKENWELL SHOREDITCH St Paul's Cathedral
17 BETHNAL GREEN MILE END WHITECHAPEL
18 BOW BROMLEY STEPNEY LIMEHOUSE
19 CANNING TOWN BLACKWALL
20 NOTTING HILL SHEPHERDS BUSH HOLLAND PARK
21 KENSINGTON S. KENSINGTON CHELSEA
22 KNIGHTSBRIDGE BELGRAVIA GREEN PARK
23 WESTMINSTER LAMBETH
24 NEWINGTON WALWORTH
25 BERMONDSEY ROTHERHITHE WAPPING
26 SURREY DOCKS DEPTFORD
27 ISLE OF DOGS GREENWICH
28
29 PARSONS GREEN FULHAM
30 WALHAM GREEN BATTERSEA PARK
31 SOUTH LAMBETH STOCKWELL CLAPHAM BRIXTON
32 CAMBERWELL PECKHAM HERNE HILL EAST DULWICH
33 HATCHAM DEPTFORD NEW TOWN NUNHEAD
34 LEWISHAM BLACKHEATH LEE
The Tower
R. Thames
Hammersmith Bridge
Putney Bridge
Wandsworth Bridge
Battersea Bridge
Albert Bridge
Victoria Bridge
Vauxhall Bridge
Lambeth Bridge
Westminster Bridge
Waterloo Bridge
Blackfriars Bridge
Southwark Bridge
London Bridge
10 11 12 13 14 15 16 17 18 19 20 21 22 23 24 25 26 27 28 29 30 31 32
D E F G H I J K L M N O P Q R S T

KEY TO THE 'NINE INCH' MAPS

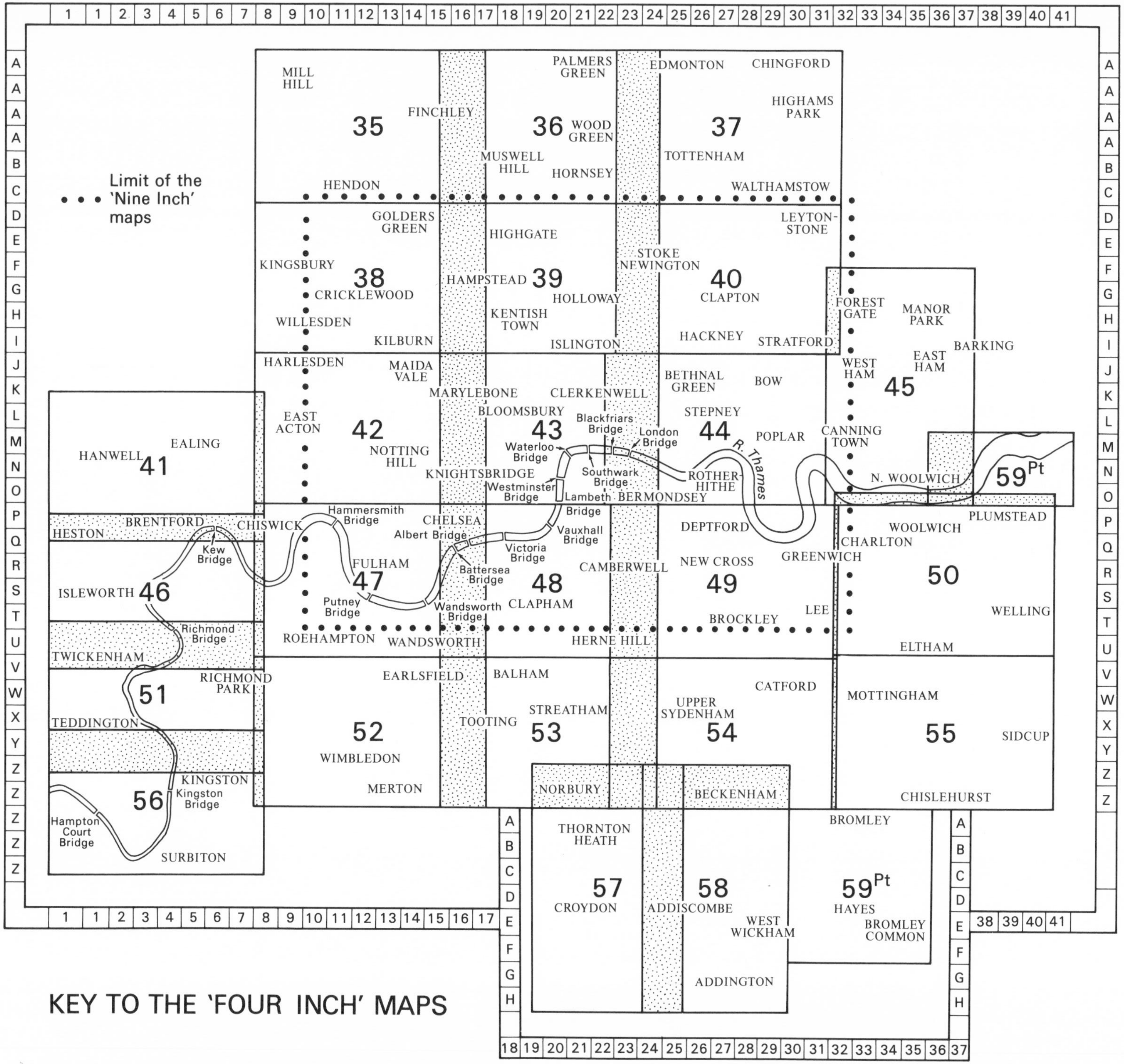

Limit of the 'Nine Inch' maps
35
MILL HILL
FINCHLEY
HENDON
36
PALMERS GREEN
WOOD GREEN
MUSWELL HILL
HORNSEY
37
EDMONTON
CHINGFORD
HIGHAMS PARK
TOTTENHAM
WALTHAMSTOW
38
GOLDERS GREEN
KINGSBURY
CRICKLEWOOD
WILLESDEN
KILBURN
39
HIGHGATE
HAMPSTEAD
HOLLOWAY
KENTISH TOWN
ISLINGTON
40
STOKE NEWINGTON
LEYTON-STONE
CLAPTON
HACKNEY
STRATFORD
41
HANWELL
EALING
42
HARLESDEN
MAIDA VALE
EAST ACTON
NOTTING HILL
43
MARYLEBONE
BLOOMSBURY
CLERKENWELL
KNIGHTSBRIDGE
Blackfriars Bridge
Waterloo Bridge
Westminster Bridge
Southwark Bridge
London Bridge
Lambeth Bridge
44
BETHNAL GREEN
BOW
STEPNEY
POPLAR
R. Thames
ROTHER-HITHE
BERMONDSEY
45
FOREST GATE
MANOR PARK
EAST HAM
BARKING
WEST HAM
CANNING TOWN
N. WOOLWICH
59Pt
46
BRENTFORD
HESTON
Kew Bridge
ISLEWORTH
Richmond Bridge
47
CHISWICK
Hammersmith Bridge
FULHAM
Putney Bridge
ROEHAMPTON
WANDSWORTH
Wandsworth Bridge
48
CHELSEA
Albert Bridge
Battersea Bridge
Victoria Bridge
Vauxhall Bridge
CAMBERWELL
CLAPHAM
HERNE HILL
49
DEPTFORD
NEW CROSS
GREENWICH
BROCKLEY
LEE
50
PLUMSTEAD
WOOLWICH
CHARLTON
WELLING
ELTHAM
51
TWICKENHAM
RICHMOND PARK
TEDDINGTON
52
EARLSFIELD
WIMBLEDON
MERTON
53
BALHAM
TOOTING
STREATHAM
54
CATFORD
UPPER SYDENHAM
55
MOTTINGHAM
SIDCUP
CHISLEHURST
56
KINGSTON
Kingston Bridge
Hampton Court Bridge
SURBITON
57
NORBURY
THORNTON HEATH
CROYDON
58
BECKENHAM
ADDISCOMBE
WEST WICKHAM
ADDINGTON
59Pt
BROMLEY
HAYES
BROMLEY COMMON

KEY TO THE 'FOUR INCH' MAPS

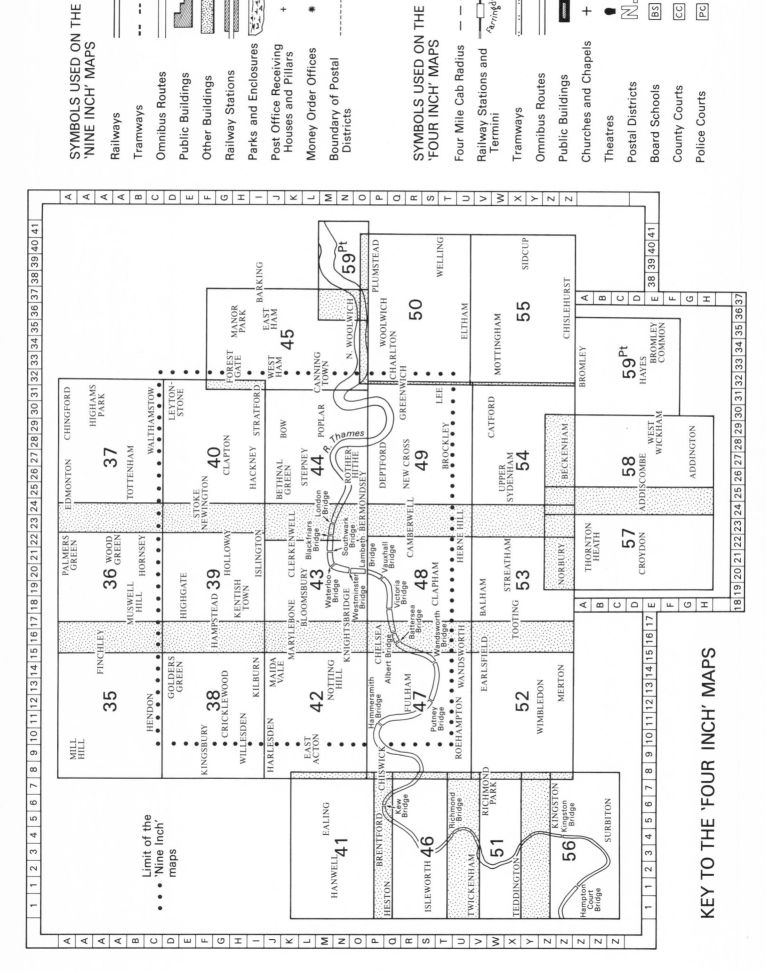

SYMBOLS USED ON THE 'NINE INCH' MAPS

- Railways
- Tramways
- Omnibus Routes
- Public Buildings
- Other Buildings
- Railway Stations
- Parks and Enclosures
- Post Office Receiving Houses and Pillars
- Money Order Offices
- Boundary of Postal Districts

SYMBOLS USED ON THE 'FOUR INCH' MAPS

- Four Mile Cab Radius
- Railway Stations and Termini (Farringdon St.)
- Tramways
- Omnibus Routes
- Public Buildings
- Churches and Chapels
- Theatres
- Postal Districts (N.)
- Board Schools (BS)
- County Courts (CC)
- Police Courts (PC)

1

For same area on 4 inch scale, see sheets 38-39
15
16
D
E
F
Spaniards Fm
Bishops Wood
Bunkers Hill
George Lane
Turners Wood
North Wood
Kenwood Farm
The Spaniards P.H.
Heath Fm
Manor Ho.
Golders Hill
School
NORTH END
The Elms
SPANIARDS ROAD
NORTH END ROAD
Heath Lodge
Reservoir
Hill House
Cedar Lawn
Childs Hill Well
Vale of Health
Sub. & Hampstead Heath Amateur Club
Hampstead Ponds
(New River Cos Water Wks)
Heath Brew
Jackstraws Castle
Castle Hotel
HAMPSTEAD HEATH
WEST HEATH ROAD
THE HEATH
Whitestone Pond
The Grange
G.W.Bacon, F.R.G.S. 127 Strand, London.
Adjoining 5 Sheet

17
18
Board Sch.
Gravelpit Wood
Southwood Hall
Church Road
All Saints Ch.
Highgate Coll. School
Bishops Rd.
Bloomfield Road
HIGHGATE
NORTH HILL
Grange Rd.
The Park
Lane
D
Southwood Ho.
Park Ho. Penitentiary
Jacksons Lane
Southwood Lawn
Oak Lodge
Broadlands Road
The Bull P.H.
Hornsey Local Bd.
Southwood Lawn Road
The Red Lion
The Limes
Southwood
Bishops Wood Rd.
Bishops Wood Road
Nat. Sch.
Highgate School Boarding Ho.
Cricket Ground
Southwood Place
Parsonage
North Grove
Baptist Chap.
LANE
Kenwood Towers
Site of Highgate
Police Sta.
Beechwood
Water Works
Pond Square
HIGH STREET
SOUTH GROVE
The Grove
Fitzroy Park
Bishops Gate
Fairseat
Adjoining 2 Sheet
HIGHGATE
The Limes
St. Michaels Church
Catacombs
Fitzroypark Farm
Southampton Lodge
WEST HILL
Highgate Lo.
Holly Ter.
Highgate Cemetery
Holly Lo.
Mortuary Chap.
St. Pancras Infirmary
Merton Lodge
Merton Lane
Bromwich Walk
Highgate Cemetery
HIGHGATE RISE
Millfield Lane
Highgate (New River Co. Water Wks.) Ponds
Southampton Villas
Swains Lane
F
St. Annes Church
Holly Village
Parsonage
St. Albans Rd.
Adjoining 6 Sheet
17
0 1 2 3 4 Furlongs
SCALE 0 10 Chains ¼ Mile 30 Chains ½ MILE

For same area on 4 inch scale, see sheet 39

19 20

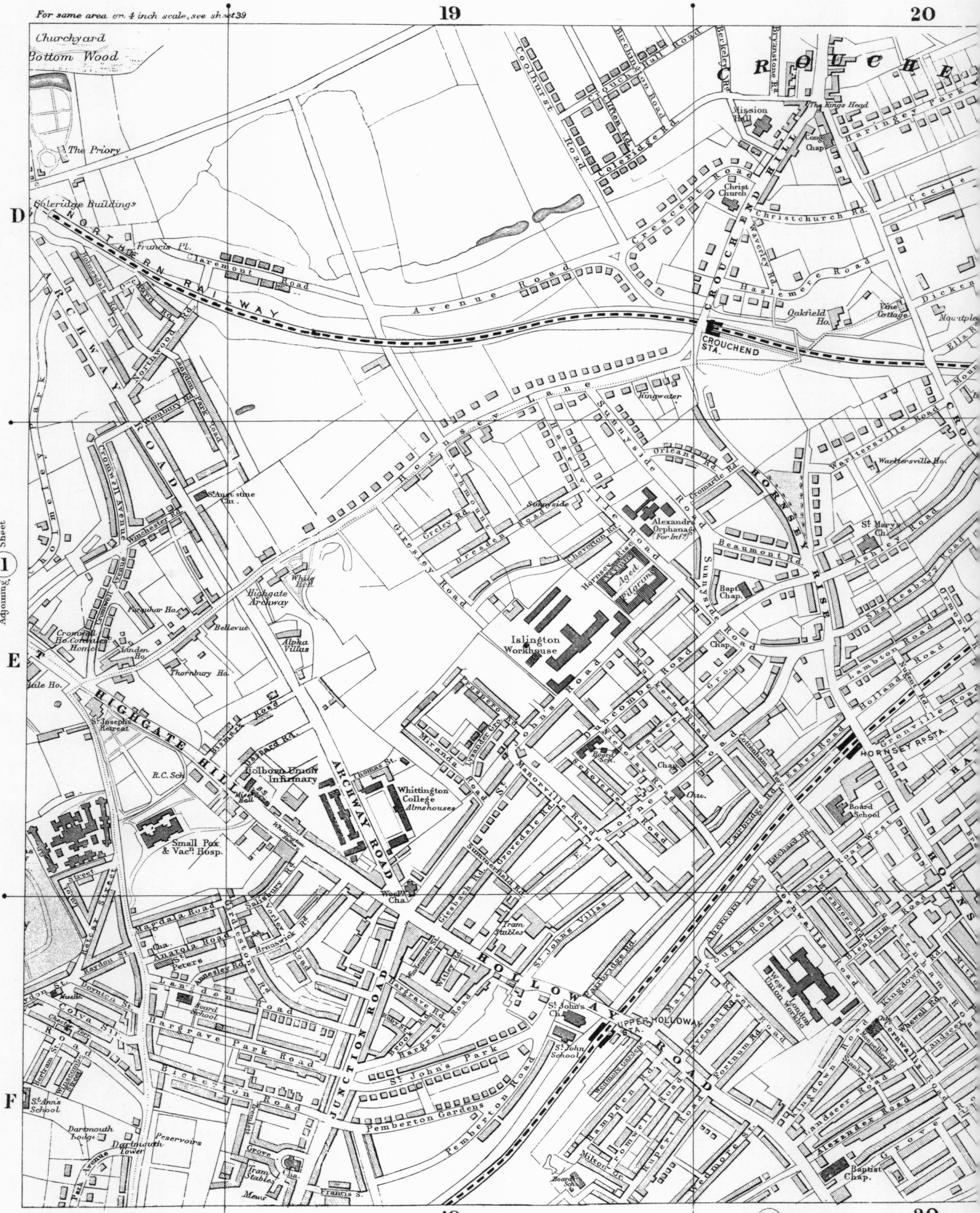
Churchyard
Bottom Wood
The Priory
Coleridge Buildings
NORTHERN RAILWAY
Francis Pl.
Claremont Road
Avenue Road
Crescent Road
Coleridge Rd.
Clifton Rd.
Colehurst Road
Birchington Road
Berkeley Rd.
Bryanstone Rd.
CROUCH
Mission Hall
The Kings Head
Cong. Chap.
Haringey Park
Christ Church
Christchurch Rd.
CROUCH END HILL
Haslemere Road
Waverley Rd.
Oakfield Ho.
Vine Cottage
CROUCHEND STA.
Hornsey Lane
Kingwater
Sunnyside
Sunnyside Road
Orleans Rd.
Cromartie Rd.
HORNSEY RISE
Warltersville Road
Warltersville Ho.
St. Mary's Ch.
Ashley Road
Shaftesbury Road
Beaumont Rd.
Bapt. Chap.
Alexandra Orphanage (For Inf.)
Aged Pilgrims
Islington Workhouse
Hornsey Rise
Greley Rd.
Dresden Road
Gresley Road
Ashmount
Hazelville Road
ARCHWAY ROAD
Northwood Rd.
Cromwell Avenue
Winchester Rd.
St. Augustine Ch.
Highgate Archway
White Hart
Alpha Villas
Farquhar Ho.
Bellevue
Cromwell Ho. Convalescent Home
Linden Ho.
Thornbury Ho.
HIGHGATE HILL
St. Joseph's Retreat
Bismarck Road
Despard Rd.
Holborn Union Infirmary
R.C. Sch.
Whittington College Almshouses
Thomas St.
ARCHWAY ROAD
Small Pox & Vacn. Hosp.
Prospero Rd.
Miranda Road
St. Johns Road
Manorville Road
Duncombe Road
Cottenham Road
Lambton Road
Holland Rd.
Granville Road
HORNSEY RD. STA.
Board School
Chap.
Chu.
Fairbridge Rd.
Magdala Road
Anatola Road
St. Peters
Annesley Rd.
Salisbury Rd.
Brunswick Rd.
Cheverton Rd.
HOLLOWAY ROAD
Hargrave Road
Hargrave Park Road
Junction Road
St. Johns Park
St. Johns Villas
Tram Stables
Bickerton Road
Pemberton Gardens
Pemberton Road
St. John's Ch.
UPPER HOLLOWAY STA.
St. John School
Abercorn Rd.
Marlborough Road
Cornwallis Road
West London Union Workho.
Blenheim Rd.
Kingdown Rd.
Whewell Rd.
Landseer Road
Alexander Road
Grove
Baptist Chap.
Hampden Rd.
Cromwell Road
Rupert Road
Wedmore St.
Milton Gr.
St. Ann's School
Dartmouth Lodge
Dartmouth Tower
Reservoirs
Francis S.
Mews

D
E
F

Adjoining (1) Sheet

19 Adjoining (7) Sheet 20

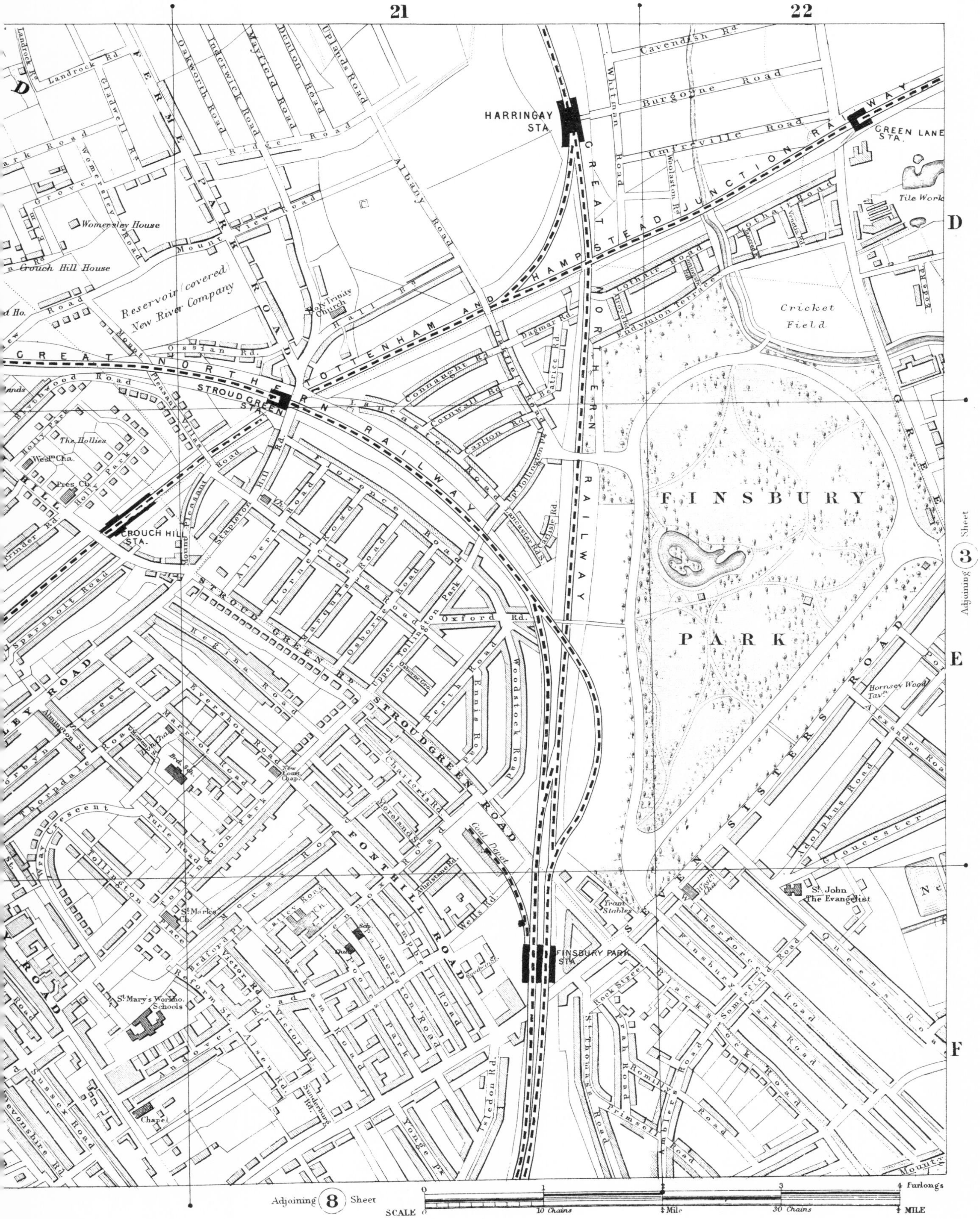
21
22
D
E
F
HARRINGAY STA.
GREEN LANE STA.
STROUD GREEN STA.
CROUCH HILL STA.
FINSBURY PARK STA.
GREAT NORTHERN RAILWAY
TOTTENHAM AND HAMPSTEAD JUNCTION RAILWAY
FINSBURY PARK
Cricket Field
Reservoir (covered) New River Company
Womersley House
Crouch Hill House
Holy Trinity Church
The Hollies
Tile Work
Hornsey Wood Tavn.
St. John The Evangelist
St. Marys Workho. Schools
Coal Depot
Tram Stables
Chapel
Cavendish Rd
Burgoyne Road
Umfreville Road
Whitman Road
Uplands Road
Denton Road
Mayfield Road
Inderwick Road
Oakworth Road
Landrock Rd
Gladwell Rd
Womersley Road
Ridge Road
Albany Road
Mount View Road
Ferme Park Road
Ossian Rd
Dagmar Rd
Endymion Terrace
Connaught Rd
Cornwall Rd
Carlton Rd
Oxford Rd.
Lancaster Road
Florence Road
Stapleton Hall Rd
Stroud Green Rd
Stroudgreen Road
Regina Road
Evershot Road
Marriot Road
Osborne Road
Woodstock Road
Perth Road
Ennis Road
Fonthill Road
Moray Road
Tollington Park
Turle Road
Sparsholt Road
Seven Sisters Road
Adolphus Road
Alexandra Road
Gloucester
Queens Road
Wilberforce Road
Somerfield Road
Blackstock Road
Finsbury Park Road
Romilly Road
St. Thomas's Road
Rock Street
Primsell
Victor Rd
Andover Rd
Alsen Rd.
Sussex Road
Devonshire Rd
Yonge Pk
Adjoining 3 Sheet
Adjoining 8 Sheet
SCALE
Furlongs
10 Chains
¼ Mile
30 Chains
½ MILE

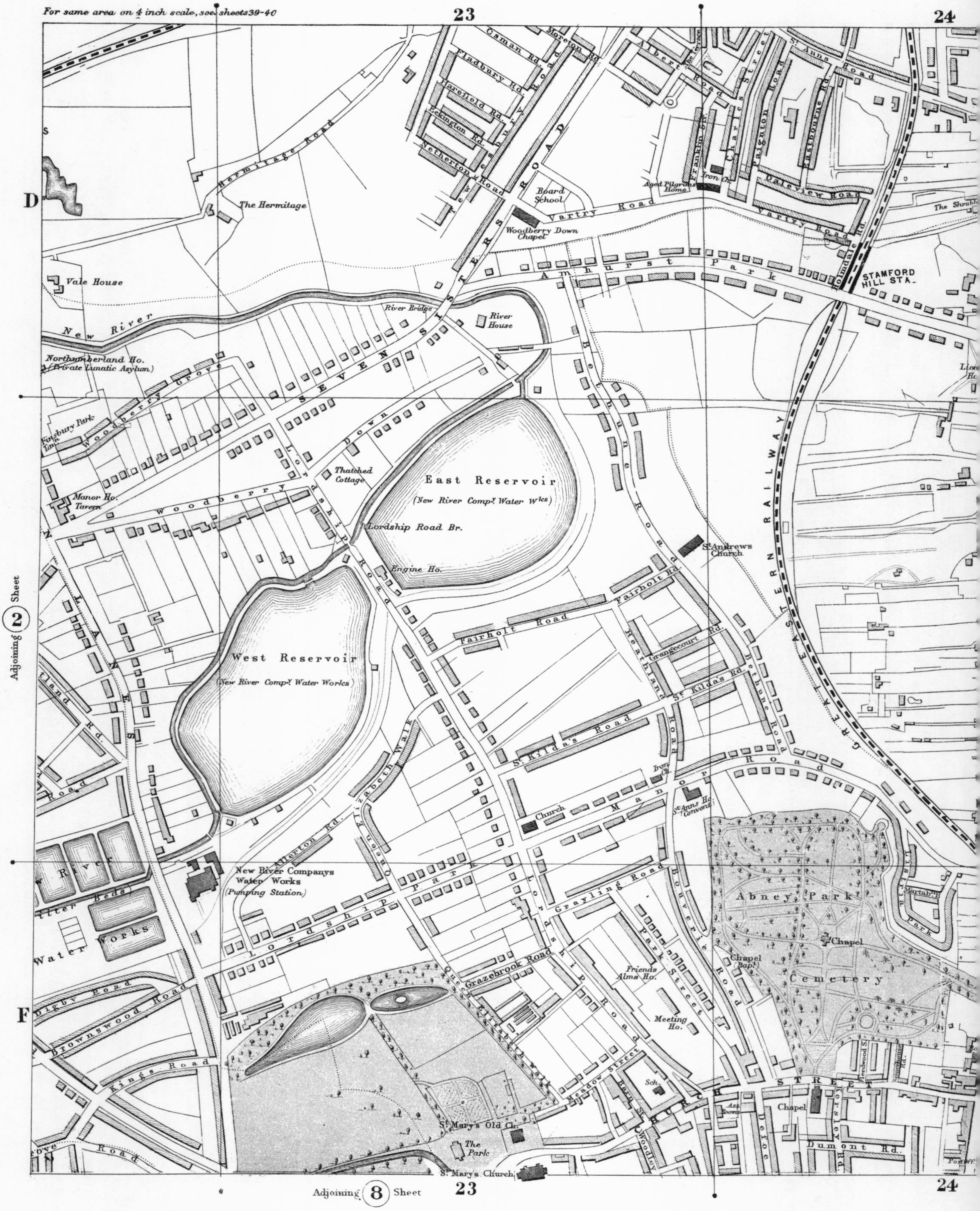
For same area on 4 inch scale, see sheets 39-40
23
24
D
F
Adjoining 2 Sheet
Adjoining 8 Sheet
23
24
Hermitage Road
The Hermitage
Vale House
New River
Northumberland Ho. (Private Lunatic Asylum)
Woodberry Grove
Finsbury Park Tavn.
Manor Ho. Tavern
Woodberry Down
Thatched Cottage
Lordship Road
Lordship Road Br.
Engine Ho.
East Reservoir
(New River Compy. Water Wks)
West Reservoir
(New River Compy. Water Works)
Seven Sisters Road
River Bridge
River House
Woodberry Down Chapel
Board School
Vartry Road
Amhurst Park
Netherton Road
Fladbury Rd.
Harefield Rd.
Pulford Rd.
Dateview Road
Eastbourne Rd.
Aged Pilgrims Home
Iron Ch.
STAMFORD HILL STA.
GREAT EASTERN RAILWAY
Bethune Road
St. Andrews Church
Fairholt Road
Fairholt Rd.
Grangecourt Rd.
St. Kilda's Rd.
St. Kilda's Road
Heathland Road
Manor Road
Church
Iron Ch.
St. Anns Ho. (Convent)
Elizabeth Walk
Allerton Rd.
Lordship Park
Grayling Road
New River Companys Water Works (Pumping Station)
Filter Beds
Water Works
Digby Road
Brownswood Road
Kings Road
Grove Road
Grazebrook Road
Queen Elizabeth's Walk
Friends Alms Ho.
Meeting Ho.
Park Street
Bouverie Road
Abney Park
Chapel
Chapel (Bapt.)
Cemetery
Church Street
Chapel
Dumont Rd.
St. Mary's Old Ch.
The Park
St. Mary's Church

25
26
D
E
F
Baileys Lane
Olinda Road
Ravensdale Road
Rookwood Road
Leabourne Rd.
Egerton Road
Castlewood Road
Craven Walk
Craven Lodge
CLAPTON COMMON
Summit Ho.
Portland Avenue
STAMFORD HILL
Gothic Hall
Clapton Terr.
Mews
St. Thomas's Ch.
Darenth Road
Grove Ho.
Avenue Ho.
Osbaldeston Road
UPPER CLAPTON ROAD
Spring Hill
Spring Lane
Spring Ho.
Willow Field Cottage
Springfield Ho.
Springfield Private Rd.
Hadham Ho.
Cazenoves Ho.
Grove Lane
Chapel Road
Clapton Hall
Stamford Hill Brewery
Cazenove Road
Burford Ho.
Warwick Road
STOKE NEWINGTON STA.
Alkham Rd.
Kyverdale Rd.
Fountayne Road
Winslade Rd.
Rossington St.
Northwold Road
Mount Pleasant
Mountpleasant Lodge
St. Mathews Church
Mount Pleasant
School
High Hill Ferry
RIVER LEA
High Bridge
Horse Shoe Pond
Coppermill Bn
Coppermill Stream
WALTHAMSTOW MARSHES
Walthamstow Mills
GREAT EASTERN RAILWAY
Inver Rd.
Detmold Rd.
Southwold
Comberme Rd.
CLAPTON STA.
Ickburgh Rd.
Evering Road
Reighton Road
Narford Road
Norcot Rd.
Benthal Rd.
Jenner Rd.
Sandford Pl.
STOKE NEWINGTON COMMON
Wes. Cha.
Ch.
Adjoining 9 Sheet
SCALE
0 1 2 3 4 Furlongs
0 10 Chains ¼ Mile 30 Chains ½ MILE

For same area on 4 inch scale, see sheet 38

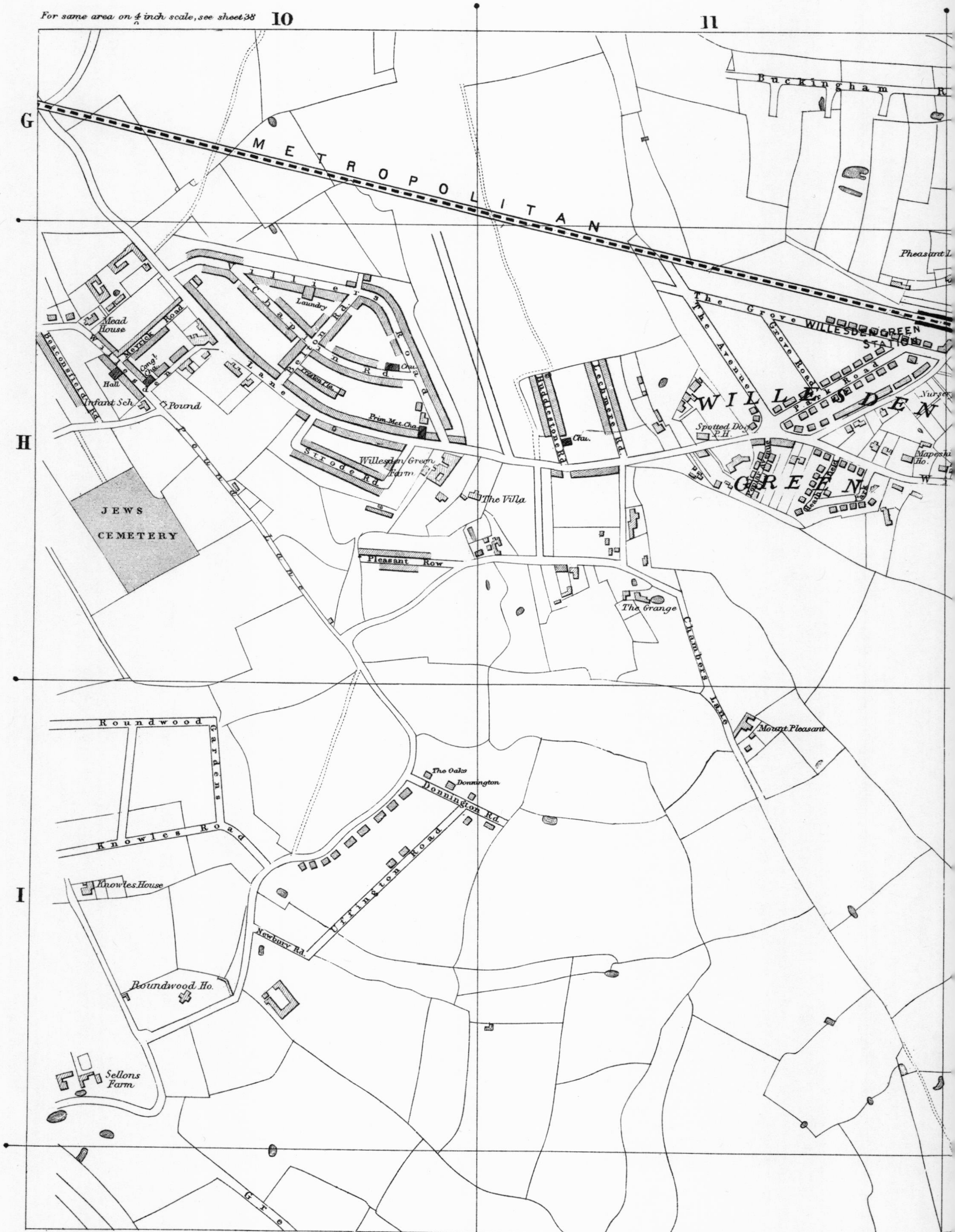
10
11
G
H
I
METROPOLITAN
Buckingham Rd
Pleasant
Villiers Road
Chapter Rd
Laundry
Meyrick Road
Mead House
Beaconsfield Rd
Congl. Cha.
Hall
Infant Sch.
Pound
Pound Lane
Prim. Met. Cha.
Strode Rd
Willesden Green Farm
The Villa
JEWS CEMETERY
Pleasant Row
Huddlestone Rd
Chu.
The Grange
The Grove
The Avenue
Grove Road
Park Road
WILLESDEN GREEN STATION
WILLESDEN
GREEN
Spotted Dog P.H.
Mapeshill Ho.
Chambers Lane
Mount Pleasant
Roundwood Gardens
Knowles Road
Knowles House
The Oaks
Donnington
Donnington Rd
Uffington Road
Newbury Rd
Roundwood Ho.
Sellons Farm
10
11
Adjoining 12

G.W. Bacon, F.R.G.S. 127 Strand, London.

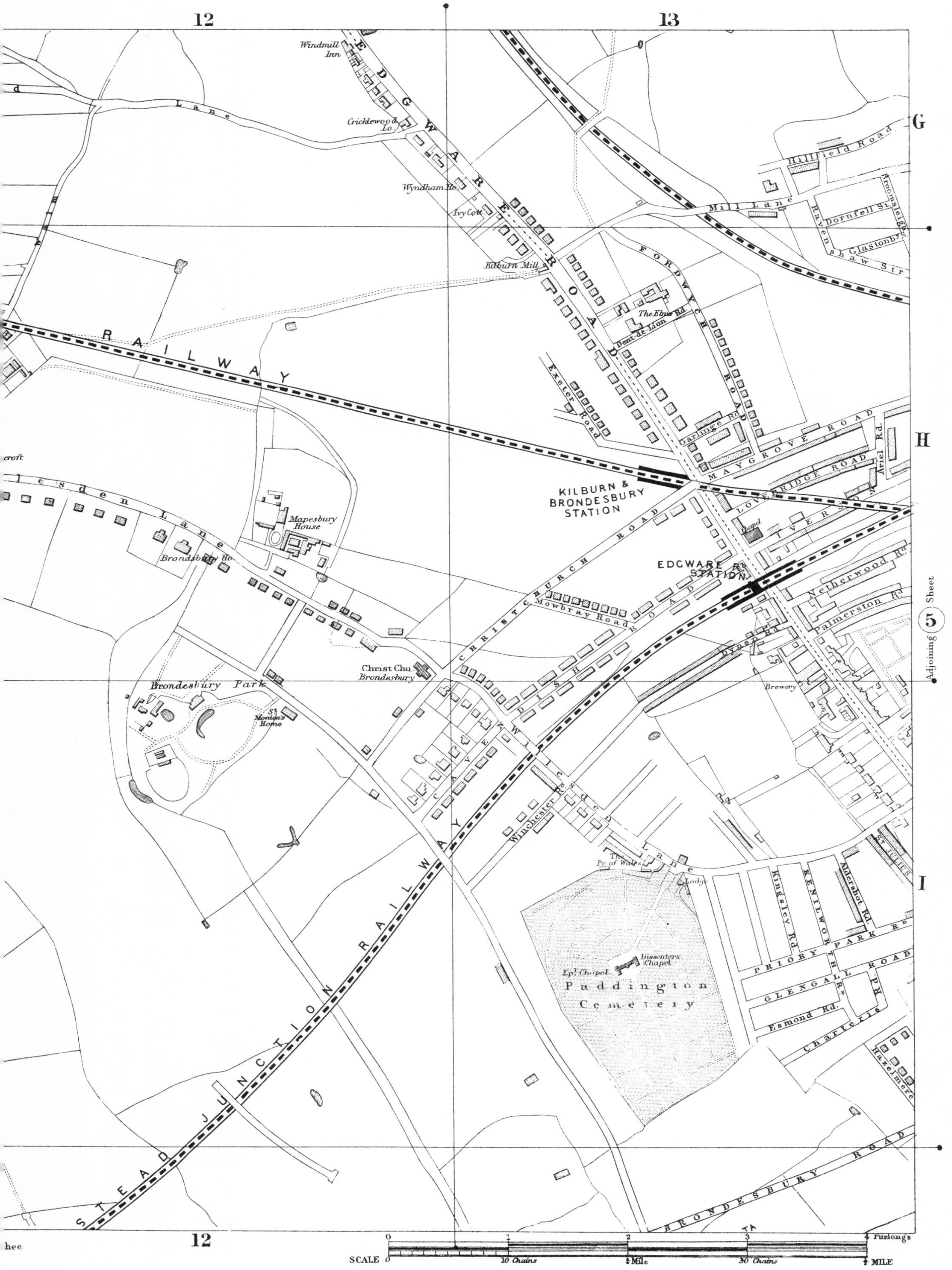
12
13
G
H
I
Windmill Inn
EDGWARE ROAD
Lane
Cricklewood Lo.
Wyndham Ho.
Ivy Cott.
Kilburn Mill
Hillfield Road
Mill Lane
Dornfell St.
Ravenshaw Str.
Glastonbury
Broomsleigh
FORDWYCH ROAD
The Elms Rd.
Dent-de-Lion Rd.
RAILWAY
Exeter Road
Garlinge Rd.
MAYGROVE ROAD
LOVERIDGE ROAD
Ariel Rd.
IVERSON
KILBURN & BRONDESBURY STATION
CHRISTCHURCH ROAD
Chapel
EDGWARE Rd. STATION
Netherwood Rd.
Palmerston Rd.
Adjoining Sheet 5
Mowbray Road
ROAD
Dyne Rd.
Brewery
Mapesbury House
Brondesbury Ho.
croft
Lane
Christ Chu. Brondesbury
Brondesbury Park
St. Monica's Home
Winchester Rd.
The Pr. of Wales
Lane
Lodge
Kingsley Rd.
KENILWORTH RD.
Aldershot Rd.
St. Julian's
PRIORY PARK Rd.
GLENGALL ROAD
Esmond Rd.
Charteris RD.
Hazelmere
Ep. Chapel
Dissenters Chapel
Paddington Cemetery
JUNCTION RAILWAY
STEAD
BRONDESBURY ROAD
12
SCALE
0
1
2
3
4 Furlongs
10 Chains
¼ Mile
30 Chains
½ MILE

HAMPSTEAD
WEST END
HAMPSTEAD HEATH
FINCHLEY ROAD
HIGH STREET
ROSSLYN STREET
HAVERSTOCK
Church Row
Grave Yard
St. John's Church
Greenhill Road
Ellerdale Rd.
Frognal
Holford Rd.
Heath Street
The Grove
Fortune Green
Temple Park
West Middlesex Water Wks.
New West End
Cannon Hill
Sumatra Road
Solent Road
Narcissus
Aldred Str.
Lyndhurst
Belsize Park
Belsize Cres.
Fitzjohns Avenue
Nutley Terrace
Canterbury Ho.
Treherne Ho.
West End Lane
Finchley Rd. Stan.
West End Stan.
West Hampstead Stan.
Hampstead Junction Railway
Midland Railway
Blackburn Road
Weech Rd.
Stone Yard
Oakhill Lodge
Branch Hill Lodge
Sailors Orphan Girls Home
Adjoining 1 Sheet
F
G
H
15
16

Sheet
6
I
J
Furlongs
MILE
Chains
SCALE
Strathray Gards.
Kings College Road
Harley Road
Crosfield Road
Winchester Rd.
AVENUE ROAD
ORDNANCE ROAD
St. JOHN'S WOOD BARRACKS
Saint Johns Wood Park
College Crescent
SWISS COTTAGE
FINCHLEY ROAD
Queens Terrace
Albion Road
Marlborough Hill
MARLBOROUGH ROAD STA.
LOUDOUN RD. STA.
All Saints Church
LOUDOUN ROAD
Fairfax Road
BOUNDARY ROAD
Fairhazel Gardens
Broadhurst Gardens
Canfields Gardens
BELSIZE ROAD
NORTH WESTERN RAILWAY
ALEXANDRA ROAD
ST. JOHNS WOOD
Adjoining 13 Sheet
Carlton Place
PRIORY ROAD
St. Georges Road
Cleve Road
Woodchurch Rd
Acol Road
ABBEY ROAD
KILBURN VALE
Hilltop Road
Gladys Rd.
Kylemore Rd
Lowfield Rd
Dynham Road
Kingsgate Road
Flaxley Road
Smyrna Rd
EDGWARE ROAD
KILBURN
LONDON & NORTH WESTERN RAILY.
Oxford Road
Signal Works
Chichester Road
Alexandra Road
Randolph Ga.
VICTORIA VILLAS
Alger Road
Kelson St
Sheet
4

F
G
H
19
18
17
Adjoining 2 Sheet
Adjoining 1 Sheet
For same area on 4 inch scale, see sheets 39, 43.
KENTISH TOWN
HAVERSTOCK HILL
HIGHGATE
DARTMOUTH PARK
DARTMOUTH PARK HILL
JUNCTION ROAD
HIGHGATE ROAD
FORTESS ROAD
KENTISH TOWN STAᴺ
TOTTENHAM & HAMPSTEAD
MIDLAND RAILWAY
HAMPSTEAD JUNCTION RAILWAY
GOSPEL OAK
MALDEN ROAD
WEEDINGTON ROAD
PRINCE OF WALES ROAD
HAVERSTOCK
Leighton Road
Leverton Street
Lismore Rd.
Savernake Rd.
Rona Rd.
Estelle Rd.
Constable Rd.
Shirlock Rd.
Roderick Rd.
Agincourt Rd.
Nassington Road
Tanza Road
South Hill Park Road
South Hill Park Gardens
Parliament Hill
Hampstead Ponds
Fleet Road
Small Pox Hospital
SOUTH END GREEN
The White Horse
Board School
Southampton Road
Maitland Park
Carlton Street
Bassett Street
Grafton Road
Alma Street
Cathcart Str.
Coal Depot
Engine Ho.
Oak Village
Haverstock Road
Upper Park Road
Park Road
Lawn Road
Haverstock Terrace

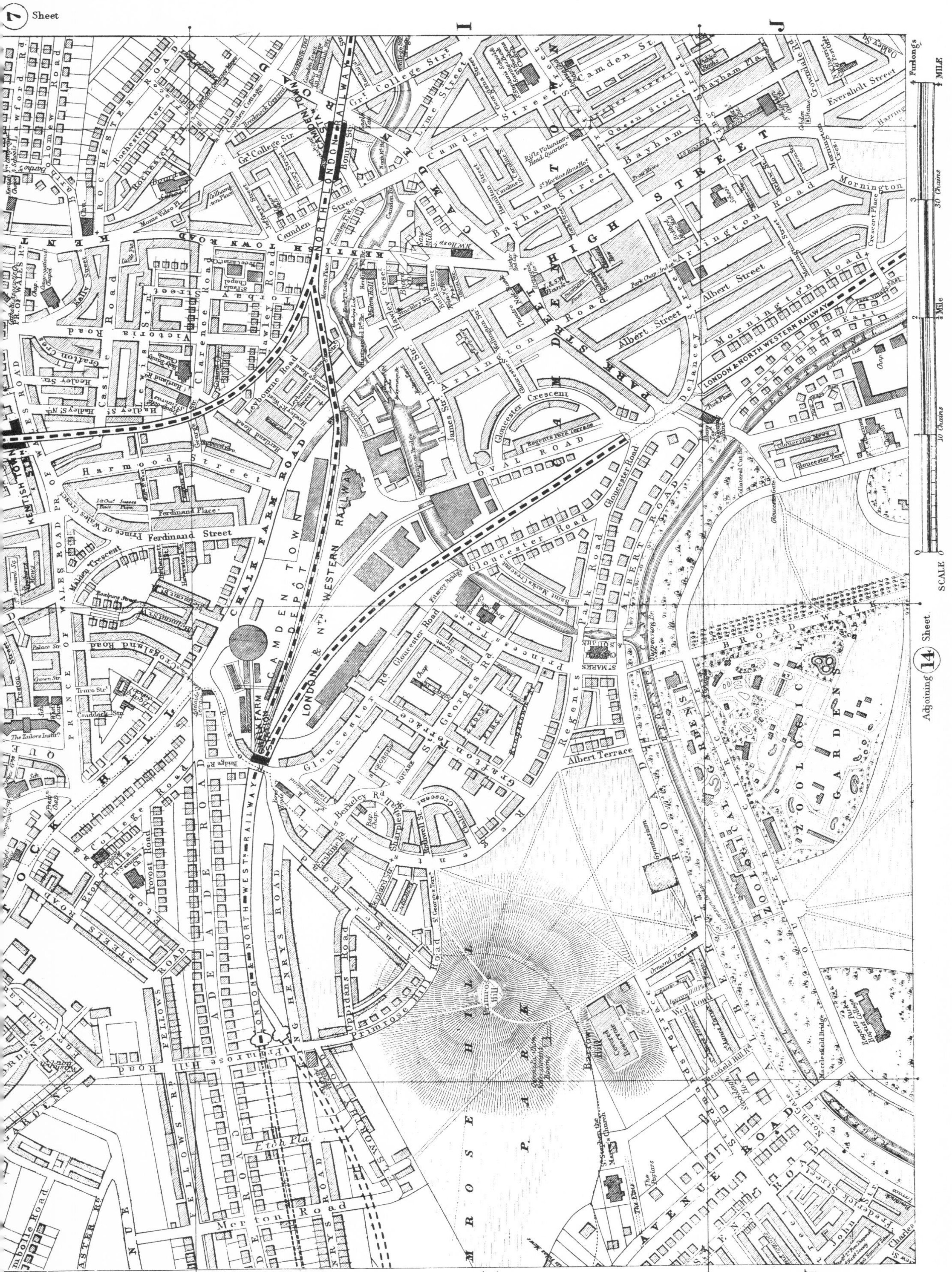
Sheet
Adjoining 14 Sheet
Sheet
SCALE
MILE
Furlongs
30 Chains
10 Chains
KENTISH TOWN ROAD
CAMDEN TOWN
HIGH STREET
PARK STREET
CAMDEN STREET
BAYHAM STREET
ARLINGTON ROAD
ALBERT STREET
MORNINGTON ROAD
LONDON & NORTH WESTERN RAILWAY
CHALK FARM ROAD
HARMOOD STREET
FERDINAND STREET
OVAL ROAD
GLOUCESTER CRESCENT
GLOUCESTER ROAD
ALBERT TERRACE
ADELAIDE ROAD
KING HENRYS ROAD
PRIMROSE HILL ROAD
MERTON ROAD
PRIMROSE HILL
REGENTS PARK
ZOOLOGICAL GARDENS
REGENTS CANAL

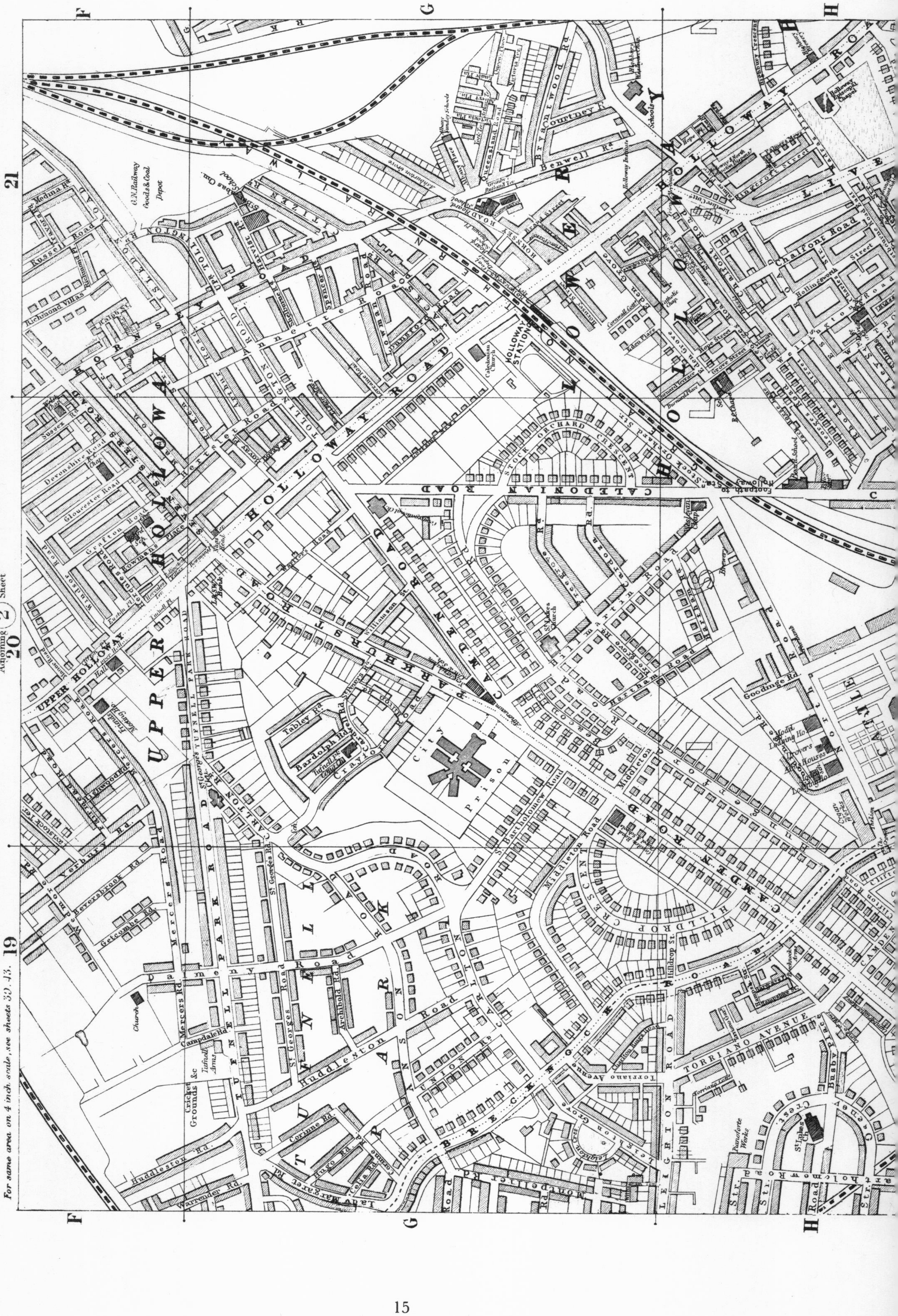
UPPER HOLLOWAY
HOLLOWAY ROAD
HOLLOWAY STATION
CALEDONIAN ROAD
CAMDEN ROAD
City Prison
TUFNELL PARK ROAD
STOCK ORCHARD CRESCENT
HILLDROP CRESCENT
TORRIANO AVENUE
Adjoining Sheet 2
For same area on 4 inch scale, see sheets 32, 43.

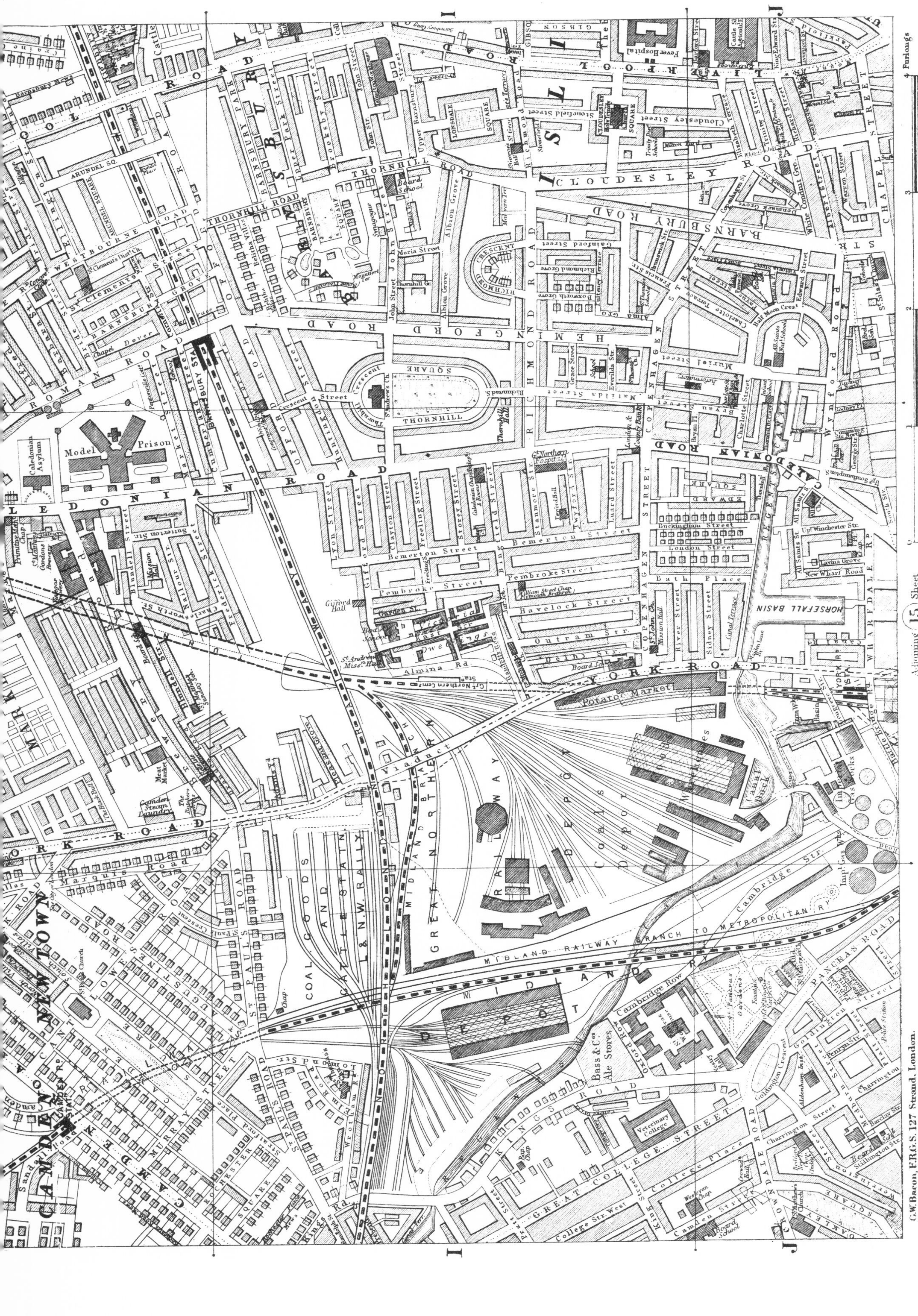
CALEDONIAN ROAD
YORK ROAD
THORNHILL ROAD
THORNHILL SQUARE
CLOUDESLEY ROAD
BARNSBURY ROAD
BARNSBURY PARK
HEMINGFORD ROAD
RICHMOND ROAD
COPENHAGEN STREET
LIVERPOOL ROAD
ISLINGTON
BARNSBURY
Model Prison
Caledonian Asylum
Bemerton Street
Pembroke Street
Havelock Street
Outram Str.
Potato Market
REGENTS CANAL
HORSEFALL BASIN
Canal Basin
GREAT NORTHERN RAILWAY DEPOT
COAL DEPOT
COAL GOODS AND CATTLE STATION L&NW RAILY
MIDLAND DEPOT
MIDLAND RAILWAY BRANCH TO METROPOLITAN RY
Cambridge Row
Bass & Co's Ale Stores
Veterinary College
KING'S ROAD
GREAT COLLEGE STREET
CAMDEN NEW TOWN
CAMDEN SQUARE
ST PAULS ROAD
MURRAY STREET
ROCHESTER SQUARE
PANCRAS ROAD
Imperial Gas Works
Adjoining 15 Sheet
SCALE
4 Furlongs
1 MILE
G.W.Bacon, F.R.G.S. 127 Strand, London.

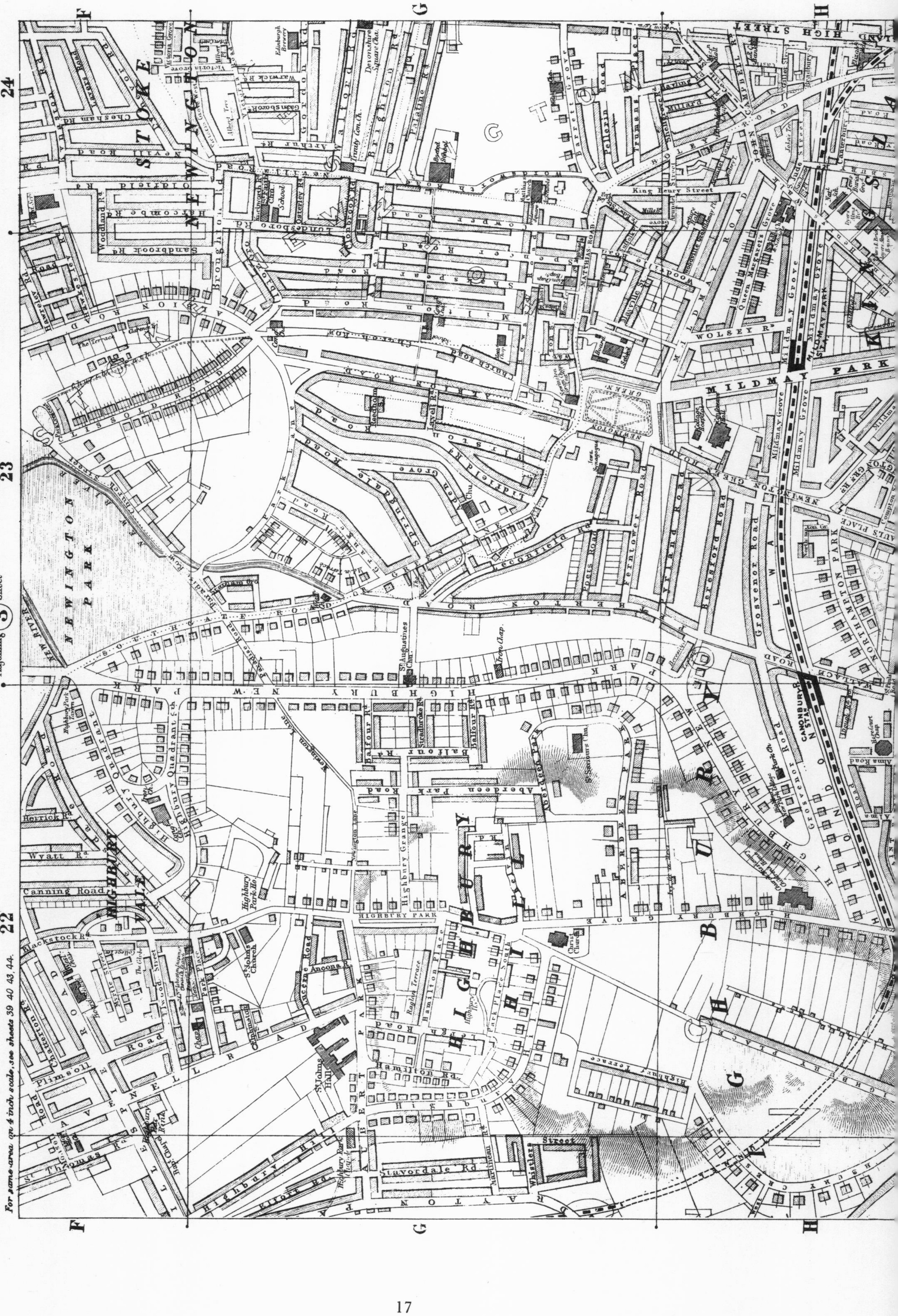
Adjoining Sheet 3
For same area on 4 inch scale, see sheets 39 40 43 44.
STOKE NEWINGTON
NEWINGTON PARK
HIGHBURY
HIGHBURY VALE
MILDMAY PARK
HIGHBURY NEW PARK
SOUTHGATE ROAD
Highbury Grove
CANONBURY STAT.N
Aberdeen Park Road
Mildmay Road

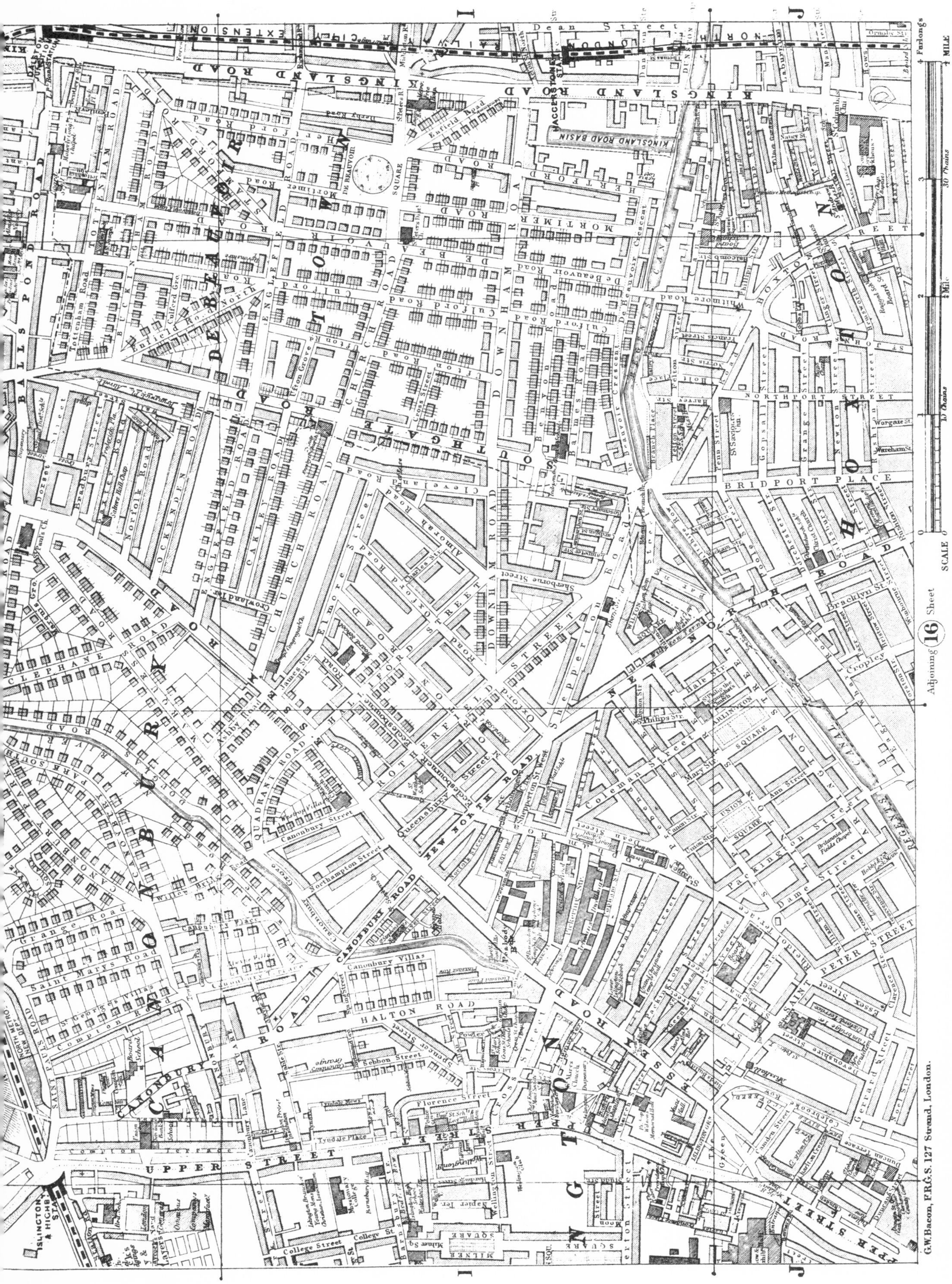
KINGSLAND ROAD
KINGSLAND ROAD BASIN
HAGGERSTONE STA.
DALSTON JUNCTION STATION
NORTH LONDON RAILWAY CITY EXTENSION
DE BEAUVOIR SQUARE
MORTIMER ROAD
HERTFORD ROAD
DOWNHAM ROAD
CHURCH ROAD
BALLS POND ROAD
SOUTHGATE ROAD
ESSEX ROAD
NEW NORTH ROAD
BRIDPORT PLACE
NORTHPORT STREET
HOXTON STREET
REGENTS CANAL
CANONBURY ROAD
CANONBURY VILLAS
HALTON ROAD
UPPER STREET
SAINT PETER STREET
PACKINGTON STREET
COLEMAN STREET
ROTHERFIELD STREET
QUADRANT ROAD
NORTHAMPTON STREET
GRANGE ROAD
SAINT MARYS ROAD
ISLINGTON & HIGHBURY STN.
SCALE
MILE
Furlongs
Chains
Adjoining 16 Sheet
G.W. Bacon, F.R.G.S. 127 Strand, London.

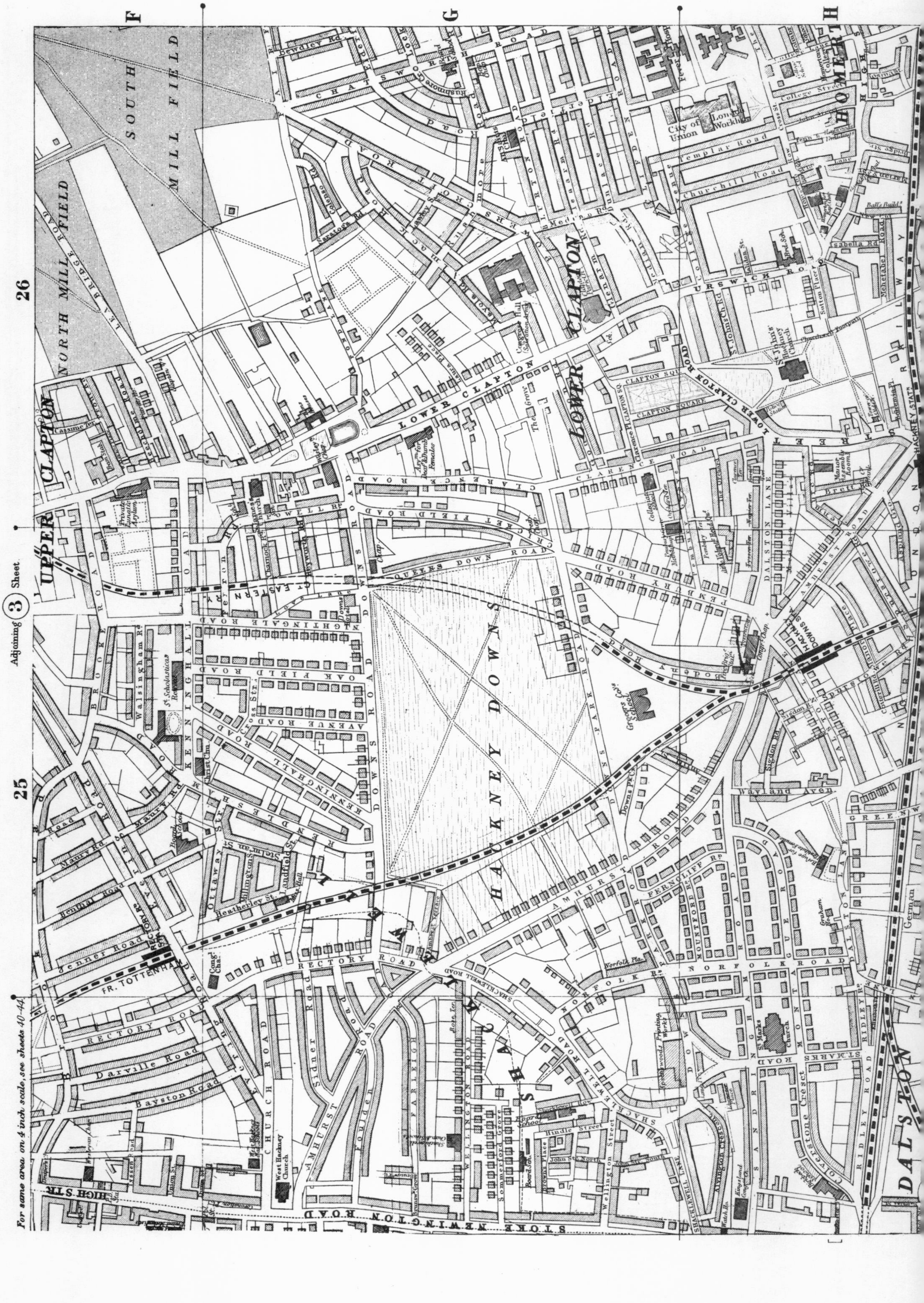
F
G
H
25
26
Adjoining 3 Sheet
For same area on 4 inch scale, see sheets 40–44
NORTH MILL FIELD
SOUTH MILL FIELD
UPPER CLAPTON
LOWER CLAPTON
HACKNEY DOWNS
DALSTON
STOKE NEWINGTON ROAD
LOWER CLAPTON ROAD
CLAPTON SQUARE
CLARENCE ROAD
PEMBURY ROAD
AMHURST ROAD
RECTORY ROAD
DOWNS ROAD
NORFOLK ROAD
Grocers' Co's School
West Hackney Church
St. Marks Church
St. John's Hackney Church
City of London Union Workhouse
Templar Road
Churchill Road
Urswick Road
Darville Road
Bayston Road
Jenner Road
Kenninghall Road
Nightingale Road
Shacklewell Road

Adjoining 10 Sheet
Adjoining 8 Sheet
Adjoining 17 Sheet
G.W.Bacon, F.R.G.S. 127 Strand, London.
SCALE
MILE
Furlongs
LONDON FIELDS
MARE STREET
Bethnal Green
Union Workhouse
Frampton Park Road
Navarino Road
Greenwood Road
Lansdowne Road
Queens Road
Richmond Road
Eleanor Road
Horton Road
London Terrace
Broadway
Haggerstone Road
Brunswick Street
Great Cambridge
Regents Canal
Imperial Gas Works
Homerton Terrace
Chatham Place
Victoria Park Road
Well Street
St Thomas Road
Shore Road
Sidworth St.
Woodland Street
Holly Street
Dalston Lane
Albion Square
Haggerstone
Dalston
St. Michaels & All Angels Ch.
Town Hall
Broughton Road
Albert Road
Lavender Grove
Malvern Road
Ash Grove
Pritchards Road
Whiston Str.
Laburnum Street
Clarissa Street
Pellows St. North

27
28
29
F
G
H
GREAT EASTERN RAILWAY
RIVER LEA
HACKNEY CUT
EAST LONDON WATERWORKS CANAL
East London Waterworks Bridge
Pond Lane Bridges
Brick Lock Bridge
Homerton Brick Lock
White Bridge
Homerton Road
Homerton Bridge
Marsh Gate Bridge
Marsh Road
Marsh Hill
Temple Mill Road
Temple Mill Bridge
White Hart
Wick Bridge
Wick Lane Bridge
Tar Works
Indiarubber Works
Presburg Str.
Oswald St.
Mandeville Street
Rock Rd.
Redwald Rd.
Glenarm Road
Dunlace Rd.
Clifden Road
Goldsmiths Oilcloth Works
Ashenden Rd.
Daubeney Road
Durrington Road
Pincey Rd.
GLYN ROAD
Cooperscale Road
Hackney Union
Infirmary
St. Barnabas Ch.
Church Terrace
Board School
Tyne Str.
HOMERTON STA.
HACKNEY

For same area on 4 inch scale, see sheets 40-44

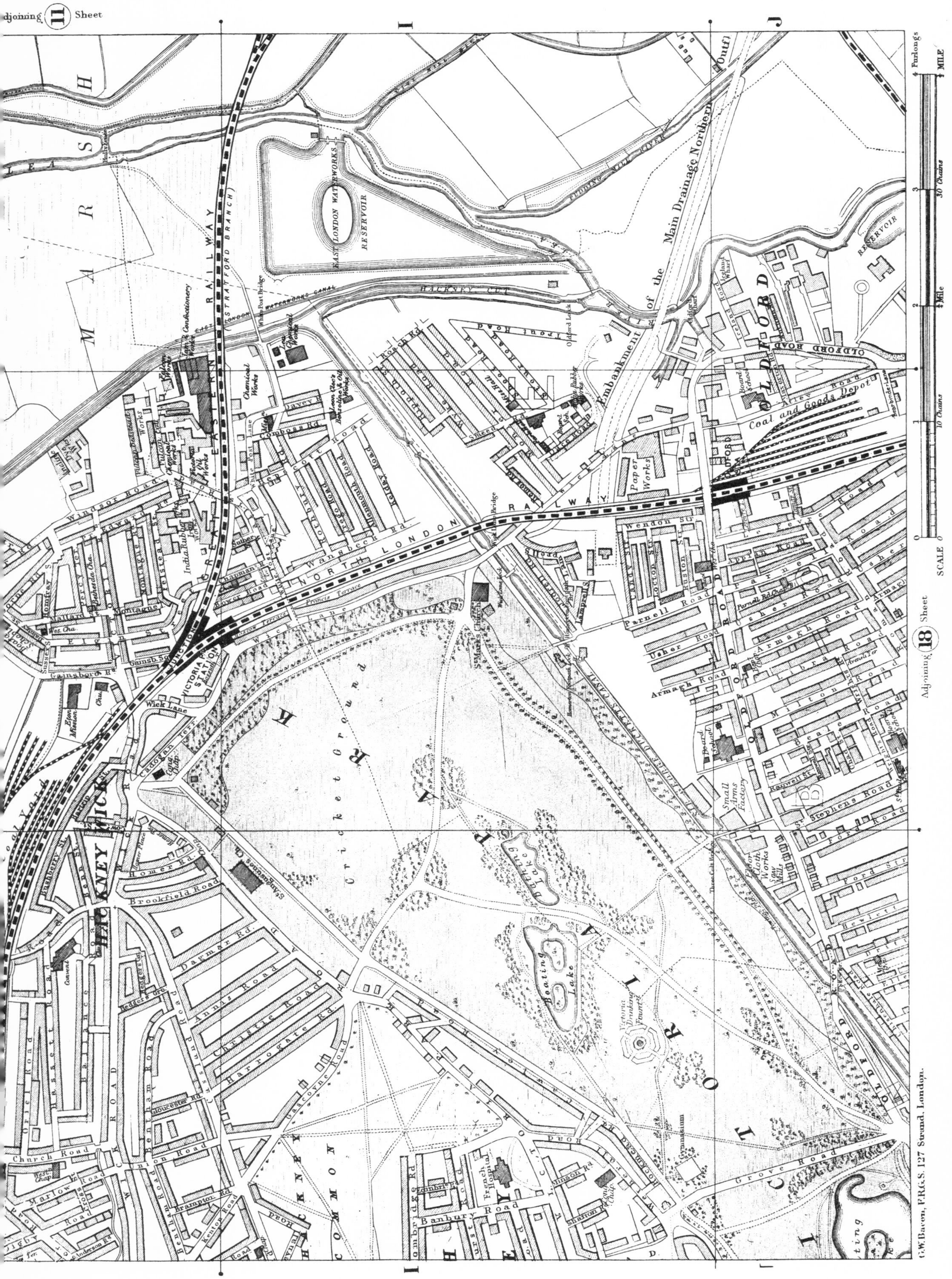

Adjoining 11 Sheet
Adjoining 18 Sheet
EAST LONDON WATERWORKS RESERVOIR
HACKNEY CUT
EAST LONDON WATERWORKS CANAL
GREAT EASTERN RAILWAY (STRATFORD BRANCH)
NORTH LONDON RAILWAY
Embankment of the Main Drainage Northern Outfall
VICTORIA STATION
JUNCTION
HACKNEY WICK
OLD FORD
Coal and Goods Depot
Paper Works
Chemical Works
India Rubber Works
Small Arms Factory
Board School
VICTORIA PARK
Cricket Ground
Boating Lake
Bathing Lake
Gymnasium
French Hospital
HACKNEY COMMON
Grove Road
Old Ford Road
Wick Lane
Wick Road
Windsor Road
Brookfield Road
Dagmar Rd.
Christie Road
Harrogate Rd.
Annis Road
Gascoyne Road
Church Road
Marlow Road
Banbury Road
Parnell Road
Armagh Road
Usher Road
Stephens Road
Milton Road
REGENTS CANAL
SCALE
0 1 2 3 4 Furlongs
10 Chains 30 Chains
½ Mile 1 MILE
G.W. Bacon, F.R.G.S. 127 Strand, London.

For same area on 4 inch scale, see sheet 40.

Adjoining (10) Sheet

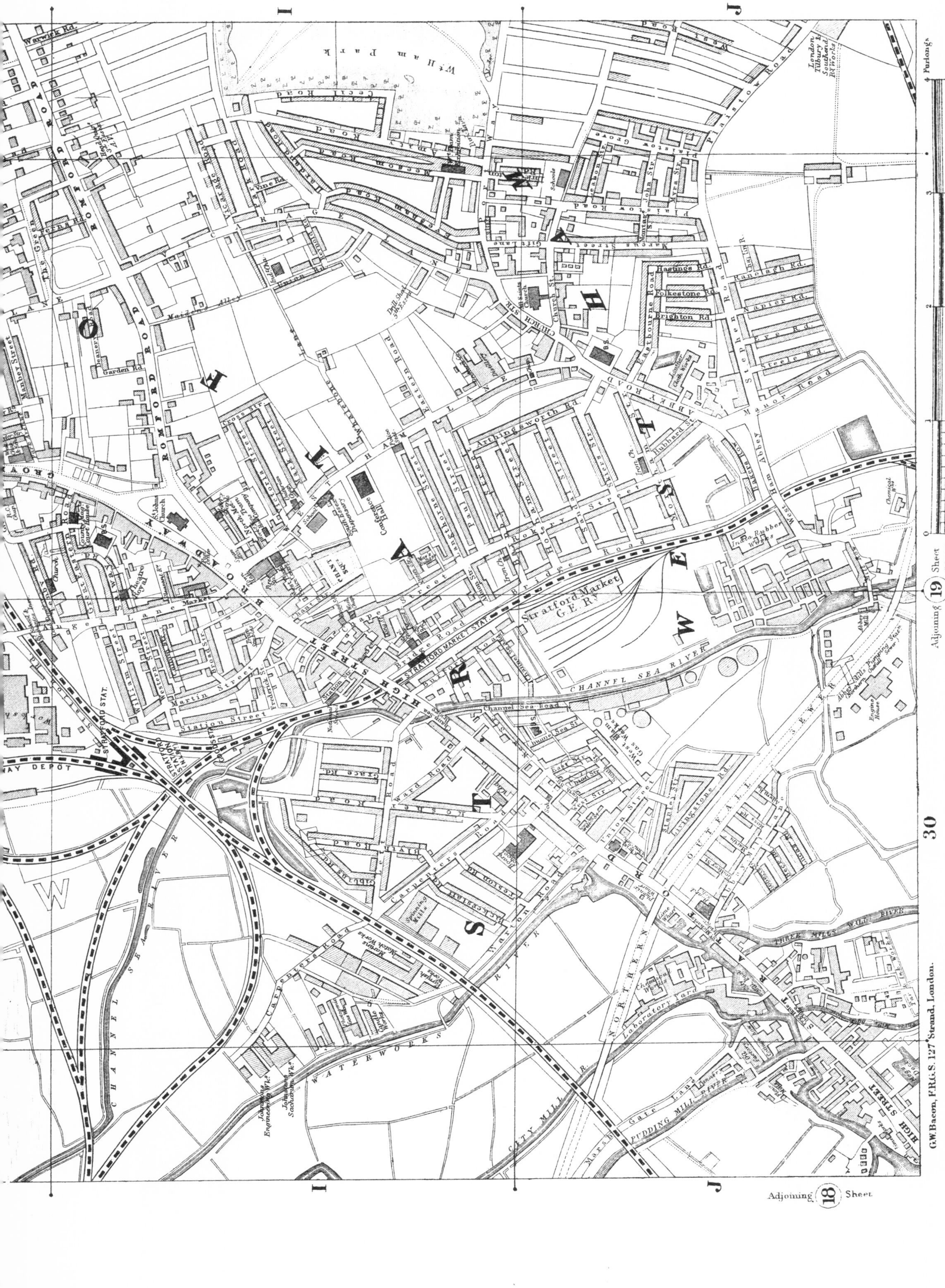
I
J
Warwick Rd.
Ham Park
Cecil Road
West Road
Plaistow Road
London Tilbury & Southend Rly. Works
Plaistow Grove
Romford Road
Vicarage Lane
Church St.
Eastbourne Road
Hastings Rd.
Folkestone Rd.
Brighton Rd.
Ranelagh Rd.
Napier Rd.
Steele Rd.
Stephen's Rd.
Abbey Road
Manor Road
West Ham Abbey
Arthingsworth Rd.
Maiden's Alley
Garden Rd.
Manbey Street
Broadway
Angel Lane
Great Eastern Road
High Street
Bridge Road
Stratford Market G.E.R.
Stratford Market Stat.
India Rubber Works
Chemical Wks.
Channel Sea River
Channel Sea Road
Stratford Stat.
Station Street
Martin Street
William Street
Grace Rd.
Livingstone Rd.
Union St.
Gibbins Rd.
Carpenters Road
Warton Road
Northern Outfall Sewer
Abbey Mills Pumping Stat.
Three Mills Wall River
Laboratory Yard
Marsh Gate Lane
Pudding Mill River
City Mill R.
Waterworks
W
W E S T   H A M
S T R A T F O R D
30
SCALE
1/4 Mile
Adjoining 19 Sheet
Adjoining 18 Sheet
G.W. Bacon, F.R.G.S. 127 Strand, London.

For same area on 4 inch scale, see sheet 42

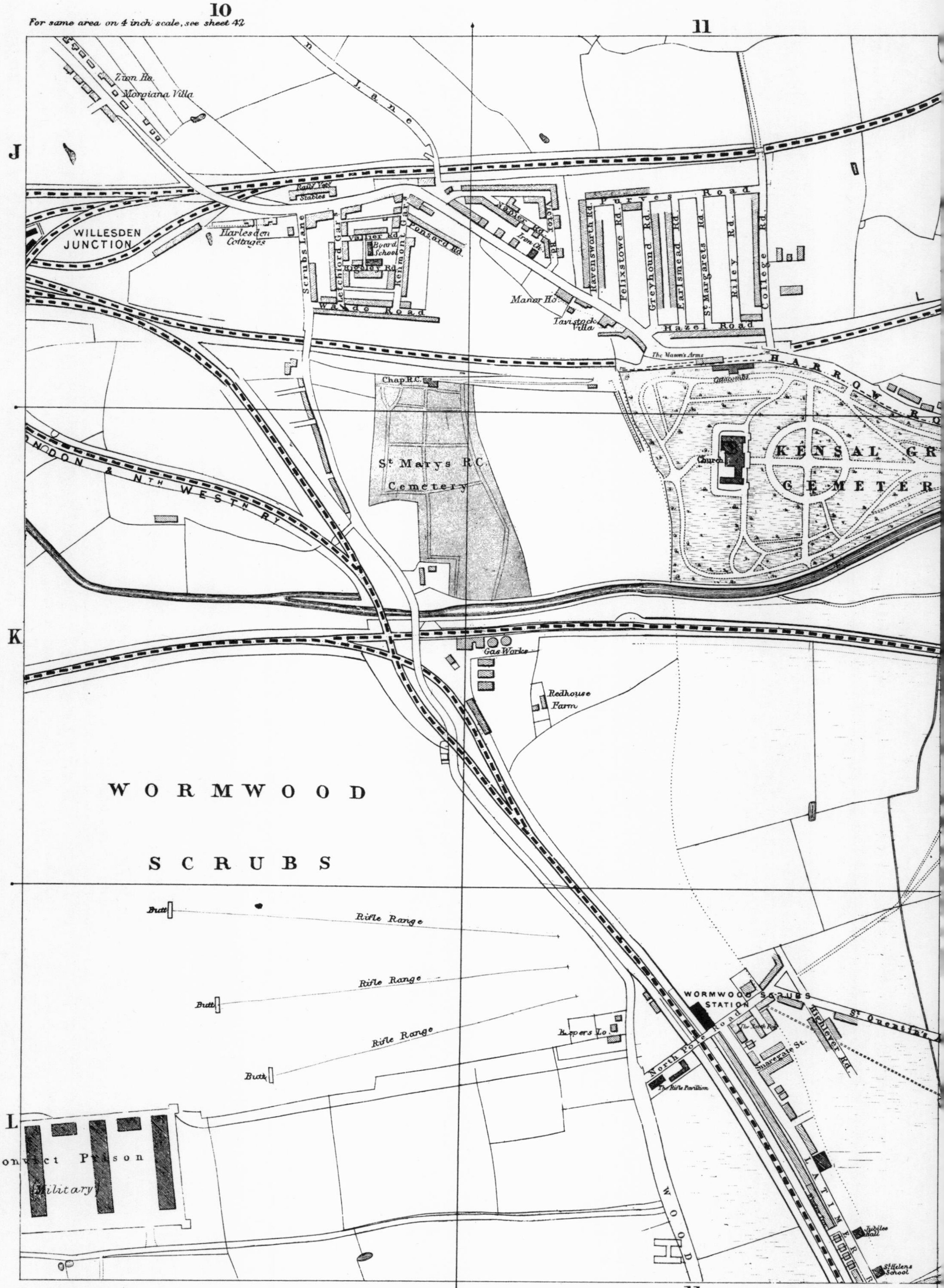
10
11
J
K
L
Zion Ho.
Morgiana Villa
Lane
WILLESDEN JUNCTION
Harlesden Cottages
Stables
Scrubs Lane
Letchford Gar.
Board School
Ponsard Rd.
Wando Road
Napier Rd.
Iron Ch.
Purves Road
Ravensworth Rd.
Felixstowe Rd.
Greyhound Rd.
Farismead Rd.
St. Margarets Rd.
Riley Rd.
College Rd.
Manor Ho.
Tavistock Villa
Hazel Road
The Mason's Arms
Catacombs
HARROW RD
Chap R.C.
St. Marys R.C. Cemetery
KENSAL GR
Church
CEMETER
LONDON & NTH WESTN RY
Gas Works
Redhouse Farm
WORMWOOD SCRUBS
Butt
Rifle Range
WORMWOOD SCRUBS STATION
North Pole Road
Keepers Lo.
The Rifle Pavilion
Sharegate St.
St. Quentin's
Convict Prison
(Military)
WOOD
LATIMER
Jubilee Hall
St. Helens School

G.W. Bacon F.R.G.S. 127 Strand, London

12
13
KENSAL GREEN STATION
QUEENS PARK WEST KILBURN STA.
LONDON AND NORTH WESTERN R
Albert Road
Denmark Road
Rupert Rd
Salisbury Rd
Canterbury Road
Carlton Road
Malvern Rd
St Lukes Church
St Lukes Schools
Neeld Road
Ashmore Road
Kensal Green Lane
Farm
Oliphant Street
Nutbourne Street
Marne Street
Lothrop Street
Kilravock Street
Beethoven Street
Third Avenue
Herries Street
Lancefield Street
Dart Street
Boord Sch.
St Judes Church
Fordingley Road
Shirland Road
Shirland Mews
Lydford Rd
Warlock Rd
Barnsdale Rd
Mozart St
Albert Street
Saw Mills
Farrant Street
Caird Street
Enbrook Street
Droop Street
Second Avenue
Fourth Ave
Fifth Ave
Galton St
St Johns Church
Chapel
GRAND JUNCTION CANAL
HARROW ROAD
KENSAL ROAD
Western Gas Works
Public Offices
Elgin Road
Fernhead Road
Portnall Road
Bravington Rd
Kennet Rd
KENSAL NEW TOWN
Absalom Rd
Appleford Road
Southam Street
South Row
GREAT WESTERN RAILWAY
Board School
Edinburgh Road
Bransford St
Braunston St
Treverton St
Raymede St
Hewer St
Rackham St
St Marylebone Infirmary
Ladbroke Grove
Portobello Road
Telford Rd
Faraday Rd
Golborne Road
St Ervans Road
Swinbrooke Road
Bevington Road
Blagrove Road
Franciscan Convent
Cricket Field
St Charles Sq
St Charles R.C. College Playground
Chesterton Road
Bassett Road
Oxford Gardens
Cambridge Gards
St Helens Church
HAMMERSMITH AND CITY JUNCTION RAILWAY
NOTTING HILL STATION
Lancaster Road
Cornwall Road
Westbourne Park Road
Tavistock Road
St Lukes Road
Great Western Road
Westbourne Schools
WESTBP STATION
GOODS STAT
Talbot Road
Burlington Rd
Westmoreland Rd
Powis Gardens
J
K
L
Adjoining Sheet 13
0 1 2 3 4 Furlongs

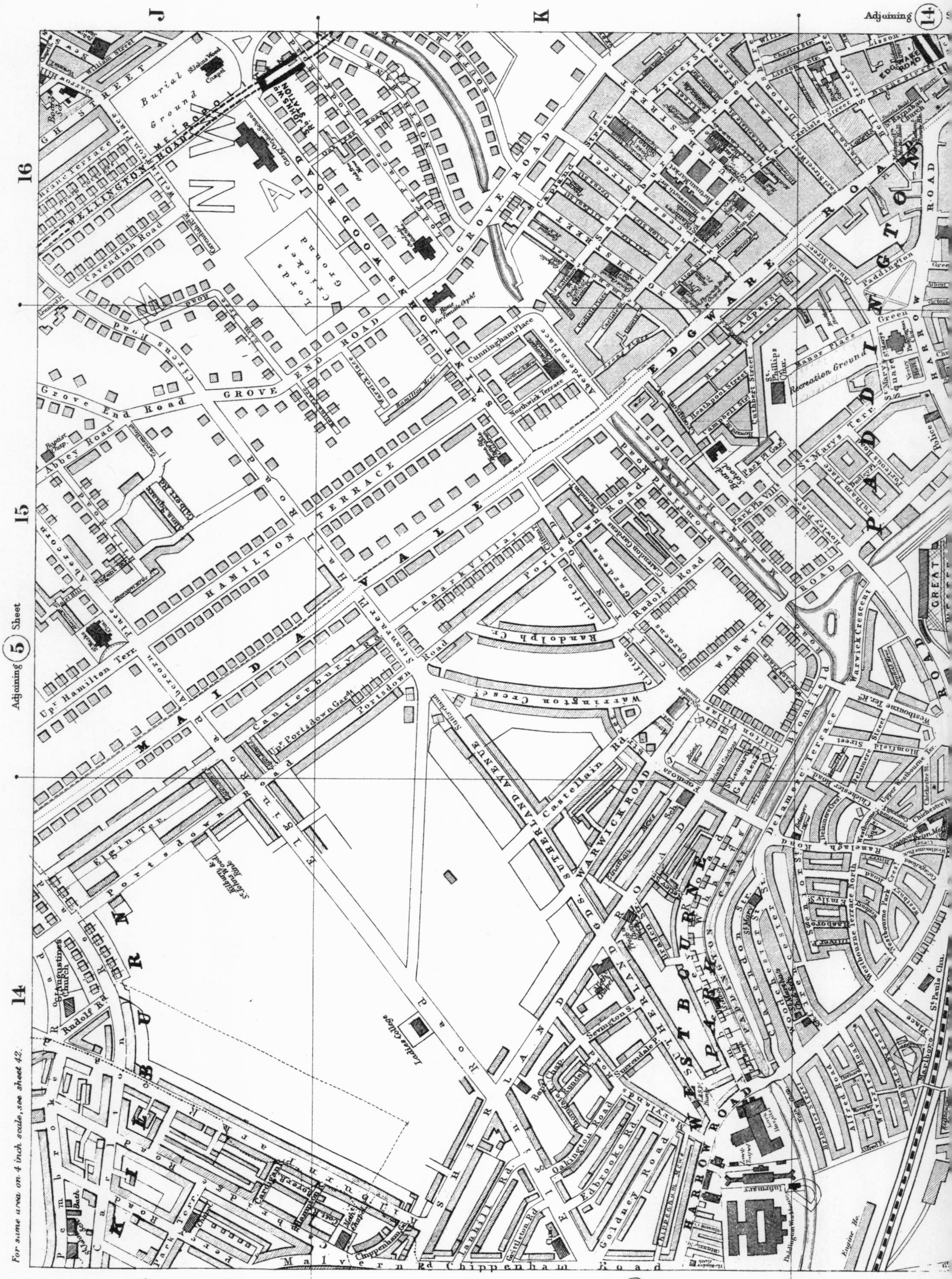
J
K
Adjoining 14 Sheet
16
15
14
Adjoining 5 Sheet
Adjoining 12 Sheet
For same area on 4 inch scale, see sheet 42.
MAIDA VALE
HAMILTON TERRACE
GROVE END ROAD
Lords Cricket Ground
Burial Ground
St. Johns Wood Chapel
WELLINGTON ROAD
METROPOLITAN RAILWAY
ST JOHNS WOOD ROAD
Cavendish Road
Circus Road
Abbey Road
Grove End Road
EDGWARE ROAD
Aberdeen Place
Cunningham Place
Northwick Terrace
Warwick Place
Hall Road
Blomfield Road
Clifton Road
Clifton Gardens
Randolph Cr.
Warrington Crescent
Lanark Villas
Portsdown Road
Canterbury Villas
Upr. Portsdown Gardens
Elgin Terr.
Portsdown Road
Castellain Rd.
SUTHERLAND AVENUE
WARWICK ROAD
Randolf Road
WARWICK CRESCENT
Westbourne Terrace
Delamere Terrace
Chichester Road
PADDINGTON
HARROW ROAD
WESTBOURNE PARK
Recreation Ground
St. Marys Square
Manor Place
Paddington Green
St. Augustines Church
Rudolf Rd.
KILBURN
Ladies College
Shirland Road
Oakington Road
Edbrooke Rd.
Goldney Road
Chippenham Road
Malvern Rd.
Sevington St.
Surrendale Pl.
Infirmary
St. Pauls Chu.
Alfred Road
GREAT WESTERN

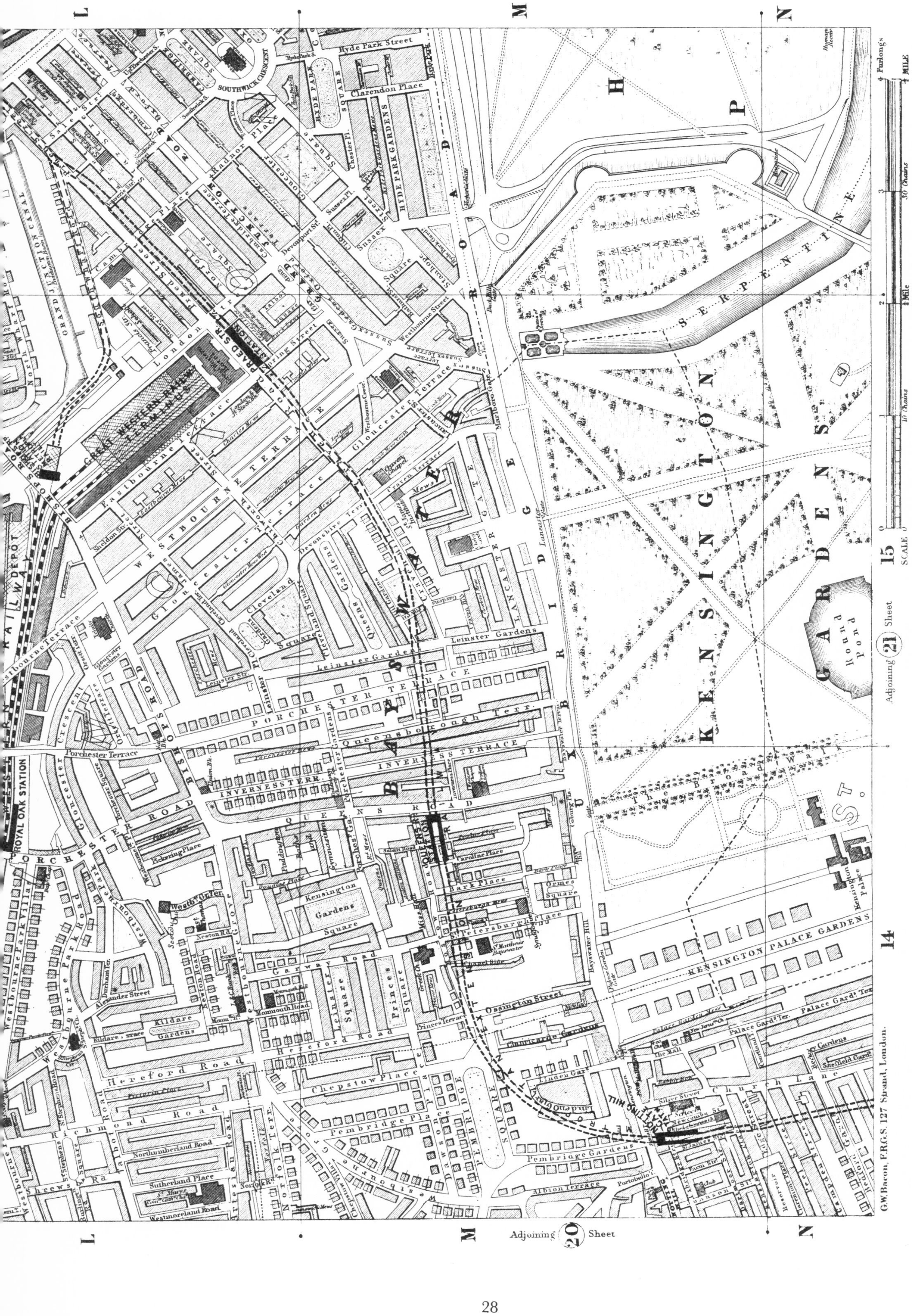
L
M
N
HYDE PARK
SERPENTINE
KENSINGTON GARDENS
Round Pond
Adjoining 21 Sheet
Adjoining 20 Sheet
15
14
SCALE
4 Furlongs
1 MILE
30 Chains
½ Mile
10 Chains
G.W.Bacon, F.R.G.S. 127 Strand, London.
BAYSWATER
BAYSWATER ROAD
GREAT WESTERN RAILWAY TERMINUS
ROYAL OAK STATION
PRAED STR. STATION
GRAND JUNCTION CANAL
WESTBOURNE TERRACE
GLOUCESTER TERRACE
PORCHESTER TERRACE
INVERNESS TERRACE
Queens Road
Leinster Gardens
LANCASTER GATE
KENSINGTON PALACE GARDENS
Kensington Palace
Hereford Road
Pembridge Square
Pembridge Gardens
Chepstow Place
Westbourne Grove
Kensington Gardens Square
NOTTING HILL
Church Lane
Sussex Square
Hyde Park Square
Hyde Park Street
Hyde Park Gardens
Clarendon Place
Southwick Crescent
Radnor Place
Sussex Gardens
Westbourne Street
Craven Terrace
Cleveland Square
Porchester Road
Richmond Road
Ledbury Road
Westbourne Park Villas
Palace Gardens Terrace
Kildare Gardens
Garway Road
Leinster Square
Prince's Square
Ossington Street
Linden Gardens
Albion Terrace
Northumberland Road
Sutherland Place
Westmoreland Road

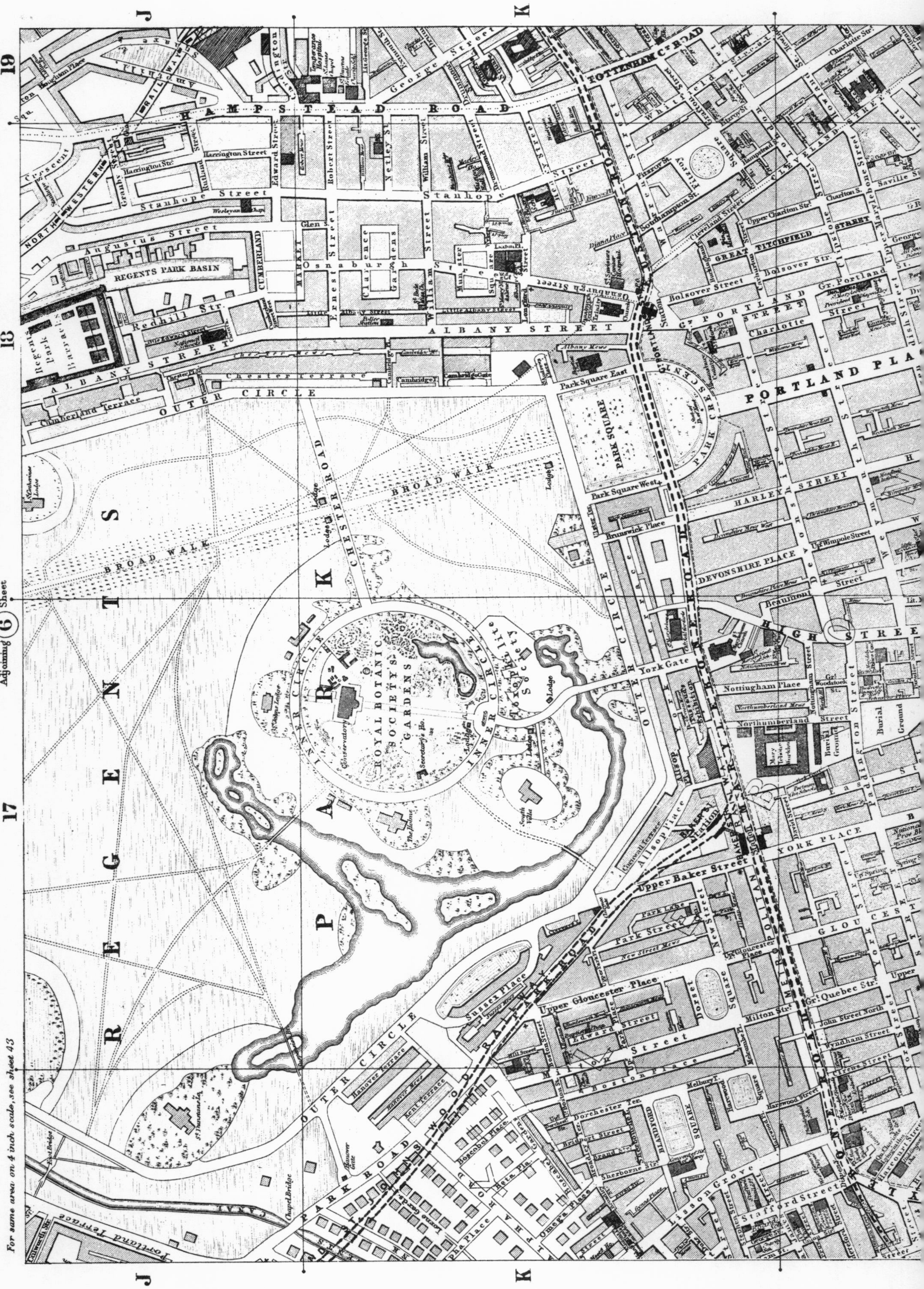
J
K
19
18
17
HAMPSTEAD ROAD
TOTTENHAM CT ROAD
ALBANY STREET
OUTER CIRCLE
REGENTS PARK BASIN
Regents Park Barracks
PARK SQUARE
Park Square East
Park Square West
PORTLAND PLACE
BROAD WALK
CHESTER ROAD
INNER CIRCLE
ROYAL BOTANIC SOCIETY'S GARDENS
Toxophilite Society
REGENTS PARK
York Gate
Upper Baker Street
DEVONSHIRE PLACE
HIGH STREET
YORK PLACE
DORSET SQUARE
BLANDFORD SQUARE
PARK ROAD
CANAL
Portland Terrace
Adjoining 6 Sheet
For same area on 4 inch scale, see sheet 43

L
M
N
REGENT STREET
OXFORD STREET
NEW BOND STREET
LANGHAM PLACE
CAVENDISH SQUARE
HANOVER SQUARE
BERKELEY SQUARE
GROSVENOR SQUARE
PORTMAN SQUARE
MONTAGU SQUARE
BRYANSTON SQUARE
PORTLAND STREET
TITCHFIELD STREET
BERNERS
Wells Street
Poland Street
Princess's Theatre
Sackville Street
Saville Row
Old Burlington Street
Old Bond Street
Burlington Arcade
Royal Acad.
Albemarle Street
Dover Street
Berkeley Street
Stratton Street
Bolton Street
Clarges Street
Half Moon Street
Curzon Street
Queen Street
Chesterfield Str.
Charles Street
Hill Street
Duke Street
Bury Street
Conduit Street
George Street
Princes Street
Holles Street
Chandos Street
Harley Street
Queen Anne Street
Welbeck Street
Wigmore Street
Stratford Place
Mandeville Pla.
Thayer Street
Manchester Square
Spanish Place
Duke Street
Brook Street
Davies Street
Mount Street
South Audley Street
North Audley Street
Upper Grosvenor Street
Upper Brook Street
Park Street
Park Lane
Orchard Street
Portman Street
Gloucester Street
Baker Street
Quebec Street
Montagu Street
Great Cumberland Place
Seymour Place
Seymour St.
Edgware Road
Connaught Place
Connaught Square
Stanhope Place
Albion Street
Brown Street
Shouldham Street
Molyneux Street
Norfolk Crescent
St George (Hanover Sq.) Burial Gd. (closed)
Drinking Fountain
Barracks
Rangers House
Deputy Rangers Ho.
HYDE PARK
GEORGE ST
Adjoining 22 Sheet
17
SCALE
4 Furlongs
1 MILE
30 Chains
½ Mile
10 Chains
G. W. Bacon, F.R.G.S. 127 Strand, London.

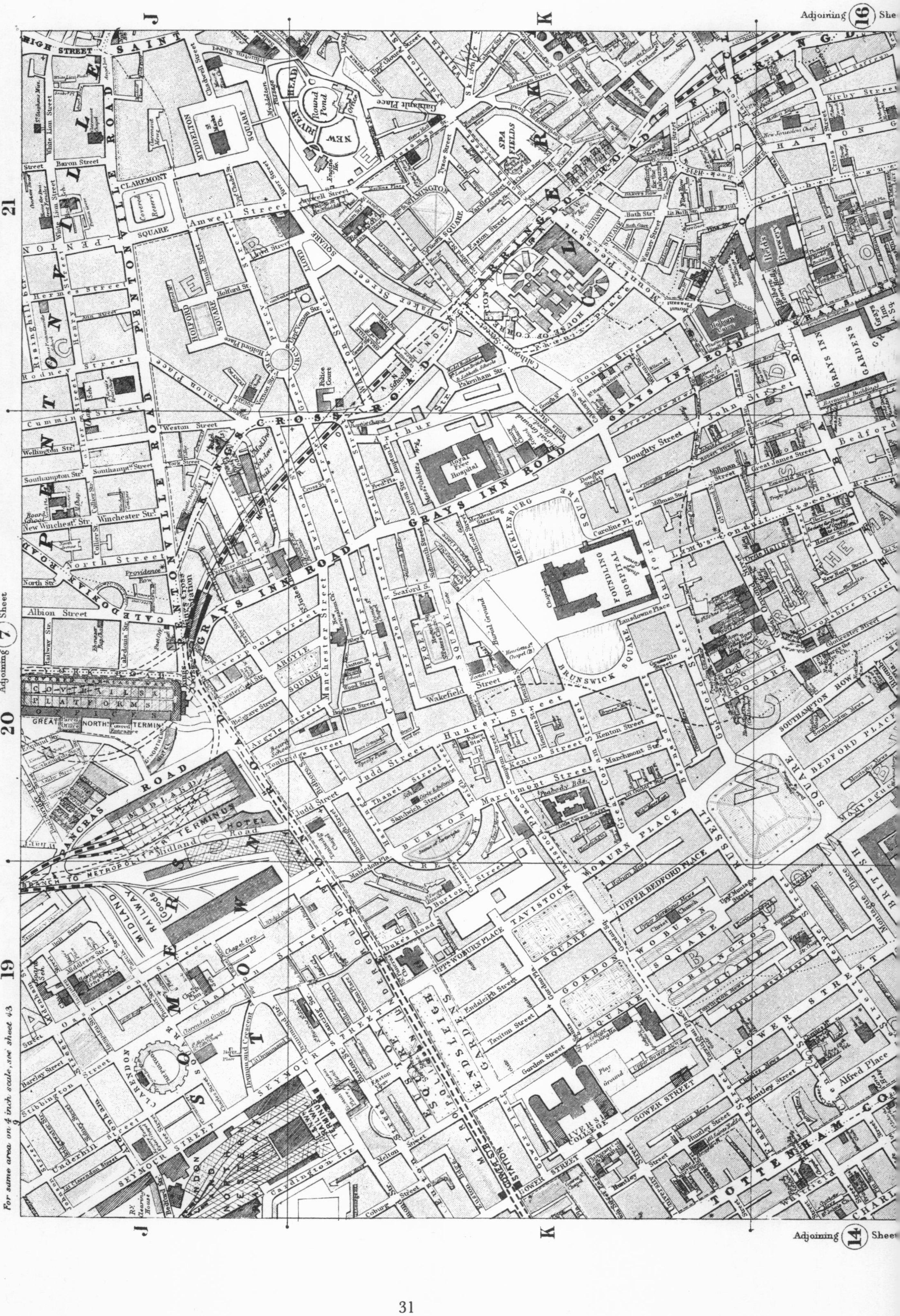
Adjoining 16 Sheet
Adjoining 7 Sheet
Adjoining 14 Sheet
For same area on 4 inch scale, see sheet 43
J
K
21
20
19
PENTONVILLE ROAD
CALEDONIAN ROAD
GRAYS INN ROAD
KINGS CROSS ROAD
FARRINGDON ROAD
EUSTON ROAD
MIDLAND RAILWAY
ST. PANCRAS ROAD
GREAT NORTHERN TERMINUS
PLATFORMS
MIDLAND RAILWAY TERMINUS
HOTEL
SOMERS TOWN
CLERKENWELL
MYDDELTON SQUARE
CLAREMONT SQUARE
HOLFORD SQUARE
PERCY CIRCUS
SPA FIELDS
HOUSE OF CORRECTION
Royal Free Hospital
MECKLENBURG SQUARE
FOUNDLING HOSPITAL
BRUNSWICK SQUARE
ARGYLE SQUARE
REGENT SQUARE
BURTON CRESCENT
RUSSELL SQUARE
TAVISTOCK SQUARE
WOBURN SQUARE
TORRINGTON SQUARE
GORDON SQUARE
EUSTON SQUARE
UNIVERSITY COLLEGE
ENDSLEIGH GARDENS
GOWER STREET
BEDFORD PLACE
SOUTHAMPTON ROW
QUEEN SQUARE
GRAYS INN GARDENS
GUILFORD STREET
UPPER BEDFORD PLACE
WOBURN PLACE
TOTTENHAM COURT ROAD
CLARENDON SQUARE
SEYMOUR STREET
Hunter Street
Judd Street
Marchmont Street
Doughty Street
Amwell Street
Baron Street
Wakefield Street
Tonbridge Street
Euston Square Station

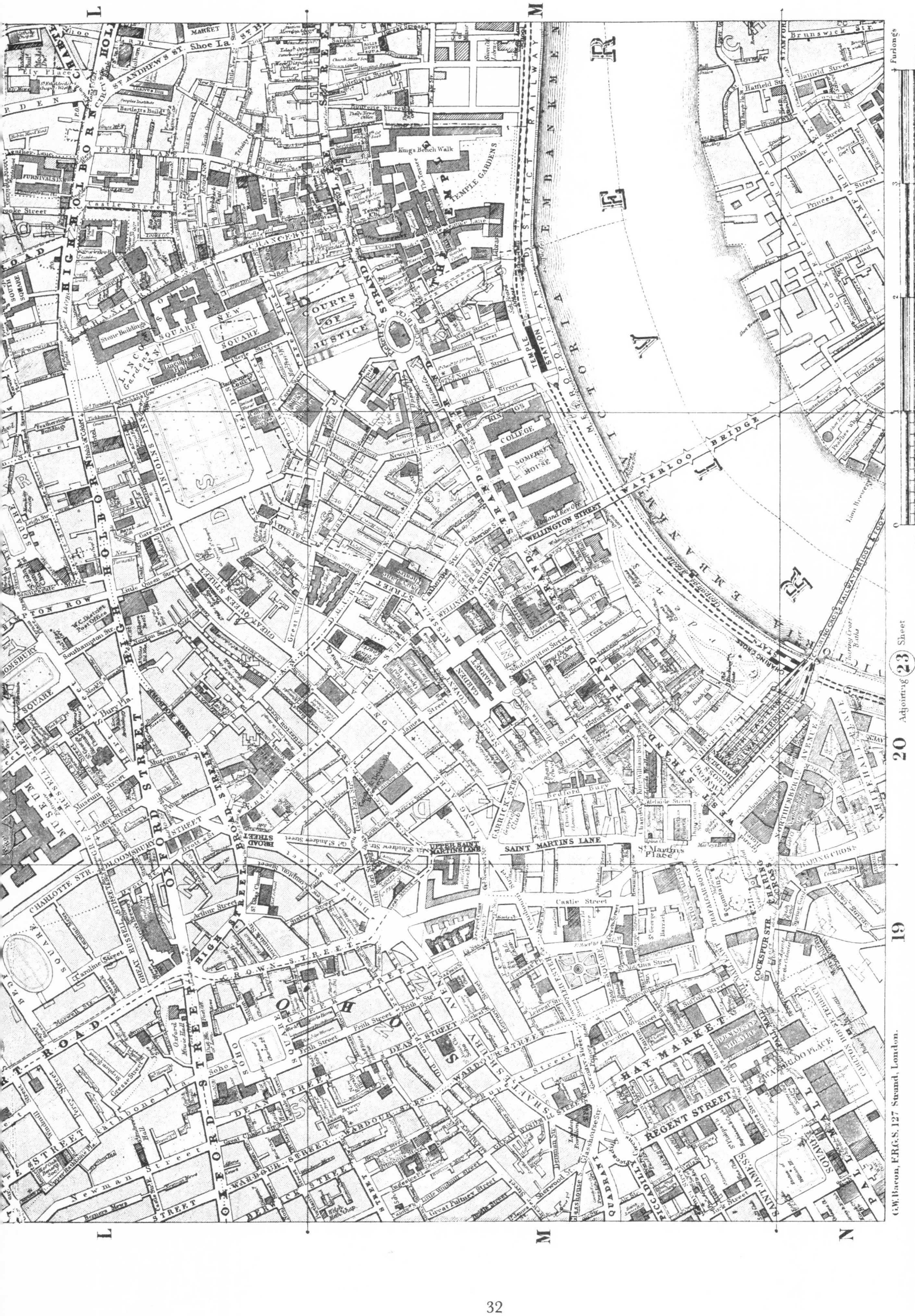
L
M
N
SCALE
Furlongs
MILE
Adjoining 23 Sheet
20
19
G.W. Bacon, F.R.G.S. 127 Strand, London.
COURTS OF JUSTICE
TEMPLE GARDENS
Kings Bench Walk
TEMPLE STATION
VICTORIA EMBANKMENT
WATERLOO BRIDGE
SOMERSET HOUSE
KINGS COLLEGE
WELLINGTON STREET
STRAND
CHARING CROSS
HIGH HOLBORN
NEW SQUARE
Stone Buildings
CHANCERY LANE
FETTER LANE
Shoe La
SAINT MARTINS LANE
UPPER SAINT MARTINS LANE
COVENT GARDEN MARKET
BROAD STREET
OXFORD STREET
CROWN STREET
DEAN STREET
WARDOUR STREET
REGENT STREET
HAY MARKET
COCKSPUR STR.
QUADRANT
PICCADILLY
WATERLOO PLACE
PALL MALL
Newman Street
Rathbone Pl
Soho
Frith Street
Castle Street
Museum Str.
Southampton Str.
Bury Pl.
Caroline Street
Morwell Str.
Charlotte Str.
Bedford Street
Garrick Str.
Long Acre
Newcastle Street
Brunswick Str.
Hatfield Street
Duke Street
Princes Street
Cornwall Road
Stamford Street

Adjoining 17 Sheet
Adjoining 8 Sheet
Adjoining 15 Sheet
For same area on 4 inch scale, see sheets 43-44
J
K
24
23
22
KINGSLAND ROAD
HACKNEY ROAD
HIGH STREET SHOREDITCH
COMMERCIAL STR.
GREAT EASTERN RAILWAY
Hoxton Street
Hoxton St.
CURTAIN ROAD
GREAT EASTERN STREET
HOXTON SQUARE
Pitfield Str.
Haberdash. Alms Hous.
Aske's Hospital
CHARLES SQUARE
NEW NORTH ROAD
EAST ROAD
CITY ROAD
OLD STREET
FINSBURY SQUARE
ARTILLERY GROUND
Bunhill Fields Bur. Ground (Closed)
St. Lukes Hospital
ST. LUKE
Shepherdess Walk
WENLOCK BASIN
CITY ROAD BASIN
Wharf Road
Central Street
Goswell Road
NORTHAMPTON SQUARE
ST. JAMES
CLERKENWELL
SAINT JOHN STREET
SAINT JOHN STR.
ALDERSGATE STREET
JOHN STREET ROAD
FARRINGDON STR. STATION
Burial Ground

L
M
MINORIES
THE TOWER
GREAT TOWER HILL
Thames Subway
CUSTOM HOUSE QUAY
FENCHURCH STREET
FENCHURCH ST. RAILWAY TERMINUS
BISHOPSGATE STREET WITHOUT
BISHOPSGATE STREET WITHIN
LIVERPOOL STR.
FINSBURY CIRCUS
MOORGATE STREET
MOORGATE STR. STATION
BANK OF ENGLAND
ROYAL EXCHANGE
KING WILLIAM STREET
KING WILLIAM ST.
GRACECHURCH STREET
EAST CHEAP
MONUMENT
LONDON BRIDGE
CANNON STREET
CANNON ST. HOTEL
CANNON STREET TERMINUS
CHEAPSIDE
POULTRY
MANSION HO. ST.
QUEEN VICTORIA STREET
SOUTHWARK BRIDGE
SOUTHWARK BRIDGE ROAD
Barclays Brewery
DERSGATE STREET
POST OFFICE
ST. MARTINS LE GRAND
NEWGATE STREET
Little Britain
St. Bartholomews Hospital
Christs Hospital
ST. PAULS CATHEDRAL
ST. PAULS CHURCH YARD
LUDGATE HILL
HOLBORN VIADUCT
SNOW HILL
FARRINGDON STREET
NEW BRIDGE STREET
LONDON CHATHAM & DOVER RAILWAY
BLACKFRIARS BRIDGE
Burrell Street
Bennett Street
SOUTHWARK
THAMES
22
SCALE
Furlongs
MILE
Adjoining 24 Sheet
G.W. Bacon, F.R.G.S. 127 Strand, London.

Adjoining (18)

Adjoining (9) Sheet

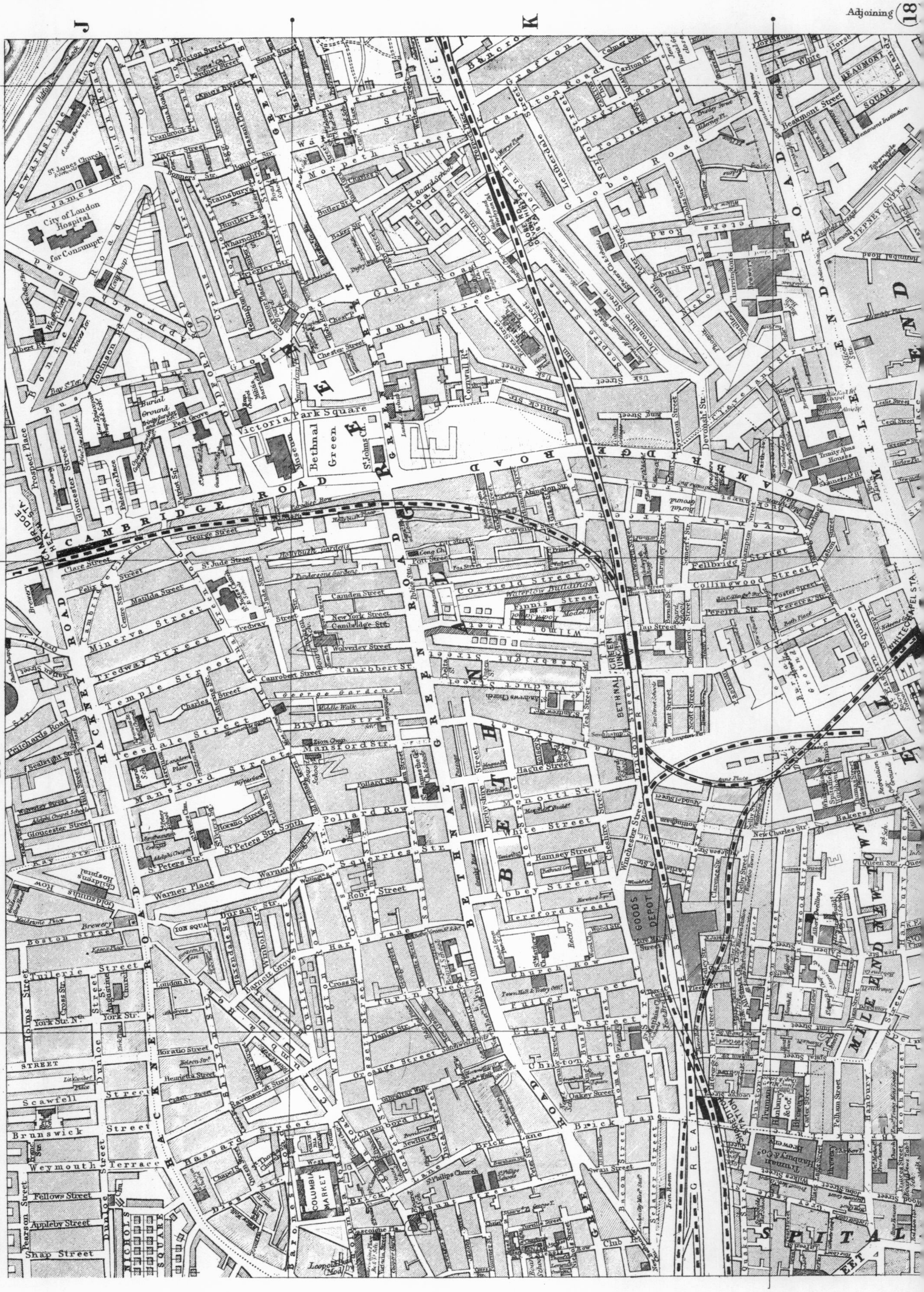

For same area on 4 inch scale, see sheet 44.

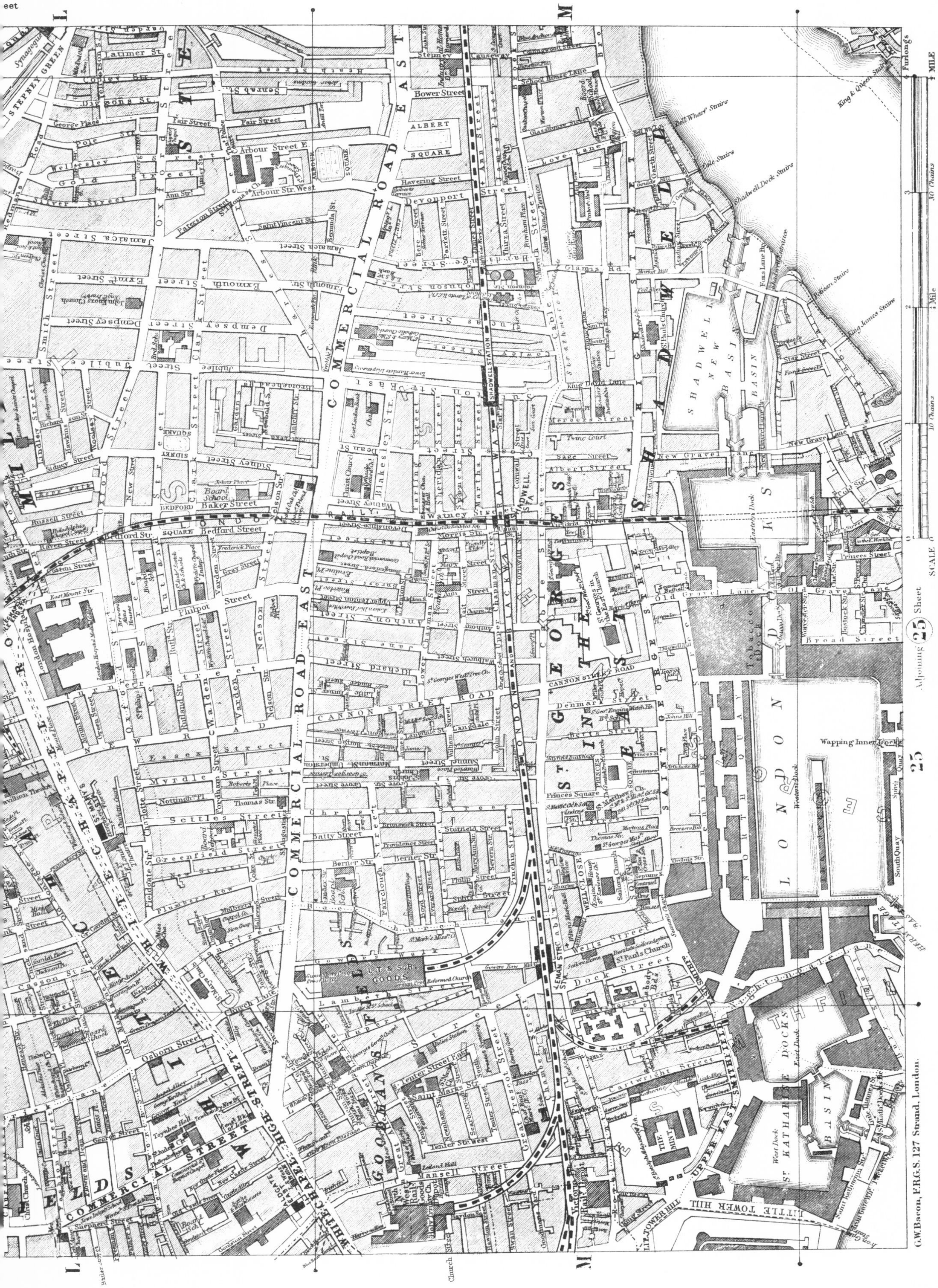
COMMERCIAL ROAD EAST
SHADWELL STATION
SHADWELL NEW BASIN
LONDON DOCKS
ST. KATHARINE DOCKS
THE MINT
Wapping Inner Dock
Western Dock
Tobacco Dock
Eastern Dock
East Dock
West Dock
Cannon Street Road
Cable Street
Leman Str.
Upper East Smithfield
Little Tower Hill
Whitechapel High Street
Commercial Street
Goodmans Fields
Mansell Street
Prescot Street
Great Alie Street
Dock Street
Wells Street
Princes Square
St. George's Street
New Road
Sidney Street
Jubilee Street
Dempsey Street
Exmouth Street
Jamaica Street
Arbour Square
Albert Square
Bower Street
Devonport Street
Old Gravel Lane
New Gravel Lane
Broad Street
Glamis Rd.
Stepney Green
Settles Street
Myrdle Street
Essex Street
Berner Str.
Fieldgate Str.
Batty Street
Christian Street
Philpot Street
Nelson Street
Varden Street
Walden Street
Sage Street
Albert Street
King David Lane
King James Stairs
Shadwell Dock Stairs
Free Trade Wharf
King & Queen Stairs
Adjoining 25 Sheet
SCALE
1/2 MILE
1/4 Mile
4 Furlongs
30 Chains
10 Chains
G.W. Bacon, F.R.G.S. 127 Strand, London.
L
M
25

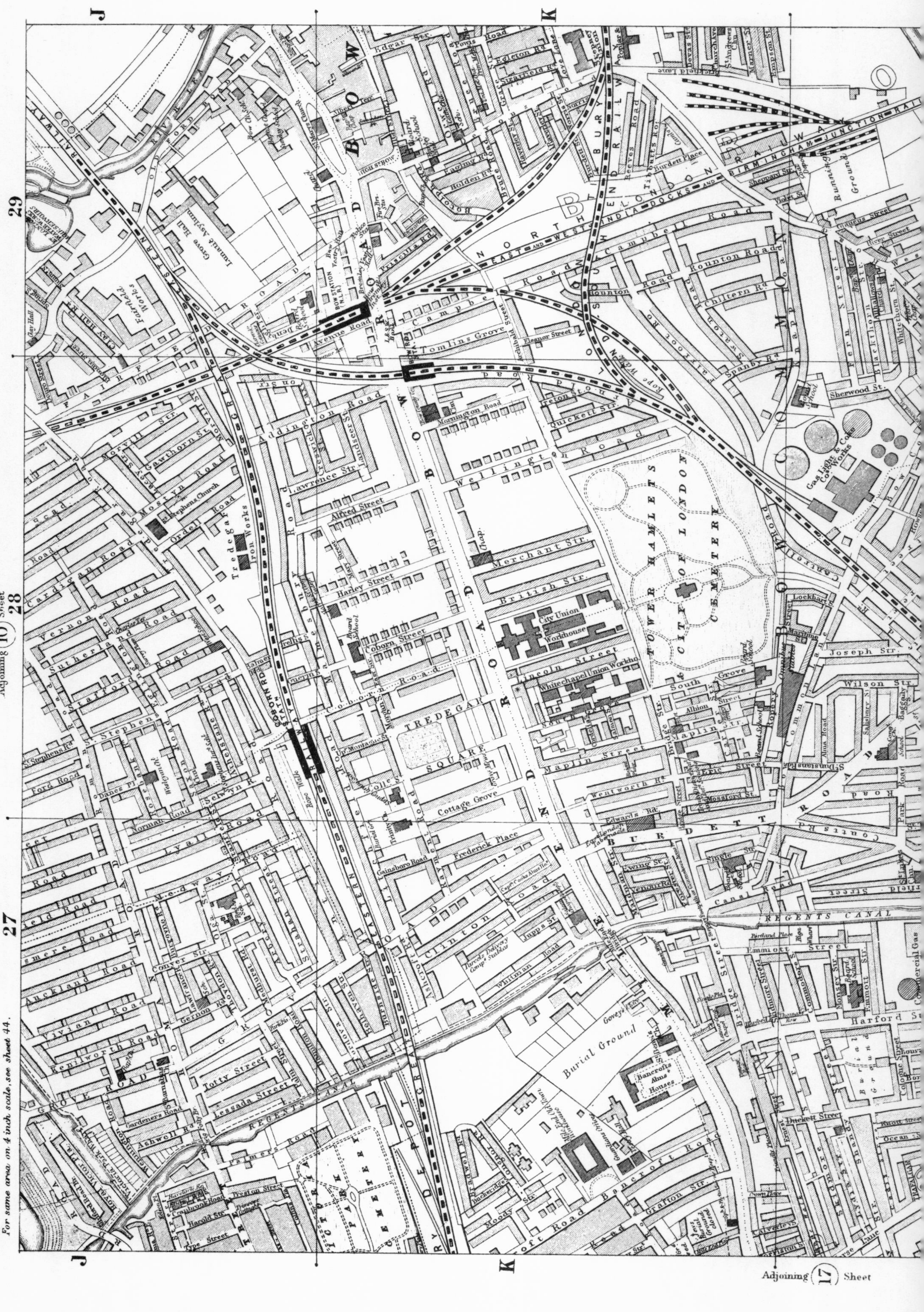
J
K
29
28
27
Adjoining (10) Sheet
For same area on 4 inch scale, see sheet 44.
Adjoining (17) Sheet
BOW
BOW ROAD
Bow Station (N.L.R.)
Grove Hall Lunatic Asylum
Fairfield Works
Clay Hall
FAIRFIELD ROAD
Tomlins Grove
Campbell Road
Eleanor Street
Archibald Street
Rounton Road
Chiltern Rd
Spanby Rd
Sherwood St.
Gas Light & Coke Co's Works
Birmingham Junction Railway
East and West India Docks and Birmingham Junction Railway
North London Railway
Blackthorn St.
Whitethorn St.
Fern Street
Addington Road
Lawrence Str.
Alfred Street
Harley Street
Coborn Street
Coborn Road Station
Mornington Road
Wellington Road
Merchant Str.
British Str.
City Union Workhouse
Whitechapel Union Workhouse
Lincoln Street
Tower Hamlets & City of London Cemetery
Tredegar Iron Works
Tredegar Square
Mostyn Road
St. Stephen's Church
Cardigan Road
Vernon Road
Sutherland Road
Stafford Road
Ford Road
Norman Road
Lyal Road
Medway Road
Cottage Grove
Frederick Place
Gainsboro Road
Clinton Road
Mile End Road
Burdett Road
Joseph Str.
Wilson St.
Maplin Street
Wentworth Rd.
Edwards Rd.
Regents Canal
Emmott Street
Harford St.
Burial Ground
Bancrofts Alms Houses
Bancroft Road
Grafton Str.
Moody St.
Grove Road
Kenilworth Road
Totty Street
Lessada Street
Ashwell Rd.
Gardeners Road
Auckland Road
Vivian Road
Gernon Rd.
Duckett Street
Ocean St.
Commercial Gas
Eastern Counties Railway
Great Eastern Railway

L
M
WEST INDIA DOCK
WEST INDIA (Import)
LIMEHOUSE
POPLAR
EAST INDIA DOCK ROAD
WEST INDIA DOCK ROAD
COMMERCIAL ROAD EAST
REGENTS CANAL DOCK
LONDON AND BLACKWALL RAILWAY
HIGH STREET
Burdett Road
Salmons Lane
Limehouse Station
West India Docks Station
St. Annes Chu.
Stepney Church
Bridge Road
Limehouse Basin
Morris Road
Chrisp Street
Augusta Str.
Upper North Street
Penny Fields
Three Colt Street
Narrow Street
Belgrave Street
Bromley Street
Carr Street
Blount Street
Brenton Street
Samuel Street
Conder Street
Repton Street
Rhodes Well Road
Ropemakers Fields
Adjoining 26 Sheet
Adjoining 28 Sheet
SCALE
Furlongs
MILE
30 Chains
½ Mile
10 Chains
G.W. Bacon, F.R.G.S. 127 Strand, London.

K
L
30
31
EAST LONDON CEMETERY
WEST HAM ABBEY MARSH
NORTHERN OUTFALL SEWER
GREAT EASTERN RAILWAY
NORTH WOOLWICH BRANCH
Level Crossing
CANNING TOWN
Imperial Gas Works
Commercial Gas Works
Chemical Works
BOW CREEK
RIVER LEA
BROMLEY STATION
Bromley Workhouse
St. Leonards Street
Brunswick Road
Teviot Street
Nairn St.
Bromley Hall Rd.
Board School
Iron Works
Lea Wharf
Hancock Road
Adjoining 11 Sheet
Adjoining 18 Sheet
For same area on 4 inch scale, see sheets 44.

M
N
THAMES
BOW CREEK (RIVER LEA)
THAMES IRON WORKS AND SHIP BUILDING COMPANY
Thames Plate Glass Works
EAST INDIA DOCK BASIN
EAST INDIA DOCK (Import)
EAST INDIA DOCK (Export)
EAST INDIA DOCK ROAD
WEST INDIA DOCK (Poplar Dock) (Railway Dock)
WEST INDIA DOCK BASIN (Blackwall)
PRESTON NEW ROAD
Brunswick Street
Brunswick Wharf
Brunswick Hotel
Brunswick Stairs
Blackwall Point
Blackwall Point Dry Dock
BLACKWALL REACH
BUGSBY'S MARSHES
Victoria Docks Pier Entrance
DRY DOCKS
LONDON RAILWAY
G.W.R.
SOUTH DOCK STA.
BASIN
Blackwall Entrance to South Dock
POPLAR STATION
CANNING TOWN STATION
Orchard
East Quay
West Quay
North Quay
South Quay
Chemical & Manure Works
Blackwall Ordnance Wks.
30
SCALE
4 Furlongs
½ MILE
1 Mile
Adjoining 27 Sheet
Adjoining 26 Sheet
G.W.Bacon, F.R.G.S. 127 Strand, London.

10

For same area on 4 inch scale, see sheet 42

11

L
M
N
O
A
M
M
LANE
WOOD LANE
Old Oak Fm.
Wormholt Fm.
Thorpebanks
Woodlane Farm
Gynam Farm
Wood Ho.
U X B R I D G E   R O A D
St. Lukes Chu.
Oaklands Cha.
St. Stephens Chu.
St. Thomas Chu.
Albion Brewery
Parsonage
Warwick Ho.
Ellerslie Road
Ethelden Rd.
Bloemfontein Rd.
Loftus Road
Bloemfield Road
Frithville Gardens
Macfarland Road
Adelaide Road
Oakland Gro.
L. Omnibus Co. Stables
Boscombe Road
Cunningham Road
Godolphin Road
St. Stephens Avenue
Devonport Road
Wabeck Road
Coverdale Road
Bulwer Street
Thornfield Road
Findon Road
Roxwell Rd.
Percy Road
Haydn Park Road
GREEN
SHEPHERDS BUSH STATION
SHEPHERDS BUSH
GREEN
Goodwin Road
Melina Rd.
Cathnor Road
Station Road
Davisville Road
Westville Road
Greenside Road
Orchard Road
Lefroy Rd.
G O L D H A W K   R O A D
Southbrook St.
Mayfield Road
Avenue Road
Richford St.
Augustus Rd.
Oakley Rd.
Benbow Rd.
Carthew Vil.
Beaucler Rd.
Coulter Rd.
Brackenbury Rd.
Tabor Road
Agate Road
Hebron Rd.
Marco Rd.
Aldensley Rd.
Adie Road
Wellesley Av.
Paddenswick Road
Wingate Road
Wellington Terrace
Anglesea Villas
Cardross St.
Nasmyth Street
Ravenscourt
Rylett Road
Starch Green
H A M M E R S M I T H   &   C I T Y   J U N C T I O N
SHEPHERDS BUSH ROAD STATION
Silgrave Road
Gopler Grove
Cromwell Grove
Melrose Gardens
Batoum Gardens
Lena Gardens
Shepherds Bush Road
Westwick
BROOK GREEN

G.W. Bacon, F.R.G.S. 127 Strand, London.

11

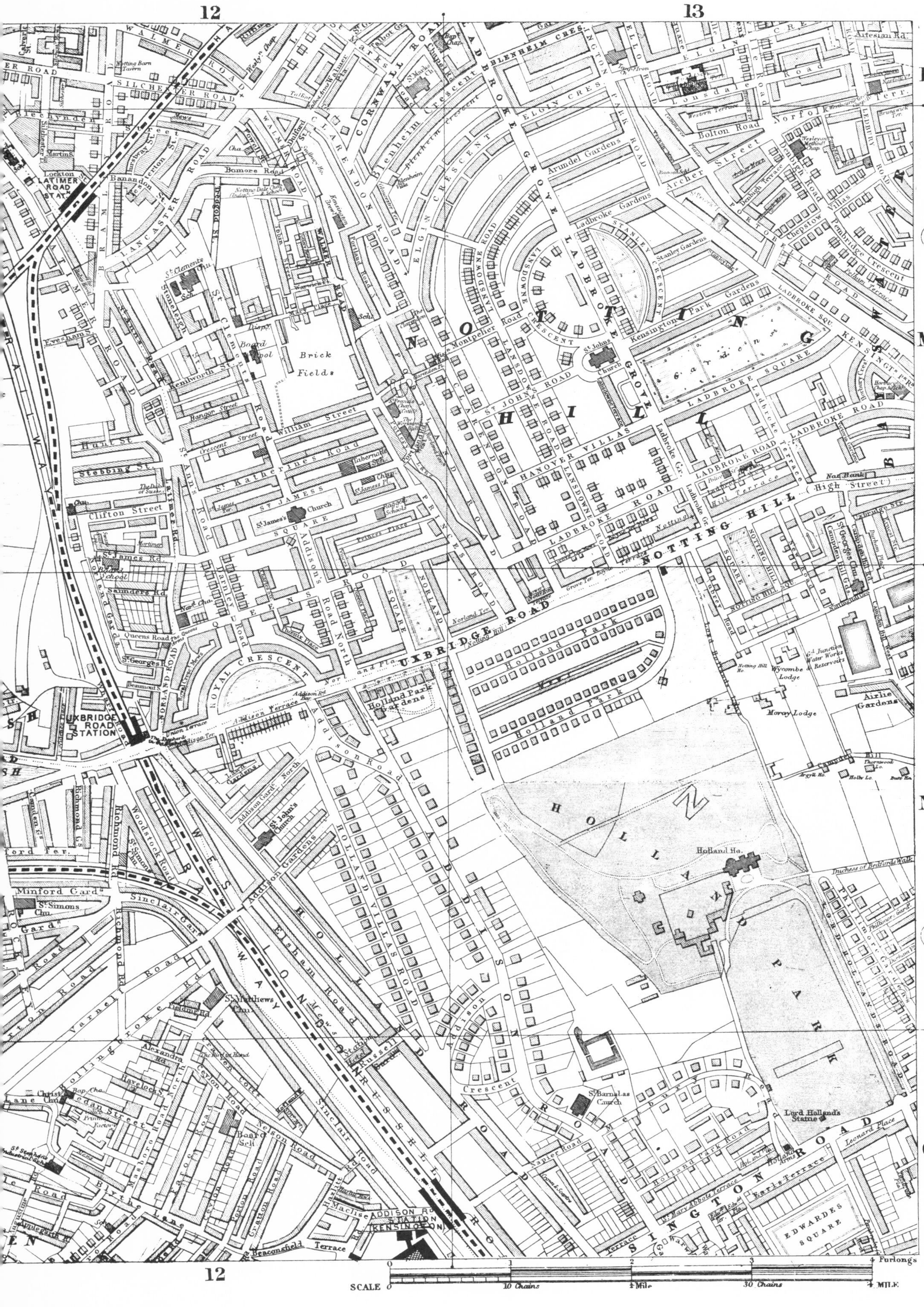
12
13
L
M
N
O
Adjoining Sheet 13
Adjoining Sheet 21
NOTTING HILL
HOLLAND PARK
LATIMER ROAD STAT.
UXBRIDGE ROAD STATION
ADDISON ROAD STATION KENSINGTON
Walmer Road
Silchester Road
Blechynden
Lancaster Road
Bomore Road
Clarendon Road
Cornwall Road
Blenheim Crescent
Elgin Crescent
Ladbroke Grove
Arundel Gardens
Ladbroke Gardens
Stanley Crescent
Stanley Gardens
Kensington Park Gardens
Ladbroke Square
Lansdowne Crescent
Lansdowne Road
Montpelier Road
St Johns Church
Kensington Park Road
Westbourne Grove
Bolton Road
Archer Street
Denbigh Terrace
Chepstow Villas
Pembridge Crescent
Pelham Terrace
Kensington Gardens Square
Ladbroke Road
Ladbroke Terrace
High Street
Hanover Villas
Brick Fields
Board School
Kenilworth St.
St Clements Road
William Street
St Katherines Road
Crescent Street
Hunt St.
Stebbing St.
Clifton Street
St James's Church
St James Square
Princes Place
Addisons Road North
Norland Square
Norland Road
Queens Road
Royal Crescent
St. Georges Rd.
Uxbridge Road
Holland Park
Holland Park Gardens
Addison Road
Addison Gardens
Addison Terrace
St John's Church
Holland Villas Road
Holland Road
Holland Ho.
Lord Holland's Statue
Wycombe Lodge
Moray Lodge
Airlie Gardens
Campden Hill
Notting Hill Square
Gd. Junction Water Works Reservoirs
Duchess of Bedford's Walk
Phillimore Gardens
Woodstock Road
Richmond Rd.
Minford Gardns
St Simons Chu.
Sinclair Gardns
Sinclair Road
Elsham Road
Russell Road
St Matthews Chu.
Alexandra Rd.
Havelock Rd.
Nelson Road
Blythe Lane
Beaconsfield Terrace
Maclise Rd.
St Barnabas Church
Napier Road
Holland Park Road
Kensington Road
Earls Terrace
Edwardes Square
Leonard Place
St Mary Abbots Terrace
SCALE
10 Chains
¼ Mile
30 Chains
½ MILE
Furlongs

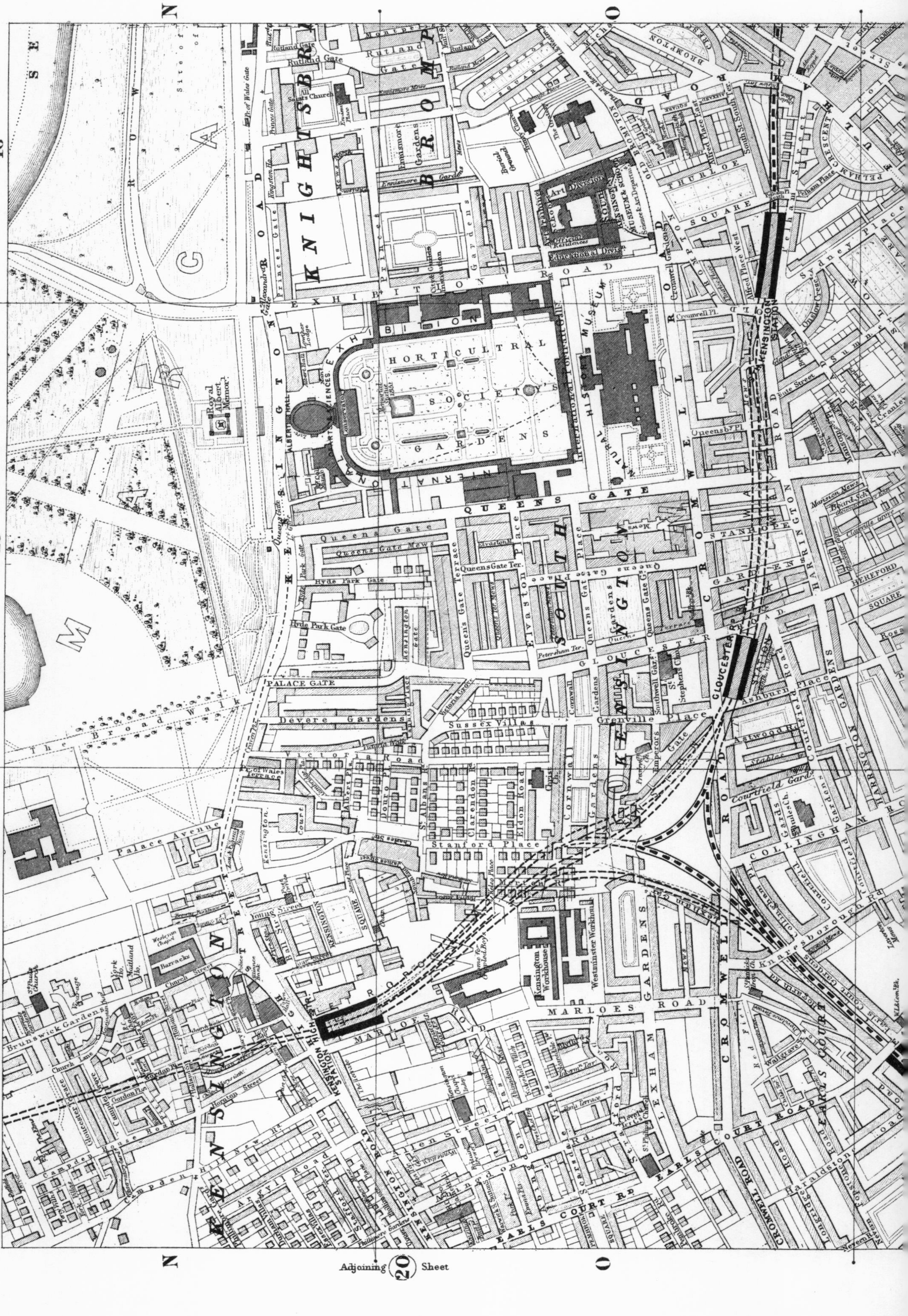

Adjoining 13 Sheet

Adjoining 20 Sheet

For same area on 4 inch scale, see sheets 42-47

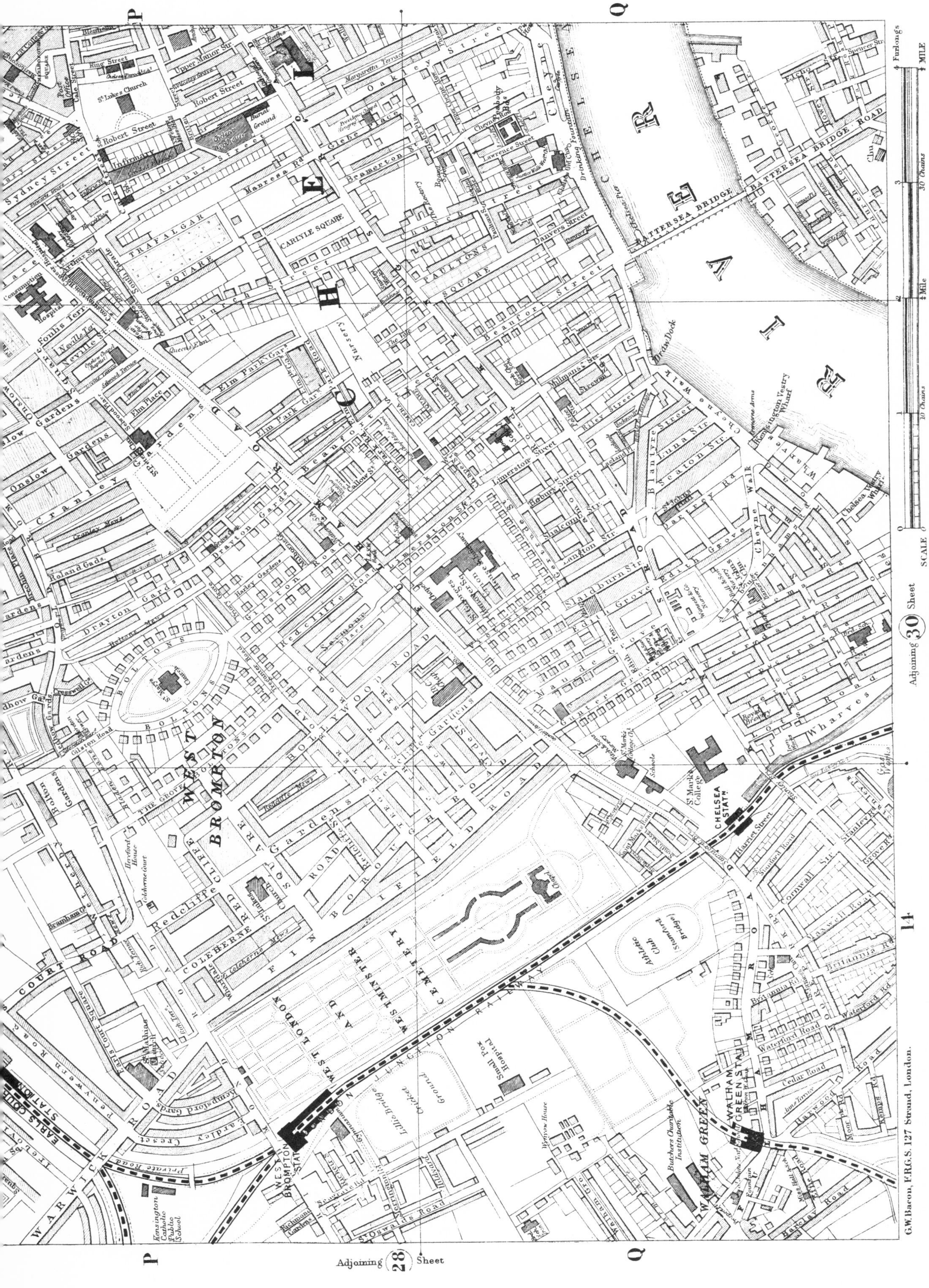
P
Q
CHELSEA
WEST BROMPTON
WALHAM GREEN
RIVER
St. Lukes Church
Infirmary
Sydney Street
Robert Street
Upper Manor Str.
King Street
Margaretta Terrace
Oakley Street
Cheyne
Glebe Place
Manresa Rd.
Arthur Street
Beamerton St.
Lawrence Street
Danvers Street
Carlyle Square
Trafalgar Square
Paultons Square
Church Street
Beaufort Street
Battersea Bridge
Battersea Bridge Road
Elm Park Gardens
Onslow Gardens
Cranley Gardens
Cranley Mews
Foulis Terr.
Neville Terr.
Neville St.
Consumption Hospital
Fulham Road
Drayton Gardens
Roland Gds.
Harley Gardens
Bolton Gardens
The Boltons
Gilston Road
Tregunter Road
Redcliffe Road
Seymour Place
Limerston Street
Hobury Street
Stadium Str.
Langton Str.
Slaidburn Str.
Edith Grove
Lots Road
Blantyre Street
Luna Str.
Seaton Str.
Riley Street
Millmans Street
Draw Dock
Cheyne Walk
Kensington Vestry Wharf
Chelsea Vestry Wharf
Wharves
Maude Grove
Uverdale Road
Burnaby Street
Royal Brewery
St. Marks College
Chelsea Statn.
Harriet Street
Stanley Road
Cromwell Str.
Kings Road
Britannia Road
Waterford Road
Cedar Road
Moore Park Road
Barclay Road
Walham Green Statn.
Butchers Charitable Institution
Athletic Club
Stamford Bridge
Small Pox Hospital
Lillie Bridge Cricket Ground
West London and Westminster Cemetery
West London Junction Railway
Finborough Road
Ifield Road
Redcliffe Gardens
Redcliffe Square
Coleherne Road
Earls Court Road
Earls Court Station
Earls Court Square
Penywern Road
Kempsford Gardens
Eardley Crescent
Warwick Road
West Brompton Statn.
Private Road
Kensington Catholic Public School
St. Oswalds Road
Richmond Gardens
SCALE
Furlongs
Mile
Chains
Adjoining 30 Sheet
14
Adjoining 28 Sheet
G.W. Bacon, F.R.G.S. 127 Strand, London.

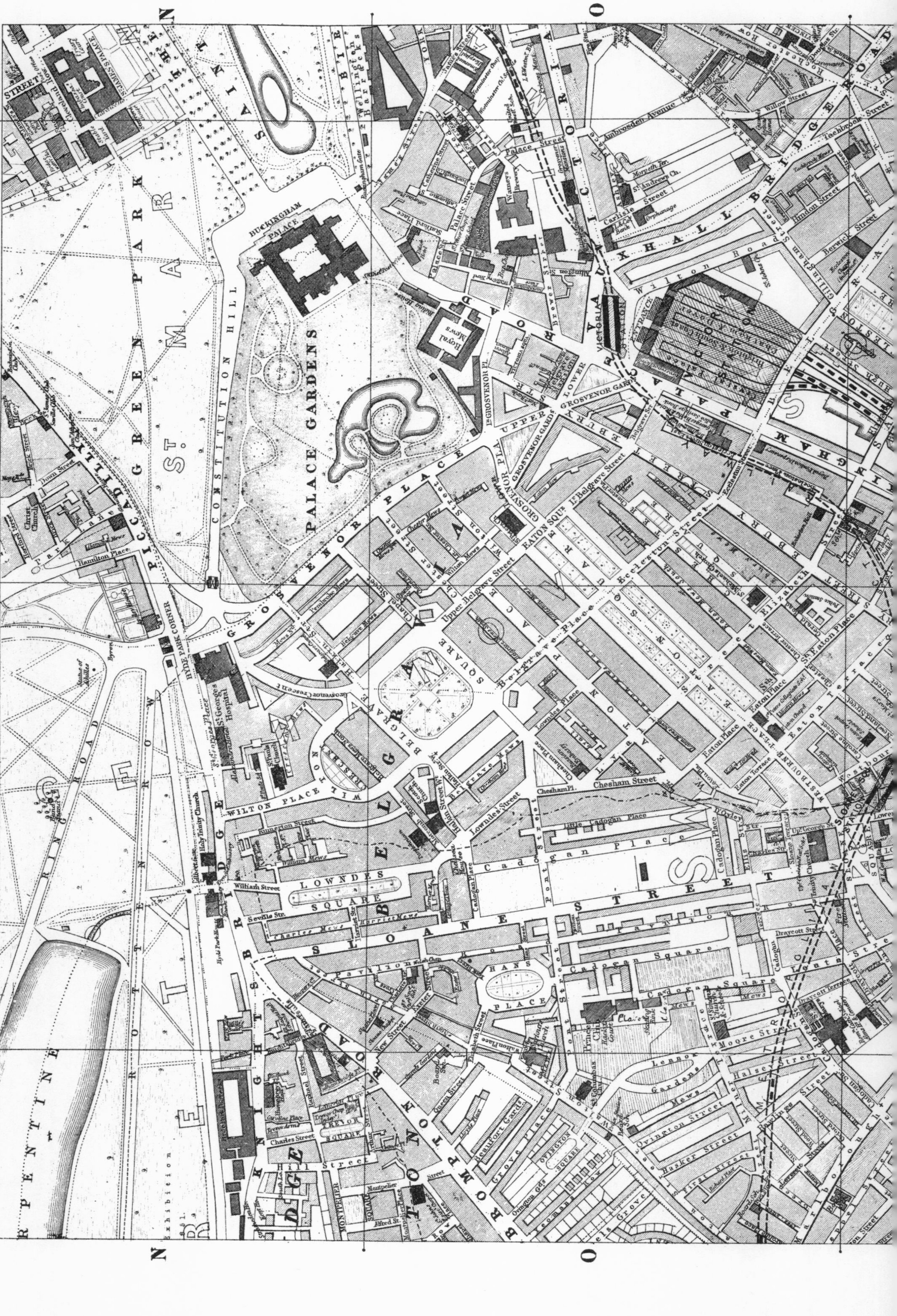

Adjoining (14) Sheet

For same area on 4 inch scale, see sheets 43·48

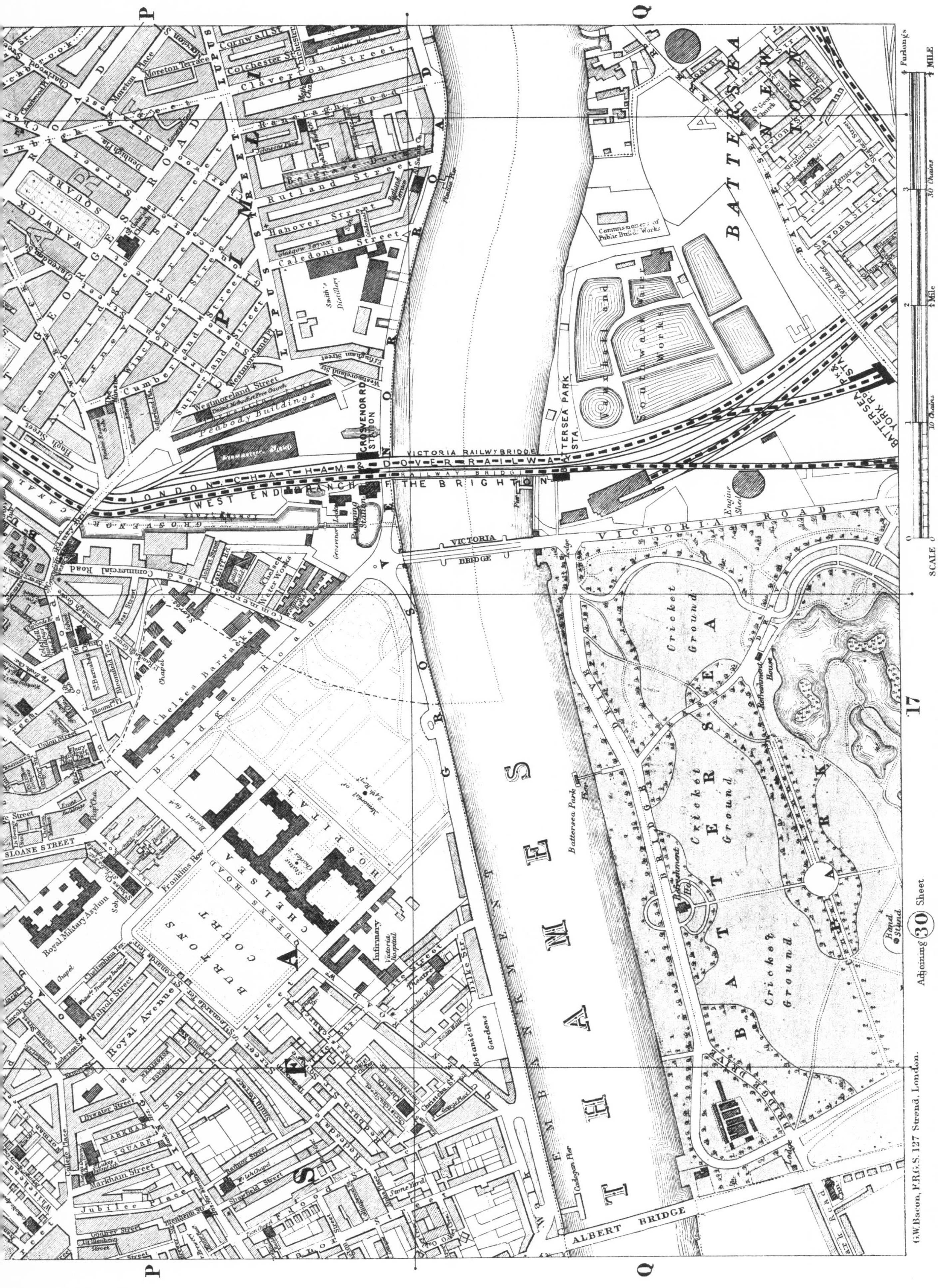
P
Q
P
Q
17
THAMES
BATTERSEA PARK
BATTERSEA NEW TOWN
VICTORIA BRIDGE
ALBERT BRIDGE
VICTORIA RAILWAY BRIDGE
LONDON CHATHAM & DOVER RAILWAY
WEST END BRANCH OF THE BRIGHTON
GROSVENOR RD STATION
BATTERSEA PARK STA.
BATTERSEA PARK & YORK RD. STA.
GROSVENOR ROAD
VICTORIA ROAD
Chelsea Barracks
Chelsea Bridge Road
Chelsea Water Works
Royal Military Asylum
HOSPITAL
Burtons Court
Queens Road
Franklins Row
Victoria Hospital
Infirmary
Botanical Gardens
Cadogan Pier
Battersea Park Pier
Cricket Ground
Refreshment House
Band Stand
Lodge
Southwark Works
Vauxhall Works
Commissioners of Public Build. Works
Engine Shed
Smith's Distillery
Peabody Buildings
Belgrave Dock
Pumping Station
SLOANE STREET
Royal Avenue
Markham Square
Markham Street
Jubilee Place
Smith Street
Commercial Road
Warwick Square
St. George's Road
Lupus Street
Rutland Street
Hanover Street
Caledonia Street
Claverton Street
Ranelagh Road
Moreton Terrace
Moreton Place
Cornwall St.
Colchester St.
Westmoreland Street
Cumberland Street
Sutherland Street
Winchester Street
Denbigh Place
Adjoining 30 Sheet
SCALE
Furlongs
Mile
10 Chains
30 Chains
G.W. Bacon, F.R.G.S. 127 Strand, London.

Adjoining 24
Adjoining 22 Sheet
Adjoining 15 Sheet
For same area on 4 inch scale, see sheets 43-48
N
O
19
20
21
WESTMINSTER BRIDGE
LAMBETH BRIDGE
WESTMINSTER BRIDGE ROAD
KENNINGTON ROAD
WATERLOO ROAD
WHITEHALL
PARLIAMENT STREET
GREAT GEORGE STREET
MILLBANK STREET
MARSHAM STREET
TUFTON STREET
PAGE STREET
REGENCY
LAMBETH PALACE
LAMBETH
WESTMINSTER
HOUSES OF PARLIAMENT
PALACE OF WESTMINSTER
NEW PALACE YARD
ST. THOMAS'S HOSPITAL
THAMES EMBANKMENT
WATERLOO STATION
GAS LIGHT & COKE Co's WORKS
Dean's Yard
Westminster School
ST. JAMES'S PARK
BIRDCAGE WALK
Millbank

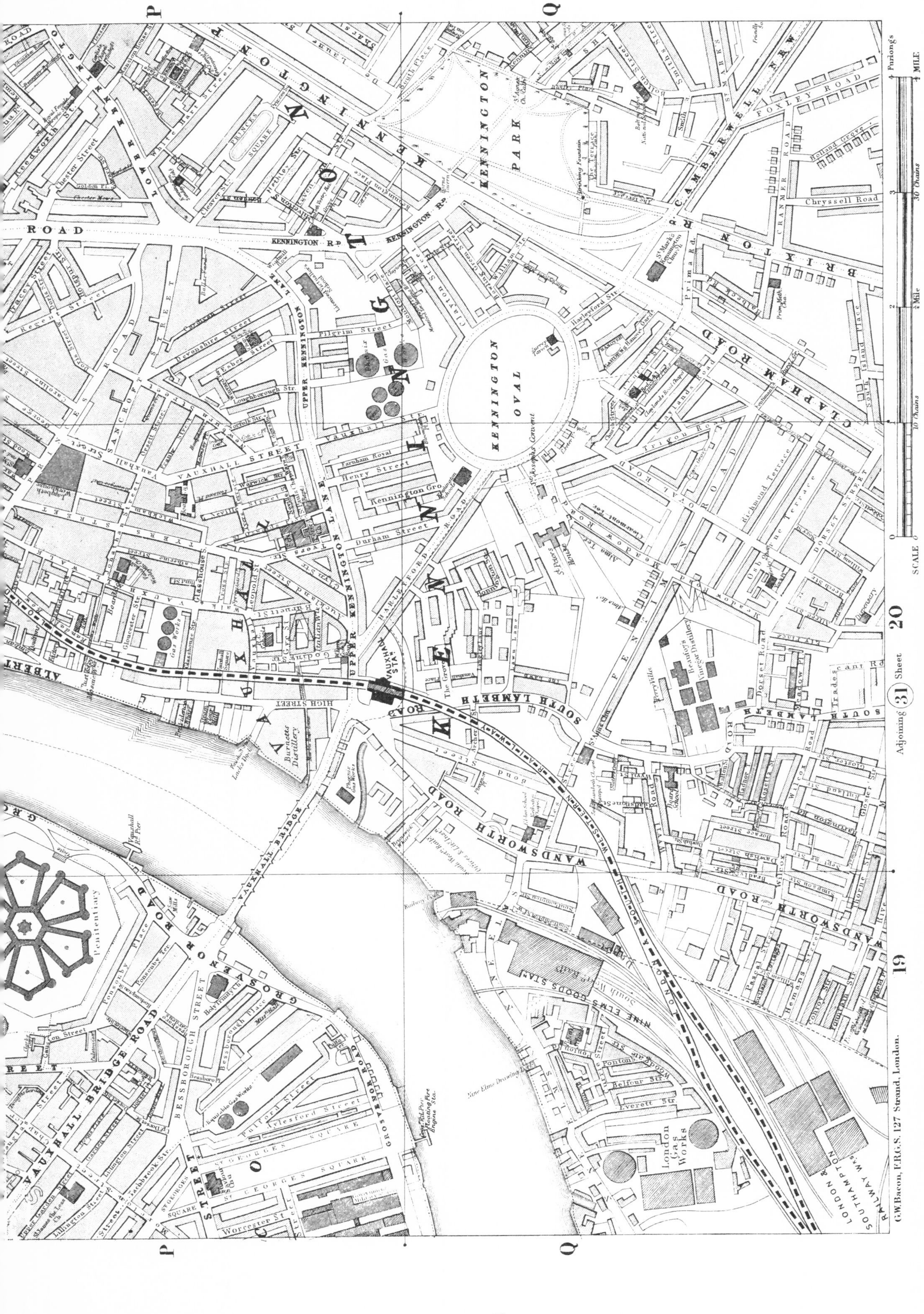

P
Q
KENNINGTON PARK
KENNINGTON OVAL
KENNINGTON ROAD
CAMBERWELL NEW RD
BRIXTON RD
CLAPHAM ROAD
UPPER KENNINGTON LANE
VAUXHALL STREET
SOUTH LAMBETH ROAD
WANDSWORTH ROAD
NINE ELMS GOODS STA.
VAUXHALL BRIDGE
VAUXHALL BRIDGE ROAD
GROSVENOR ROAD
BESSBOROUGH STREET
Penitentiary
London Gas Works
Burnetts Distillery
LONDON & SOUTHAMPTON RAILWAY Wks.
Chryssell Road
Foxley Road
Holland Grove
Cranmer Road
Trigon Road
Richmond Terrace
Durham Street
Kennington Gro.
Henry Street
Farnham Royal
Loughborough Str.
Devonshire Street
Pilgrim Street
Harleyford Str.
Clayton Street
Princes Square
Chester Street
Gloucester Str.
Gas Works
High Street
Everett Str.
Belfour Str.
Aylesford Street
Lillington Street
St. George's Square
Worcester Str.
Dorset Road
Wilcox Road
Horace Street
Heyford
St. Joseph's Convent
St. Peter's House
Adjoining 31 Sheet
20
19
SCALE
4 Furlongs
½ Mile
30 Chains
10 Chains
¼ MILE
G.W. Bacon, F.R.G.S. 127 Strand, London.

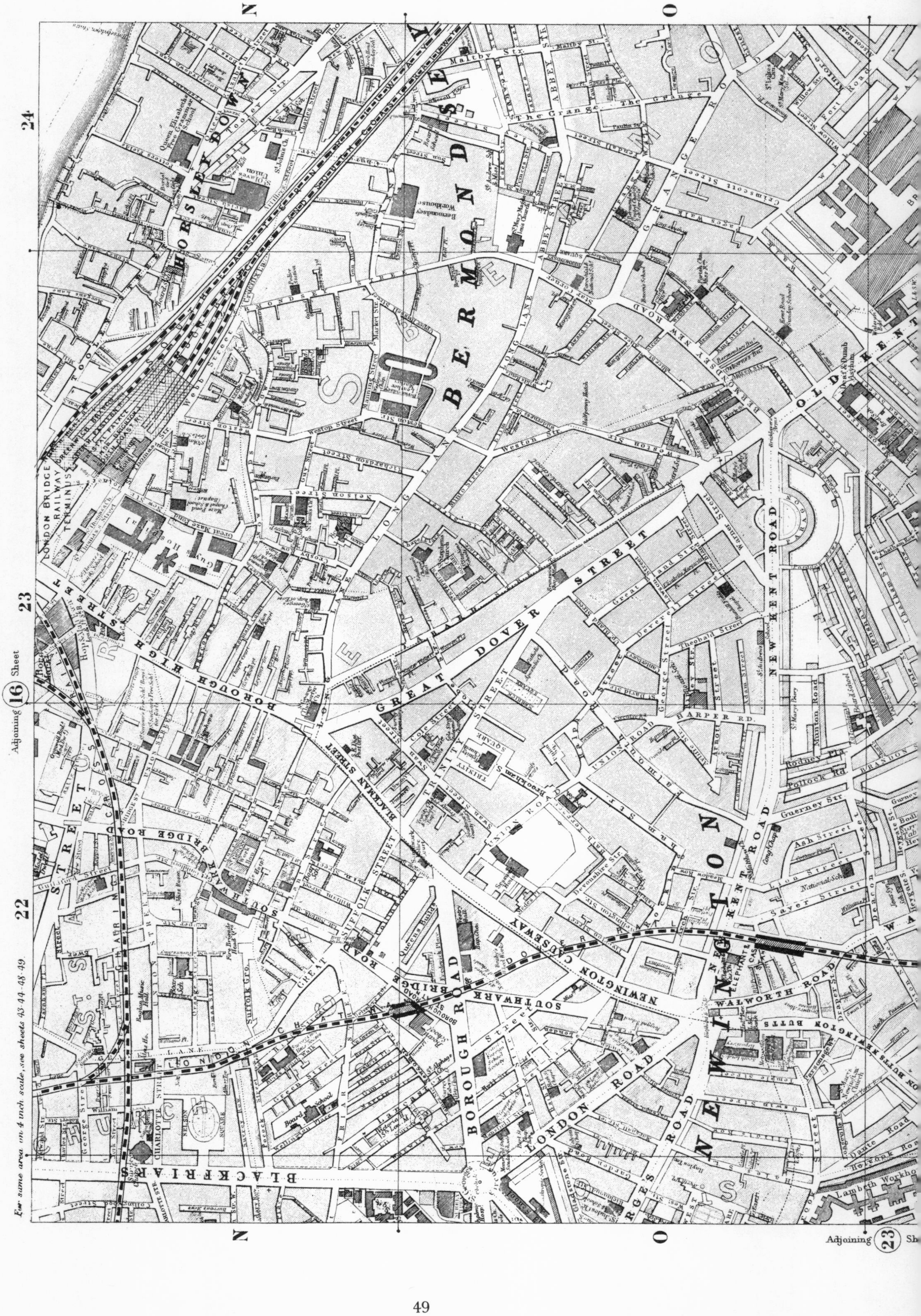
N
O
24
23
22
Adjoining 16 Sheet
For same area on 4 inch scale, see sheets 43·44·48·49.
Adjoining 23 Sheet
BERMONDSEY
NEWINGTON
LONDON BRIDGE RAILWAY TERMINUS
BOROUGH HIGH STREET
GREAT DOVER STREET
NEW KENT ROAD
OLD KENT
NEWINGTON CAUSEWAY
WALWORTH ROAD
SOUTHWARK BRIDGE ROAD
BOROUGH ROAD
LONDON ROAD
BLACKFRIARS

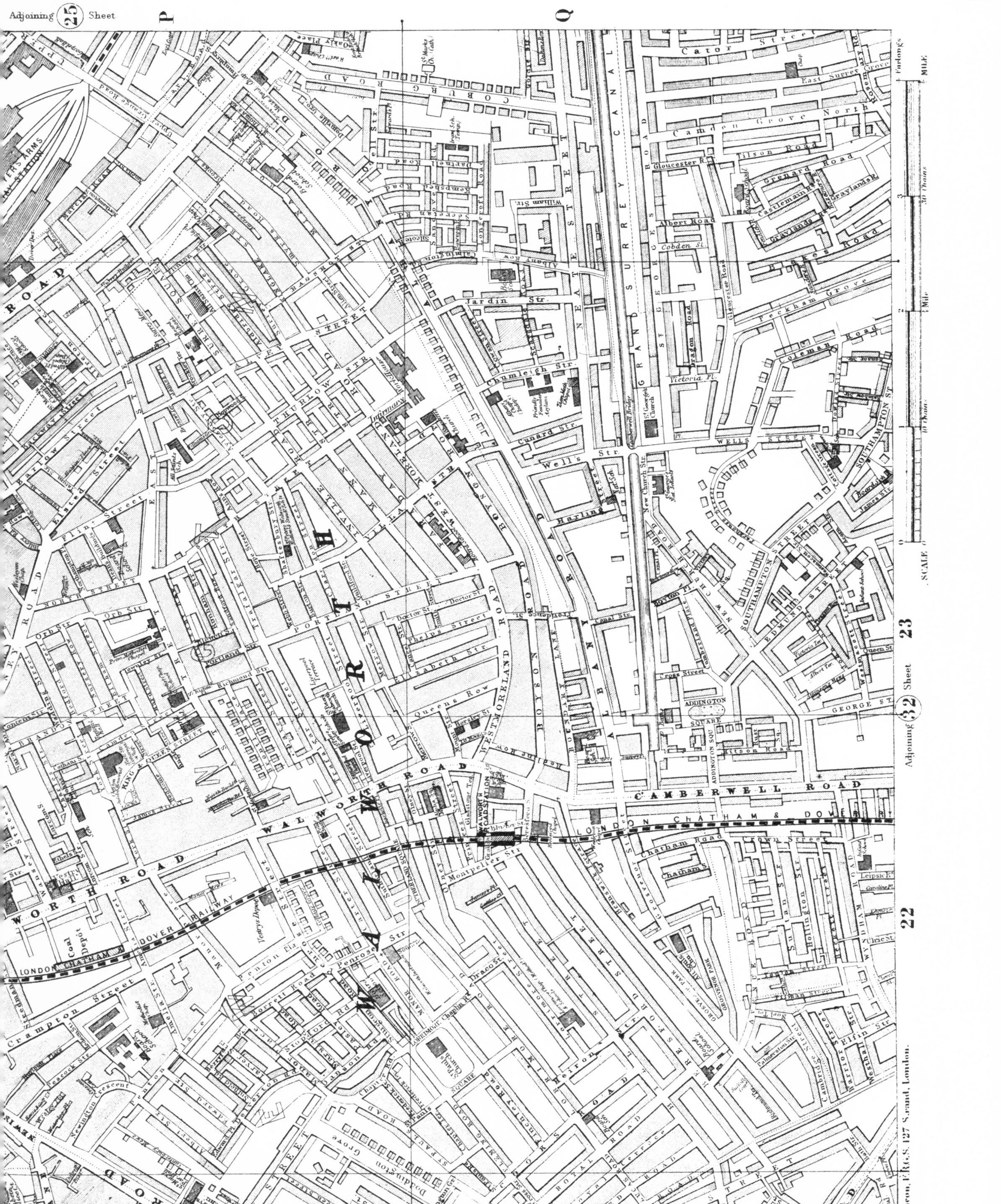

Adjoining 25 Sheet
P
Q
Cator Street
Coburg Road
East Surrey Grove
Camden Grove North
Tilson Road
Gloucester R.
Grenard Road
Castlemain R.
Graylands R.
Albert Road
Cobden St.
Albany Row
Peckham Grove
Jardin Str.
Coleman Road
Dragon Road
Chumleigh Str.
Victoria Pl.
St. George's Church
Camberwell Bridge
Cunard Str.
Wells Street
Well's Str.
Southampton St.
Harling
New Church Str.
Southampton Street
Edmund Street
Canal St.
Boyson Road
Boyson Lane
Albany Road
Grand Surrey Canal
Neate Street
Cross Street
Addington Square
Ritson Road
Camberwell Road
London Chatham & Dover Ry
Chatham Road
Crown Street
Leipsic Rd
Wyndham Road
Westmoreland Road
Walworth Road Station
Walworth Road
Montpelier Str
Beresford Street
Portland Street
Doctor St
Phelps Street
Elizabeth Str
Queens Row
Thurlow Str
East Street
Orb Str
Flint Street
North Street
Manor Place
Penton Pl.
Penrose Str
Crampton Street
Peacock Str
Newington Crescent
Coal Depot
London Chatham & Dover Railway
W A L W O R T H
23
22
Adjoining 32 Sheet
SCALE
Mile
Furlongs
30 Chains
10 Chains
G.W. Bacon, F.R.G.S. 127 Strand, London.

Adjoining 26 Sheet
Adjoining 17 Sheet
Adjoining 24 Sheet
Albion Dock
Canada Dock
Canada Yard
Albion Yard
Surrey Gas Works
Dock Office
LOWER POOL
THAMES TUNNEL
EAST LONDON RAILY.
Tunnel Pier
Church Stairs
Hanover Stairs
New Crane Stairs
King Edwards Stairs
Elephant Stairs
Princes Stairs
Rotherhithe Stairs
Platform Wharf
Wapping New Stairs
Thames Police Station
WAPPING
WAPPING BASIN
Wapping Old Stairs
Union Stairs
Hermitage Stairs
Gun Wharf
UPPER POOL
THE POOL
SOUTHWARK PARK
LOWER ROAD
Neptune Street
Paradise St.
Paradise Place
Princes Street
Adam St.
Rotherhithe Workhouse
Parish St.
Cherry Garden Str.
Marygold Street
Salisbury Street
West Lane
Lucas St.
Prospect St.
Major Rd.
Keyton Road
Stork Road
Drummond Road
Spa Road
St. James's Rd.
Jamaica Road
Dockhead
Neckinger St.
Neckinger Road
Abbey Street
Layard Road
Camilla Rd.
Vauban St.
Amelia Row
Board School
Ascot Road
Grange Rd.
Tooley St.
Stanworth St.
Queen's Place
Raymond Street
Anchor & Hope Alley
Lower Well Alley
Bird Street
Johns Street
London Street
Virginia Row
Georges Row
Southwark Park Road
For same area on 4 inch scale, see sheets 44, 49.
N
O
25
26

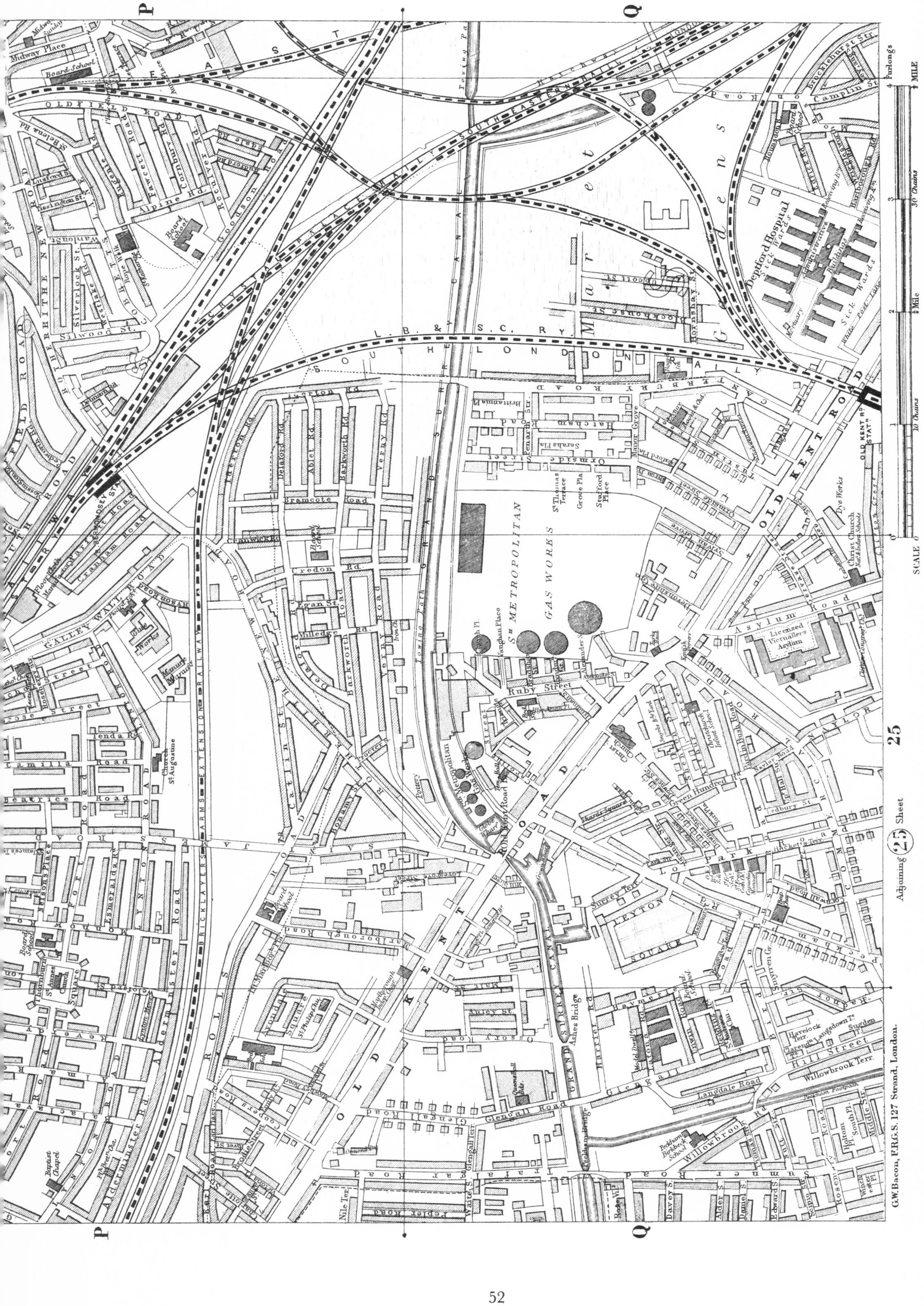
P
Q
25
Adjoining 25 Sheet
SCALE
MILE
Furlongs
Chains
G.W. Bacon, F.R.G.S. 127 Strand, London.
Deptford Hospital
Sick Wards
Administrative Buildings
Mortuary
White Post Lane
OLD KENT RD. STAT.
OLD KENT ROAD
S^T METROPOLITAN GAS WORKS
Licensed Victuallers Asylum
Asylum Road
Christ Church
Dye Works
Canterbury Road
South London Railway
L.B. & S.C. Ry.
South Eastern Railway
Bricklayers Arms Extension Railway
Grand Surrey Canal
Towing Path
Ruby Street
Leyton Square
Glengall Road
Ashes Bridge
Hill Street
Willowbrook Terr.
Langdale Road
Peckham Birkbeck School
Bramcote Road
Credon Rd
Egan St
Barkworth Road
Verney Road
Catlin St
Pottery
Galleyway Road
Rotherhithe New Road
Silwood St.
Oldfield Road
Alpine Rd.
Midway Place
Board School
Cranham Road
Beatrice Road
Camilla Road
Tenda Rd
Church St. Augustine
Baptist Chapel
Alderminster Rd.
Ossory Road
Hatcham Road
Sarahs Pla.
St. Thomas Terrace
Grove Pla.
Stafford Place
Manor Grove
Naylor Road
Ledbury St.
Green Hundred Rd.
Park Road
Peckham Road
Pepler Road
Nile Ter.

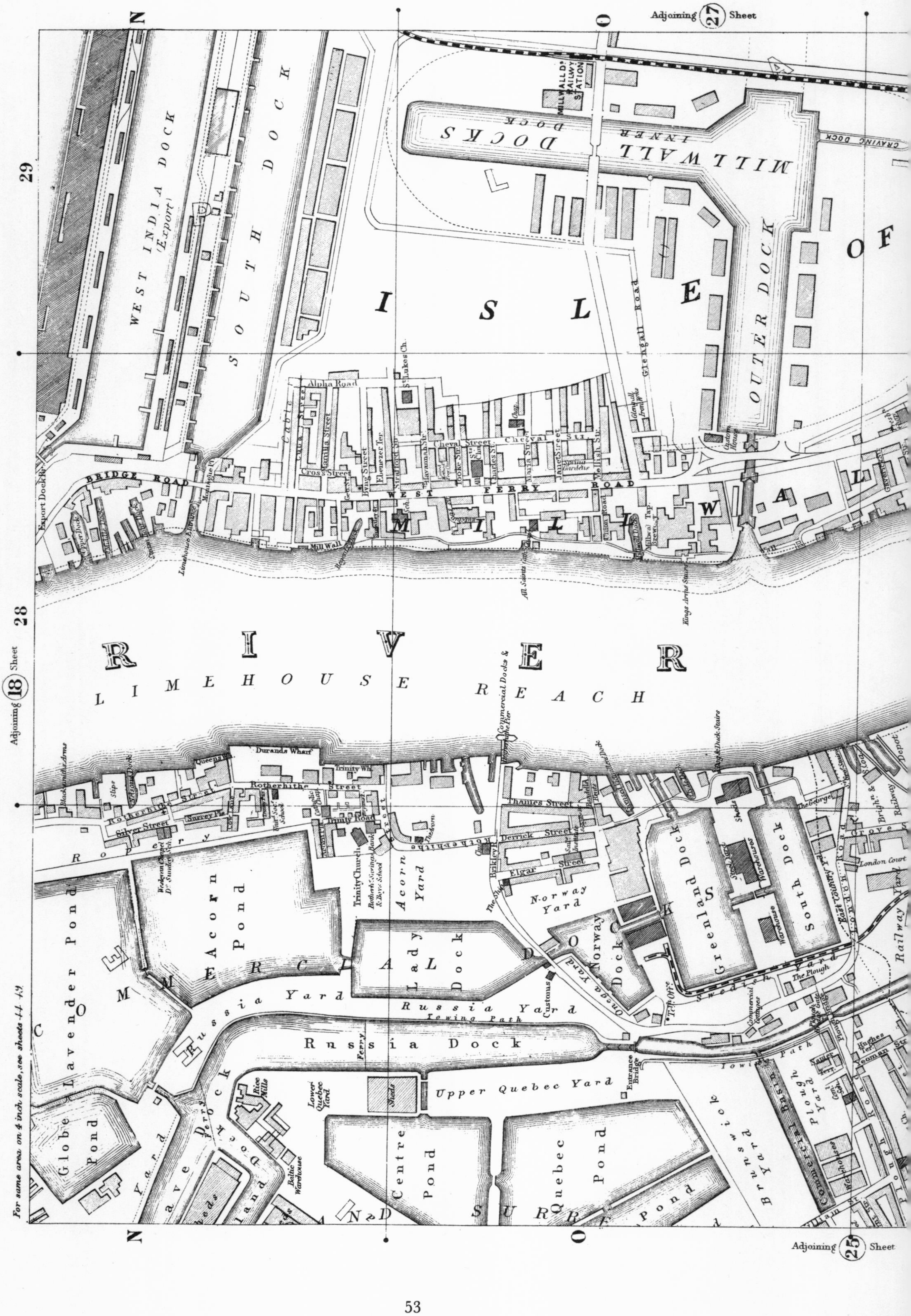
Adjoining 27 Sheet
WEST INDIA DOCK (Export)
SOUTH DOCK
MILLWALL DOCKS
INNER DOCK
OUTER DOCK
MILLWALL RAILWAY STATION
CRAVING DOCK
ISLE OF
MILL WALL
Glengall Road
Alpha Road
Cheval Street
Cross Street
BRIDGE ROAD
WEST FERRY ROAD
St Lukes Ch.
Export Dock
Limehouse Entrance
Millwall Tap Brewery
Kings Arms Stairs
All Saints
Adjoining 18 Sheet
RIVER
LIMEHOUSE REACH
Commercial Docks & Greenland Pier
Durands Wharf
Queens Wh.
Trinity Wh.
Blacksmiths Arms
Rotherhithe Street
Silver Street
Surrey Pl.
Trinity Road
Thames Street
Derrick Street
Elgar Street
Ropery
Acorn Pond
Acorn Yard
Trinity Church
Lavender Pond
Norway Yard
Norway Dock
Lady Dock
Greenland Dock
South Dock
Onega Yard
Customs
Russia Yard
Towing Path
Russia Dock
Upper Quebec Yard
Lower Quebec Yard
Entrance Bridge
Rice Mills
Baltic Warehouse
Globe Pond
Centre Pond
Quebec Pond
Brunswick Yard
Plough Yard
Commercial Basin
The Plough
Swedish Yard
Grove
London Court
Railway Yard
Railway Depot
COMMERCIAL DOCKS
SURREY
For same area on 4 inch scale, see sheets 44 49
Adjoining 25 Sheet

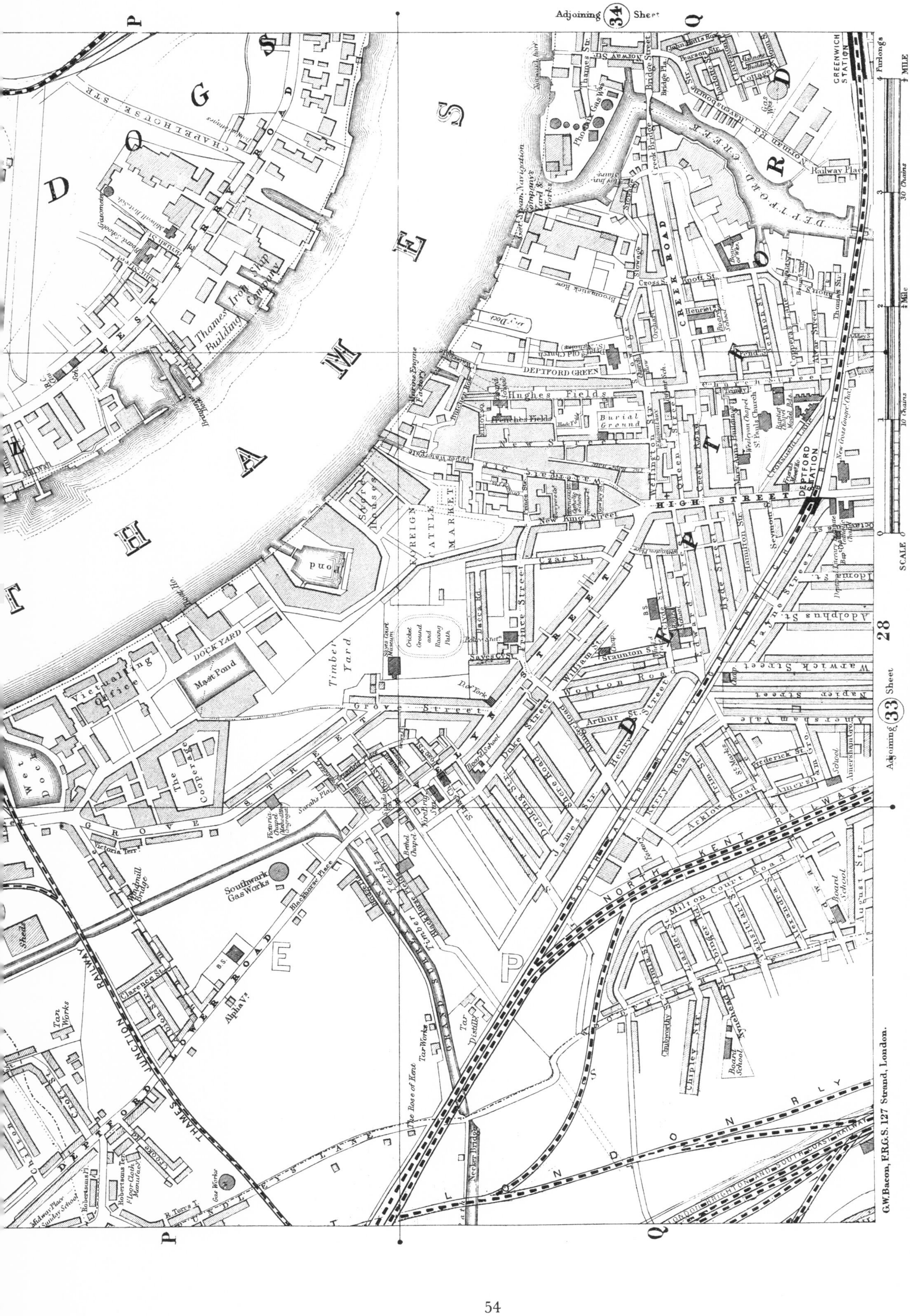
Adjoining 34 Sheet
Adjoining 33 Sheet
28
SCALE
Mile
G.W. Bacon, F.R.G.S. 127 Strand, London.
THAMES
DOGS
DEPTFORD
Thames Iron Building Company
Deptford Green
High Street
Creek Road
Deptford Creek
Church Street
Hughes Fields
Burial Ground
St. Pauls Church
Wesleyan Chapel
Deptford Station
Greenwich Station
Foreign Cattle Market
Dock Yard
Mast Pond
Victualling Office
Wet Dock
The Cooperage
Timber Yard
Cricket Ground and Racing Path
Sayes Court Museum
Grove Street
Evelyn Street
Southwark Gas Works
Lower Road
Thames Junction Railway
South Eastern Railway
North Kent Railway
London Brighton and South Coast Railway
Tan Works
Tar Works
Tar Distillery
Neckinger Bridge
Milton Court Road
Amersham Vale
Napier Street
Warwick Street
Adolphus Street
Payne Street
Board School

For same area on 4 inch scale, see sheets 44-49.

Adjoining (19) Sheet

Adjoining (18) Sheet

P
Q
THAMES
GREENWICH REACH
GREENWICH
Nth. GREENWICH RAILWAY STATION
MAZE HILL STATION
SOUTH EASTERN RAILWAY
ROYAL HOSPITAL CEMETERY
Union Workhouse
Telegraph Construction and Maintenance Companys Works
Portland Cement Works
Thames Soap Factory
Enderby's Wharf
Cubitt Town Pier
London Oil Storage Compy.
Millwall Wharf
Plough Wharf
Marsh Lane
Marsh Street
Bellot Str.
Waldridge Street
Church Street East
Northumberland Street
Tyler New Town
Tyler Str.
George Street
Edward Street
Park Street
Lower Park St.
Park Row
King William Street
Church Street
BRIDGE STREET
Railway Road
Ship Street
Ferry Street
Horse Ferry
Steam Ferry
ROYAL NAVAL SCHOOLS
ROYAL HOSPITAL
Adjoining 26 Sheet
Adjoining 34 Sheet
SCALE
30
G.W.Bacon, F.R.G.S. 127. Strand, London.

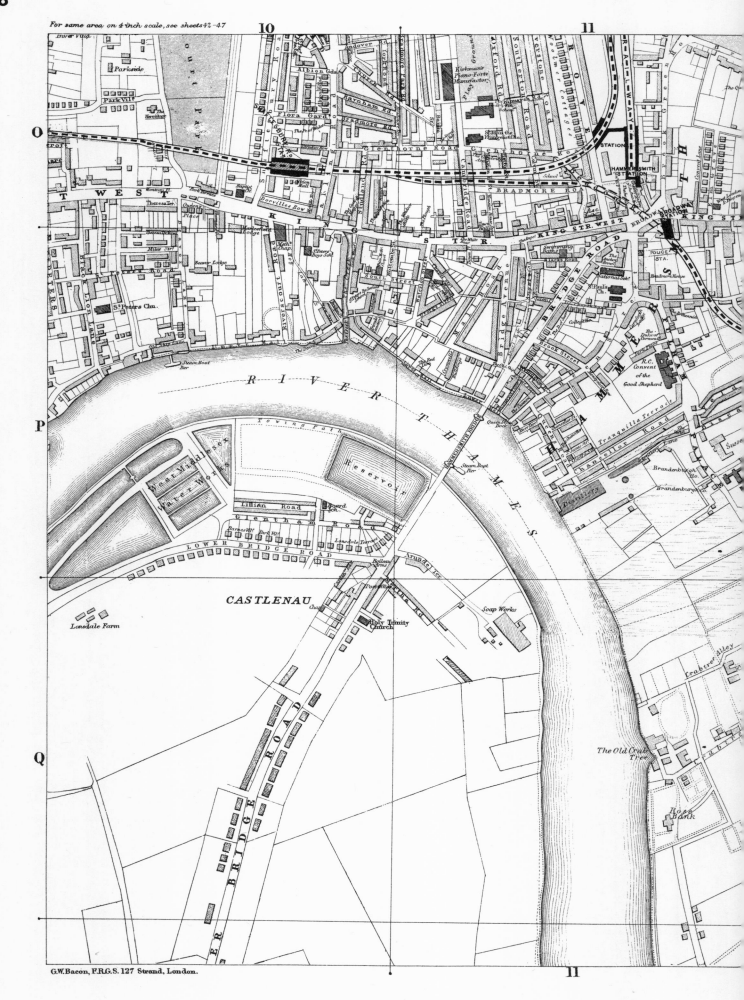

For same area on 4 inch scale, see sheets 42-47

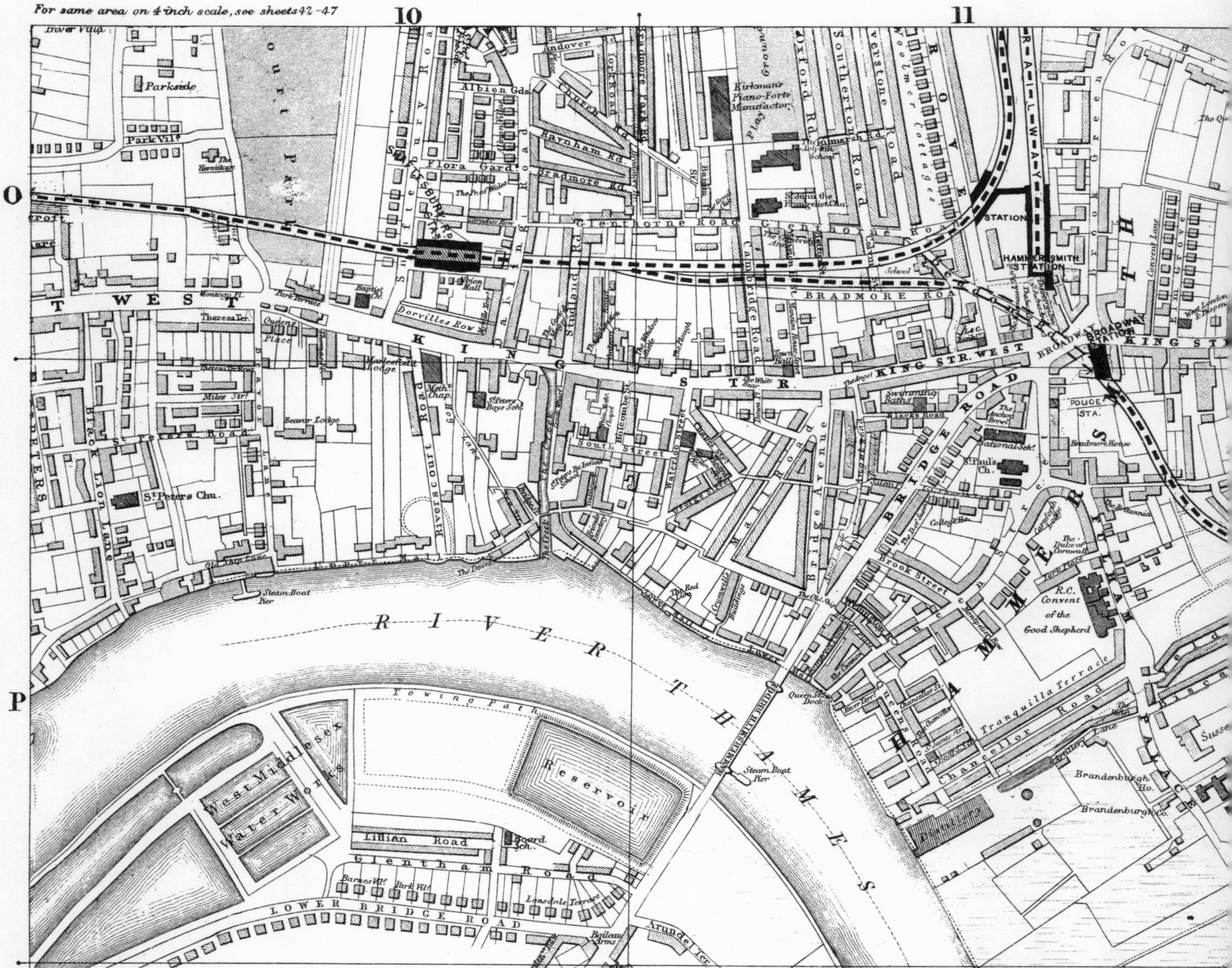

G.W. Bacon, F.R.G.S. 127 Strand, London.

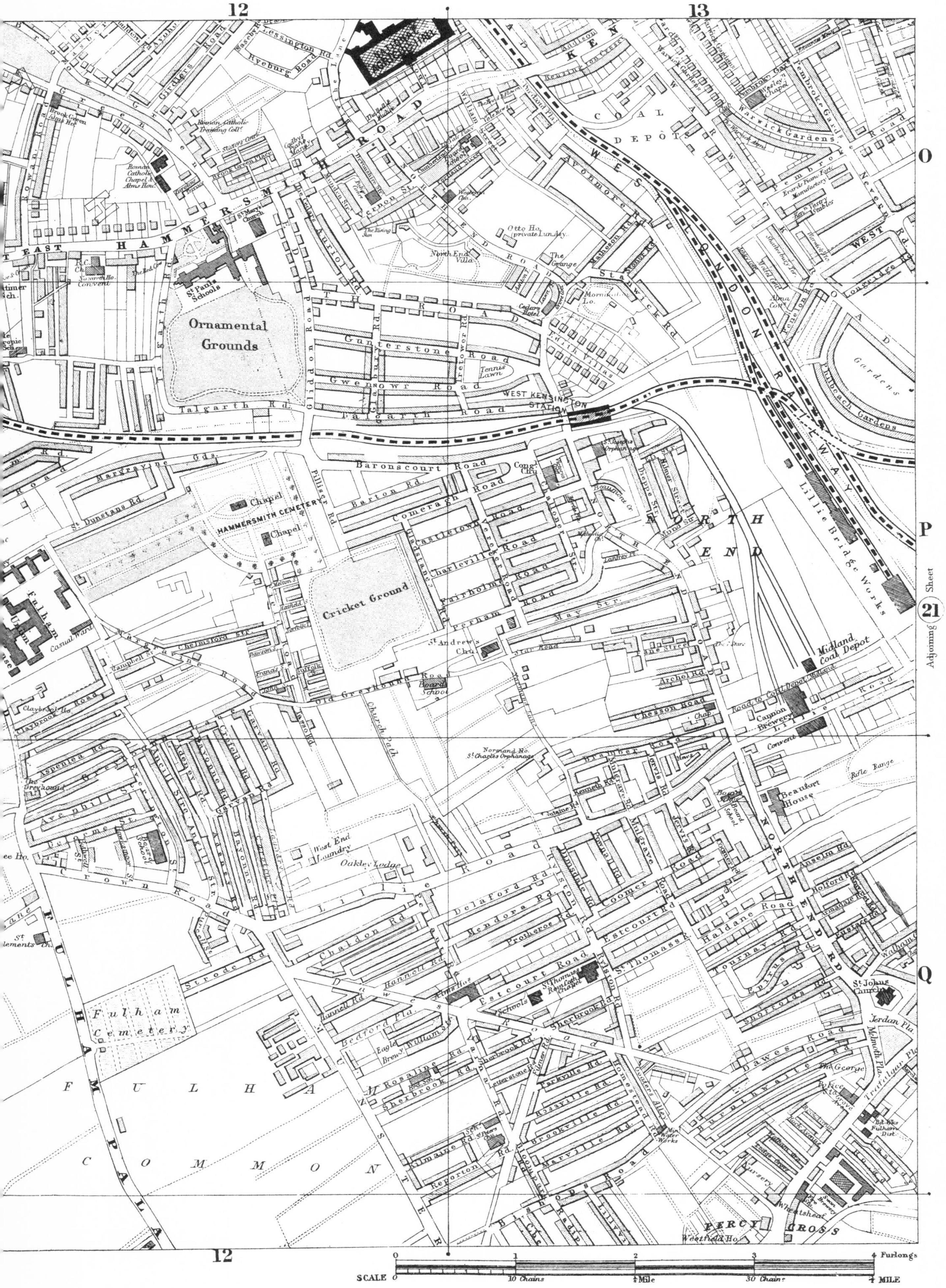
12
13
O
P
Q
Adjoining Sheet 21
Ornamental Grounds
St Pauls Schools
HAMMERSMITH CEMETERY
Chapel
Chapel
Cricket Ground
WEST KENSINGTON STATION
WEST LONDON RAILWAY
COAL DEPOT
NORTH END
Lillie Bridge Works
Midland Coal Depot
Cannon Brewery
Beaufort House
Fulham Cemetery
FULHAM COMMON
FULHAM PALACE RD
PERCY CROSS
Talgarth Road
Gunterstone Road
Gwendwr Road
Baronscourt Road
Barton Rd
Comeragh Road
Castletown Road
Charleville Road
Fairholme Road
Perham Road
May Str
Margravine Gds
Margravine Road
St Dunstans Rd
Chelmsford Str
Old Greyhound Road
Church Path
Lillie Road
Chesson Road
Archel Rd
Star Road
Avonmore Rd
Stanwick Rd
Edith Villas
Pembroke Gardens
Warwick Gardens
Philbeach Gardens
Aspenlea Rd
Crown Road
Strode Rd
Chaldon Rd
Delaford Rd
Mendora Rd
Protheroe Rd
Estcourt Road
Dawes Road
Sherbrook Rd
Rosaline Rd
Parkville Rd
Rosaville Rd
Brookville Rd
Harville Rd
Reporton Rd
Haldane Road
Tournay Rd
Anselm Rd
St Johns Church
West End Laundry
Oakley Lodge
Otto Ho.
The Grange
North End Villa
Normand Ho. St Charles Orphanage
St Andrews Chu.
Board School
Alms Hos
Eagle Brewy
Westfield Ho.
Wheatsheaf
The George
Hammersmith Road
East Hammersmith
0 1 2 3 4 Furlongs
SCALE 0 10 Chains ¼ Mile 30 Chains ½ MILE

For same area on 4 inch scale, see sheet 47.

Adjoining 28 Sheet

12
R
S
T
FULHAM
PUTNEY
FULHAM PALACE
Bishops Avenue
Bishops Walk
Palace Gardens
All Saints Fulham Church
St. James' Home
Craven Cottage
Devil's Alley
Colehill House
Colehill Lane
The Model House
HIGH STREET
Church Street
Church Row
FULHAM & PUTNEY BRI.
PUTNEY BRIDGE
PUTNEY BRIDGE (OLD)
Willow Bank
Ranelagh House
Barnes Elms Park
Towing Path
River Bank
London Rowing Club
Half Moon Cricket Ground
LOWER RICHMOND ROAD
Windsor Pla.
Putney Pier
Windsor St.
Gardners Lane
International School
St. Mary's Church
Cedar Lodge
THE CEDARS
PUTNEY SQUARE
Coopers Arms Lane
Coopers Arms
Charlwood Road
Clarendon Rd.
Spencer Rd.
Botham Villas Road
Stanbridge Rd.
Sefton St.
Fairfax Ho.
Montserrat Rd.
The Lawn
Werter Road
Disraeli Road
Post Office
PUTNEY STATION
UPPER RICHMOND ROAD
Chapel Grave Yard
Police Sta.
Ravenna Road
Burston Road
St. Johns Church
St. Johns Rd.
PUTNEY HILL
St. Johns Road East
Carlton Rd.
Oxford Road
Rockland Rd.
College Street
Bective Road
Oak Hill Road
St. Stephen's Church
Riding School
Fulham Park Gardens
Burlington Road
Munster Rd.
The Durell Arms
Emanuel Church
Oxford Cong. Chap.
Bapt. Chap.
12

G.W.Bacon, F.R.G.S. 127 Strand, London.

13
14
COMMON
ROAD
KINGS ROAD
SANDS END
GAS WORKS
PARSONS GREEN
The Green
Peterborough House
Market Gardens
HURLINGHAM PARK
Hurlingham House
Broom House
Lonsdale Ho.
Broomhouse Dock
Elizabethan Charity School
Broom House Lane
Bryans Lane
Daisy La.
Southfield Fm.
Chemical Works
Malt Ho.
WANDSWORTH BRIDGE
WANDSWORTH BRIDGE ROAD
THE TOWN MEADOW
St. Cyprians Orphanage
Edenhurst
Pitt Place
Church
Rectory Place
Mission Hall
Crown Brewery
Chapel
Grove Ho.
Sandilands Rd.
Maynards Distillery
Pier
WANDSWORTH
WANDSWORTH STATION
LONDON & SOUTH WESTERN
WINDSOR BRANCH
RICHMOND
Point Pleasant
Oak Hill Road
Santos Road
Ferrier Str.
White House
Lion Str.
Tonsley Hill
Fullerton Road
Board School
Swing Br.
Adjoining Sheet 30
13
SCALE
0 1 2 3 4 Furlongs
10 Chains
¼ Mile
30 Chains
½ MILE

For same area on 4 inch scale, see sheets 47-48
14
Adjoining 21 Sheet
15
R
S
T
Adjoining 29 Sheet
EEL BROOK COMMON
IMPERIAL GAS WORKS
SANDY END
Chelsea Creek
Railway Wharf
Railway Dock
WEST LONDON
St. Mary's Church
BATTERSEA REACH
Peterborough House
WANDSWORTH BRIDGE ROAD
KINGS ROAD
Market Gardens
THE TOWN MEADOWS
Bryans Lane
Southfield Fm.
Daisy La.
Elizabethan Charity School
Lonsdale Ho.
Broomhouse Dock
Chemical Works
Malt Ho.
Grove Ho.
Chapel
Price's Patent Candle Company
Battersea Creek
Starch Works
Watney's Distillery
Mendip Rd.
YORK ROAD
Holman St.
Creek St.
School
Saw Mills
Wharf
Dale Pla.
Ship Lane
Jews Row
Warple Way
Board School
Maysoule Road
Harbutt Road
Cologne Road
Weston St.
Fishmongers Alms Houses
WANDSWORTH STATION
Ferrier Str.
Gas Works
White House
Swing Br.
Bap. Chap.
WINDSOR BRANCH
LONDON & SOUTH WESTERN
WANDSWORTH
Park Road
G.W.Bacon, F.R.G.S. 127 Strand, London.
14
15

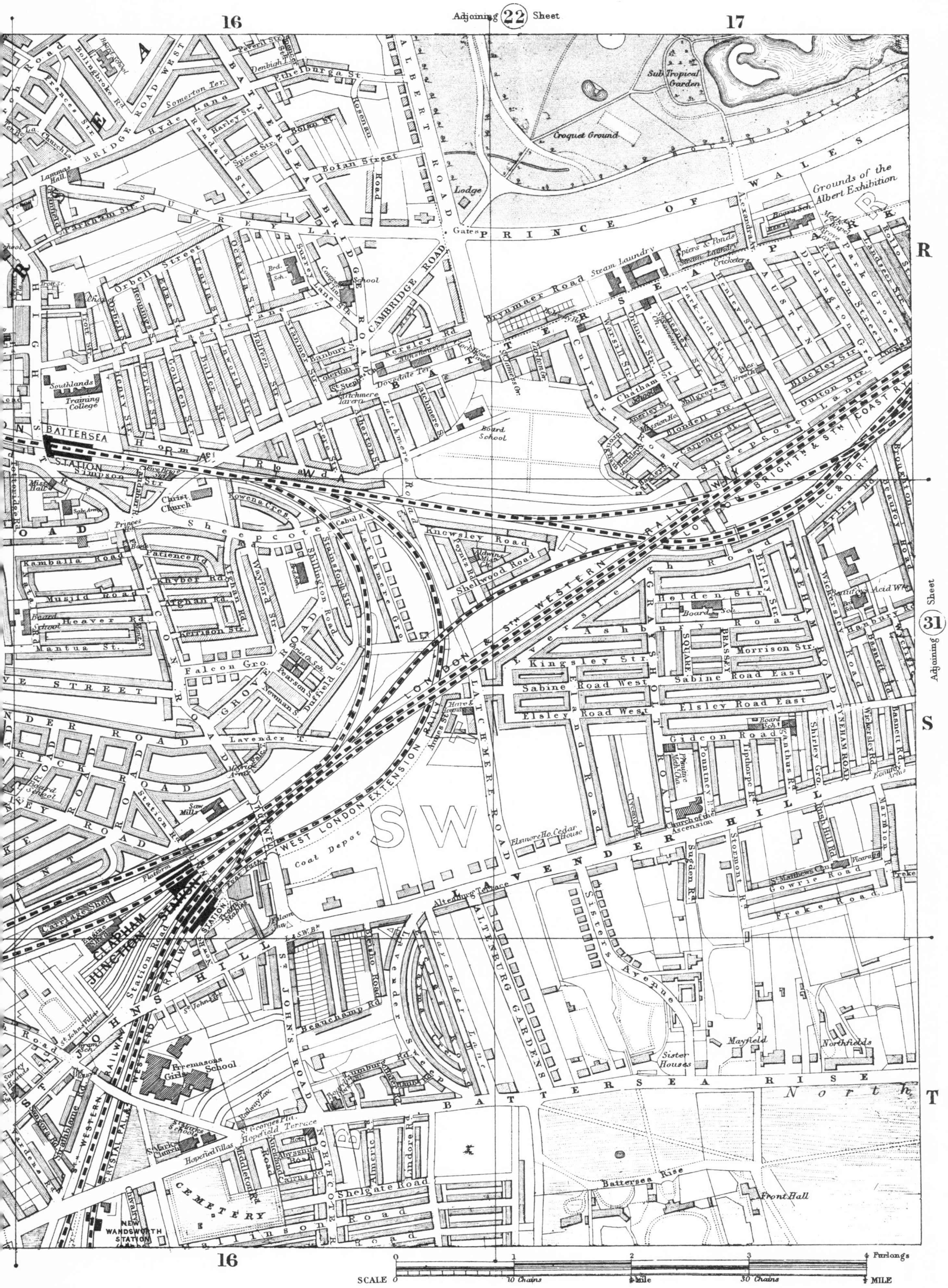
Adjoining 22 Sheet
16
17
Sub Tropical Garden
Croquet Ground
Lodge
Gates
PRINCE OF WALES
Grounds of the Albert Exhibition
Board Sch.
Spiers & Ponds Steam Laundry
Steam Laundry
Brynmaer Road
ALBERT ROAD
CAMBRIDGE ROAD
BATTERSEA BRIDGE ROAD
BATTERSEA PARK
Bolan Street
Surrey Lane
Orbell Street
Southlands Training College
BATTERSEA STATION
Christ Church
Sheepcote
Kamballa Road
Patience Rd
Khyber Rd
Musjid Road
Heaver Rd
Mantua St.
Morrison Str.
Falcon Gro.
Falcon Road
Grove Road
Lavender T.
Knowsley Road
Shellwood Road
Shillington Str.
Stainforth Str.
Latchmere Gro.
LATCHMERE ROAD
LONDON & STH WESTERN
WEST LONDON EXTENSION RAILY
Coal Depot
SW
Holden Str.
Board Sch.
Ashbury Road
Kingsley Str.
Sabine Road West
Sabine Road East
Elsley Road West
Elsley Road East
Gideon Road
TYNEHAM ROAD
Church of the Ascension
Elsmore Ho.
Cedar House
LAVENDER HILL
Altenburg Terrace
ALTENBURG GARDENS
Sisters Avenue
Sister Houses
Mayfield
Northfields
Gowrie Road
Freke Road
Stormont R.
Sugden Rd.
St Matthews Ch.
Vicarage
CLAPHAM JUNCTION STATION
Carriage Shed
Platform
Station Road
ST JOHNS HILL
ST JOHN'S ROAD
Beauchamp Rd
Lavender Lane
Freemasons Girls School
Railway Tav.
St Georges Pl.
Hopefield Terrace
Hopefield Villas
St Marks Church
CEMETERY
NEW WANDSWORTH STATION
NORTHCOTE R
Shelgate Road
BATTERSEA RISE
Battersea Rise
North
Front Hall
Adjoining 31 Sheet
R
S
T
SCALE
Furlongs
10 Chains
¼ Mile
30 Chains
½ MILE

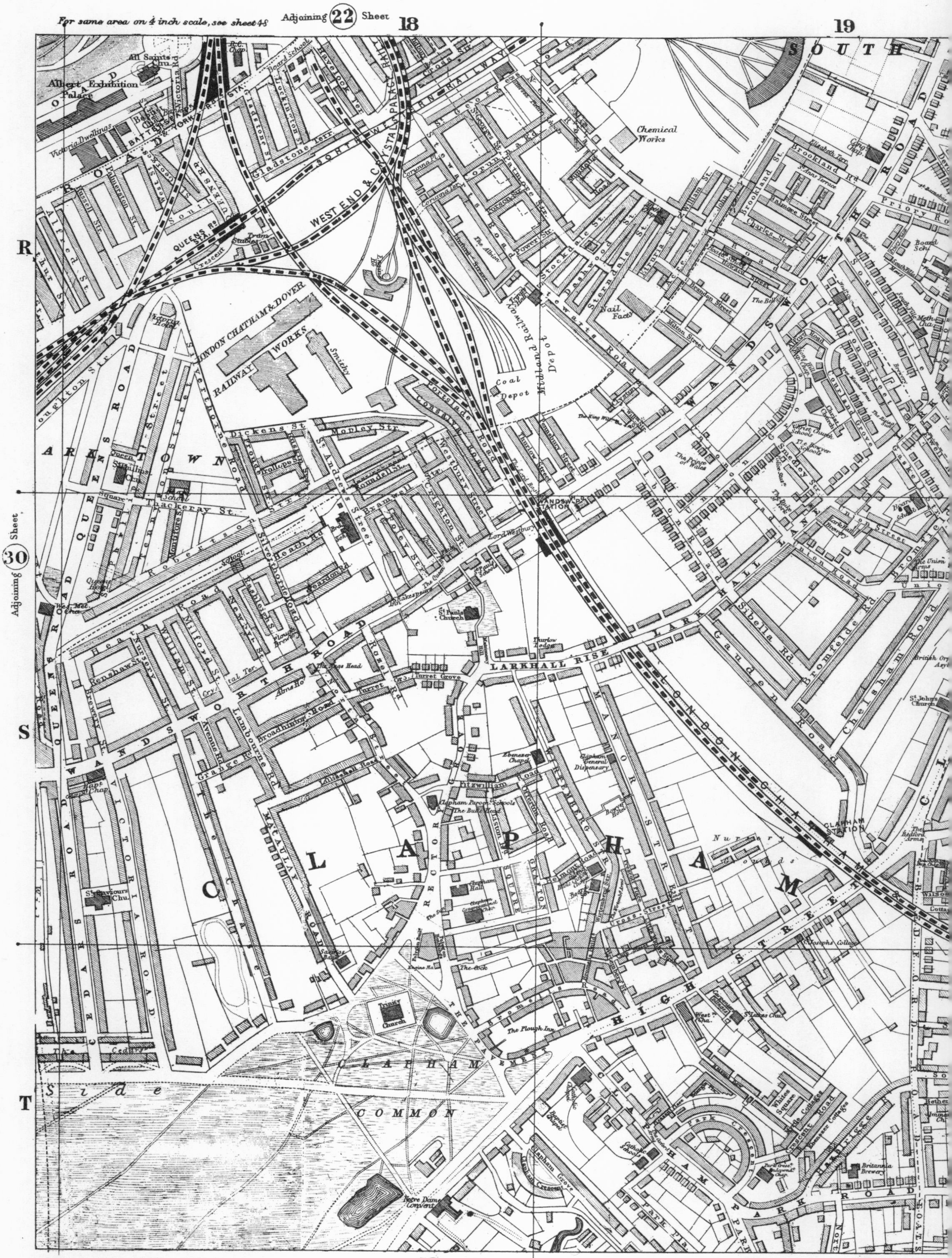
For same area on 4 inch scale, see sheet 48
Adjoining 22 Sheet
18
19
Adjoining 30 Sheet
R
S
T
SOUTH
CLAPHAM
CLAPHAM
COMMON
LONDON CHATHAM & DOVER RAILWAY WORKS
WEST END & CRYSTAL PALACE RAILWAY
LARKHALL RISE
HIGH STREET
Albert Exhibition Palace
Chemical Works
G.W. Bacon, F.R.G.S. 127 Strand. London.
18
19

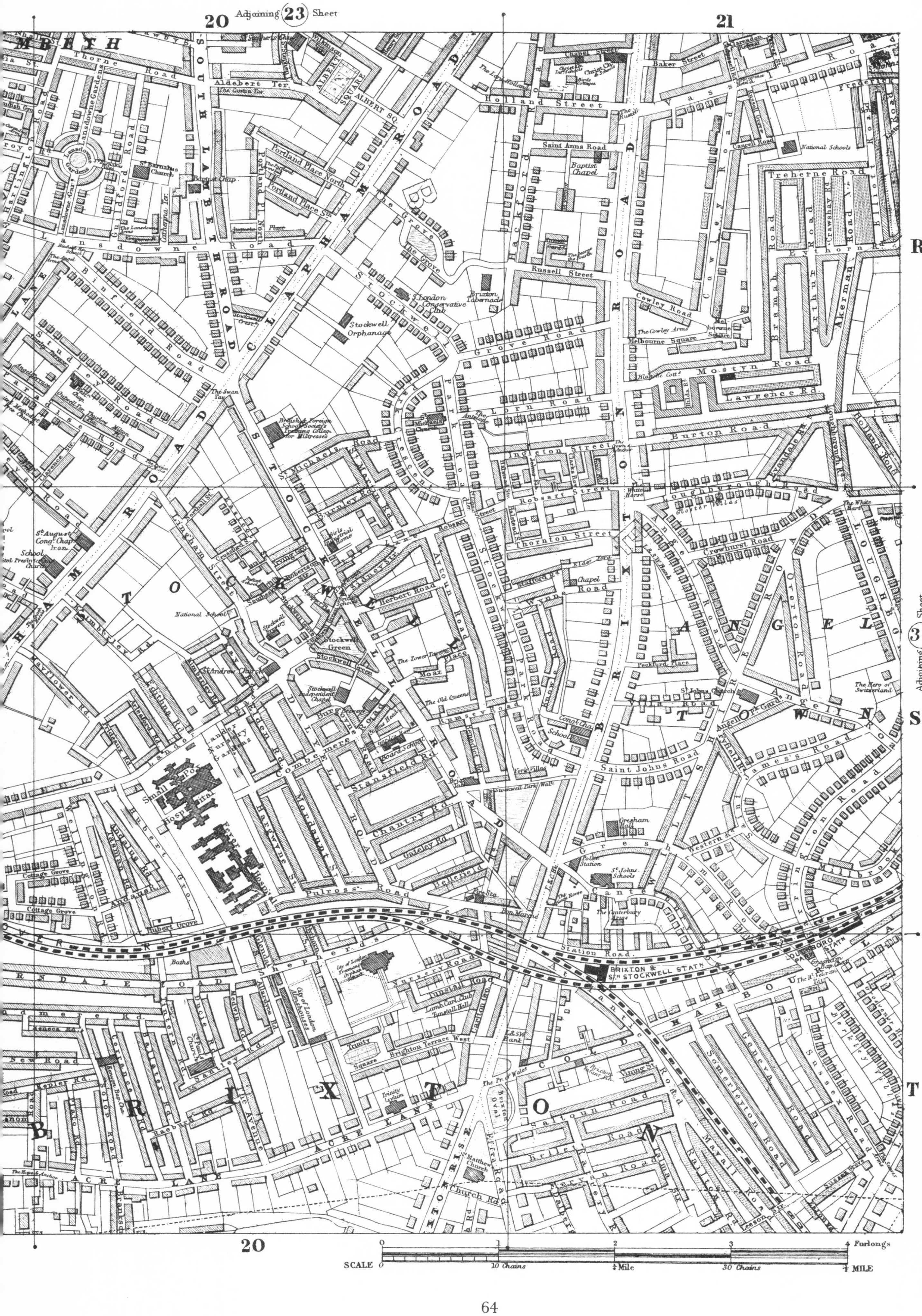

Adjoining 23 Sheet
20
21
Adjoining 32 Sheet
STOCKWELL
BRIXTON
ANGELL TOWN
Clapham Road
South Lambeth Road
Brixton Road
Stockwell Road
Landsdowne Road
Holland Street
Saint Anns Road
Russell Street
Grove Road
Lorn Road
Burton Road
Loughborough Road
Robsart Street
Thornton Street
Crowhurst Road
Overton Road
Angell Road
Saint Johns Road
St. James's Road
Gresham Road
Canterbury
Coldharbour Lane
Acre Lane
Atlantic Road
Railton Road
Mayall Road
Somerleyton Road
Geneva Road
Sussex Road
Effra Road
Stockwell Orphanage
Stockwell Green
Stockwell Park Road
Binfield Road
Combermere Road
Stansfield Rd.
Chantry Rd.
Mordaunt St.
Hospital
Hubert Grove
Pulross Road
Station Road
BRIXTON & STH STOCKWELL STATN
Brighton Terrace West
Trinity Square
Tunstall Road
Nursery Road
Cowley Road
Mostyn Road
Lawrence Rd.
Treherne Road
Baker Street
National Schools
Baptist Chapel
Brixton Tabernacle
Gresham Hall
St. Johns Schools
Police Station
Brixton Oval
St. Matthew's Church
Church Rd.
Millbrook
Western Rd.
Wynne Road
Herbert Road
Aytoun Road
Ramsay Road
Ingleton Street
20
0 1 2 3 4 Furlongs
SCALE 0 10 Chains ¼ Mile 30 Chains ½ MILE

For same area on 4 inch scale, see sheets 43 - 49

22 Adjoining 24 Sheet 23

R

S

T

Adjoining 31 Sheet

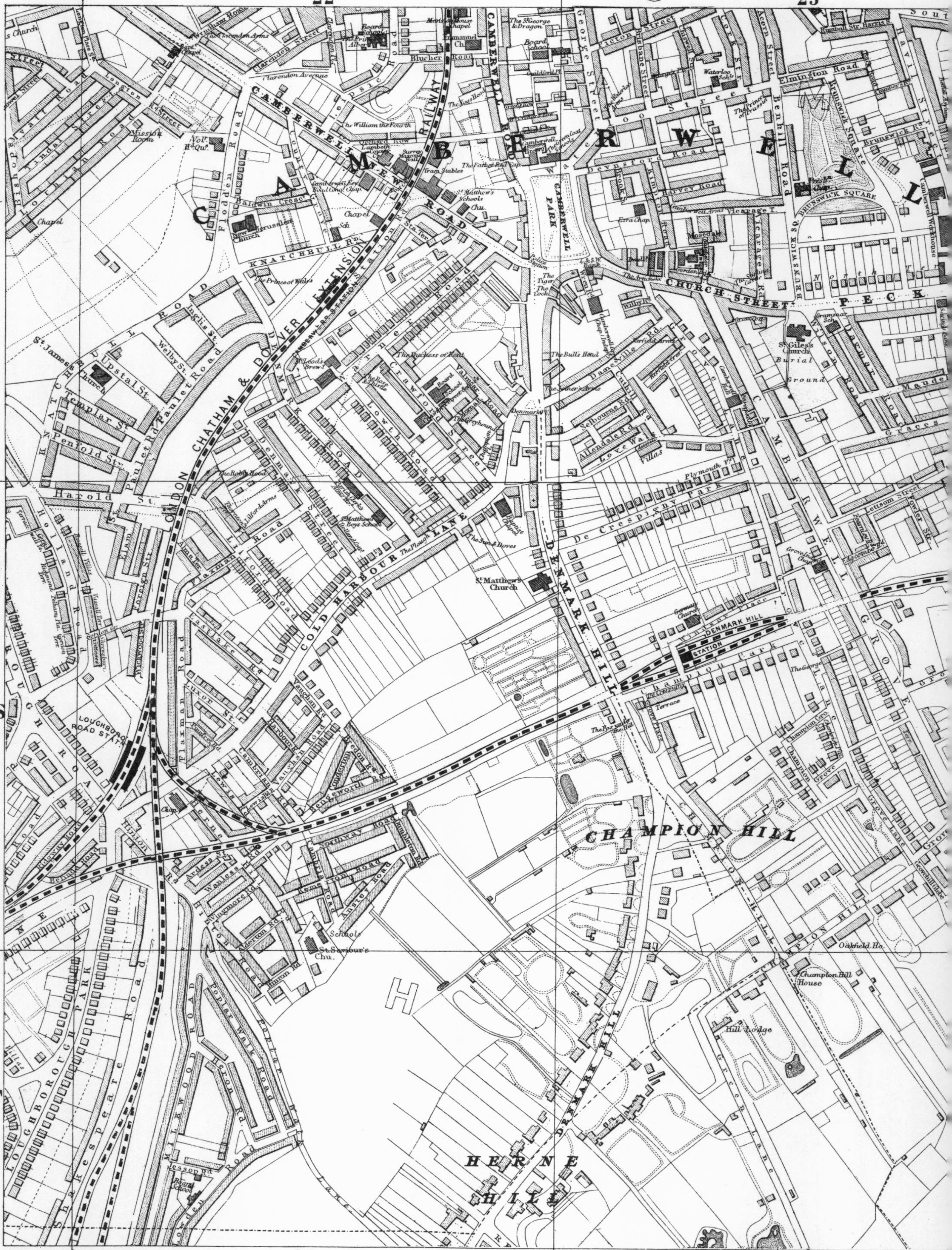

G.W.Bacon, F.R.G.S. 127 Strand, London.

22 23

Adjoining 25 Sheet
24
25
PECKHAM
PECKHAM RYE
EAST DULWICH
PECKHAM RYE
COMMON
HIGH STREET
QUEENS ROAD
CHADWICK RD
Choumert Road
GOOSE GREEN
EAST DULWICH RD
Camden District Church
Camden Grove
Hanover Park
Rye Lane
Peckham Rye Statn
Museum of Fire Arms
Bournemouth Rd
Parkstone Rd
Atwell Road
Copeland Road
Bellenden
Lordship Lane
Crystal Palace Rd
Northcross Road
Fountain
The Gardens
Camberwell Workho.
Nunhead Cresct
Teachers Orphanage
Boards School
R
S
T
Adjoining 33 Sheet
24
SCALE
0
1
2
3
4 Furlongs
10 Chains
½ Mile
30 Chains
¾ MILE

For same area on 4 inch scale, see sheet 49

Adjoining (25) Sheet

26 27

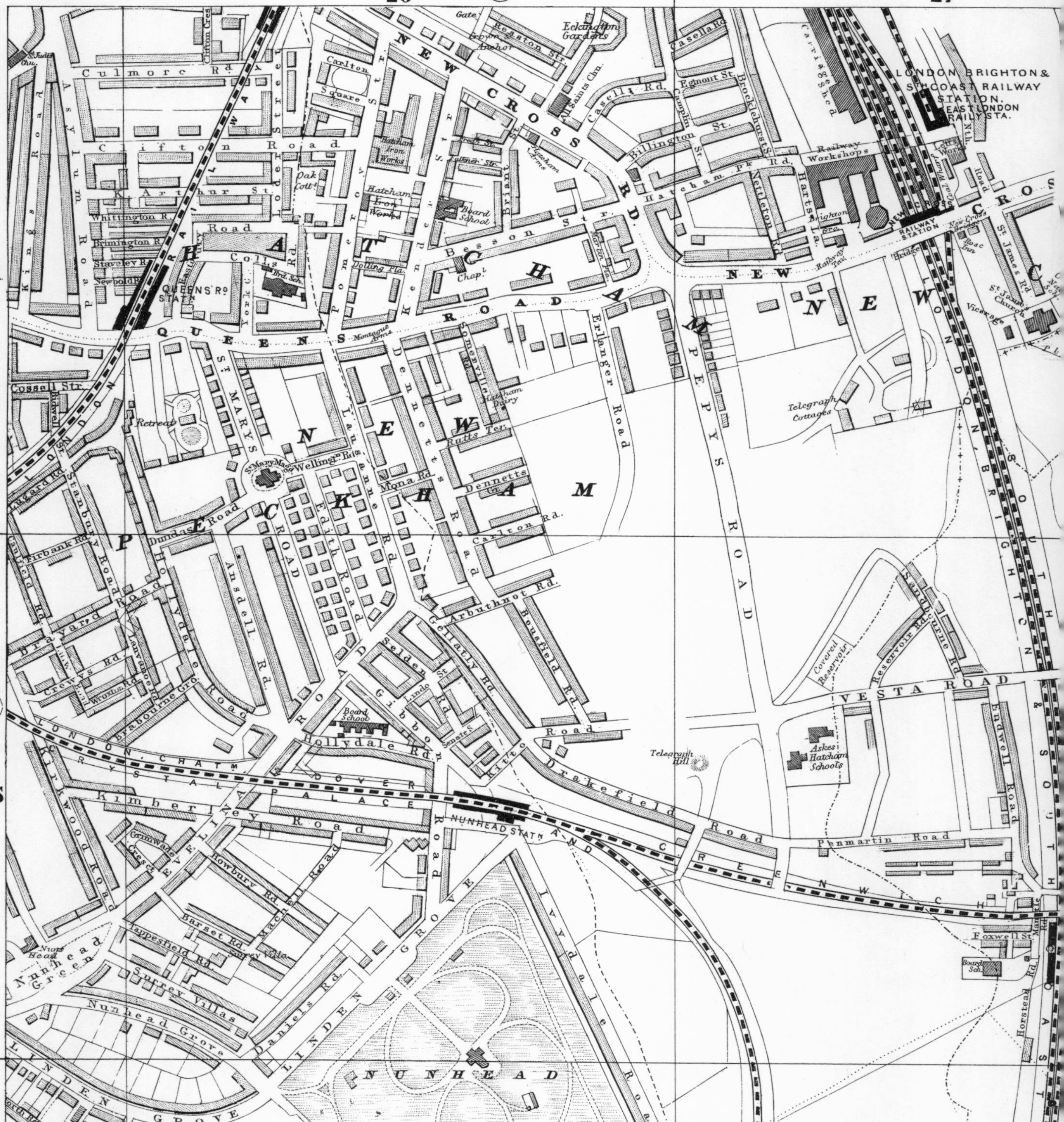

R

S

Adjoining (32) Sheet

T

26 27

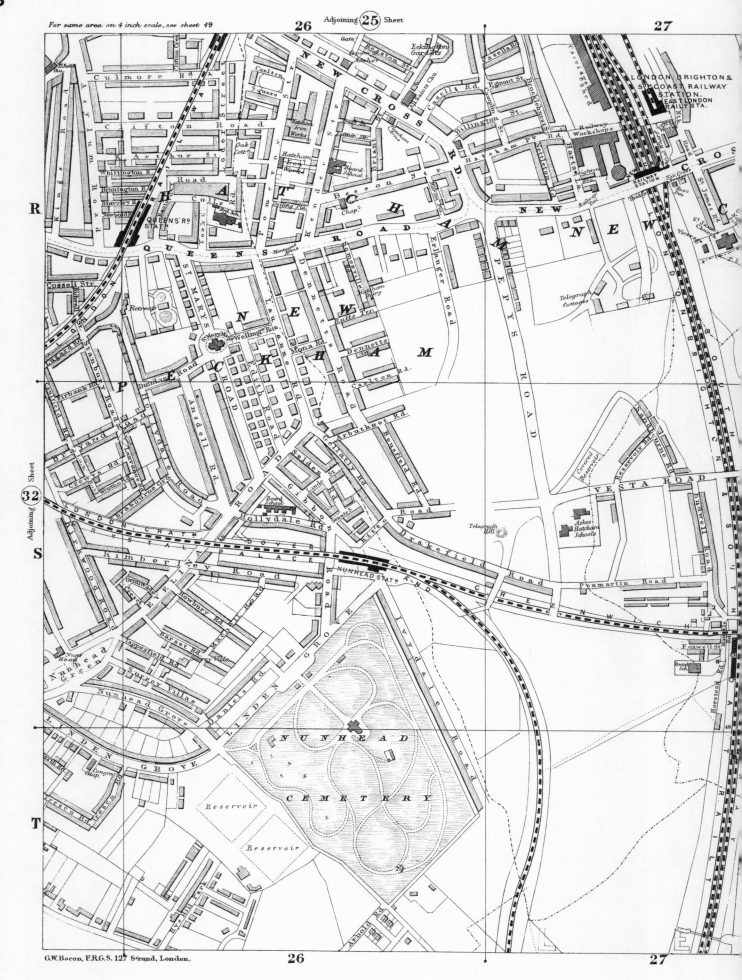

G.W.Bacon, F.R.G.S. 127 Strand, London.

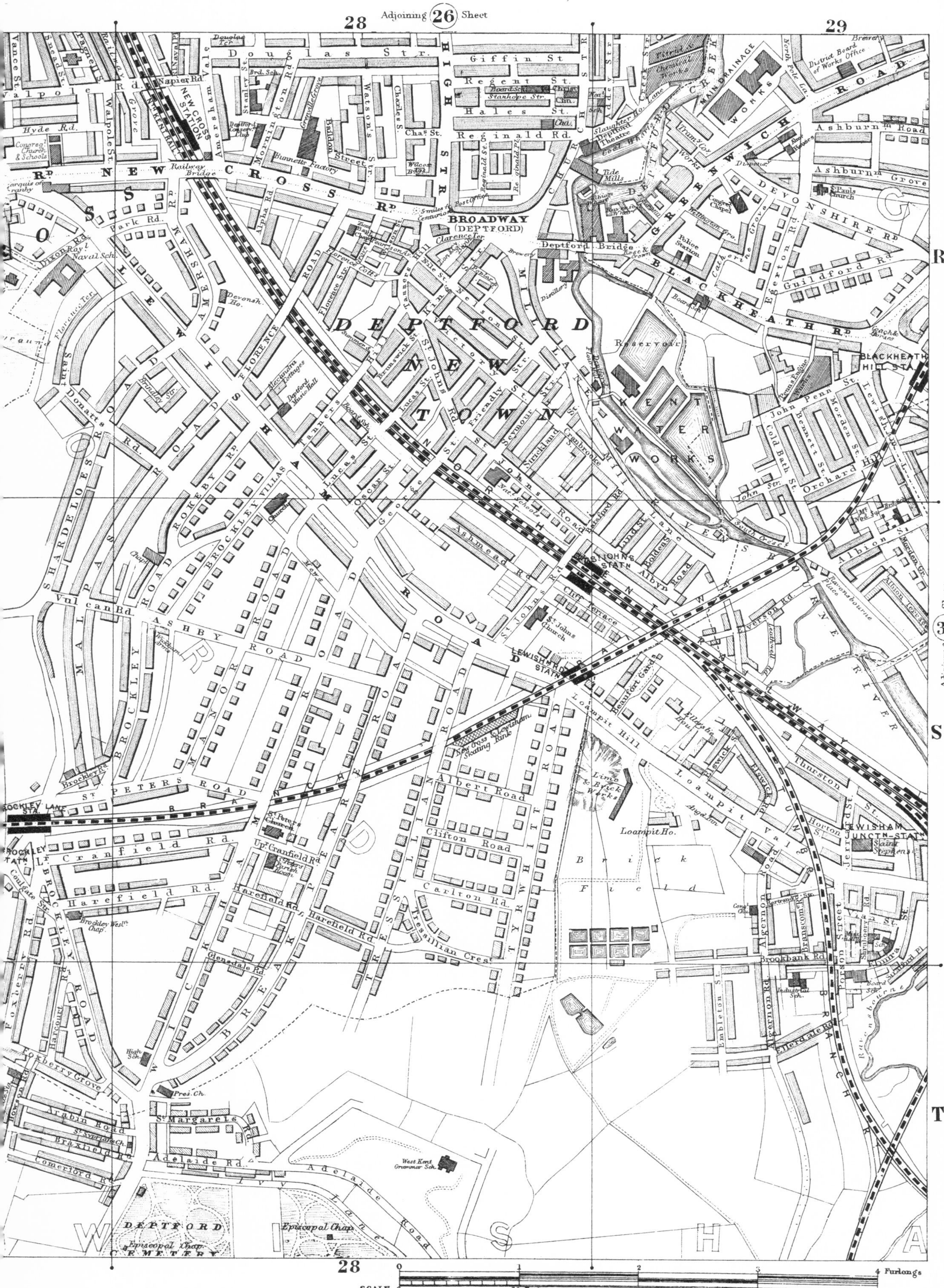
Adjoining 26 Sheet
28
29
Adjoining 34 Sheet
Douglas St.
Giffin St.
Regent St.
Hales St.
Reginald Rd.
Stanhope Str.
Napier Rd.
Walpole St.
Hyde Rd.
New Cross Station
Amersham Vale
Railway Bridge
New Cross Rd.
Broadway (Deptford)
Clarence Ter.
High Str.
Church St.
Deptford Bridge
Creek
Main Drainage Works
Greenwich Road
Ashburnm Road
Ashburnm Grove
Devonshire Rd.
Guildford Rd.
Blackheath Rd.
Blackheath Hill Sta.
Police Station
Reservoir
Kent Water Works
Deptford New Town
Florence Road
Tanners Hill
Mill Lane
Friendly St.
Seymour St.
Lucas St.
Lewisham Road
Brockley Road
Rokeby Rd.
Brockley Villas
Church
Chapel
Devonsh. Ho.
Deptford Music Hall
Alexandra Cottages
Brindley St.
Donatts Rd.
Shardeloes Rd.
Malpas Road
Vulcan Rd.
Ashby Road
Manor Road
Ashmead Road
St Johns Stat.
St Johns Church
St Johns Rd.
Lewisham Rd. Stat.
Loampit Hill
Loampit Vale
Loampit Ho.
Lime & Brick Works
Brick Field
Beaufort Gardens
Albyn Road
Lewisham Junctn. Stat.
Thurston St.
Ravensbourne River
John Penn St.
Orchard Hill
Albion St.
St Peters Road
St Peters Church
Brockley Lane Stn.
Brockley Statn.
Cranfield Rd.
Harefield Rd.
Brockley West Chap.
Albert Road
Clifton Road
Carlton Rd.
Tressillian Road
Tressillian Cres.
Tyrwhitt Road
Wickham Road
Breakspear Road
Glensdale Rd.
Foxberry Rd.
Harcourt Rd.
Foxberry Grove
High Sch.
Pres. Ch.
St Margarets Rd.
Arabin Road
Braxfield Rd.
Comerford Rd.
Adelaide Rd.
Ivy Lane
Adelaide Road
West Kent Grammar Sch.
Deptford Episcopal Chap.
Cemetery
Episcopal Chap.
Brookbank Rd.
Embleton St.
Algernon Road
Vernon Rd.
Ellerdale Rd.
Industrial Sch.
Branch Railway
New Cross & Lewisham Skating Rink
Scale
0 1 2 3 4 Furlongs
10 Chains
¼ Mile
30 Chains
½ Mile

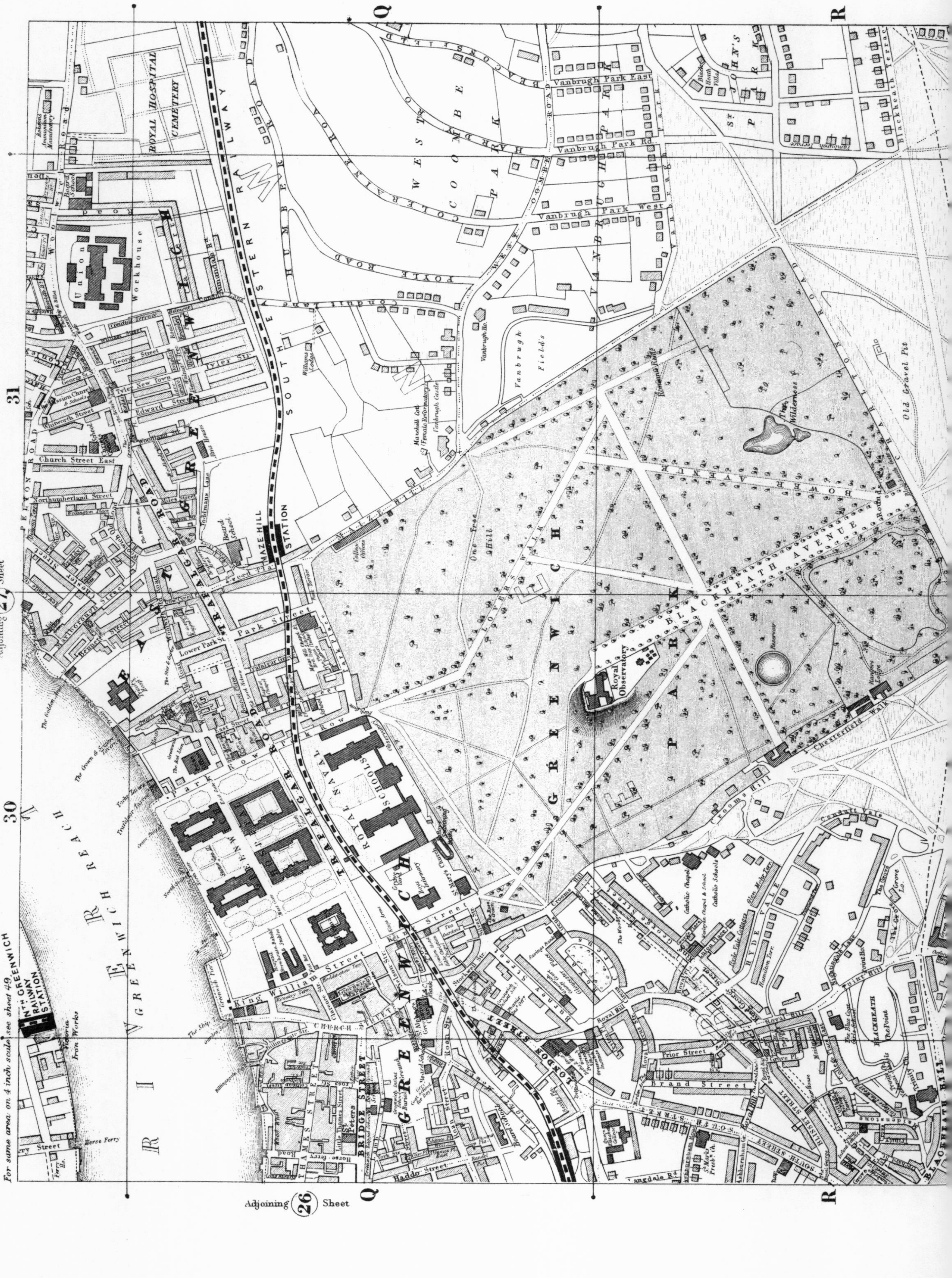
Q
R
31
30
Adjoining 27 Sheet
Adjoining 26 Sheet
For same area on 4 inch scale see sheet 49
GREENWICH PARK
GREENWICH
GREENWICH REACH
RIVER
ROYAL HOSPITAL CEMETERY
Workhouse
Union
SOUTH EASTERN RAILWAY
MAZE HILL STATION
WESTCOMBE PARK
Vanbrugh Park East
Vanbrugh Park Rd.
Vanbrugh Park West
VANBRUGH PARK
Vanbrugh Fields
Conduit Lane
Royal Observatory
Reservoir
One Tree Hill
Lovers Walk
BLACKHEATH AVENUE
ROYAL NAVAL SCHOOLS
TRAFALGAR ROAD
Park Row
Park Street
King William Street
LONDON STREET
BRIDGE STREET
THAMES STREET
Church Street East
Northumberland Street
Chesterfield Walk
Crooms Hill
Royal Hill
Brand Street
Prior Street
Conduit Vale
HYDE VALE
BLACKHEATH HILL
Old Gravel Pit
The Wilderness
Haddo Street
Horse Ferry Road
Langdale Rd
Nth GREENWICH RAILWAY STATION
Horse Ferry

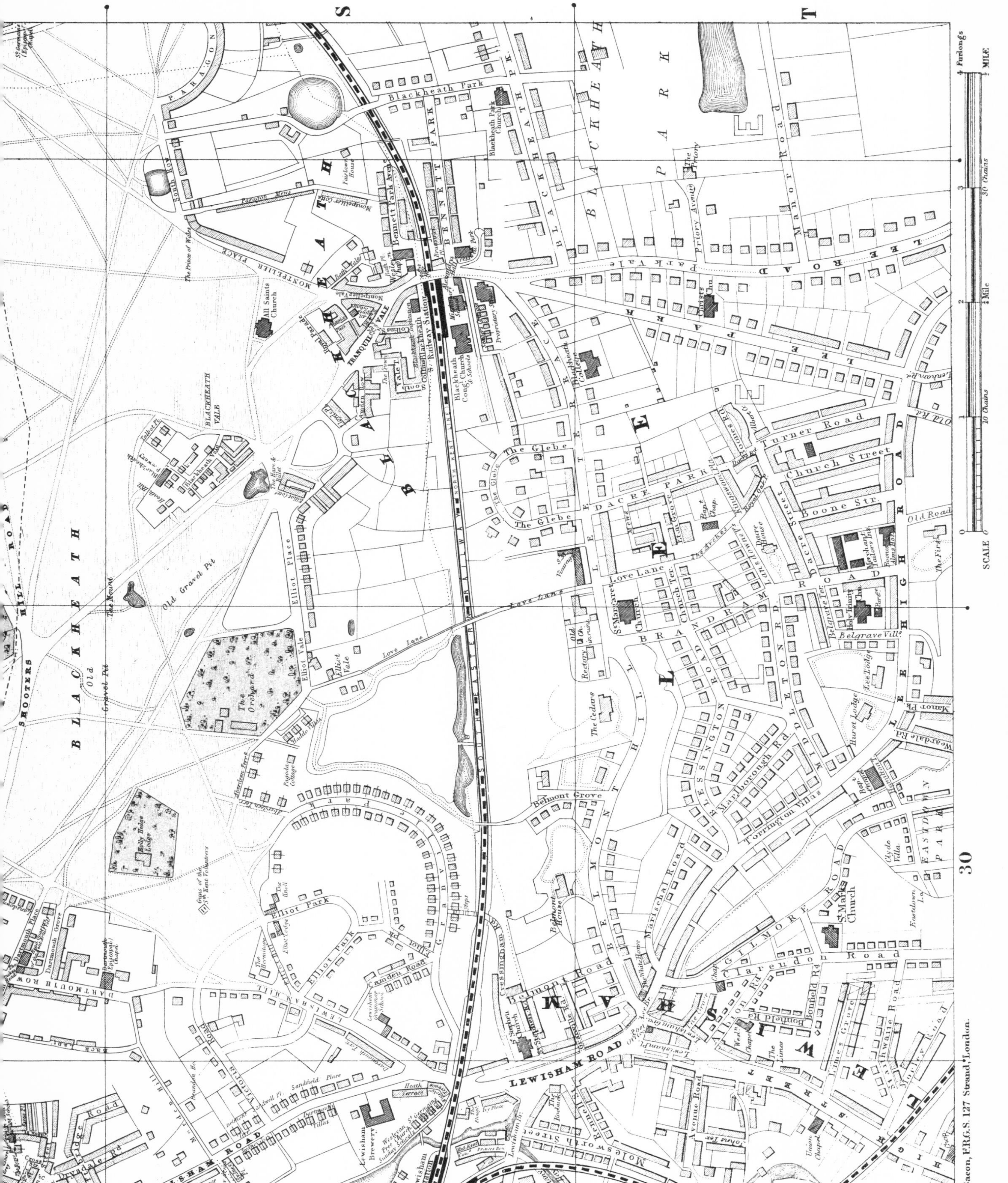

BLACKHEATH
LEE
LEWISHAM
Shooters Hill Road
Old Gravel Pit
The Mount
Dartmouth Row
Dartmouth Place
Dartmouth Grove
Dartmouth (Episcopal) Chapel
Holly Hedge Lodge
Morden Hill
Victoria Road
Lewisham Road
Lewisham Brewery
Lewisham Station
Lewisham Hill
Elliot Park
Elliot Place
Elliot Vale
The Orchard
Pagoda Cottage
Blackheath Vale
All Saints Church
Montpellier Place
South Row
Paragon
The Prince of Wales
Royal Parade
Tranquil Vale
Bennett Park Avenue
Blackheath Railway Station
Bennett Park
South Eastern Railway
North Kent Line
Blackheath Cong. Church & Schools
Proprietary School
Blackheath Park
Blackheath Park Church
Blackheath Pk.
The Glebe
Blackheath Terrace
Blackheath College
Love Lane
Cressingham Rd.
St. Stephen Church
Belmont House
Belmont Grove
Belmont Hill
The Cedars
Rectory
Old Ch. in ruins
St. Margaret's Church
Church Ter.
Dacre Park
Mews
Brandram Road
Marischal Road
Blessington Road
Marlborough Rd.
Torrington Villas
Middleton Rd.
Lansdowne Pl.
Dacre House
Dacre Street
Boone Str.
Church Street
Turner Road
Christs Chu.
Priory Avenue
The Priory
Park Vale
Lee Park
Lee Road
Manor Road
Belgrave Ter.
Belgrave Vill.
Holy Trinity Chu.
Merchant Tailors Ins.
Boones Alms Hos.
Lee High Road
Old Road
Hurst Lodge
Lee Lodge
Clyde Villa
Eastdown Park
Weardale Rd.
Manor Pk.
The Firs
St. Mark's Church
Gilmore Road
Clarendon Road
Bonfield Rd.
Limes Grove
Staithwaite Road
Morley Road
High Street
Avenue Road
Molesworth Street
Union Chapel
30
G.W. Bacon, F.R.G.S. 127 Strand, London.
SCALE
Furlongs
10 Chains
¼ Mile
30 Chains
½ MILE

Adjoining 33 Sheet

MILL HILL
Upper Hale
Holcombe House
Belmont
Post Off.
St. Paul's Chu.
Nat. Sch.
Grammar Sch.
Kings Head Inn
Littleberries Ho.
Almshouses
Angel Inn
The Priory
Drivers Hill
Wentworth Ho.
Milespitt Farm
Milespitt
Bittacy House
Burtonhole Farm
Burton Hole
Stoneyfields
Gibbs Green
Lower Hale
Hale Lodge
Snakerham Farm
Hale
Deans Lane Farm
Uphill Farm
Lawrence Street Farm
Shakespeare Rd.
Melton Rd.
Birkbeck Road
Marion Rd.
Victoria Road
Daws Lane
Flower Lane
Mill Hill
Rose Villa
Goldbeaters Farm
Copthall Park
Featherstone Ho.
Dale Street Farm
Copt Hall
Page Street
Good News Fm.
Sanders Lane Fm.
Saunders Lane
Orange Hill
Sheveshill Common Field
Tithe Fm.
Brick Barn
MIDLAND RAILWAY
The Bald Faced Stag
Red Hill
Kingsbury Home for Orphans
Red Hill Fm.
Shoeland Fm.
Grove House
Collin Dale
Collindale Lodge
Collin Deep Lane
Silk Stream
Grove Park
Mount Pleasant
Hay Lane
Hyde Cottage
Roe Green House
Roe Green
Springfield Ho.
Hyde Farm
Manor Fm.
THE HYDE
Hyde Con. Chur.
The Kings Arms
Red Lion
Hyde Lodge
Hyde House
Rookery Farm
Green Man
Pipers Green
KINGSBURY GREEN
Kingsbury Villa
Kingsbury House
Cowleaze House
Rise Fm.
Silk Bridge
EDGWARE ROAD
Ancient Street
HENDON
Hendon Hall
Downage Wood Ho.
Ivy Ho.
The Vicarage
St. Mary's Ch.
Church Fm.
Churchend Fm.
Glebe
Grove Ho.
Alms Hos.
Ravensfield Ho.
Wesleyan Chap.
R.C. Chap.
Dial Ho.
Esmeralda Ho.
Harwood Ho.
The Burroughs
The White Bear
St. Stephens Home
St. Georges Mission
Burroughs Farm
Pound
Paddock Fm.
Congregational Sch.
The Bell Inn
Nursery
Hendon House
Brent Lo.
Foster House
Albert Cott
Salisbury Pl.
Butchers Lane
Ashley Lane
Burroughs Lane
Hall Lane
Bunns Lane
Brabourne Heigh
Selvage Lane
Lawrence Street
Hammers Lane
Wise Lane
Dale Street
8
9
10
11
12
A
B
C
G.W.Bacon, F.R.G.S. 127 Strand, London.

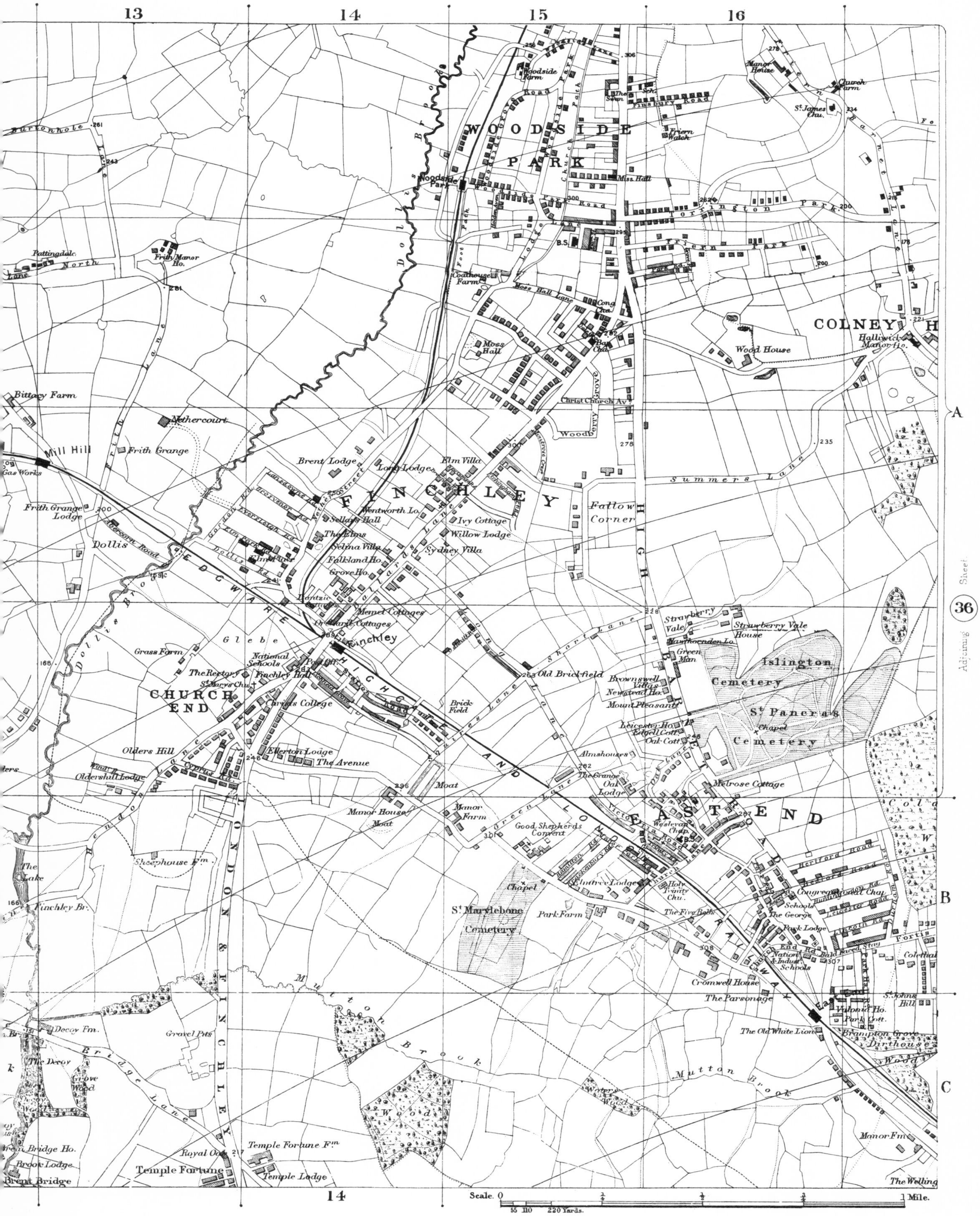
13
14
15
16
WOODSIDE
PARK
Woodside Farm
Woodside Park
The Swan
Finsbury Road
Manor House
Church Farm
St. James Chu.
Friern Watch
Moss Hall
B.S.
Coathouse Farm
Moss Hall Lane
Cong. Cha.
Bap. Cha.
COLNEY H
Halliwick Manor Ho.
Wood House
Pattingdale
Frith Manor Ho.
North
Bittacy Farm
Nethercourt
Mill Hill
Gas Works
Frith Grange
Frith Grange Lodge
Dollis
Christ Church Av.
Summers Lane
Brent Lodge
Long Lodge
Elm Villa
FINCHLEY
Fallow Corner
HIGH
Wentworth Lo.
Sellars Hall
Ivy Cottage
Willow Lodge
The Elms
Selma Villa
Sydney Villa
Falkland Ho.
Grove Ho.
Memel Cottages
Orchard Cottages
Finchley
EDGWARE
Glebe
Grass Farm
National Schools
The Rectory
St. Marys Chu.
Finchley Hall
Post Off.
CHURCH END
Christs College
Old Brickfield
Brick Field
Short Lane
Strawberry Vale
Strawberry Vale House
Hawthornden Lo.
Green Man
Islington Cemetery
St. Pancras Chapel Cemetery
Brownswell Villas
Newstead Ho.
Mount Pleasant
Leicester Ho.
Oak Cott.
Almshouses
The Grange
Oak Lodge
Melrose Cottage
Olders Hill
Oldershill Lodge
Ellerton Lodge
The Avenue
Moat
Manor House
Manor Farm
Good Shepherds Convent
EAST END
Wesleyan Chap.
Holy Trinity Chu.
Elmtree Lodge
The Five Bells
Hertford Road
St. Marylebone Cemetery
Chapel
Park Farm
Cromwell House
The Parsonage
Schools
The George
Park Lodge
Nation. & Indust. Schools
Sheephouse Fm.
The Lake
Finchley Br.
Decoy Fm.
The Decoy
Grove Wood
Gravel Pits
Wood
Mutton Brook
Waters Wood
The Old White Lion
Brampton Grove
Manor Fm
Brent Bridge Ho.
Brook Lodge
Brent Bridge
Royal Oak
Temple Fortune Fm
Temple Fortune
Temple Lodge
The Welling
LONDON & FINCHLEY
A
B
C
Adjoining Sheet 36
Scale. 0 ¼ ½ ¾ 1 Mile.
55 110 220 Yards.

16
17
18
19
A
B
C
Adjoining Sheet 35
Cemetery Station
Great Northern Cemetery
Manor House
Church Farm
St. James Chu.
Bridge Ho.
Foot Path
Friern Watch
Torrington Park
Friern Park
Miss Hill
The Waterfall
Beaver Hall
Clock & Watchmakers Asylum
Arno's Grove Wood
COLNEY HATCH
Halliwick Manor Ho.
The Hermitage
Wood House
Chapel
County Lunatic Asylum
NEW SOUTHGATE
New Southgate
Gas Works
Bounds Green Farm
Christchurch Ave.
Summers Lane
Fallow Corner
St. Peters
Muswell Hill Fm.
Strawberry Vale
Strawberry Vale House
Hawthornden Lo.
Green Man
Old Brickfield
Brownswell Villas
Newstead Ho.
Mount Pleasant
Islington Cemetery
St. Pancras Cemetery
Chapel
Leicester Ho.
Almshouses
The Grange
Oak Lodge
Melrose Cottage
Coppetts Farm
ALEXANDRA PARK
MUSWELL HILL ESTATE
Finchley Entrance
Lake
Water Village
Archery Grd.
ALEXANDRA
Palace Station
ALEXANDRA PALACE
Japanese Village
Grand Stand
Cedar Lod.
Laurel Bank Cot.
Carisbrook Cott.
Melford Lodge
Caen Wood Lodge
Essex Lo.
EAST END
Coldfall Wood
Tatterdown Fl.
The Hermitage
Almshouses
North Lodge
Wellfield
Hertford Road
Congregational Chap.
Schools
The George
Park Lodge
Elmtree Lodge
Holy Trinity Chu.
Park Farm
The Five Bells
Fortis Cott.
The Limes
Muswell Hill
The Grove
MUSWELL HILL
Fortismere
Fortis Green Road
Brewery
Fortis Green
Colehall Ho.
The Firs
St. James Chu.
The Parsonage
Horticult. Gardens
Grove Lodge
Rutland Villa
Entrance
The Priory
Vale Cot.
Cromwell House
The Parsonage
The Hall
Valonia Ho.
Park Cott.
Brampton Grove
Dirthouse Wood
The Old White Lion
ALEXANDRA PALACE BRANCH RAILWAY
Upton Farm
Lalla Rookh Cott.
Rose Cot.
PRIORY RD.
S
Mutton Brook
Waters Wood
Elizabeth Cottage
Gravelpit Wood
Hildridge Wood
Manor Fm.
Muswell Hill Cottages
Churchyard Bottom Wood
The Wellington Inn
Park Villas

G.W.Bacon, F.R.G.S. 127 Strand, London.

20
21
22
23
24
PALMERS GREEN
Aldermans Hill
Palmers Green
Broomfield House
Broomfield Farm
Hazelwood Ho.
Hedge Lane
Hazelwood Farm
The Lodge
THE NEW RIVER
Firs Farm
Ivy Cottage
Huxley Farm
Kings Arms Lane
Huxley Flour Mills
PYMM
PARK
Wyer Hall Road
Millfield Ho.
Tanners Hall
Wyer Hall
Pymmes Brook
Cartridge Factory
Union Workhouse
Lodge
Church
Bowes Road
Cock Inn
Stafford Rd.
Tilekiln Lane
School
Tilekiln Farm
Bowes Manor
Green Lanes
Rifle Butt
UPPER EDMONTON
A
BOWES PARK
Lyndhurst Road
Maryland Road
Clayhill Farm
Clayhill Lodge
The Compasses
Bowes Pk.
Myddleton Road
Chitts Hill Ho.
Woodside Road
Clarence Villa
Tent Farm
White Hart Lane
St. Katherine Training College (Ladies)
Moselle Villa
Moselle Ho.
Wolves Lane
Tottenham Park
Tottenham Cemetery
The Moselle
WOOD GREEN
Adjoining Sheet 37
Nightingale Hall
Palace Gate Sta.
Wood Green
The Fishmongers Almshouses
Trinity Rd
Snakes Lane
Allhallows Chu.
The Priory
Rose Cot.
Printers Almshouses
Royal Masonic Institute
Elm Lodge
Bruce Castle
Wood Green
Station
Lordship Lane
Graingers Farm
Broadwater Farm
Green Lanes Sta.
Bruce Grove
X
Swimming Baths
Croquet Ground
Reservoirs
Stables
Dovecote Villas
B
Downhills
Mount Pleasant
Tottenham Cross
HORNSEY
West Green
WEST GREEN
Three Compasses
St. Marys Church
Hornsey
Glebe
Church Path
Fairfax Road
Effingham Road
Falkland Road
Lightfoot Rd.
Elmbank
Church Hill Cot.
Rokesley Ho.
Holy Innocents
Brixton Ho.
Haringey House
Black Boy Lane
Seaford Road
Rosslyn Road
Seven Sisters
C
Rose Cot.
St. Anns Rd.
St. Johns Lo.
St. Marys Priory
Warham Road
Abresford Lo.
Lightfoot Ho.
20
21
Scale.
1 Mile.
220 Yards.

23
24
25
26
27
LOWER EDMONTON
Firs Farm
Ivy Cottage
Huxley Flour Mills
PYMMES PARK
EDMONTON
Police Sta.
Wes. Cha.
Millfield Ho.
Weir Hall
Tanners Hall
Silver St.
Cartridge Factory
Union Workhouse
Lodge
Church Road
Angel Road
Dyson's Farm
The Blue Anchor
Cooks Ferry
Locks Wharf
Angel Ho.
Angel Works
Indep. Cha.
Rifle Butt
UPPER EDMONTON
Edmonton & Tottenham Ragged School
Brook Ho.
Waggon Horse La.
Tottenham and Edmonton Gas Wks.
Whitebraid Hill Farm
Clayhill Lodge
The Compasses
Nursery
Brewery
Northumberland Park
Willoughby Farm
Rifle Butts
St. Katherine Training College (Ladies)
Moselle Villa
Moselle Ho.
White Hart Lane
Tottenham Park
Tottenham Cemetery
The Moselle
Fletcher Ho.
St. Johns Ch.
Bruce Ter.
Willoughby Ho.
The Grove
PARK
WILD MARSH
Higham Hill Ferry
Asplin Farm
Park
Adjoining Sheet 36
Allhallows Chu.
The Priory
Rose Cot.
National
Manor Road
Brewery
Ruskin Rd.
800 Yards
RIVER
Bruce Castle
TOTTENHAM
TOTTENHAM MARSH
Essex Hall
Higham House
Lordship Lane
Broadwater Farm
Broad Mead
Stoneleigh Lock
Foot Br.
Friends Meet.g House
Almshouses
India Rubber Factory
Down Lane Crossing
Clendish Marsh
Mitchley Marsh
Bruce Grove
X
Upland Ho.
Higham Lodge
GREAT EASTERN RAILWAY
RESERVOIRS
B
Downhills
Mount Pleasant
Hale Farm
Tottenham Cross
Tottenham
Tottenham Lock
Tottenham Mills
Ferry Bridge
Ferry Lane
Royal Standard
Stonydown Cotts.
West Green
Aldborough Ho.
High Cross Ch.
Cattle Pens
Baker's Pyrotechnic Works
Cricket Ground
Seven Sisters
Foot Bridge
C
East London Water Works Reservoirs
Page Gr.
South Tott.
G.W. Bacon. F.R.G.S. 127 Strand, London.
Adjoining 40

28
29
30
31
CHINGFORD
Old Chingford Chu.
Caroline Mount
Lit. Fridayhill
Hatch Grove
Manor Farm
Gunners Grove
Larkswood Lo.
CHINGFORD HATCH
Hatch Lane
Prince of Wales
Chingford Lane
Australia Road
Church Path
Chapel Road
New Road
Prince Albert
Chingfordhall Lane
Larks Farm
Larks Old Farm
Canister Ho.
Nightingale Hall
Higham Farm
Normanshire Farm
Chingford Hall
Chase Lane
Larks Wood
Inks Green
Hale End Road
Rolls
Ainslie Wood
HIGHAMS
WOODFORD SIDE
Hale End
The Avenue
Jacks Farm
Higham Hall
A
Folly Lane
CHINGFORD ROAD
The Ching
Foot Bridge
HALE END
Beech Hall
Willow Cott.
Forest Hall
Mamerley Ho.
Forest Lodge
Salisbury Hall
Brick Field
Oakhill Lodge
The Crooked Billet
Sky Peals
Blind Lane
Billet Lane
St. Johns Fm.
Manor Ho.
Friars Watch
Mill Cott.
The Napier's Arms
CHAPEL END
Farm
HIGHAM HILL
The Victory
Thorphall Fm.
EPPING
St. Johns Chu.
Nat. Sch.
Higham Hill Tavern
Wilderness
Black Horse
Bellevue House
East London Water Works
Hagger Lane
Common
The Winns
The Priory
Northbank
Woodend Ho.
Claystreet Fm.
The Bell Inn
Clay Street
B
Brooks Croft
Woodbank
Waltham Stow Ho.
Elm Lo.
The Elms
TOWER HAMLET
The Parsonage
St. Peters Pla.
St. Peters Chu.
Smiths Cott.
Providence Row
Wood Street
College
Manor Ho.
Rectory Manor
Salters Buildings
Castle Ho.
Forest Sch.
Elm Cott.
Shern Lodge
St. Marys Chu.
Infant School
Victoria Hall
RAILWAY
Buck Lane
Buck Ho.
Buxton Ho.
Shern Hall
Forest Road
C
Eagle Pond
WALTHAMSTOW
R.C. Chap.
Whips Cross
EPPING FOREST
SNARES BROOK
Orphan Asylum
Forest Lane
St. James St.
Scale. 0 ¼ ½ ¾ 1 Mile.
55 110 220 Yards.
23
29

For same area on 9 inch scale, see sheets 4 & 5.

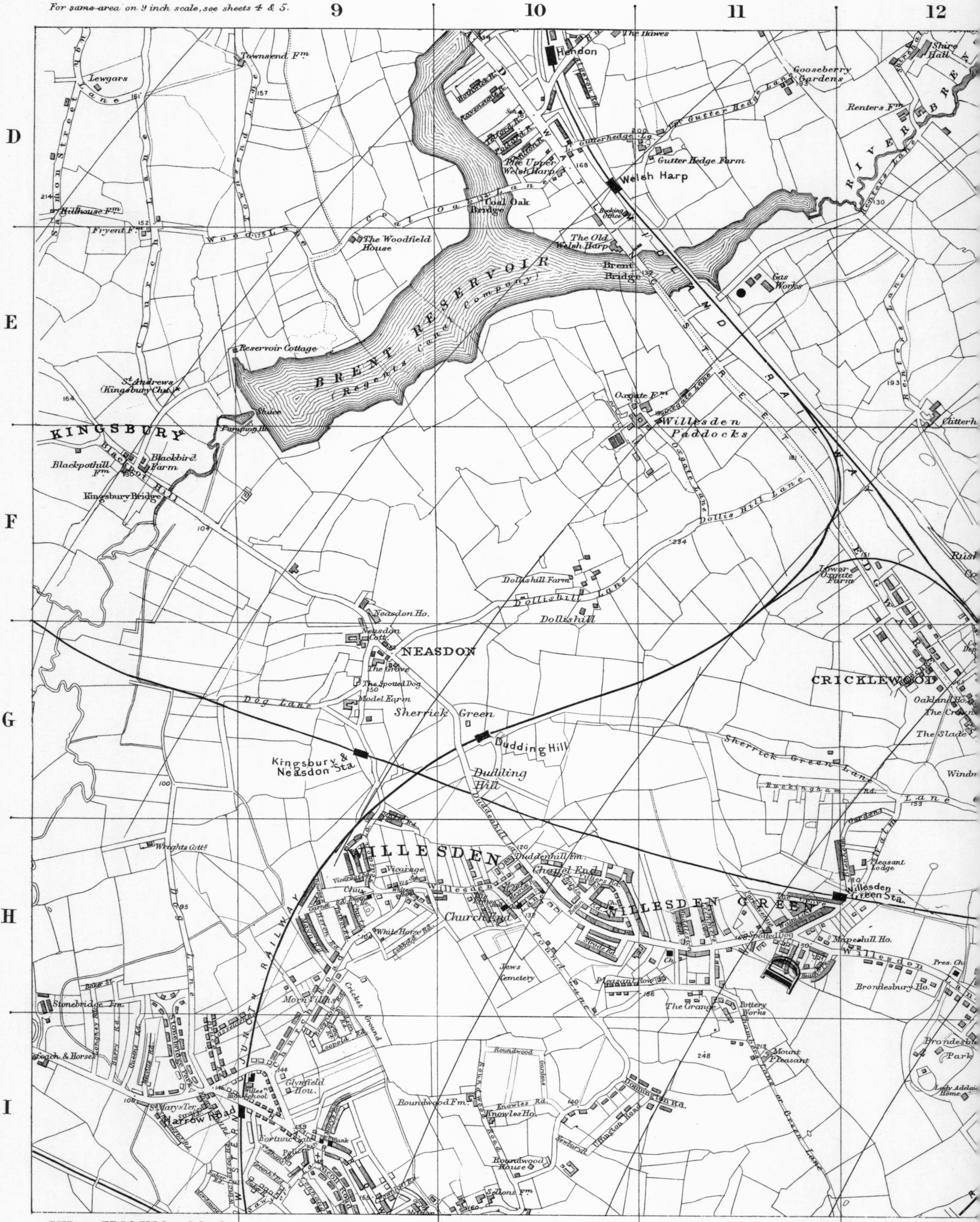
9
10
11
12
D
E
F
G
H
I
Hendon
The Hawes
Townsend Fm
Lewgars
Shire Hall
Gooseberry Gardens
Renters Fm
Gutter Hedge Lane
Gutterhedge La.
Gutter Hedge Farm
The Upper Welsh Harp
Welsh Harp
Booking Office
Coal Oak Bridge
Coal Oak Lane
Hillhouse Fm
Fryent Fm
Wood Lane
Salmon Street
Church Lane
Townsend Lane
The Woodfield House
The Old Welsh Harp
Brent Bridge
Gas Works
River Brent
Renters Lane
BRENT RESERVOIR
(Regents Canal Company)
Reservoir Cottage
St Andrews (Kingsbury Chu.)
Sluice
Pumping Ho.
KINGSBURY
Blackpothill Fm
Blackbird Farm
Blackpot Hill
Kingsbury Bridge
Oxgate Fm
Oxgate Lane
Willesden Paddocks
EDGWARE ROAD
MIDLAND RAILWAY
Dollis Hill Lane
Dollishill Farm
Dollishill Lane
Dollishill
Lower Oxgate Farm
Neasdon Ho.
Neasdon Cott.
NEASDON
The Grove
The Spotted Dog
Model Farm
Dog Lane
Sherrick Green
Dudding Hill
Kingsbury & Neasdon Sta
Dudding Hill
CRICKLEWOOD
Oakland Ho.
The Slade
Sherrick Green Lane
Buckingham Rd.
Lane
Pleasant Lodge
Willesden Green Sta.
Wrights Cottg.
WILLESDEN
Vicarage
Duddenhill Fm.
Chapel End
Church End
WILLESDEN GREEN
Spotted Dog
Mapeshill Ho.
Willesden Lane
Pres. Ch.
Brondesbury Ho.
Dog Lane
White Horse Rd.
Jews Cemetery
Pleasant Row
The Grange
Pottery Works
Mount Pleasant
Cricket Ground
JUNCTION RAILWAY
Stonebridge Fm.
Coach & Horses
Glynfield Hou.
Harrow Road
St Marys Ter.
Willes. High School
Roundwood
Roundwood Fm.
Knowles Rd.
Knowles Ho.
Tomlinson Rd.
Roundwood House
Sellons Fm
Brondesbury Park
Lady Adelaide Home

G.W.Bacon, F.R.G.S. 127 Strand, London.

Adjoining 35 Sheet
13
14
15
16
17
D
E
F
G
H
I
Adjoining 39 Sheet
Adjoining 42 Sheet
Albert Row
Alba Lodge
The Elms
Stilton Lo.
GOLDERS
GREEN
Gloucester Lodge
Elm Lodge
Grove Cott.
Grove House
The Oaks
Golders Lodge
Temple Fortune Lane
Hoop Lane
Wild Hatch
Bunkers Hill
Turners Wood
Moat
Lodge Hill
Site of Bishops Lodge
Bishops Wood
Spaniards End
Golders Green
Golders Green Or Hodford Farm
Kenwood Farm
North Wood
Kenwood (Mansfield House)
Caen Wood Towers
Ken Wood
The Spaniards Tavern
Heath Fm.
NORTH END
Ivy Ho.
Spaniards Road
The Elms
Fitzroy Farm
Highgate Ponds
Heath Lodge
Hill Ho.
HAMPSTEAD HEATH
CHILDS HILL
The Castle
West Heath Rd.
Jack Straws Castle
Vale of Health
Hampstead Ponds
New River Co.s Water Wks.
Tumulus
Parliament Hill
Pattison Rd.
Platts Lane
Redington Rd.
East Heath Rd.
Temple Park
Covered Reservoir
Kidderpore Hall
Willow Road
Farm
West Croft Farm
Newmans Hunting Est.
Hampstead Cemetery
New West End
HAMPSTEAD
Church Row
John Str.
Hampstead Heath
Soldiers Daughters Home
FLEET ROAD
Hackney College
Hillfield Road
Gd. Junc. Water Works
HAMPSTEAD
Small Pox Hospital
Finchley Rd
Ivy Lodge
Midland Railway
West End
Coal Depot
Belsize Avenue
Haverstock Hill
Kilburn Brondesbury
Hampstead Junc. Railway
Blackburn Rd.
West Hampstead
Broadhurst Gardens
Fitzjohn Avenue
Belsize Park
Belsize Square
Lancaster Road
Eton Avenue
Edgware Road
High Road
Priory Road
Fairfax
Adelaide Road
King Henrys Road
Acol Rd.
Goldhurst Road
Belsize Road
Alexandra Road
Boundary Road
Springfield Rd.
Clifton Hill
Eton & Middlesex Cricket Ground
PRIMROSE HILL
Paddington Cemetery
Kilburn
St. John's Wood
Avenue Road
0
1 Mile.
220 Yards

For same area on 9 inch scale, see sheets 6, 7, 8.

Adjoining (36) Sheet

G.W.Bacon, F.R.G.S. 127 Strand, London.

17 18 19

Adjoining (43) Sheet

20
21
22
23
24
CROUCH END
Harringay
Green Lanes Sta
HAMPSTEAD JUN
Stroud Green Sta
Crouch Hill
Tile Works
The Hermitage
Cricket Ground
NEW RIVER
Stamford Hill
Amhurst Park Road
Lion Ho.
FINSBURY PARK
New River Company's Works Reservoir
St. Andrews Church
STAMFORD HILL
Abney Park Cemetery
Pumping Station New River Company's Wks.
Finsbury Park
Brownswood Road
NEWINGTON PARK
Newington Park
SEVEN SISTERS RD.
Highbury Quadrant
Park Lane
Aubert Park North
Highbury Gr.
Holloway
ISLINGTON
HIGHBURY
Mildmay Park
Mildmay Avenue
Balls Pond Rd
Dalston Jnc.
Kingsland High Street
Stoke Newington
St. Pauls Road
CANONBURY
Caledonian Road
Slaughter Houses
Richmond Road
Downham Road
Balmes Rd.
De Beauvoir Crescent
Canal R.
Copenhagen
D
E
F
G
H
I
Adjoining Sheet 40
Scale. 0 ¼ ½ ¾ 1 Mile.
55 110 220 Yards.

23
24
25
26
27
D
E
F
G
H
I
Adjoining Sheet 39
STAMFORD HILL
Stamford Hill
UPPER CLAPTON
Clapton
LEYTON MARSH
Lea Bridge
NORTH MILL FIELD
SOUTH MILL FIELD
Abney Park Cemetery
Newington Park
STOKE NEWINGTON
Stoke Newington
HACKNEY DOWNS
LOWER CLAPTON
HOMERTON
KINGSLAND
DALSTON
HACKNEY
HACKNEY COMMON
LONDON FIELDS
Dalston Junc.
New River Companys Works Reservoir
Walthamstow Mill
Pumping Sta.
Copperwill Fm.
High Hill Ferry
Springfield Ho.
High Bridge
Amhurst Park Road
Ravensdale Road
Egerton Rd.
Northfield Rd.
Lordship Rd.
Church St.
Albion Road
Green Lanes
Mildmay Park
Mildmay Avenue
Balls Pond R.
Tottenham Rd.
Buckingham Rd.
Englefield Road
De Beauvoir Square
Kingsland Road
Stoke Newington High Street
Downs Road
Downs Park Road
Dalston Lane
Amhurst Road
Sandringham Road
Shacklewell Lane
Rectory Road
Kenninghall Rd.
Brooke Road
Northwold Road
Lea Bridge Road
Clarence Road
Mare Street
Well Street
Cassland Road
Victoria Park Road
King Edwards Road
Richmond Road
Forest Road
Wilton Road
Graham Road
Albion Rd.
Lenthall Rd.
Shrubland Gro.
Broadway
Brownlow Rd.
Canal
Homerton High Street
Wick Road
Liverpool

G.W.Bacon, F.R.G.S. 127 Strand, London.

Adjoining 37 Sheet
28
29
30
31
D
E
F
G
H
I
Adjoining 45 Sheet
Adjoining 44 Sheet
Scale.
Mile.
220 Yards.
E S S E X
Knotts Green
Cemetery
Forest Ho.
Forest Place
Forest Fm.
Wallwood Ho.
Leyton Green
Leyton Corner
The Poplars
Leyton Ho.
Mark House
Lea Bridge Road Nursery
LEYTON STREET
Wallwood Fm.
Leytonstone
National Sch.
Leytonstone House
Green Man
Park Villa
The Hare & Hounds
Sunny Side
Leyton House St. Agnes Orphanage
Lea Bridge Gas Works
Etloe Ho.
Ive Farm
LOW LEYTON
The Great Ho.
Leyton College
Grove Fm.
The American Nursery
Home for poor Children
Lancaster Rd.
Lansdowne Rd.
LEYTON MARSH
HACKNEY MARSH
RIV LEA
GREAT EASTERN RAILWAY
WOODFORD & LOUGHTON RAILWAY
Leyton Town Hall
Ruckholt Fm.
Quartermile Lane
St. Patricks R.C. Cemetery
Harrow Green
Leyton
Holloway Down
West Ham Union
Lead Mill Stream
Temple Mills
East London Water Works Canal
Marsh Rd. Br.
Marsh Road
Wick Bridge
Brick Field
Chobham Fm.
West Ham Cemetery
Chandos Rd.
Chobham Road
Henniker Rd.
STRATFORD NEWTOWN
Maryland Point
Forest Lane
High Meads
Channelsea River
Victoria Park
GREAT EASTERN AND NORTH LONDON JUNC. RY.
East London Water Wks. Reservoir
STRATFORD MARSH
Stratford
Romford Road
Broadway
Nobshill Mill
Stratford Market
Waterworks River
Duckett's Canal

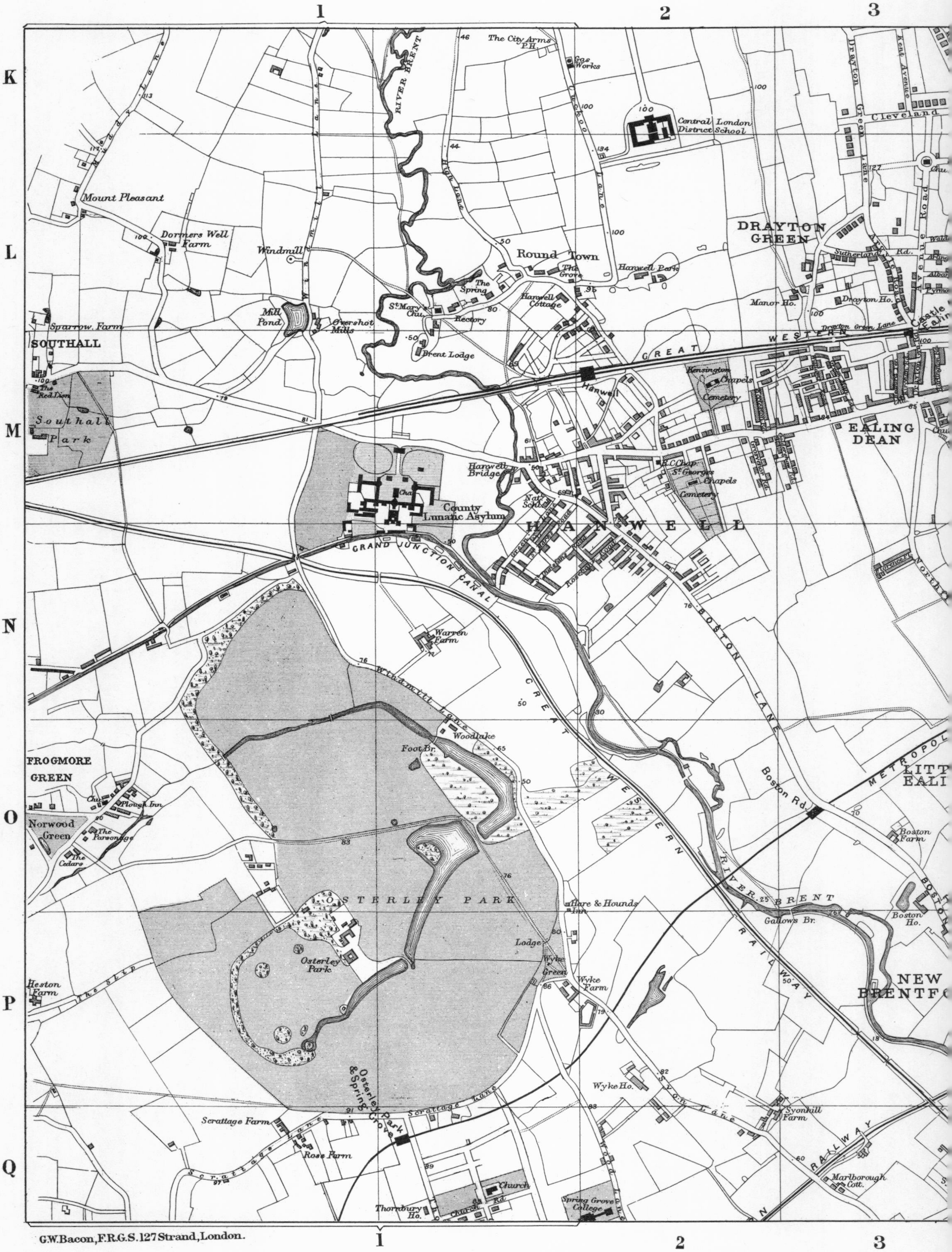
Mount Pleasant
Dormers Well Farm
Windmill
Mill Pond
Overshot Mills
Sparrow Farm
SOUTHALL
The Red Lion
Southall Park
River Brent
The City Arms P.H.
Gas Works
Central London District School
Cuckoo Lane
Hanwell Park
Round Town
The Grove
The Spring
St. Mary's Chu.
Rectory
Hanwell Cottage
Brent Lodge
DRAYTON GREEN
Drayton Green Lane
Cleveland
Sutherland Rd.
Manor Ho.
Drayton Ho.
GREAT WESTERN
Hanwell
Kensington Chapels Cemetery
EALING DEAN
Hanwell Bridge
R.C.Chap.
St. Georges Chapels Cemetery
County Lunatic Asylum
H A N W E L L
GRAND JUNCTION CANAL
BOSTON LANE
Warren Farm
Wincmill Lane
Woodlake
Foot Br.
FROGMORE GREEN
Plough Inn
Norwood Green
The Parsonage
The Cedars
OSTERLEY PARK
Osterley Park
Hare & Hounds Inn
Lodge
Wyke Green
Wyke Farm
Boston Rd.
METROPOL
LITT EALI
Boston Farm
RIVER BRENT
Gallows Br.
Boston Ho.
NEW BRENTF
Heston Farm
The Slip
Osterley Park & Spring Grove
Scrattage Lane
Scrattage Farm
Rose Farm
Wyke Ho.
Syon Lane
Synhill Farm
RAILWAY
Marlborough Cott.
Church
Church Rd.
Thornbury Ho.
Spring Grove College
G.W.Bacon, F.R.G.S. 127 Strand, London.

4
5
6
7
K
L
M
N
O
P
Q
Castlebar Park
Mount Avenue
College
Mount Park Hill
Mount Park Rd.
Montpelier Rd.
Castlebar Park
CASTLEBAR HILL
Water Works Reservoir
Hangerhill Ho.
The Elms
Hanger Lane
Mason's Green Lane
Hanger Vale
Mason's Green
Remains of Moat
Friars Place Farm
Hanger Lane Farm
Castlebar Rd.
Haven Green
Ealing C.W.
Madeley Road
Gordon Road W.
RAILWAY
BROADWAY
Hamilton Rd.
College
St Matthews Church
North Common Road
Freeland Road
Linton Road
Gunnersbury Avenue
Greenfield Road
Layer Rd.
Stanway Rd.
Acacia Rd.
The Lodge
UXBRIDGE ROAD
Ashton Ho.
Matlock Lane
Manor Ho.
High Str.
The Grove
The Grange
Ealing Common
Fordhook
METROPOLITAN DISTRICT RAILWAY
Birch Rd.
ACTON
Mills
The Elms
The Steyne
Hill Ho.
Shakespear Road
Chaucer Rd.
EALING
Ealing Common
West Lo.
East Lo.
Acton Hill
HIGH STREET
Chu.
Vicarage
Elm Grove
Bathing Pond
Chu.
Baillies Walk
Mill Hill Park
Gunnersbury Lodge
GUNNERSBURY
Manor Ho.
New Farm
Pope's Lane
South Ealing
DISTRICT RAILWAY
The Limes
Village Park
Pope's Cross
Gunnersbury Ho.
Gunnersbury Park
Bollo Bridge Lane
South Acton
The Elms
Acton Green
Ealing Park
Chapels Cemetery
Ponds
Ealing Sewerage
Little Boston
Carlyle Road
Cole's Hole
Grove Ho.
Claypond Lane
The Brook
Claypond Ho.
Coal Depôt
London Style Farm
Sydney Ho.
Wellesley Road
Gunnersbury Lane
CHISWICK
HIGH ROAD
Turnham Green
Vestry Hall
Royal Horti. Society's Gd.
Grosvenor Road
Barrowgate Road
Little Sutton Ho.
Little Sutton
Grand Junct. Water Works
Gasometers
HIGH STR.
Kew Bridge
Strand on the Green
Sutton Court Lo.
Sutton Court
BRENTFORD
Brentford Ait
Herbarium
Kew Green
Toll House
KEW PALACE
Museum
Palace Grounds
Gate
KEW
Museum
Park Lane
Chiswick Park Cricket Club Ground
LONDON
Chiswick
HIGH STREET
Chu.
Sch.
Adjoining Sheet 42
Adjoining Sheet 47
4
5
Scale. 0
1/4
1/2
3/4
1 Mile.
55 110 220 Yards

For same area on 9 inch scale, see sheets 12, 13, 20, 21.

9
10
11
12
J
K
L
M
N
O
Adjoining Sheet 41
HARLESDEN GREEN
Harlesden Ho.
Lower Place
Acton Lane
MIDLAND AND STH
Willesden Junction
HAMPSTEAD JUNCTION
NORTH WEST
LONDON AND
Naptha Works
Steam Laundry
St Mary's Roman Cathc. Cemetery
KENSAL GREEN
Kensal Green Cemetery
Gd Junctn Canal
Grand Junction Canal
Peoples Garden
Old Oak Commom
GREAT WESTERN RAILWAY
Lunatic Asylum
Gas Wks
Redhouse Fm
Gas Light & Coke Co's Works
Wells Hou.
Wales Fm
WORMWOOD SCRUBS
Recreation Ground
Marylebone Infirmary
NORTH AND STH WESTERN JUNCTION RAILWAY
The Friars
Friars Place
Wormwood Scrubs
Keepers Lo.
Butts
Gun Club
Reilly & Co Shooting ground
Convict Prison
Duncane Rd.
WEST LONDON
WOOD LANE
Orchard Pla.
The Grange
EAST ACTON
Goldsmiths Arms
Manor Hou.
Old Oak Rd.
HAMMERSMITH
Old Oak Fm
Woodlane Fm
Wormholt Fm
Thorpebank
Eynam Fm
Churchfield Road East
Nursery
Kings Arms
ACTON VALE
UXBRIDGE RD
SHEPHERDS BUSH
Oldfield Hou.
STARCH GREEN
Shepherds Bush
Shepherds Bush Green
Uxbridge Road
NTH & STH WESTERN JUNCTN RAILWY
Stamford Brook
GOLDHAWK ROAD
St Mary Iron Ch.
The 7 Stars
Ravenscourt Park
Shaftesbury Rd.
THE GROVE
WEST KENSINGTON
BROOK GREEN
Acton Green
Back Comn
Hammersmith
Glenthorne Road
KING STREET WEST
Devonshr Pla.
Police Stn
Hammersmith Broadway
KING ST EAST

G.W. Bacon, F.R.G.S. 127 Strand, London.

Adjoining 38 Sheet
13
14
15
16
J
K
L
M
N
O
Adjoining 43 Sheet
Adjoining 47 Sheet
0
1 Mile.
55 110 220 Yards
Queens Park
West Kilburn Sta.
Recreation Ground
L.G.O.C. Yard
Wes. Ch.
College
Baptist College
St. Dunstans
MAIDA VALE
WOOD
MARYLEBONE
PADDINGTON
Paddington Workhouse
GRT. WESTERN RAILWAY
HARROW RD
EDGWARE RD
Bishops Rd
Royal Oak
Paddington Basin
Praed St.
BAYSWATER
BAYSWATER ROAD
Ladbroke Square
Notting Hill Gate
NOTTING HILL
KENSINGTON PALACE
KENSINGTON PALACE GARDENS
Basin
KENSINGTON GARDENS
HYDE PARK
SERPENTINE
Humane Socy. House
W.
KENSINGTON
Holland House
KENSINGTON HIGH ST.
KENSINGTON GORE
KNIGHTSBRIDGE
Royal Albert Hall
IMPERIAL INSTITUTE
NATURAL HISTORY MUSEUM
The Oratory
Princes Gardens
Kensington Union House
Home for Crippled Boys
SOUTH KENSINGTON
CROMWELL ROAD
BROMPTON ROAD
PELHAM STREET
HARRINGTON RD
WESTMINSTER

For same area on 9 inch scale, see sheets 14, 15, 16, 22, 23, 24.

Adjoining (39) Sheet

17 18 19

G.W. Bacon, F.R.G.S. 127 Strand, London.

Adjoining (48) Sheet

20
21
22
23
24
J
K
L
M
N
O
PENTONVILLE ROAD
CITY ROAD
HOLBORN
VIADUCT
NEWGATE ST.
CHEAPSIDE
FLEET STR.
LUDGATE H.
CORNHILL
LEADENHALL ST.
ALDGATE
BLACKFRIARS BRIDGE
BLACKFRIARS ROAD
BOROUGH ROAD
WESTMINSTER BRIDGE RD.
LAMBETH ROAD
NEW KENT ROAD
T
H
A
M
Adjoining 44 Sheet
0
¼
½
¾
1 Mile.
220 Yards.

24
25
26
J
K
L
M
N
O
43
Adjoining
SHOREDITCH
HACKNEY ROAD
BETHNAL GREEN ROAD
CITY ROAD
OLD STREET
SHOREDITCH
BISHOPSGATE ST.
HOUNDSDITCH
CHEAPSIDE
CORNHILL
LEADENHALL ST.
ALDGATE
WHITECHAPEL HIGH ST.
WHITECHAPEL ROAD
COMMERCIAL ROAD
MILE END
TOWER
ST. CATHARINE DOCK
LONDON DOCKS
LONDON DOCKS
LONDON BRIDGE
THAMES
UPPER POOL
LOWER POOL
WAPPING
SHADWELL
TOOLEY STREET
BOROUGH HIGH ST.
BERMONDSEY
BERMONDSEY
NEW KENT ROAD
SOUTHWARK PARK
ROTHERHITHE
JAMAICA ROAD
G.W.Bacon, F.R.G.S. 127 Strand, London.
24
25
26
Adjoining

27
28
29
J
K
L
M
N
O
BOW ROAD
GREAT EASTERN RAILWAY
LONDON TILBURY & SOUTHEND RAIL
WEST HAM ABBEY MARSH
BROMLEY MARSH
Imperial Gas Works
Commercial Gas Works
City of London and Tower Hamlets Cemetery
Bromley
Four Mills Distillery
Three Mills Distillery
Pumping Station
West Ham Abbey Print Works
Chemical Works
St Thomas Mill Flour
Soap Works
Five Bells Br.
East London Water Wks
COMMERCIAL RD EAST
E. INDIA DOCK RD
EAST INDIA DOCK RD
HIGH STREET
POPLAR
LIMEHOUSE
REGENT'S CANAL DOCKS
WEST INDIA DOCKS
EAST INDIA DOCKS
North Quay
South Quay
Blackwall Basin
South Dock Basin
MILLWALL DOCKS
MILLWALL DOCK
Millwall Docks Sta.
Millwall Junc.
Blackwall
Poplar
Lavender Pond
Acorn Pond
Lady Pond
Centre Pond
Quebec Pond
Russia Dock
Greenland Dock
South Dock
LIMEHOUSE REACH
DEPTFORD
BLACKWALL REACH
BUGSBYS REACH
Pea Ness
Blakeley Ordnance Company's Works
Chemical Works
Iron Boat Building Yard
Cement Works
Thames Soap Wks
Thames Ironwks
Canal Dock Yd.
Graving Docks
Ship Building Yard
Cubitt T. Pier
CLEMENTS ROAD
BOW COMMON
Adjoining Sheet 45
27
28
29
0
1 Mile.
55 110 220 Yards.

G.W.Bacon, F.R.G.S. 127 Strand, London.

Adjoining 40 Sheet

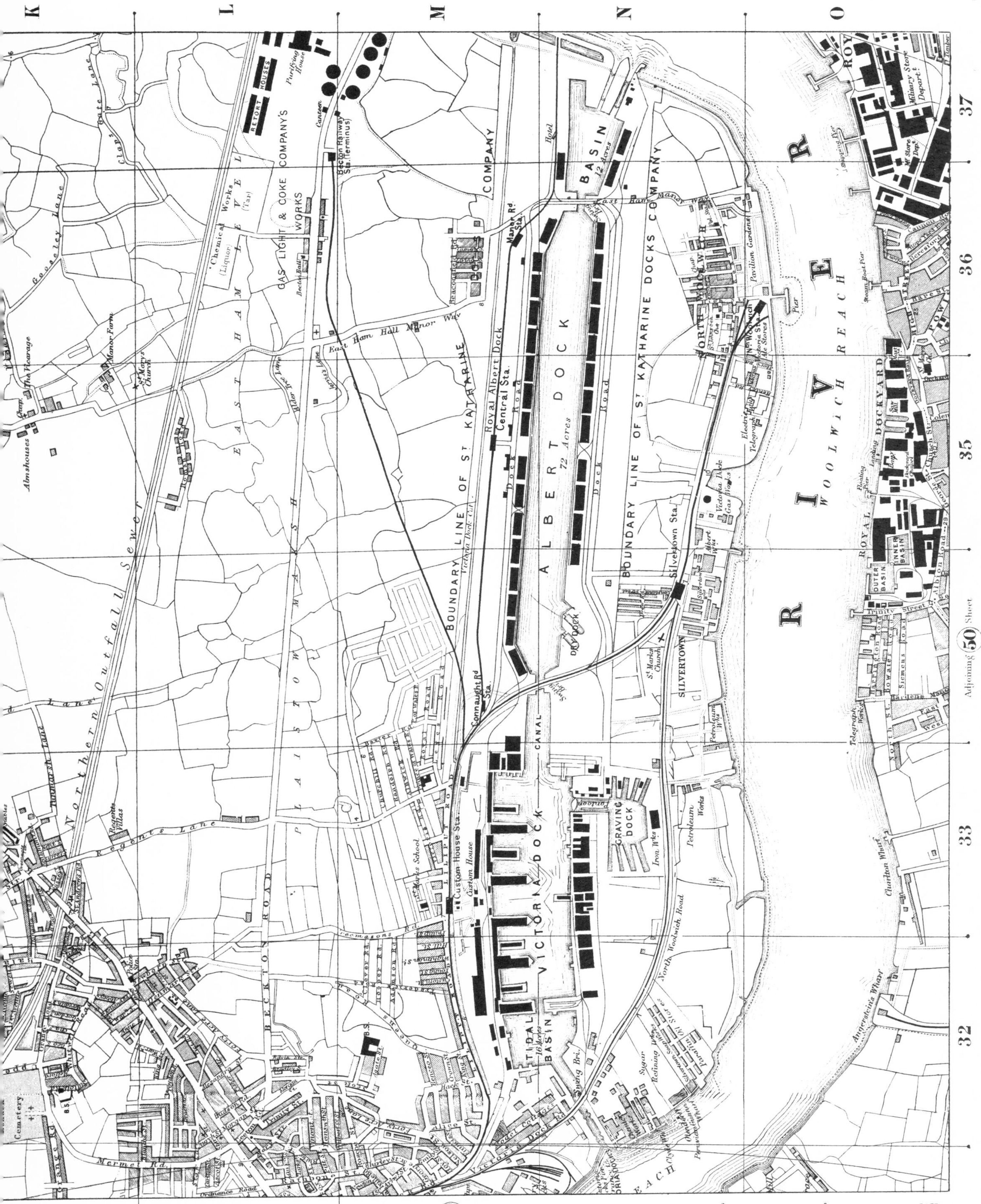

K
L
M
N
O
ALBERT DOCK
72 Acres
VICTORIA DOCK
TIDAL BASIN
16 Acres
BASIN
12 Acres
GRAVING DOCK
CANAL
BOUNDARY LINE OF ST KATHARINE DOCKS COMPANY
GAS LIGHT & COKE COMPANY'S WORKS
RETORT HOUSES
Purifying House
Beckton Railway Sta. (Terminus)
EAST HAM LEVEL
PLAISTOW MARSH
BECKTON ROAD
Northern Outfall Sewer
Chemical Works
Royal Albert Dock Central Sta.
Connaught Rd Sta.
Custom House Sta.
Custom House
Manor Rd Sta.
Silvertown Sta.
SILVERTOWN
St Marks Church
NORTH WOOLWICH
North Woolwich Road
Pavilion Gardens
Pier
Victoria Gas Works
Petroleum Works
Iron Wks
Sugar Refining Wks
RIVER
WOOLWICH REACH
ROYAL DOCKYARD
INNER BASIN
OUTER BASIN
Trinity Street
Charlton Wharf
Angerstein's Wharf
Telegraph Works
Regents Lane
East Ham Hall Manor Way
East Ham Manor Way
Gooseley Lane
The Vicarage
Manor Farm
St Marys Church
Almshouses
Cemetery
Ordnance Road
Adjoining 50 Sheet
Adjoining 44 Sheet
0 ¼ ½ ¾ 1 Mile.
55 110 220 Yards
37
36
35
33
32

1
2
3
P
Q
R
T
U
Heston Farm
Osterley Park
Wyke Green
Wyke Farm
NEW BRENTF
Osterley Park & Spring Grove
Scrattage Lane
Scrattage Farm
Rose Farm
Wyke Ho.
Syon Lane
Syonhill Farm
Marlborough Cott.
Thornbury Ho.
Church Rd
Spring Grove College
Lampton Hall
Lampton
Coach & Hor Inn
Syon Lodge
Bush Ho.
Rose & Crown P.H.
Thanet Ho.
Brentford Union Workhouse
Brentford Union Schools
The Lawn
The Elms
Lampton House
SPRING GROVE
Nat. School
Smallbury Green
Spring Grove & Isleworth
Bridge Ho.
Hounslow Town
Police Sta.
WOODLANDS
Brewery
Vicarage
Lodge Park Ho.
Nat. Sch.
Militia Barracks
R.C. Chap.
Convent
Isleworth Ait
South St.
Bank
The Priory
Cottage Hosp.
Worton Ho.
Royal Oak P.H.
Worton Lane
Happisbry Ho.
Holme Court
Isleworth Ho.
HOUNSLOW
ISLEWORTH
Worton Hall
Worton Farm
Coach & Horses P.H.
Talbot Rd.
Gordon Ho.
RIVER CRANE
Oak Lane
Mogden Ho.
Royal Naval Female School
Hounslow & Whitton
Walnut Tree Ho.
Mogden Lane
St. Margarets Lo.
Whitton Dean
Whitton Farm
Whitton Park
Kneller Hall
Park Place
Orchard Cot.
St. Margarets
Alton Cot.
Tithe Farm
The Admiral Nelson
Burlington Lo.
Brook Ho.
Neville Ho.
Perryn Ho.
Heath Ho.
WESTERN RAILWAY
Marsh Fm.
LONDON AND SOUTH
CRANE
York Ho.
Orleans Ho.
TWICKENHAM
Twickenham Cemetery
HEATH ROAD
KING ST.
CHURCH ST.
Pie Island
G.W.Bacon, F.R.G.S. 127 Strand, London.

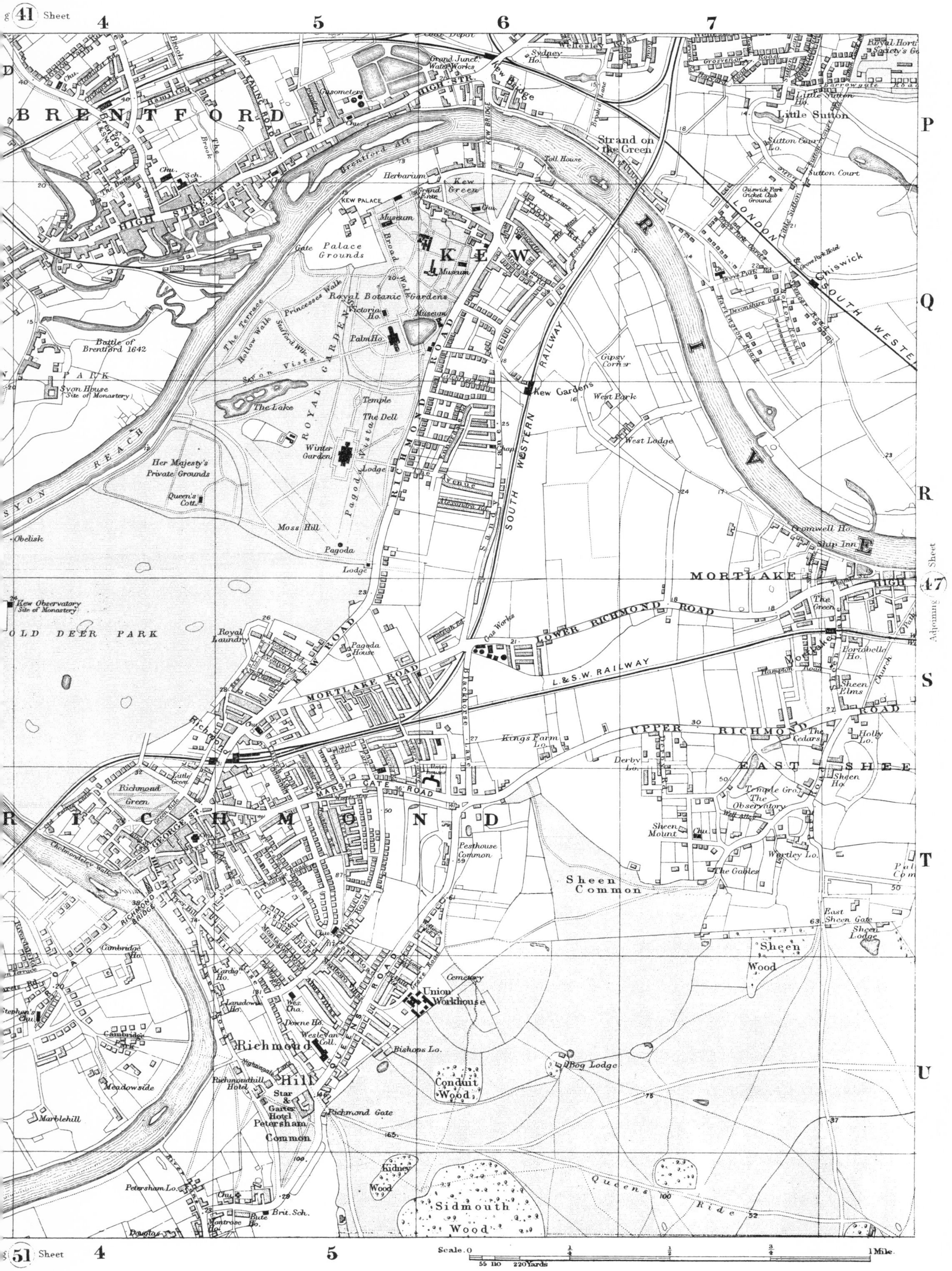
41 Sheet
4
5
6
7
BRENTFORD
EALING ROAD
HIGH STREET
Brentford Ait
Gasometers
Grand Junct. Water Works
HIGH STR.
KEW BRIDGE
Kew Bridge
Sydney Ho.
Wellesley Ho.
Grosvenor
Royal Horti. Society's Gs
Barrowgate Road
Little Sutton Ho.
Little Sutton
Sutton Court Lo.
Sutton Court
Strand on the Green
Toll House
Herbarium
Grand Entr.
Kew Green
KEW PALACE
Museum
Palace Grounds
KEW
Royal Botanic Gardens
Victoria Ho.
Palm Ho.
Princesses Walk
The Terrace
Hollow Walk
Syon Vista
ROYAL GARDENS
Broad Walk
The Lake
Temple
The Dell
Winter Garden
Pagoda Vista
Lodge
Her Majesty's Private Grounds
Queen's Cott.
Moss Hill
Pagoda
Battle of Brentford 1642
PARK
Syon House
Site of Monastery
SYON REACH
Obelisk
Kew Observatory
Site of Monastery
OLD DEER PARK
Royal Laundry
Pagoda House
KEW ROAD
RICHMOND ROAD
SOUTH WESTERN RAILWAY
Kew Gardens
Gipsy Corner
West Park
West Lodge
Chiswick Park Cricket Club Ground
LONDON & SOUTH WESTERN
Chiswick
Grove Park Rd.
Devonshire Gds.
RIVER
THAMES
Cromwell Ho.
Ship Inn
MORTLAKE
HIGH
The Green
LOWER RICHMOND ROAD
Gas Works
L.&S.W. RAILWAY
MORTLAKE ROAD
Blackhorse Lane
Portobello Ho.
Sheen Elms
Church
UPPER RICHMOND ROAD
The Cedars
Holly Lo.
Kings Farm Lo.
Derby Lo.
EAST SHEEN
Sheen Ho.
Temple Gro.
The Observatory
Sheen Mount
Wortley Lo.
The Gables
RICHMOND
Richmond Green
Little Green
GEORGE ST.
MARSH GATE ROAD
Almshouses
Pesthouse Common
Sheen Common
East Sheen Gate
Sheen Lodge
Sheen Wood
Cholmondeley Walk
RICHMOND BRIDGE
Cambridge Ho.
Cemetery
Union Workhouse
Lansdown Ho.
Wes. Cha.
Downe Ho.
Wesleyan Coll.
QUEENS ROAD
Bishops Lo.
Richmond Hill
Richmondhill Hotel
Star & Garter Hotel
Petersham Common
Richmond Gate
Conduit Wood
Bog Lodge
Meadowside
Marblehill
Cambridge Park
Kidney Wood
Sidmouth Wood
Queens Ride
Petersham Lo.
Chu.
Brit. Sch.
Bute Ho.
Montrose Ho.
Douglas
P
Q
R
S
T
U
Adjoining Sheet 47
51 Sheet
Scale 0 ¼ ½ ¾ 1 Mile
55 110 220 Yards

9
10
11
12
P
Q
R
S
T
U
Royal Horticultural Society's Gardens
Chiswick New Town
Chiswick House
Corney Lo.
Burlington Lane
SOUTH WESTERN RAILWAY
CHISWICK
CORNEY REACH
Reservoir
THAMES
LONSDALE ROAD
Lonsdale Farm
Castelnau
Mill Lodge
Soap Works
Filter
Lillian Rd.
Glentham Road
HAMMERSMITH BRIDGE
Pier
Distillery
UPPER BRIDGE ROAD
BARNES
Barn Elms Farm
BARN ELMS PARK
Merton Lo.
St. Anne's
Barnes
Barnes Green
The Cedars
Grove Cott.
Millhill
Barnes Cemetery
Putney Cemetery
Putney Low. Common
BARNES COMMON
Beverley Brook
HIGH STREET
R.C. Chap.
Castlenau Ho.
The Limes
White Hart
Portobello Ho.
North South Mortlake Cemety.
Sheen Elms
Sandfields
LONDON & SOUTH WESTERN RAILWAY
Barnes
Woodland V.
The Woodlands
Vine Cott.
UPPER RICHMOND ROAD
Manor Ho.
Roehampton Lodge
Putney Park Lane
Roehampton Lane
All Saints
School
Dryburgh Road
Holly Lo.
SHEEN
Sheen Ho.
Palewell Lo.
The Priory
Ellenborough House
Lower Grove Ho.
Subiaco Lo.
Putney Park
Clarence
Palewell Common
East Sheen Gate
Sheen Lodge
Convent
Templeton Ho.
Grove Ho.
Trinity Ch.
Roehampton Gate
Roehampton House
Cedars
Downshire Ho.
Mount Clare
Spencer Lo.
Summerfield
Granard Lo.
Grantham Ho.
Exeter Ho.
Ashburton Ho.
Clinton Ho.
Dover Ho.
PUTNEY HEATH
ROEHAMPTON
Parochial Sch.
Bristol House
Reservoir
Chelsea
Fulham Common Fields
Fulham Cemetery
Rose Bank
Dorset Cottage
Bella Vue
St. James Home
Craven Cottage
Bishops Avenue
Bishops Walk
London Rowing Club
PUTNEY
Putney Pier
The Lawn
PUTNEY HILL
Holmwood
Denham Lo.
Lytton Grove
The Elms
Green Man
Colebrook Lo.
Adjoining Sheet 46

9 10 11 12

G.W.Bacon, F.R.G.S. 127 Strand, London.

Sheet
13
14
15
16
NORTH END
West Kensington
WALHAM GREEN
Walham Green
Chelsea
PARSONS GREEN
Parsons Green
Percy Cross
Hurlingham Park
Sands End
Chelsea Basin
Gas Works
Chemical Works
WANDSWORTH BRIDGE ROAD
WANDSWORTH BRIDGE
CHELSEA EMBANKMENT
BATTERSEA BRIDGE
ALBERT BRIDGE
Battersea
Clapham Junction
Battersea Cemetery
WANDSWORTH COMMON
Emanuel School
Roy.l Victoria Patriotic Asyl.m Girls
P
Q
R
S
T
U
Adjoining 48 Sheet
Adjoining 52 Sheet
1 Mile
220 Yards

For same area on 9 inch scale, see sheets 22, 23, 24, 30, 31, 32.

17 18 19 Adjoining (43)

P Q R S T U

Adjoining (47) Sheet

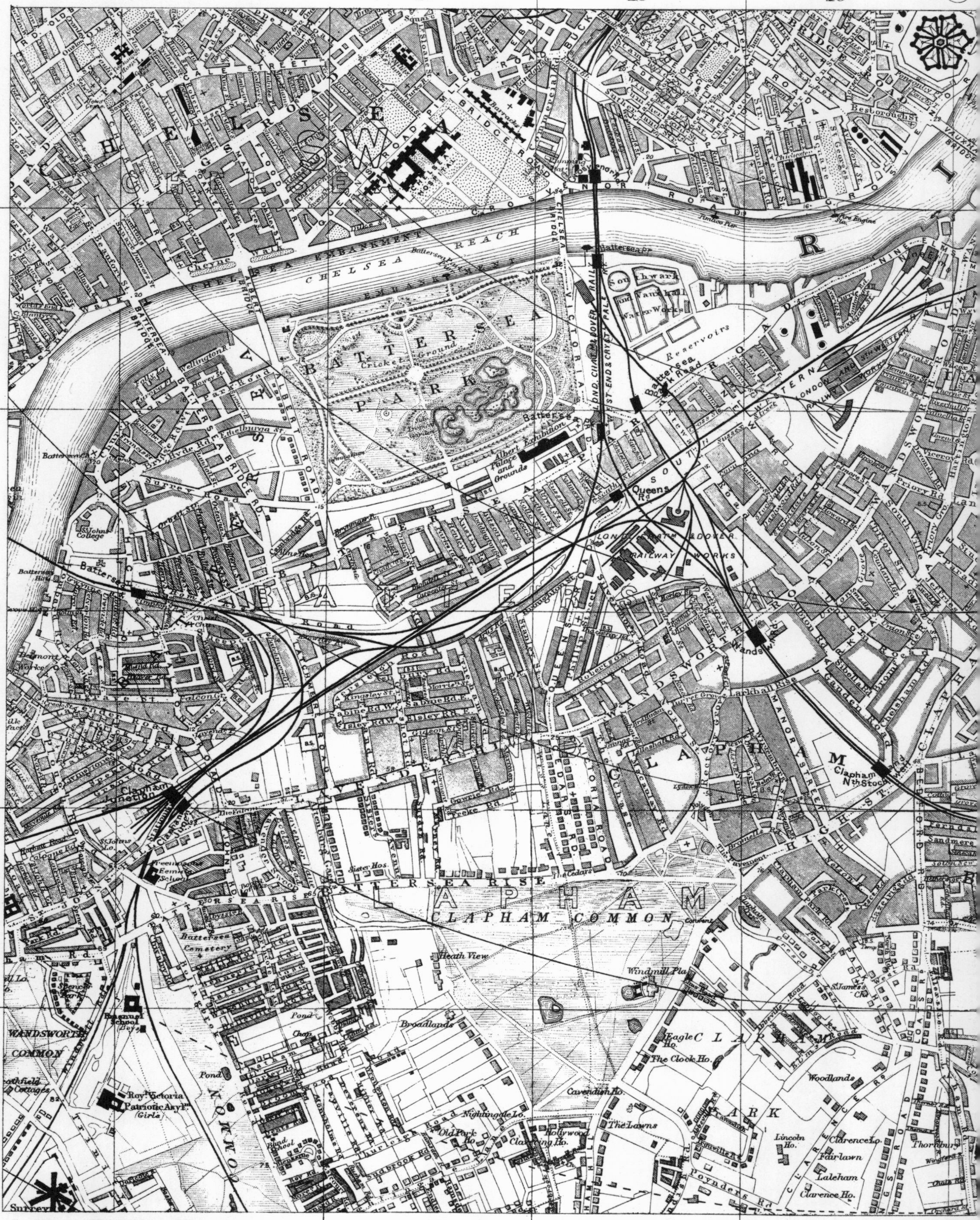

G.W. Bacon, F.R.G.S. 127 Strand, London.

17 18 19 Adjoining (53) Sheet

20
21
22
23
24
P
Q
R
S
T
U
KENNINGTON
NEWINGTON
WALWORTH
NORTH BRIXTON
CAMBERWELL
BRIXTON
CHAMPION HILL
HERNE HILL
EAST DULWICH
Kennington Oval
Camberwell New Park
Loughboro'
Denmark Hill
St. Saviour's Infirmary
Brockwell House
BROCKWELL HALL PARK
Brixton Prison
Lambeth Water Works
Model Farm
Dulwich Ho.
Herne hill Lodge
Carlton Ho.
Springfield
The Half Moon
Clarence Lodge
Raleigh Ho.
White Ho.
CAMBERWELL NEW ROAD
CAMBERWELL ROAD
BRIXTON ROAD
CHURCH ST.
PECKHAM ROAD
ALBANY ROAD
COLDHARBOUR LANE
ACRE LANE
HALFMOON LANE
WOODWARDE ROAD
Adjoining Sheet 49
0
1 Mile.
55 110 220 Yards.

For same area on 9-inch scale, see sheets 24 to 27 & 32,33,34.

28
29
30
31
P
Q
R
S
T
U
GREENWICH REACH
Millwall Pier
Royal Victualling Yard
Foreign Cattle Market
Millwall Iron Works
W. FERRY RD.
North Greenwich
Port of London Wharf
Telegraph Cable Wks
Rope Walk
Marsh St.
Paraffin Oil Wks
EAST GREENWICH
Greenwich Union Work Ho.
Royal Hospital Cemetery
Trafalgar Tav.
Royal Hospital
Royal Hosp. School
Maze Hill
WOOLWICH RAILWAY
GREENWICH
Thames Street
Creek Br.
Bridge St.
DEPTFORD
Deptford
Evelyn Street
Prince St.
Church St.
High St.
Douglas St.
Regent St.
Griffin St.
Reginald St.
New Cross
CROSS ROAD
BROADWAY
Deptford Br.
Greenwich
GREENWICH RD.
LONDON ST.
Ashburnham Rd.
Royal Observatory
GREENWICH PARK
Vanbrugh Fields
Vanbrugh Park
Charlton Road
Shooters Hill Road
BLACKHEATH
Blackheath Hill
Black Heath Rd.
Morden Hill
Lewisham Rd.
Hollyhedge Ho.
Heath House
Talbot Pla.
Blackheath Vale
Paragon
The Orchard
Eliot Place
Eliot Vale
BLACKHEATH
Blackheath
NORTH KENT RAILWAY
Lewisham Junction
St. Johns
Lewisham
Loampit Hill
HIGH ROAD
Brockley Rd.
Lewisham Road
Breakspear Rd.
St. Peters Rd.
Cranfield Rd.
Harefield Rd.
Wickham Road
Belmont Hill
Belmont
The Cedars
The Glebe
Lee Terrace
LEE
Park Villa
The Priory
Belmont Park
Dacre St.
Manor Pk. Rd.
Lee Lodge
Hurst Lo.
LEE HIGH ROAD
The Firs
LEE GREEN
Ellerdale Rd.
West Kent Gram. Sch.
Ivy Lane
Deptford Cemetery
Lewisham Cemetery
R. C. Burying Gr.
Ladywell Lane
Ladywell
St. Mary's Ch.
LEWISHAM
Eastdown Lodge
Manor Fm.
Quaggy River
Nat. School
Worcester Villa
Richmond Villa
Lewisham Park
Union Workhouse
The Priory
Alms Ho.
George Pla.
George Lane
Rosenthal
LEWISHAM ROAD
HITHER GREEN
Hither Grn. Lodge
Brockley Hall
RIVER
DARTFORD RAILWAY
Lee
Lee Public Hall
Adjoining Sheet 50
28
29
0
1 Mile.
55 110 220 Yards

Adjoining 45 Sheet
Adjoining 49 Sheet
32
33
34
35
36
O
P
Q
S
T
U
Angerstein's Wharf
Charlton Wharf
Telegraph Works
Harrington Road
Bowater Road
North St.
Siemens Road
ROYAL DOCKYARD
OUTER BASIN
INNER BASIN
Floating Pier
Landing
Saw Mill
Dockyard Chapel
Church St.
George St.
Albion Road
HIGH STREET
POWIS STREET
Dockyard Sta.
Mary's St.
King St.
Henry St.
School
Bowater Cr.
Infantry Barracks
Frances St.
Wood Street
Prospect Pl.
Artillery Place
Green Hill Schools
Hill Street
Royal Artillery Barrs.
St. Georges Church Garrison
Drill Ground
Mortar Battery
Rotunda
Magnetic Office
Battery
Bastion
Royal Military Repository
Gun Shed
Barrack Field
Barrack Dispensary
Commandant's House
Commandant's Engineer Off.
Commanding Engineers Qrs.
Female Hospital
Nightingale Pl.
WELLINGTON STREET
WOOLWICH LOWER ROAD
Pumping Sta.
National School
Charlton Sta.
Hanging Wood
Hanging Wood Lane
Charlton Lane
Little Heath
B.S.
Victoria Wks.
Gurdon Road
West Coombe Park Sta.
Victoria Road
Wellington Road
Church Lane
Charlton Grove
St. Pauls Ch.
Fair Field
Institute
St. Lukes Ch.
Fairfield Ho.
G R E E N W I C H
CHARLTON
Chapel
Charlton Ho.
Charlton Road
THE PARK
Charlton Cemetery
Marlborough Lane
School
The Cottages
WOOLWICH COMMON
Prince Imperial Statue
Hut Barracks
Royal Military Academy
Govr's Ho.
Gymnasium
Battery
Wellesley Ho.
Royal Horse Infirmary
Reservoir
Hill Farm
SHOOTERS HILL ROAD
Old Dover Rd.
St. Johns Church
Schools
St. Germans Chap.
Hervey Rd.
St. James Ch.
School
Morden College
Herbert Hospital
Fire Sta.
Police Sta.
Christ Church
SHOOTERS HILL
The Rookery
Haddon Lo.
Castle Ho.
ELTHAM COMMON
Greenwich Cemetery
Severndroog Castle
Mayfield
Castle Wood
Manor Farm
Kidbrook Green
Lower Kid Brook
Lower Kidbrooke Farm
Kidbrook Lane
Blackheath Park
Well Hall
Park Farm
The Grove
Eltham Park
St. Peters Church Parsonage
Harrowfield Cottage
Weston Park
Eltham Gas Wks.
Eltham Green
Eltham Br.
Quaggy River
Lyme Farm
Bavarian Brewery
St. Johns Ch.
Nat. Sch.
Police Sta.
Eltham Monument
Pippinhall Farm
Horn Park Lane
Mottingham Lane
G.W.Bacon, F.R.G.S. 127 Strand, London.

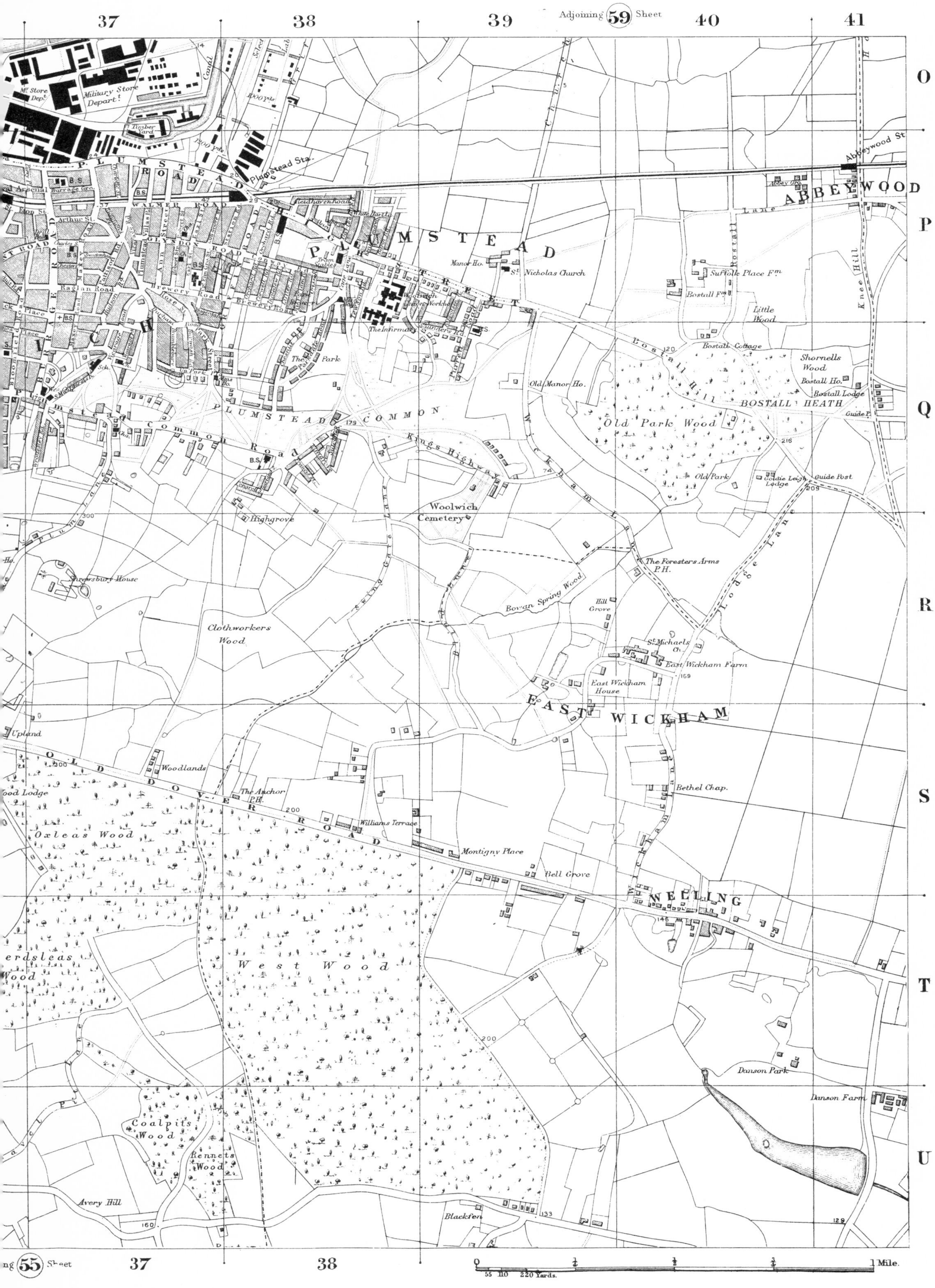
Adjoining 59 Sheet
37
38
39
40
41
O
P
Q
R
S
T
U
Military Store Depart.
Timber Yard
Canal
Plumstead Sta.
PLUMSTEAD ROAD
Burrage Gro.
Arthur St.
WALMER ROAD
GLYNDON ROAD
Raglan Road
Brewery Road
PLUMSTEAD
Manor Ho.
St. Nicholas Church
The Infirmary
The Park
PLUMSTEAD COMMON
Common Road
Kings Highway
Highgrove
Woolwich Cemetery
Shrewsbury House
Clothworkers Wood
Bovan Spring Wood
Hill Grove
Abbeywood St.
ABBEY WOOD
Lane
Bostall
Suffolk Place Fm.
Bostall Fm.
Little Wood
Bostall Cottage
Shornells Wood
Bostall Ho.
Bostall Lodge
Bostall Hill
BOSTALL HEATH
Knee Hill
Old Manor Ho.
Old Park Wood
Old Park
Goldie Leigh Lodge
Guide Post
Wickham Lane
The Foresters Arms P.H.
Lodge Lane
St. Michaels Ch.
East Wickham Farm
East Wickham House
EAST WICKHAM
Upland
Woodlands
OLD DOVER ROAD
The Anchor P.H.
Williams Terrace
Montigny Place
Bell Grove
Bethel Chap.
WELLING
Oxleas Wood
West Wood
Danson Park
Danson Farm
Coalpits Wood
Rennets Wood
Avery Hill
Blackfen
Adjoining 55 Sheet
1 Mile.
55 110 220 Yards.

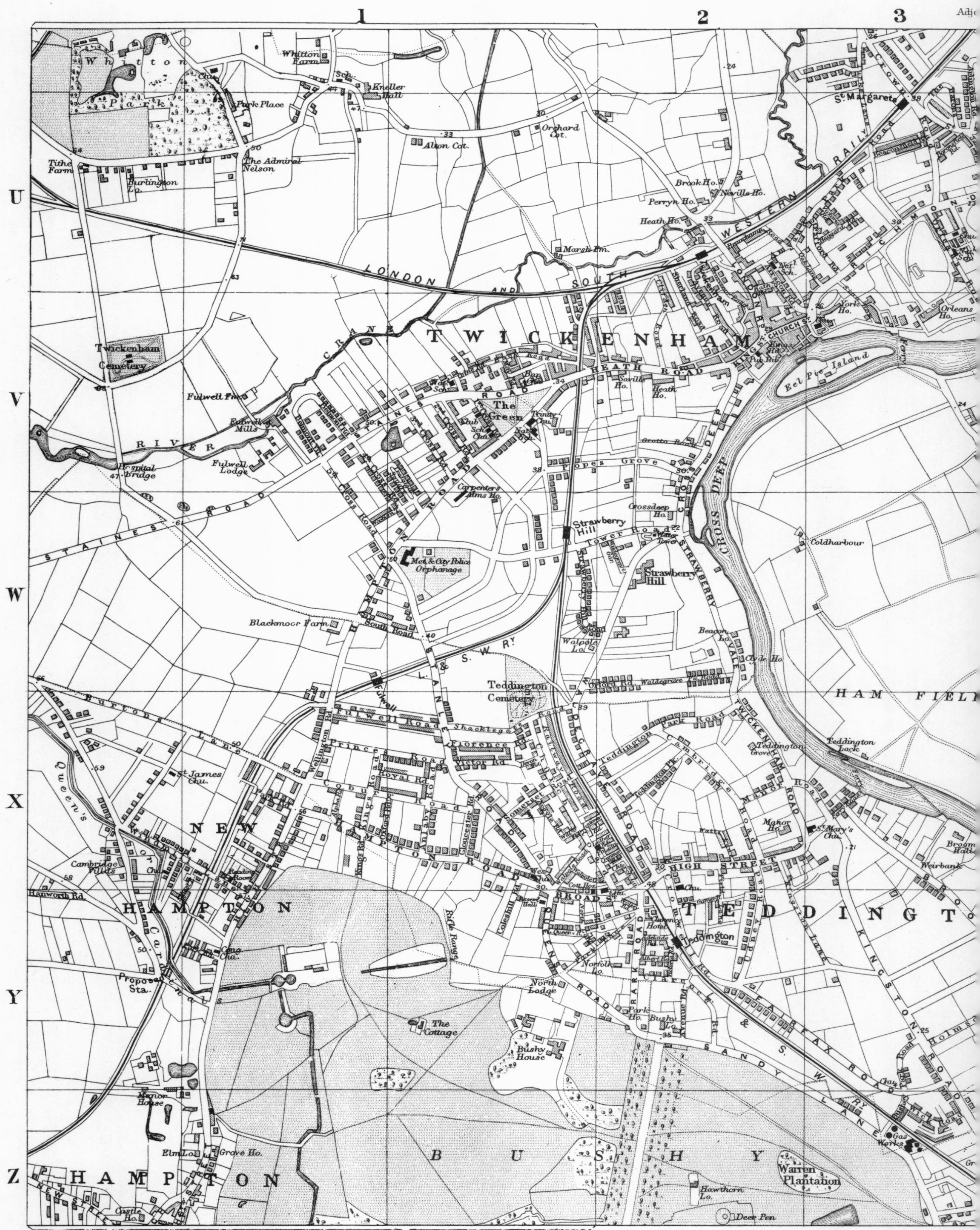
1
2
3
U
V
W
X
Y
Z
Whitton Park
Whitton Farm
Kneller Hall
Park Place
Tithe Farm
The Admiral Nelson
Burlington Lo.
Alton Cot.
Orchard Cot.
St. Margarets
Brook Ho.
Nevills Ho.
Perryn Ho.
Heath Ho.
Marsh Fm.
London and South Western Railway
Twickenham Cemetery
Fulwell Fm.
Fulwell Mills
Fulwell Lodge
Hospital Bridge
River Crane
TWICKENHAM
Heath Road
Savile Ho.
Heath Ho.
The Green
Trinity Chu.
Carpenters Alms Ho.
Popes Grove
Grotto Road
Eel Pie Island
Orleans Ho.
York Ho.
Church St.
King St.
Staines Road
Cross Road
Cross Deep
Crossdeep Ho.
Strawberry Hill
Tower Road
Water Tower
Coldharbour
Met. & City Police Orphanage
Blackmoor Farm
South Road
Beacon Lo.
Clyde Ho.
Walpole Lo.
L. & S. W. Ry.
Teddington Cemetery
Waldegrave
HAM FIELDS
Burtons Lane
Queen's
St. James Chu.
Fulwell Road
Prince Road
Florence
Victor Rd.
Royal Rd.
Coburg Road
Wellington Rd.
Teddington Park Road
Teddington Grove
Teddington Lock
Twickenham Road
Cambridge Road
Manor Ho.
St. Mary's Chu.
Broom Hall
Weirbank
NEW HAMPTON
Cambridge Villas
Hanworth Rd.
Reading Room
Hampton Road
Gloucester Rd.
Somerset Road
High Street
Broad St.
Bushy Hall
Clarence Hotel
Teddington
TEDDINGTON
Kingston Road
Rifle Range
Cong. Chu.
Proposed Sta.
North Lodge
Norfolk Lo.
Park Road
Park Ho.
Bushy Lo.
Sandy Lane
Fairfax Road
Holmesdale Road
The Cottage
Bushy House
Manor House
Elm Lo.
Grove Ho.
Castle Ho.
New Street
HAMPTON
BUSHY
Warren Plantation
Hawthorn Lo.
Deer Pen
Gas Works
Chu.
G.W.Bacon, F.R.G.S. 127 Strand, London.
Adjoi

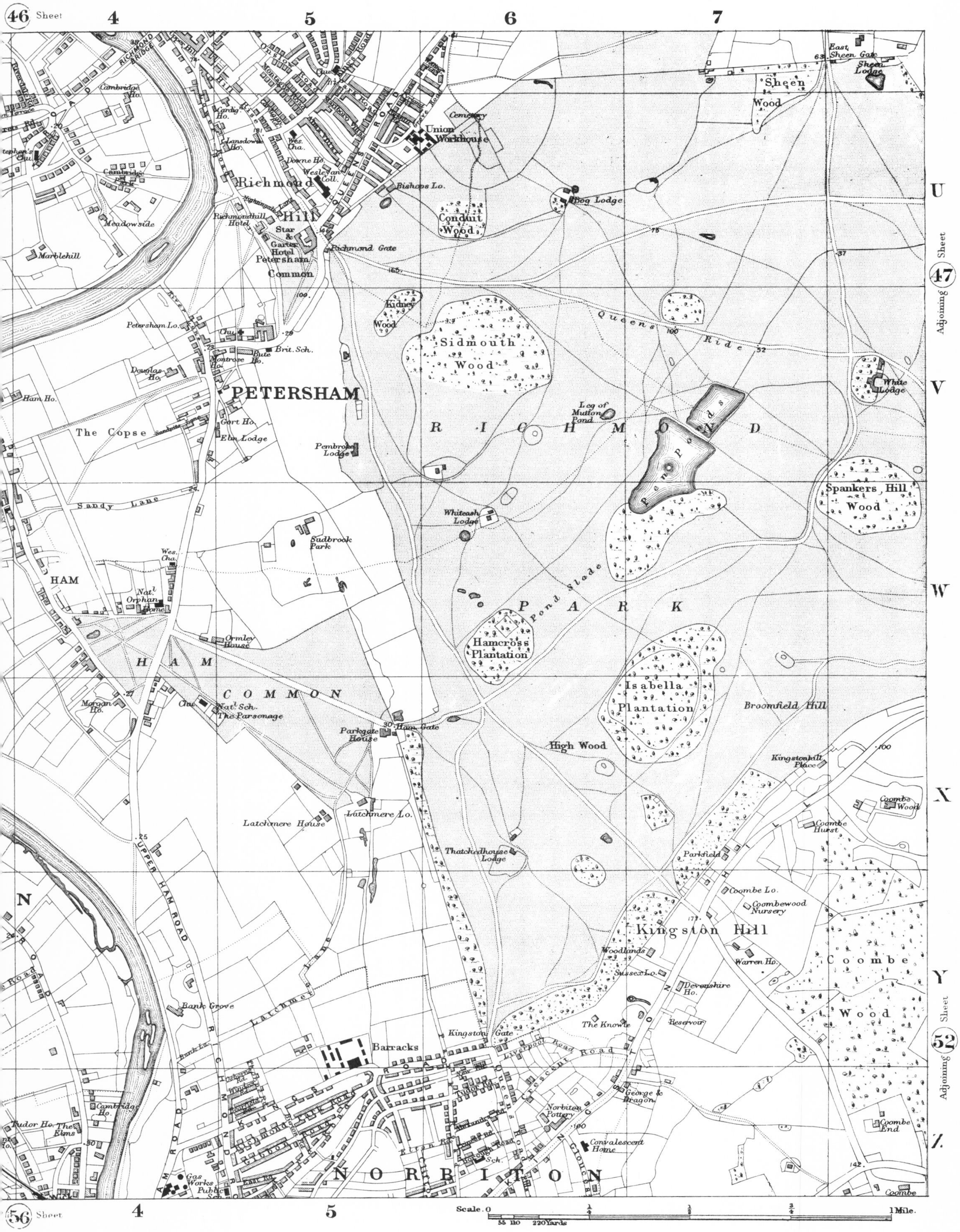
46 Sheet
4
5
6
7
U
V
W
X
Y
Z
Adjoining Sheet 47
Adjoining Sheet 52
56 Sheet
Richmond Bridge
Cambridge Ho.
Cambridge Park
Meadowside
Marblehill
Lansdown Ho.
Downe Ho.
Wes. Cha.
Wesleyan Coll.
Richmond Hill
Richmondhill Hotel
Star & Garter Hotel
Petersham Common
Cemetery
Union Workhouse
Bishops Lo.
Queens Road
Conduit Wood
Bog Lodge
Richmond Gate
East Sheen Gate
Sheen Lodge
Sheen Wood
Kidney Wood
Sidmouth Wood
Queens Ride
White Lodge
Petersham Lo.
Chu.
Brit. Sch.
Bute Ho.
Montrose Ho.
Douglas Ho.
Ham Ho.
PETERSHAM
The Copse
Gort Ho.
Elm Lodge
Pembroke Lodge
Leg of Mutton Pond
Pen Ponds
R I C H M O N D
P A R K
Spankers Hill Wood
Sandy Lane
Whiteash Lodge
Sudbrook Park
Wes. Cha.
HAM
Nat[1] Orphan Home
Pond Slade
Hamcross Plantation
Ormley House
H A M
C O M M O N
Morgan Ho.
Nat[1] Sch.
The Parsonage
Parkgate House
Ham Gate
Isabella Plantation
Broomfield Hill
High Wood
Kingstonhill Place
Coombe Wood
Coombe Hurst
Latchmere House
Latchmere Lo.
Thatchedhouse Lodge
Parkfield
Coombe Lo.
Coombewood Nursery
Kingston Hill
Upper Ham Road
Woodlands
Warren Ho.
Sussex Lo.
Devonshire Ho.
Coombe Wood
Latchmere Lane
Bank Grove
The Knowle
Reservoir
Kingston Gate
Barracks
Liverpool Road
Crescent Road
Cambridge Ho.
Tudor Ho.
The Elms
George & Dragon
Norbiton Pottery
Coombe End
Convalescent Home
Gas Works
Public Sch.
N O R B I T O N
Coombe
Scale. 0 ¼ ½ ¾ 1 Mile.
55 110 220 Yards
4
5

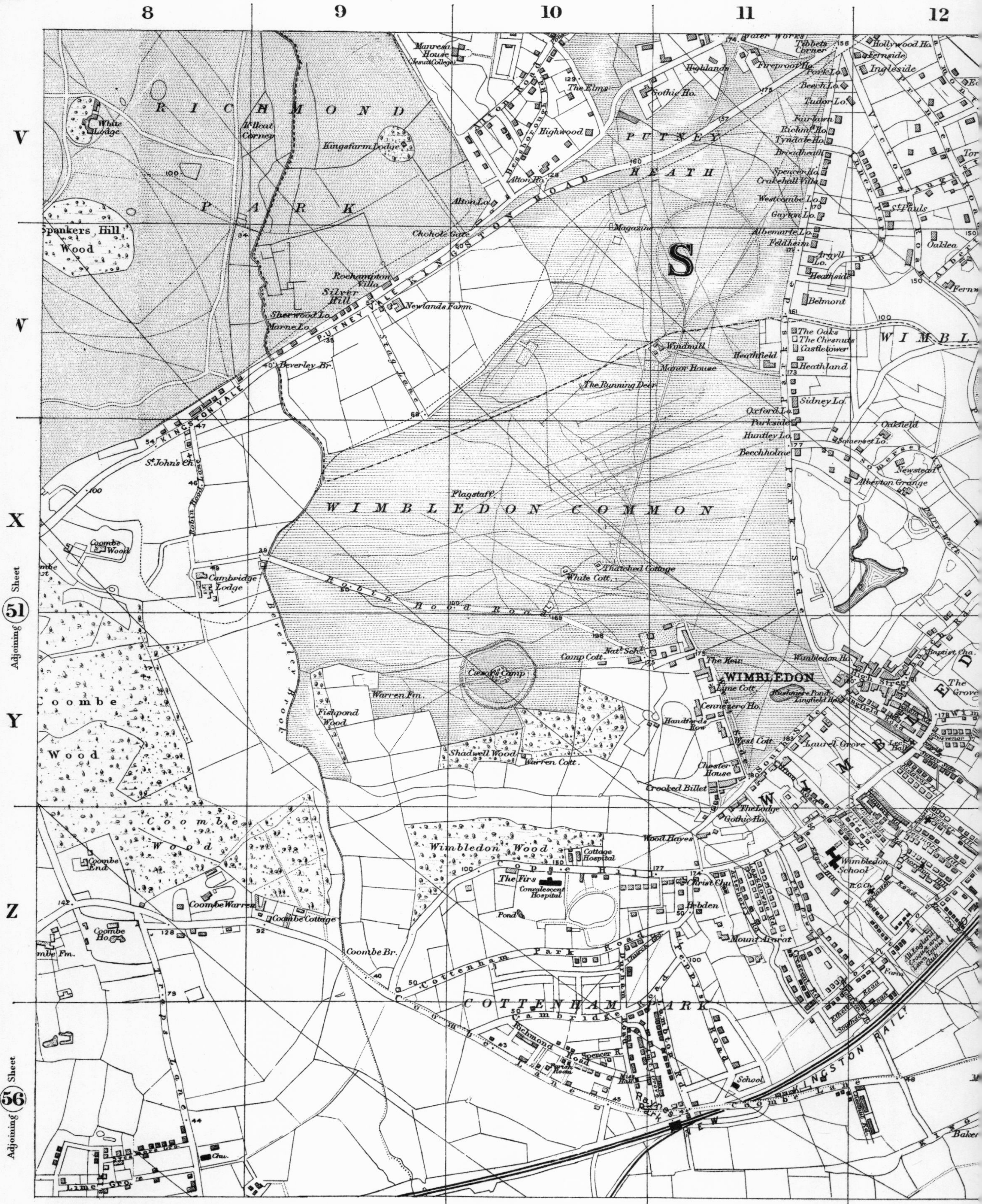
8
9
10
11
12
V
W
X
Y
Z
Adjoining Sheet 51
Adjoining Sheet 56
RICHMOND PARK
White Lodge
Spankers Hill Wood
Kingsfarm Lodge
Manresa House
The Elms
Highlands
Gothic Ho.
Highwood
Alton Ho.
Alton Lo.
PUTNEY HEATH
Tibbets Corner
Fireproof Ho.
Ingleside
Beech Lo.
Tudor Lo.
Fairlawn
Broadheath
Spencer Ho.
Westcombe Lo.
Gayton Lo.
Albemarle Lo.
Feldheim
Heathside
Belmont
St. Pauls
Oaklea
KINGSTON ROAD
Magazine
S
Roehampton Villa
Silver Hill
Newlands Farm
Sherwood Lo.
Marne Lo.
Beverley Br.
Stag Lane
Windmill
Manor House
The Running Deer
Heathfield
The Oaks
The Chesnuts
Castletower
Heathland
Sidney Lo.
Oxford Lo.
Parkside
Hunfley Lo.
Beechholme
Oakfield
Somerset Lo.
Newstead
Alverton Grange
Kingston Vale
St. John's Ch.
Flagstaff
WIMBLEDON COMMON
Coombe Wood
Cambridge Lodge
Thatched Cottage
White Cott.
Robin Hood Road
Robin Hood Lane
Beverley Brook
Nat. Sch.
Camp Cott.
Caesar's Camp
Warren Fm.
Fishpond Wood
Shadwell Wood
Warren Cott.
The Keir
WIMBLEDON
Lime Cott.
Rushmere Pond
Handfords Row
West Cott.
Laurel Grove
Chester House
Crooked Billet
The Lodge
Gothic Ho.
Wood Hayes
Wimbledon Ho.
Baptist Cha.
High Street
The Grove
Wimbledon School
Coombe Wood
Coombe End
Wimbledon Wood
Cottage Hospital
Copse Hill
The Firs
Convalescent Hospital
Pond
Christ Chu.
Hebden
Mount Ararat
Coombe Warren
Coombe Cottage
Coombe Ho.
Coombe Fm.
Coombe Br.
Cottenham Park Road
COTTENHAM PARK
Cambridge Road
Richmond Road
Spencer R.
Coombe Lane
Traps Lane
Lime Gro.
Chu.
School
Raynes Park
NEW
KINGSTON RAILY.
All England Croquet and Lawn Tennis Club
WIMBLEDON

G.W. Bacon, F.R.G.S. 127 Strand, London.

Adjoining 47 Sheet
13
14
15
16
V
W
X
Y
Z
Adjoining 53 Sheet
Balverine Villas
South Field
St Pauls
Dunsford Villas
Dunsford Fm
Mayfield Villas
Lake Farm
U
Wimbledonpark Fm
The Lake
Allen Grove Wood
Vineyardhill Wood
Vineyard Hill
Wimbledonpark House
St Mary's Ch.
Belvedere Ro.
Cemetery
Dunsford Lo.
Haydens Park
Haydens Park Rd.
Haydens Lane
Nursery
St Marks
Wimbledon
Local Board Sewage Works
Garratt Print Works
The Willows
Copper Works
Calico Print and Dye Works
Duntshill Villa
Duntshill
Earlsfield
Manure Factory
Knaresbro Lo.
Upper Wandle Ho.
Wandsworth & Clapham Workhouse
House of Correction
Wandsworth Cemetery
Burntwood Ho.
Burntwood Grange
Burntwood Lane
Burntwood Lo.
Collamore
White Lodge
Wandsworth Common
Nightingale Cot.
Fernside
St James's Indust. Sch.
R
O
W
S
County Lunatic Asylum
Springfield Farm Asylum
Garratt
Garratt Fm
Garratt Green
Garratt Lane
Althorpe
St Mary's Ch.
Summers Town
Summerstown Mission
St Clements Danes Almshouses
Bells Fm.
St Andrews Miss. Hall
Lambeth Cemetery
Manor Hou.
Fish Ponds
Park House
Park Hill
The Cedars
Lynwood
UPPER TOOTING
LOWER TOOTING
Totterdown Fm
Park Ho.
St Nicola's Ch.
Amen Corner
The Avenue
Tooting Lr. Bridge
Tooting
Tooting Hall
Swains Farm
Figge's Marsh
Tamworth Fm
The Poplars
Industrial Schools
UPPER MITCHAM
Wandsworth Lo.
Upper Tooting
NEW WIMBLEDON
Merton Pumping Station Sewage Wks.
Colliers wood
Faraday Rd.
Herschel Road
Clarence Road
Florence Road
Park Road
Recreation Ground
Flour Mill
Wandlebank Ho.
Abbey Lodge
Merton Grove
Merton Fm
MERTON
High Path
Merton Abbey
Merton Abbey Print Wks.
Copper Mills
Christ Ch.
Clifton Place
Lower Merton
Dorset Hall
Merton College
Merton Church
School
Morden
Homefield Ho.
Wandle House
Bleach Works
TOOTING MERTON AND WIMBLEDON
WIMBLEDON AND CROYDON RY
SOUTH WESTERN RAILWAY
RIVER WANDLE
0
1 Mile.
55 110 220 Yards

15
16
17
18
19
Adjoining 48
V
W
X
Y
Z
Adjoining Sheet 52
BALHAM
UPPER TOOTING
LOWER TOOTING
TOOTING COMMON
STREATHAM
LOWER STREATHAM
UPPER MITCHAM
WANDSWORTH COMMON
Wandsworth Common
County Lunatic Asylum
Springfield Farm Asylum
Burntwood Grange
Burntwood Ho.
Burntwood Lo.
Nightingale Cot.
Woodlands
Fernside
Balham Ho.
Oakfield
Woodthorpe
ATKINS ROAD
Thornton Ho.
CROVE ROAD
THORNTON ROAD
The Boundaries
The Hawthorns
The Willows
Mayfield
Upper Tooting Park
Wandsworth Lo.
Bedfordhill House
Rutherford Road
Cypress Rd.
The Priory
Hyde Fm.
Leigham Court Road
Magdalen Hospital
Woodfield
Foodfield
Norfolk House
Magnolia Cot.
The Cedars
The Elms
Park Hill
Park House
Lynwood
Fish Ponds
St. Clements Danes Almshouses
Bells Fm.
Manor Hou.
Newlands
Tooting Lodge
The Cottage
Tooting Bec Rd.
Wood Lo.
Totterdown Fields
Hillhouse Farm
Woodlands
Woodnook
Streatham Park
Kinrard
Hill House
Church Lane
Rectory Lane
Park Ho.
St. Nicola's Ch.
Grove House
Furze Down
Furzedown Fm.
Manor Park
Amen Corner
Durham Ho.
The Avenue
Waterfall Ho.
River Graveney
Tooting Lr. Bridge
Tooting
Colliers wood
Tooting Hall
Swains Farm
Roe Bridge
Streatham Common
WIMBLEDON RAILWAY
TOOTING MERTON AND WIMBLEDON RAILWAY
Biggin Farm
Christ Ch.
Chilton Place
Tamworth Fm.
Figge's Marsh
The Poplars
The Willows
The Chesnuts
Industrial Schools
Lonescombe
Lonescombe Chemical Wks.
Streatham Common
Greyhound Lane
Streatham Steeple Chase
High Elms
Emanuel Chu.
India Rubber Manufactory
Guildersfield
St. Andrew Chu.
Coventry
Fairlawn
G.W. Bacon, F.R.G.S. 127 Strand, London.

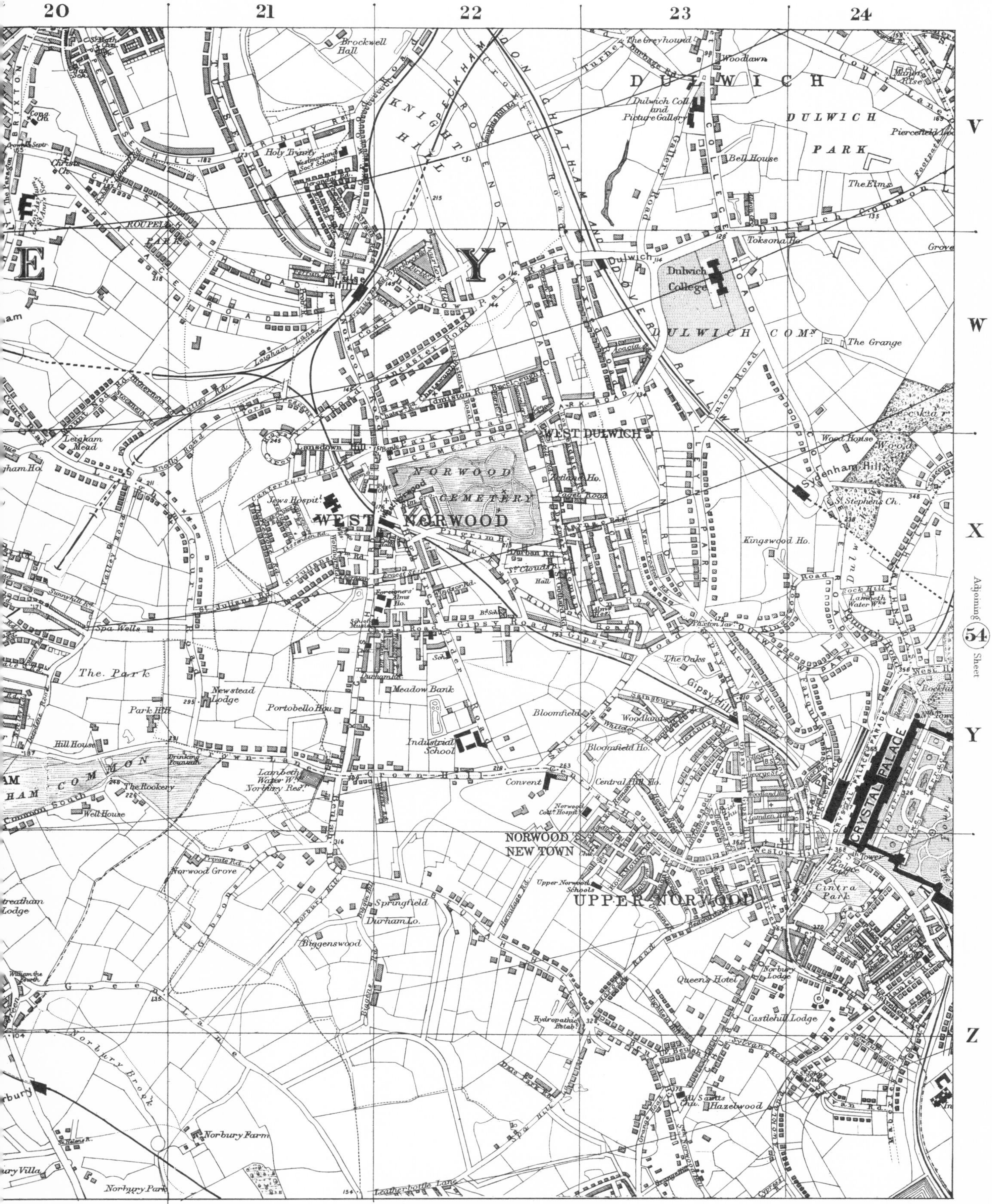

20
21
22
23
24
V
W
X
Y
Z
DULWICH
DULWICH PARK
Dulwich Coll. and Picture Gallery
Bell House
The Elms
Woodlawn
The Greyhound
Brockwell Hall
Holy Trinity
KNIGHTS HILL
ROSENDALE ROAD
Dulwich College
DULWICH COMN
The Grange
Toksowa Ho.
ROUPELL PARK
Leigham Mead
Lansdown Hill
WEST DULWICH
NORWOOD CEMETERY
WEST NORWOOD
Jews Hospitl.
Wood House
Sydenham Hill
St. Stephen's Ch.
Kingswood Ho.
Spa Wells
The Park
Newstead Lodge
Park Hill
Portobello Ho.
Meadow Bank
Bloomfield
Bloomfield Ho.
Woodlands
Industrial School
Hill House
Drinking Fountain
COMMON
The Rookery
Lambeth Water Wks. Norbury Resr.
Well House
Convent
Central Hill Ho.
The Oaks
Gipsy Hill
Gipsy Road
NORWOOD NEW TOWN
Upper Norwood Schools
UPPER NORWOOD
CRYSTAL PALACE
Westow
Cintra Park
Norwood Grove
Springfield
Durham Lo.
Biggenswood
Queen's Hotel
Norbury Lodge
Castlehill Lodge
Hydropathic Estab.
Sylvan Road
All Saints Ch.
Hazelwood
Norbury Farm
Norbury Park
Norbury Brook
Green Lane
Leatherbottle Lane
Adjoining 54 Sheet
Adjoining 57 Sheet
0
¼
½
¾
1 Mile.
55 110 220 Yards.

23
24
25
26
Adjoining 49 Sheet
V
W
X
Y
Z
Adjoining 53 Sheet
DULWICH
DULWICH PARK
Dulwich Coll. and Picture Gallery
Bell House
The Elms
Dulwich College
DULWICH COMN
The Grange
WEST DULWICH
Sydenham Hill
Kingswood Ho.
Lordship Lane
Forest Hill
UPPER SYDENHAM
Public Recreation Ground
Sydenham
Newlands
LOWER
CRYSTAL PALACE
Cricket Ground
Archery Ground
UPPER NORWOOD
Cintra Park
Queen's Hotel
Castlehill Lodge
North Surrey Industrial Schools
Infirmary
PENGE
Athletic Association
Norwood Reservoir
Holy Trinity Ch.
Kent House Sta.
G.W. Bacon, F.R.G.S. 127 Strand, London.
Adjoining 58 Sheet

54
28
29
30
31
V
W
X
Y
Z
Adjoining Sheet 55
L E W I S H A M
K E N T
Mountsfield
The Rising Sun
Woodland Ho.
Bright side
Burntash Fm.
Ravensbourne Park House
Catford Bridge
RUSHY GREEN
Cricket Ground
Sangley House
Cockshed Fm.
Sangley Farm
Catford Ho.
Blythe Ho.
Oak Cottage
Lee Cemetery
Rose Lawn
Laurel Brook
Orchard Pl.
Broad Mead
Clare Lodge
Claremont Villa
White House Fm.
Shrofield Fm.
Whitefoot Lane
Crystal Palace District Gas Wks.
Bellingham Fm.
Park House
The Hall
Nat. Sch.
Episcopal Church
Tigers Head
Corn Mill
Green Man
SOUTH END
Mill Pond
Firhill House
Lower Sydenham
Southend Lane
Gipsy Lane
Durham Hill Lane
Southend Cott.
Brickfield
Lodge
Holloway Farm
Beckenham Hill
Ash Plantation
Stumpshill Wood
Beckenham Place
Reed Beds
Summerhouse Hill Wood
Weir
Bromleyhill House
Plaistow Lodge
Farm
New Beckenham
Brackley Rd.
Park Road
Foxgrove Road
Foxgrove Rd. East
The Avenue
Westgate Rd.
Bromley Cemetery
Foot Br.
CHATHAM & DOVER RAILWAY
MID KENT RAILWAY
TONBRIDGE RAILWAY
Albemarle Road
Beckenham
BECKENHAM
The Rectory
Manor Rd.
Shortlands
Bromley Gas Works
Bromley College
BROMLEY
Beckenham Lane
Bromley Road
River Ravensbourne
River Pool
1 Mile.
55 110 220 Yards.

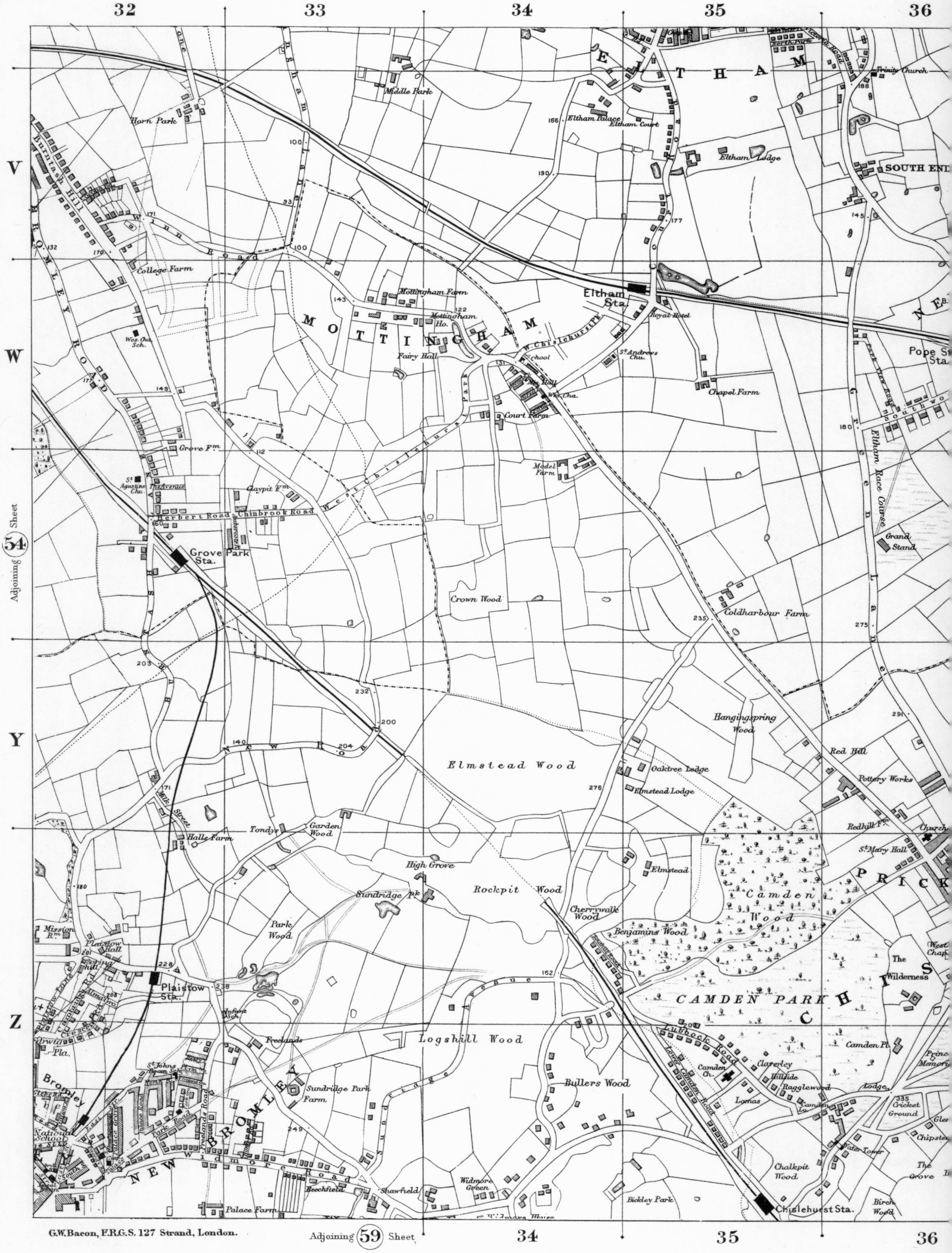
32
33
34
35
36
V
W
Y
Z
ELTHAM
Middle Park
Horn Park
Eltham Palace
Eltham Court
Eltham Lodge
SOUTH END
Trinity Church
Burnt Ash Hill
BROMLEY ROAD
College Farm
Mottingham Farm
Mottingham Ho.
MOTTINGHAM
Fairy Hall
Eltham Sta.
Royal Hotel
St. Andrews Chu.
School
Wes. Cha.
Court Farm
Chapel Farm
Pope St Sta.
Wes. Chu. Sch.
Grove Fm.
St. Augustine Chu.
The Avenue
Model Farm
Gaypit Fm.
Herbert Road
Chinbrook Road
West Chislehurst
Grove Park Sta.
Crown Wood
Coldharbour Farm
Eltham Race Course
Grand Stand
Green Lane
Hangingspring Wood
New Road
Elmstead Wood
Oaktree Lodge
Elmstead Lodge
Red Hill
Pottery Works
Redhill Fm.
Church
St. Mary Hall
Halls Farm
Tondys
Garden Wood
High Grove
Sundridge Pk.
Rockpit Wood
Elmstead
Cherrywalk Wood
Benjamins Wood
Camden Wood
PRICK
Park Wood
Mission Rm.
Plaistow Hall
Spring Hill
Plaistow Sta.
Infant Sch.
Freelands
Logshill Wood
CAMDEN PARK
CHISLEHURST
The Wilderness
Lubbock Road
Camden Ch.
Lomas
Claverley
Hillside
Ragglewood
Camden Pl.
Cricket Ground
Bullers Wood
Sundridge Park Farm
Bromley
National School
NEW BROMLEY
Widmore Road
Beechfield
Shawfield
Widmore Green
Palace Farm
Bickley Park
Chalkpit Wood
Chislehurst Sta.
Water Tower
The Grove
Birch Wood
Chipstead
34
35
36

G.W. Bacon, F.R.G.S. 127 Strand, London.

Adjoining 54 Sheet

Adjoining 59 Sheet

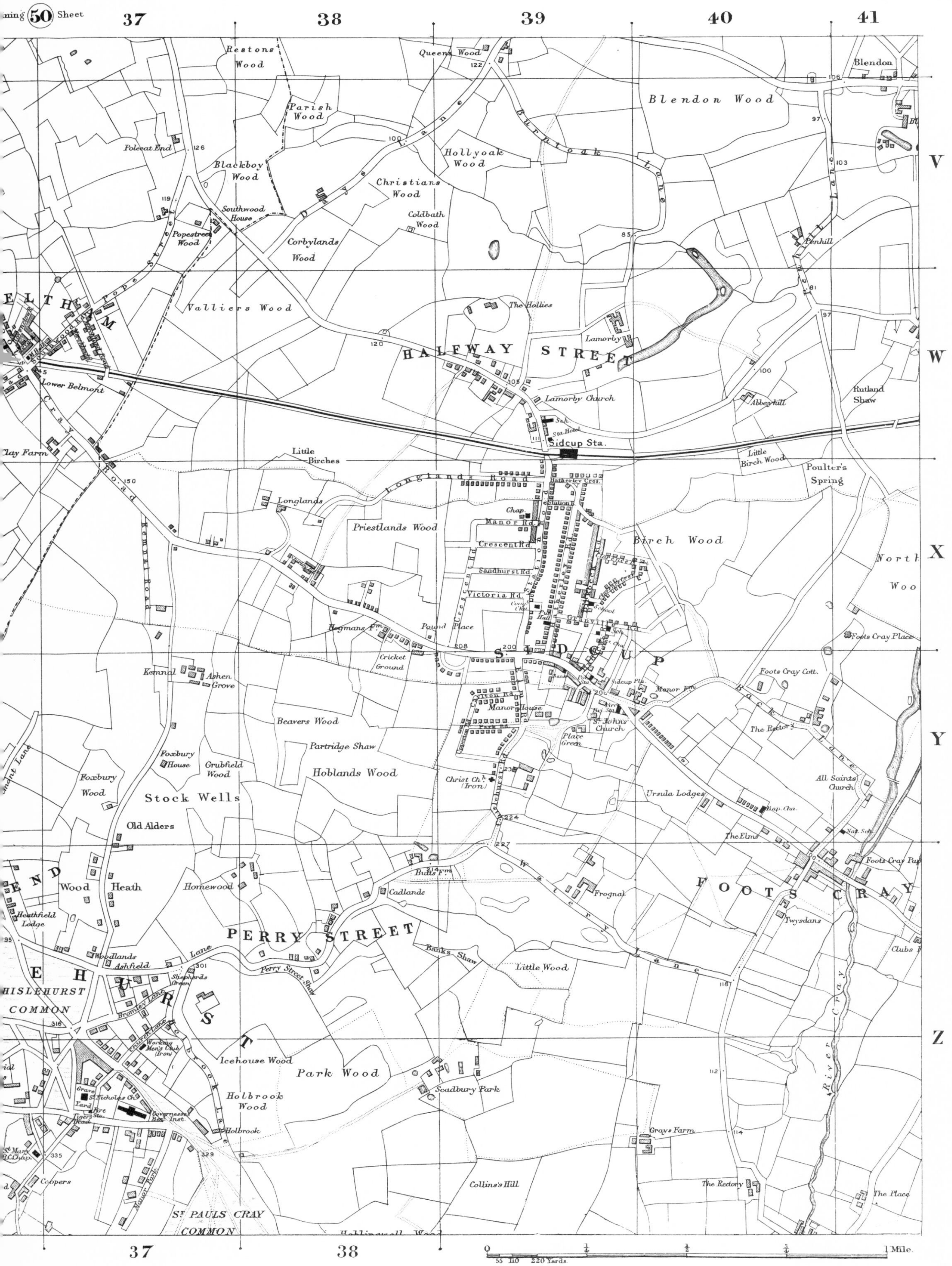
Sheet
37
38
39
40
41
Restons Wood
Queens Wood
Blendon
Blendon Wood
Parish Wood
Polecat End
Blackboy Wood
Hollyoak Wood
Christians Wood
Southwood House
Popestreet Wood
Coldbath Wood
Corbylands Wood
Penhill
ELTHAM
Valliers Wood
The Hollies
Lamorby
HALFWAY STREET
Lower Belmont
Lamorby Church
Abbeyhill
Rutland Shaw
Sidcup Sta.
Clay Farm
Little Birches
Little Birch Wood
Poulter's Spring
Longlands Road
Hatherley Cres.
Longlands
Manor Rd.
Crescent Rd.
Priestlands Wood
Birch Wood
Sandhurst Rd.
Victoria Rd.
Kemnal Road
Hogmans Fm.
Pound Place
Foots Cray Place
SIDCUP
Cricket Ground
Kemnal
Ashen Grove
Foots Cray Cott.
Manor Fm.
Manor House
Beavers Wood
The Rectory
St. Johns Church
Place Green
Partridge Shaw
Foxbury House
Grubfield Wood
Hoblands Wood
Foxbury Wood
Christ Ch. (Iron)
Stock Wells
Ursula Lodges
All Saints Church
Old Alders
The Elms
Butts Fm.
Homewood
Wood
Heath
Cadlands
Frognal
FOOTS CRAY
Heathfield Lodge
Twysdans
PERRY STREET
Woodlands
Ashfield
Banks Shaw
Little Wood
Perry Street Shaw
CHISLEHURST COMMON
Icehouse Wood
Park Wood
Scadbury Park
Holbrook Wood
Holbrook
Grays Farm
St. Nicholas Ch.
Coopers
Collins's Hill
The Rectory
The Place
ST. PAULS CRAY COMMON
River Cray
V
W
X
Y
Z
1 Mile.
220 Yards

HAMPTON
TEDDINGTON
BUSHY PARK
HAMPTON
HAMPTON WICK
Molesey Hurst
KENT TOWN
PALACE TOWN
EAST MOULSEY
WEST MOULSEY
Hampton Court Palace
HAMPTON COURT PARK
THAMES DITTON
Long Ditton
Giggshill
Rushett
Weston Green
Bushy House
The Cottage
Warren Plantation
Deer Pen
Keepers Lodge
Cavalry Barracks
The Green
Royal Mews
The Maze
Park Lodge
Stud Lodge
Chelsea Water Works
Lambeth Water Works
Ember Court
Embercourt Road
Manor Fm.
Weston Ho.
Pound Farm
Island Barn
Garricks Villa
Garricks Ait
Ash Island
Walnut Tree Island
St. Paul's Chu.
Parsonage
The Pavilion
The Cedars
Windows Bridge
Brewery
Giggshill Green
Thames Ditton
Ditton Ho.
Ditton Lo.
Manor House
Grove Ho.
Castle Ho.
Nursery
Weston Gro.
The Grove
The Priory
The Grange
Green Lane
Beauchum Road
Sandy Lane
Park Road
Hurst Road
Wolsey Road
Arnison Road
River Mole
River Ember
Summer Road
Bridge Road
London & South Western Railway
Proposed Sta.
Teddington
North Lodge
Bushy Lo.
Park Ho.
Hawthorn Lo.
Diana Fount
The Long Water
Race Course
Plough & Harrows
Up. Ditton
1
2
3
Y
Z
Adjoi

G.W.Bacon, F.R.G.S. 127 Strand, London.

Sheet 51
4
5
6
7
Kingston Hill
Coombe Lo.
Coombewood Nursery
Coombe Wood
Y
Woodlands
Sussex Lo.
Warren Ho.
Devonshire Ho.
Reservoir
The Knowle
Kingston Gate
Barracks
Bank Grove
Ham Road
Latchmere Lane
Liverpool Road
Crescent Road
George & Dragon
Norbiton Pottery
Convalescent Home
Coombe End
Coombe Ho.
Coombe Fm.
Cambridge Ho.
Tudor Ho.
The Elms
Gas Works
Canbury
N O R B I T O N
Union Workhouse
Coombe Road
Elm Road
Ceres Rd.
Tills Road
Albany Hall
Kingston Bridge
Clarence St.
London Street
The Elms
Norbiton Pla.
Kingston Hill
Cambridge Asylum
Fair Field
Fairfield
Orchard Rd.
Bonners Hill Lane
Kingston Cemetery
Gloucester Road
London and South Western Ry.
Cambridge Road
Lime Gro.
Gas Works
Acacia Gro.
Bap. Cha.
Adjoining Sheet 52
Woodbines
Oil Mills
Hogsmill River
Rifle Range
Grove Lane
Lower Marsh Lane
Norbiton Common Farm
NEW MALDEN
Z
R.C. Cha.
Anglesey Rd.
Palace Rd.
Surbiton Ho.
The Cranes
Up. Marsh Lane
Clay Hill
Ravens Ait
L. & S. W. Ry.
Grove Rd.
St. Leonards Rd.
Cleveland Road
Allbury Ho.
Church Rd.
Surbiton Hill Road
Bridge
Hogsmill River
Sow Lane
Seething Wells
S U R B I T O N
South Bank Road
Berrylands Road
Berry Lo. Farm
Southborough Park
Southborough Farm
Kingsdown Rd.
Ewell Road
Ditton Road
Shiphouse Cotts.
Neals Farm
4
5
Scale. 0 ¼ ½ ¾ 1 Mile.
55 110 220 Yards

Z
A
B
C
19
20
21
22
23
24
25
Adjoining Sheet 54
Adjoining Sheet 53
SOUTH NORWOOD
UPPER NORWOOD
THORNTON HEATH
NEW THORNTON HEATH
SELHURST PARK
ENNMORE PARK
WOODSIDE
NORBURY PARK
Norbury
Selhurst
Thornton Heath
Norwood Junct.
SOUTH COAST RAILWAY
Norbury Brook
Norbury Farm
Norbury Villa
Biggenswood
Durham Lo.
Castlehill Lodge
Queen's Hotel
Hazelwood
Norwood Reservoir
Grangewood
Recreation Ground
Selhurst Wood
Croydon Cemetery
Union Workhouse
Cricket Ground
Thornton Road
MITCHAM ROAD
The Grove
Hope Cott.
Wharncliffe Road
South Norwood Hill
Whitworth Road
Pawsons Road
Lancaster Rd.
Buckland Rd.
Ross Rd.
Grange Road
South Portland Road
Longfellow Rd.
Ryden Rd.
Hydropathic Estab.
Infirmary

D
E
F
G
H
CROYDON
CENTRAL WARD
SOUTH WARD
BEDDINGTON
WADDON
Addiscombe Road
Coombe Road
Coombe lane
Selsdon Rd
Ballards Plantation
Croham Hurst
Breakneck Hill
Duppas Hill
Cricket Ground
Croham Farm
Haling Park
Coldharbour Lane
Merebank Lane
Plough Lane
Violet Lane
Brighton Road
Waddon
South Croydon
East Croydon
West Croydon
London, Brighton & South Coast Railway
South Coast Railway
Mitcham Road
Gas Works
Bandonhill
New Barn Farm
Cross Shaws
Littleheath Wood
Thrift Wood
Shirley Rd
Stroud Green
23
22
21
G.W.Bacon, F.R.G.S. 127 Strand, London.

BECKENHAM
New Beckenham
Lower Elmers End
Upper Elmers End
Elmers End
LANGLEY PARK
Langley Park
Langley Farm
Eden Park
Kelsey Park
Crystal Palace District Cemetery
SOUTH NORWOOD
Norwood Junct.
WOODSIDE
ENMORE PARK
Long Lane Wood
The Alders
Ham Farm
Stroud Green Farm
Race Course
SOUTH EASTERN RAILWAY
Wickham Road
Adjoining 54 Sheet
Sheet 59
Z
A
B
C
24
25
26
27
28
29

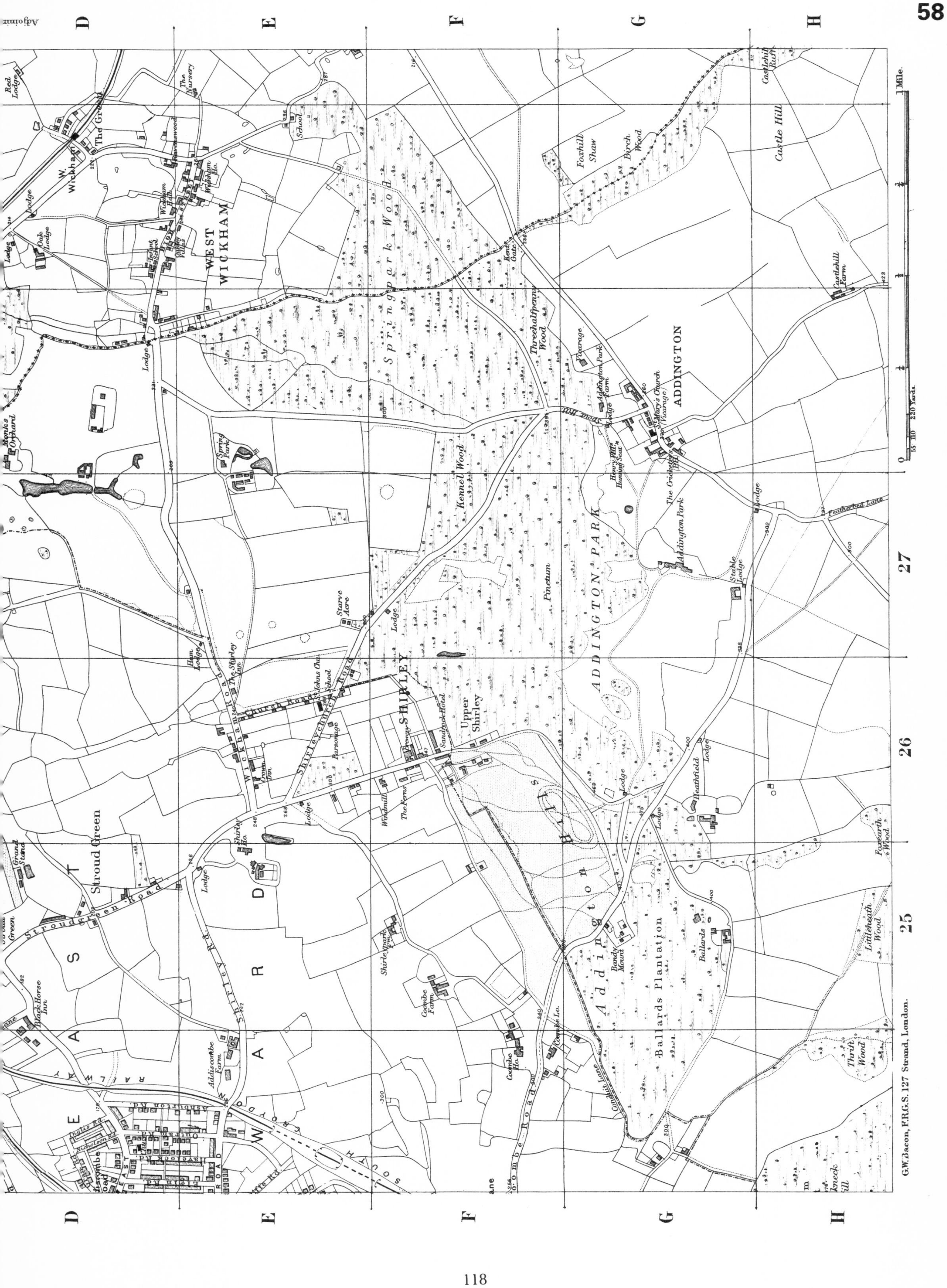
Adjoins
D
E
F
G
H
WEST WICKHAM
W. Wickham
The Green
The Nursery
Red Lodge
Oak Lodge
School
Springpark Wood
Kent Gate
Foxhill Shaw
Birch Wood
Castle Hill
Castlehill Ruin
Castlehill Farm
Threehalfpenny Wood
Vicarage
ADDINGTON
St. Mary's Church (Vicarage)
Addington Lodge Farm
Addington Park
Spout Hill
Kennel Wood
Monks Orchard
Spring Park
Pinetum
ADDINGTON PARK
The Cricketers
Heavy Hills Hunting Seat
Featherbed Lane
Starve Acre
Ham Lodge
The Shirley Inn
St. Johns Church
School
Church Road
Shirley Church Road
SHIRLEY
Upper Shirley
Sandrock Hotel
Wickham Road
Parsonage
Crown Inn
Windmill
The Ferns
Heathfield
Stable Lodge
Stroud Green
Grand Stand
Stroudgreen Road
Shirley Ho.
Shirley Rd
Shirleypark Fm.
Coombe Farm
Coombe Lo.
Coombe Ho.
Coombe Road
Bandy Mount
Ballards Plantation
Ballards
Littleheath Wood
Foxearth Wood
Thrift Wood
Black Horse Inn
Addiscombe Farm
RAILWAY
CROYDON
SOUTH
Addiscombe Rd
Coombe Lane
27
26
25
1 Mile
220 Yards
G.W. Bacon, F.R.G.S. 127 Strand, London.

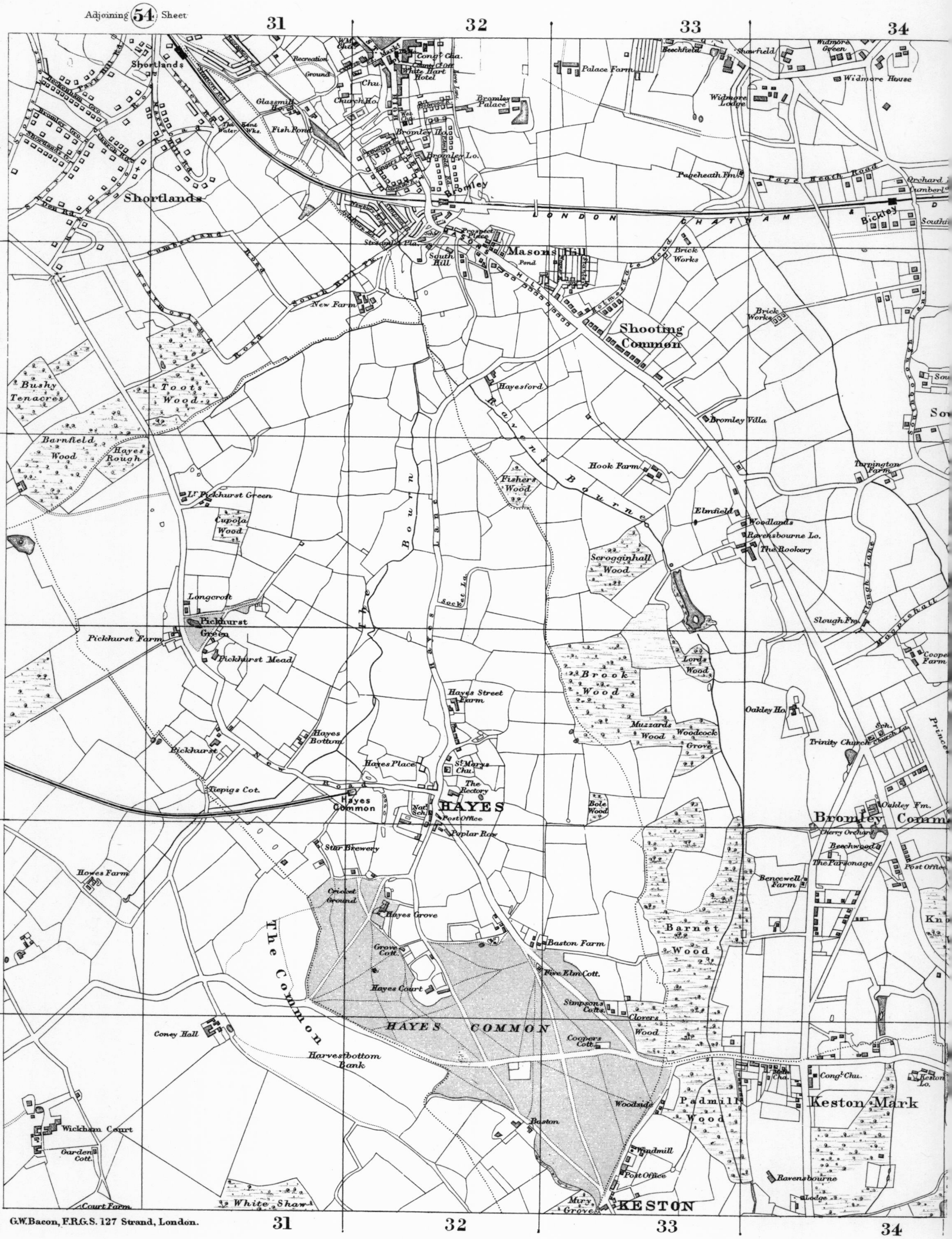
Adjoining 54 Sheet
31
32
33
34
A
B
C
D
E
F
Adjoining 58 Sheet
Shortlands
Recreation Ground
Cong¹ Cha.
White Hart Hotel
Glassmill Ho.
Church Ho.
Fish Pond
The Water Wks.
Bromley Ho.
Bromley Lo.
Bromley Palace
Palace Farm
Beechfield
Shawfield
Widmore Green
Widmore House
Widmore Lodge
Pageheath Fm.
Page Heath Road
Orchard
Bickley
London Chatham
Prospect Place
Masons Hill
South Hill
Pond
Brick Works
Cumberland Road
Warmost Road
South Hill Rd.
New Farm
Shooting Common
Bushy Tenacres
Toots Wood
Hayesford
Ravensbourne
Bromley Villa
Barnfield Wood
Hayes Rough
Hook Farm
Turpington Farm
Lᵗ. Pickhurst Green
Fishers Wood
Elmfield
Woodlands
Ravensbourne Lo.
The Rookery
Cupola Wood
Scrogginhall Wood
The Bourn
Hayes Lane
Socket La.
Longcroft
Pickhurst Green
Pickhurst Farm
Pickhurst Mead
Slough Fm.
Slough Lane
Magpiehall
Lords Wood
Brook Wood
Hayes Street Farm
Oakley Ho.
Hayes Bottom
Muzzards Wood
Woodcock Grove
Trinity Church
Church La.
Sch.
Pickhurst
New Road
Hayes Place
Sᵗ Marys Chu.
The Rectory
Tiepigs Cot.
Hayes Common
Nat¹ Sch.
HAYES
Post Office
Poplar Row
Bole Wood
Oakley Fm.
Bromley Common
Cherry Orchard
Beechwood
The Parsonage
Post Office
Star Brewery
Howes Farm
Cricket Ground
Hayes Grove
Bencewell Farm
Baston Farm
Barnet Wood
Grove Cott.
Five Elm Cott.
Hayes Court
The Common
Simpsons Cotts.
Clorers Wood
Coney Hall
HAYES COMMON
Coopers Cott.
Harvestbottom Bank
Congˡ Chu.
Keston Lo.
Keston Mark
Padmill Wood
Woodside
Wickham Court
Baston
Garden Cott.
Windmill
Post Office
Ravensbourne
Lodge
Court Farm
White Shaw
Mry. Grove
KESTON
G.W. Bacon, F.R.G.S. 127 Strand, London.

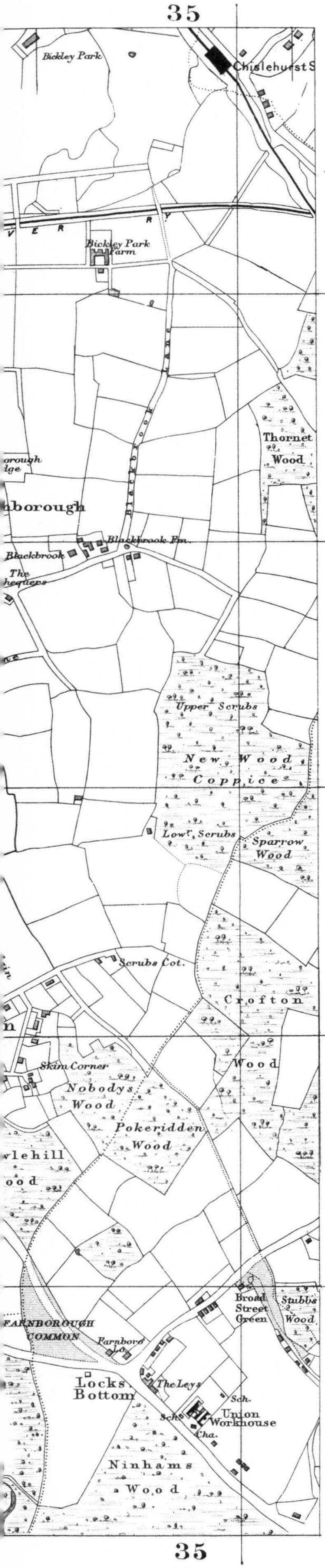
35
Bickley Park
Chislehurst S
A
Bickley Park Farm
B
Thornet Wood
Blackbrook Fm.
Blackbrook
C
Upper Scrubs
New Wood Coppice
Lowr. Scrubs
Sparrow Wood
D
Scrubs Cot.
Crofton
Skim Corner
Wood
Nobodys Wood
Pokeridden Wood
E
Broad Street Green
Stubbs Wood
FARNBOROUGH COMMON
Locks Bottom
The Leys
Sch.
Union Workhouse
Cha.
F
Ninhams Wood
35

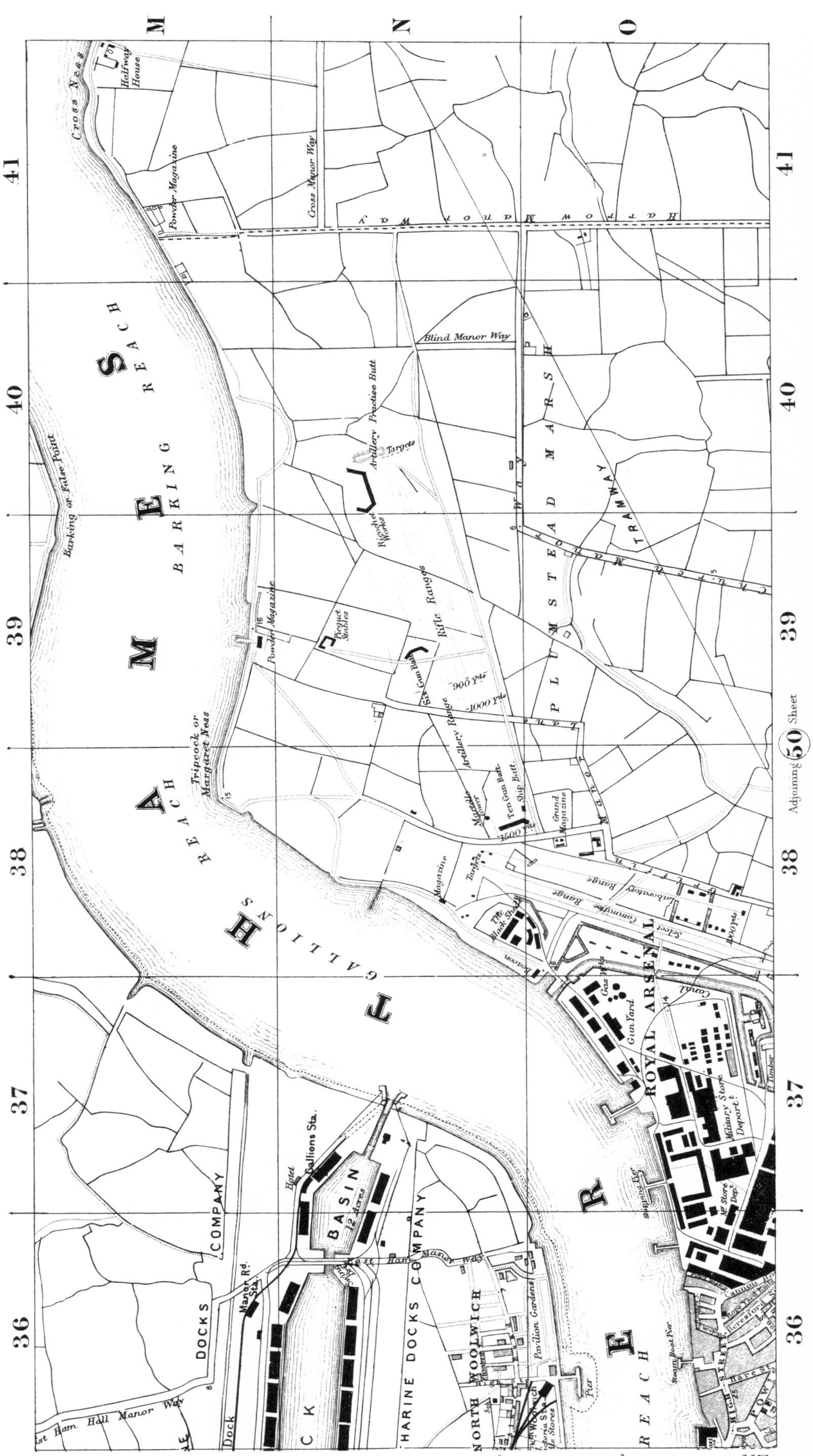
M
N
O
41
40
39
38
37
36
Cross Ness
Hollway House
Powder Magazine
Cross Manor Way
Hartow Manor Way
Blind Manor Way
BARKING REACH
Barking or False Point
Practice Butt
Artillery
Targets
Ricochet Works
Rifle Ranges
Picquet Stables
Powder Magazine
PLUMSTEAD MARSH
TRAMWAY
Tripcock or Margaret Ness
900 Yds
1000 Yds
Artillery Range
Ten Gun Batt.
Ship Batt.
Grand Magazine
Magazine
GALLIONS REACH
THAMES
ROYAL ARSENAL
Gas Works
Gun Yard
Military Store Depart.
Canal
Gallions Sta.
Hotel
BASIN 12 Acres
East Ham Manor Way
COMPANY
DOCKS
Manor Rd. Sta.
NORTH WOOLWICH
Pavilion Gardens
Pier
REACH
East Ham Hall Manor Way
Dock
Adjoining 50 Sheet
Adjoining 45 Sheet
0
1 Mile.
55 110 220 Yards.

INDEX

TO

DISTRICTS, PARISHES, PARKS, GARDENS, CEMETERIES, COMMONS, &c.

The Names of Parishes are Printed in Capitals.

N.B.—The figures in the first column refer to the number of the Map in the 9-inch survey, those in the second column to the Map of the 4-inch survey, and the letters and figures in the third column to the square on the Map in which the place will be found.

	9-*in.* *sht.*	4-*in.* *sht.mar.*
Acton	—	41...M 7
Addington Park	—	58...G 27
Addington	—	58...G 28
Agar Town NW	7	39... I 19
Abbeywood	—	50.. P 41
Abney Park Cemetery N	3	40... F 24
Alexandra Park N	—	36... B 19
Anerley SE	—	54... Z 25
Ash Island	—	56... Z 1
Balham SW.	—	53... V 17
Balls Pond N	8	39... H 23
Barking	—	45... I 37
Barnes SW	29	47... R 10
,, Cemetery SW	29	47... R 10
,, Common SW	—	47... S 9
Barnsbury N	7	39... I 21
BATTERSEA SW	30	47... R 15
Battersea Park SW	22	48... Q 17
,, Cemetery SW	30	47... T 16
Bayswater W	13	42...M 14
BECKENHAM, Kent	—	54... Z 28
Beckenham Park, Kent	—	54... Z 27
Beddington	—	57... E 19
Beddington Park	—	57... E 18
Bedford Square WC	15	43... L 19
Belgravia SW	22	43... O 17
Belgrave Square SW	22	43... O 17
Belsize Park NW	6	38... H 16
Berkeley Square W	14	43...M 18
BERMONDSEY SE	24	43... N 23
BETHNAL GREEN E	17	44... K 26
Blackheath SE	34	49... S 31
Blackheath Park	34	50 S 32
Blackwall E	19	44...M 30
Blendon	—	55... U 41
BLOOMSBURY WC	15	43... L 19
Bloomsbury Square WC	15	43... L 20
Bog Lodge Richmond-pk-rd	—	46....U 6
Bostall Heath	—	50... Q 40
BOW E	18	44... K 29
Bow Common E	18	44... L 28
Bowes Park	—	36... A 20
Brentford	—	46... P 4
Brixton SW	31	48... R 21
Brockley SE	23	49... S 27
,, Hill SE	—	54... V 27
Brockwell Hall Park SE	—	48... U 21
BROMLEY, KENT	—	54... Z 31
BROMLEY, Bow E	19	44... L 30
Brompton SW	21	42... O 16
Brook Green W	20	42... O 11
Brunswick Square WC	15	43... K 20
Bunhill Fields EC	16	43... K 23
Bushey Park	—	56... Z 1
CAMBERWELL SE	32	48... R 22
Camberwell Park SE	32	48... R 23
,, Cemetery SE	—	49... U 25
Cambridge Pk. Twickenham	—	46... U 4
Camden Park	—	55... Z 35
Camden Town NW	6	39... I 19
Camden New Town NW	6	39... H 19
Canbury, Kingston	—	56... Z 4
Canning Town E	19	44... L 31
Canonbury N	8	39... H 22
Castlebar Hill	—	41.. L 4
Castelnau SW	28	47... Q 10
Cavendish Square W	14	43... L 18
Champion Hill SE	32	48... S 23
Chapel End, Walthmst. Essex	—	37... A 29
Charing Cross SW	15	43.. M 20
Charlton, Kent	—	50... Q 33
,, Cemetery, Kent	—	50... Q 35
CHELSEA SW	21	47... P 16
Child's Hill NW	—	38... F 14
Chislehurst Common	—	55... Z 37
Chiswick SW	—	47... P 9
CHRIST CHURCH, Sthw'k SE	24	43... N 21
Church End N	—	35... A 3
CITY EC	16	43...M 23
City of London Cemetery	—	45... G 34
City & Tower Hamlets Cem. E	18	44...K 28
CLAPHAM SW	31	48... S 18
Clapham Common SW	31	48... T 18
Clapham Junction SW	30	47... S 16
Clapham Park SW	—	48... U 15
Clapton E	9	40... G 27
Clapton Common E	3	40... E 29
CLERKENWELL EC	15	43... K 27
Colney Hatch	—	36... A 16
Commercial Docks SE	26	51... N 27
Combe Hurst	—	51.. X 1
Combe Wood, Kingston Hill	—	51... X 8
Conduit Wood, Richmond-pk	—	46... U 6
Copse, The, Petersham	—	51... V 4
Cottenham Park, Surrey	—	52... Z 11
Covent Garden WC	15	43...M 20
Cricklewood NW	—	38... G 12
Cricket Ground, North-pk	—	57... B 21
,, ,, Whitehorse-rd	—	57... C 22
,, ,, Chislehurst	—	55... Z 36
Crouch End N	2	39... D 20
Croydon Cemetery	—	57... C 22
Crystal Palace SE	—	54... Y 24
Crystal Palace Dist. Cemetery	—	58... A 25
Cubitt Town E	27	44... O 30
Dalston E	9	40...H 24
Dartmouth Park NW	6	39... F 18
De Beauvoir Town N	8	40... I 24
Denmark Hill SE	32	48... S 23
DEPTFORD SE	26	49... Q 28
Deptford Cemetery SE	33	49... T 28
Deptford New Town SE	33	15... R 28
Drayton Green	—	41... L 3
Dulwich SE	—	53... V 23
,, Common SE	—	53...W 23
,, Hill SE	—	53 .. V 23
Duntshill SW	—	52... V 14
Ealing	—	41...M 4
Ealing Common	—	41...M 5
Ealing Dean	—	41...M 3
Earl's Court SW	21	42 .. O 14
Eastdown Park SE	34	49... T 30
East Dulwich SE	32	49... T 24
East End N	—	35... B 16
East Greenwich SE	27	49... P 31
East Ham	—	45... K 35
East London Cemetery E	19	45... K 32
East Moulsey	—	56... Z 1
East Smithfield E	17	44...M 24
East Sheen	—	46... T 7
East Wickham, Kent	—	50... R 40
Eaton Square SW	22	43... O 17
Eltham, Kent	—	55 .. U 35
Eltham Common	—	55... S 35
Eltham Green	—	50... U 34
Eltham Park	—	50... U 36
Enmore Park	—	58... C 24
Epping Forest E	—	37... B 31
Euston Square NW	15	43... K 19
Fairfield, Kingston	—	56... Z 5
Farwig	—	54... Z 32
Finchley N	—	35... A 14
Finsbury Park N	3	39... E 22
,, Square EC	16	43... L 23
Fitzroy Square W	14	43... K 18
Foots Cray	—	55... Z 41
Forest Gate	—	45... G 32
Forest Hill SE	—	54... V 26
Fortis Green N	—	36... B 17
Fortune Green NW	...	36... G 13
FULHAM SW	29	47... S 12
,, Cemetery SW	28	47... Q 12
Garrett Green SW	—	52...W 15
Giggshill	—	56... Z 2
Gipsy Hill SE	—	53... Y 23
Globe Town E	17	44...K 26
Golden Square W	14	43...M 19
Golder's Green NW	—	38... D 13
Goodman's Fields E	17	44...M 24
Great Ilford	—	45... G 37
GREENWICH SE	27	49... Q 30
Greenwich Cemetery, Kent	—	50.. S 35
Greenwich Park SE	27	49... R 30
Green Park SW	22	43... N 18
Grosvenor Square W	14	43...M 17
Grove Vale SE	32	49... T 24
Gunnersbury	—	41... N 6
HACKNEY E	9	40... H 26
Hackney Wick E	10	40... H 28
Hackney Common E	10	40... I 27
Hackney Downs E	9	40... G 25
Haggerston E	9	40... I 24
Hale End, Essex	—	37... A 30
Halfway Street, Kent	—	55...W 39
Hallville E	19	44...M 31
Ham	—	51...W 4
Ham Common	—	51... X 4
Hamcross Plantation	—	51...W 6
HAMMERSMITH W.	28	47... P 12
Hammersmith Cemetery W	28	47... P 11
HAMPSTEAD NW	5	33... G 15
Hampstead Cemetery NW	—	38... G 13
Hampstead Heath NW	1	38... F 15
Hampton Court Park	—	56... Z 2
Hampton Wick	—	56... Z 3
Hanwell	—	41... N 2
Hanover Square W	14	43...M 18
Harlesden Green N	12	42... J 11
Harrow Green E	11	40... G 31
Hatcham SE	33	49... R 26
Haverstock Hill NW	6	40... H 17
HENDON NW	—	35... B 11
Herne Hill SE	32	48... T 22
Higham, Essex	—	37... B 27
Higham Hill, Walthamst. Essex	—	37... A 27
,, Common, Essex	—	37... B 27
Highbury N	8	39...H 21
,, Hill N	8	39... G 22
,, Vale N	8	39... F 22
Highgate N	2	39... E 18
,, &Kentish-t. Cemet. N	2	39... E 18
Hither Green SE	—	49... U 30
Holborn WC	15	43... L 21
Holland Park W	20	42... N 13
Holloway N	7	39... G 21
Homerton E	9	40...H 26
HORNSEY N	—	36... B 20
HORSLEYDOWN SE	24	44...N 24
Horticultural Society's Gardens SW	21	42...O 15
Hoxton N	8	43... J 23
Hyde Park W	13	42...M 16
Hyde, The, NW	—	35... C 9
Ilford Cemetery	—	45... G 34
Isleworth	—	46... S 2
Isle of Dogs E	26	44... O 29
ISLINGTON N	7	39... I 21
KENNINGTON SE	23	48...Q 21
Kennington Park SE	23	48...Q 21
Kensal Green W	12	42...K 12
,, ,, Cemetery W	12	42...K 11
,, New Town W	12	42...K 13
KENSINGTON W	21	42...N 14
,, Gardens W	13	42...M 15
,, Cemetery	—	41...M 2
Kent Town	—	56... Z 1
Kentish Town NW	6	39... H 19
Kew Gardens	—	46... R 5
,, Palace	—	46... Q 5
Kidbrook SE	—	50... R 32
,, Green	—	50... S 33
,, park SE	—	50... R 32
Kidney Wood, Richmond-pk	—	51... V 5
Kilburn NW	5	38... I 14
,, Park NW	13	42... J 14
,, Vale NW	5	38... I 14
King's Cross WC	15	43... J 20
,, Square EC	16	43...K 22
Kingsbury NW	—	38... F 8
,, Green NW	—	35... C 8
Kingston Cemetery	—	56... Z 6
Kingsland E. & N.	8	40... H 24
Knightsbridge SW	21	43... N 16
Knights Hill SE	—	53... V 22
LAMBETH SE	23	43... O 21
Lambeth Cemetery SW	—	52... Y 15
Lea Bridge E	—	40... F 26
LEE SE	34	49... T 31
Lee Cemetery SE	—	54...W 31
,, Green SE	—	49... T 32
LEWISHAM SE	34	49... T 30
Lewisham Cemetery SE	33	49... T 28
,, Park SE	—	49... U 29
Leyton Street, Essex	—	40...E 29
,, Green, Essex	—	40... D 30
Leytonstone E	—	40... E 31
LIMEHOUSE E	18	44...M 27
Lincoln's Inn Fields WC	15	43... L 20
Little Ealing	—	41... O 3
,, Heath, Woolwich	—	50... Q 34
,, Ilford	—	45...H 36
,, Sutton	—	46... P 7
London Docks E	17	44...M 25
London Fields E	9	40... I 25
Long Ditton	—	56... Z 3
Lower Clapton E	9	40... G 26
Lower Elmers End	—	58... A 27
,, Holloway N	7	29... G 21
Lower Norwood SE	—	53... X 22
Lower Streatham SW	—	53... Y 19
Lower Sydenham SE	—	54... Y 27
Lower Tooting SW	—	52... X 16
Low Leyton, Essex	—	40 ... F 29
Maida Vale NW	13	42... J 15
Maze Hill SE	27	49... Q 31
Manchester Square W	14	43... L 17
Manor Park Cemetery	—	45... G 34
MARYLEBONE W	14	43... L 17
Mayfair W	14	43... N 18
Mecklenburgh Square WC	15	43...K 20
Merton, Surrey	—	52... Z 14
Mile End E	17	44... L 26
Mile End New-Town E	17	44... L 25
Millbank SW	23	48... P 19
Millwall, E	26	44... O 28
Minories E	16	44...M 24
Mitcham, Surrey	—	52... Z 16
Mitcham Common	—	57... B 18
Mortlake	—	46... S 7
Mottingham, Kent	—	55...W 34
Muswell Hill N	—	36... B 18
Neasden NW	—	38... G 9
New Brentford	—	46... P 3
New Cross SE	33	49... R 27
NEWINGTON SE	24	43... O 22
Newington Park N	8	39... F 23
Newlands SE	—	49... T 26
New Eltham	—	55...W 37
New River Head WC	15	43...K 21
New Malden	—	56... Z 8
New Peckham SE	33	49... S 26
New Southgate	—	36... A 19
New Thornton Heath	—	57... A 21
New Wandsworth SW	30	17... T 16
New Wimbledon, Surrey	—	52...Y 15
Nine Elms SW	23	48 .. Q 19
Norbury Park	—	57... A 20
North Brixton SW	31	48... R 21
North End NW	1	38... E 15
North End SW	28	47... P 13
North End	—	45... I 35
North Greenwich E	27	49... P 30
North Hill N	1	39... D 17
North Park, Croydon	—	57... C 21
North Woolwich E	—	45... N 36
Northampton Square EC	16	43... K 22
Norwood SE	—	53... X 22
Norwood Cemetery SE	—	53... X 22
Norwood, New Town SE	—	53... Z 22
Notting Hill W	20	42...M 13
Nunhead SE	32	49... R 25
Nunhead Cemetery SE	33	49... T 26
Old Brompton SW	21	47. P 15
Old Deer Park, Kew	—	46... S 4
Old Ford E	10	44... J 28
Old St. Pancras Church-yard NW	7	43... J 19
PADDINGTON W	13	42.. L 15
Paddington Cemetery N	4	38... I 13
Park, Middlesex	—	37... A 26
Park, The, Woolwich	—	50... Q 34
Parson's Green SW	29	47... R 13
Peckarman's Wood SE	—	54...W 24
Peckham SE	32	49... R 25
Peckham New Town SE	25	49... Q 25
Peckham Rye SE	32	49... S 25
Peckham Rye Common SE	32	49... T 25
Pen Ponds, Richmond-pk	—	51... V 7
PENGE SE	—	54... Z 26
Pentonville N	15	43... J 21
Percy Cross SW	28	47...R 13
Peter's Park W	13	42... K 14
Perry Street	—	55... Z 38
Petersham	—	51... V 5
Petersham Common	—	46... U 5
Piccadilly Circus W	15	43...M 19
Pimlico SW.	23	48... P 19
Plaistow	—	45... K 32
Plashet	—	45... I 34
Plumstead, Kent	—	50... P 39
Plumstead Common	—	50... Q 38
Pond Slade, Richmond-pk	—	51...W 6
POPLAR E	18	44...M 29
Portland Town NW	5	42... J 16
Portman Square W	14	43... L 17
Powis Square NW	12	42... L 3
Prick End	—	55... Z 36
Primrose Hill NW	6	39... I 17
PUTNEY SW	29	47... S 12
Putney Cemetery SW	29	47... S 11
Putney Common SW	29	47... S 11
Putney Heath SW	—	47... U 11
Queen's Park NW	12	42...K 13
Queen's Square WC	15	43...K 20
Ratcliff E	18	44...M 27
Ravenscourt Park W	20	42...O 10
Recreation Ground, Poplar E	18	44...M 29
Red Hill NW	—	35... A 8
Red Lion Square WC	15	43... L 20
Regent's Circus, Oxfd. St. W	15	43...M 19
,, ,, Piccadilly W	14	43... L 18
,, Park NW	14	43... J 17
Richmond	—	46... T 5
Richmond Cemetery	—	46... U 6
Richmond Hill	—	46... U 5
Richmond Park SW	—	52... V 9
Roehampton SW	—	47... U 10
ROTHERHITHE SE	25	44... N 26
Round Town	—	41... L 1
Roupell Park SW	—	53... V 20
Royal Hospital Cemetery SE	27	50... Q 32
Rushett	—	56... Z 3
Rushey Green SW	—	54... V 29
Russell Square WC	15	43...K 20
St. ANDREW, HOLBORN WC	15	43... L 21
St. ANNE, SOHO W	14	43... L 19
St. Katherine's Docks E	17	44...M 24
St CLEMENT DANES WC	15	43...M 21
St. GEO.-THE-MARTYR WC	15	43... L 20
St. GEORGE'S-IN-THE-EAST E	17	44...M 25
St. ,, HANOVER Sq. SW	14	43...M 18
St. George's Cemetery Hanwell	—	41...M 2
St. GILES-IN-THE-FIELDS WC	15	43... L 19
St. JAMES'S SW.	15	43... N 19
St. ,, Park SW	23	43... N 19
St. JOHN, WESTMINSTER SW	23	43... O 20
St. John's SE	33	49... S 29
St. John's Wood NW	5	38.. I 15
St. LUKE'S EC	16	43... K 22
St. Luke's Gardens EC	16	43... K 22
St. MARGARET'S, WESTM. SW	23	43... O 20
St. MARTIN-IN-THE-FLDS. WC	15	43...M 20
St. Mary's Cemetery, Battersea SW	30	47... T 16
St. Mary's Cem. Kensal-gn. NW	12	42...K 10
St. Marylebone Cemetery N	—	35... B 15
St. MARY-LE-STRAND WC	15	43...M 20
St. NICHOLAS, DEPTFORD SE	26	49... Q 28
St. OLAVE SE	16	43... N 23
St. PANCRAS NW	7	43... J 19
St. Patrick's Cemetery E	11	40... G 30
St. Patrick's Gardens E	11	40... G 30
St. PAUL, COVENT GDN. WC	15	43...M 20

INDEX

TO

PUBLIC BUILDINGS, OFFICES, AND INSTITUTIONS.

BANKS.

N.B.—Those marked * do not act as London Bankers.

Those in Italics pass the Clearing House.

BARRACKS.

BUILDING AND LAND SOCIETIES.

CITY COMPANIES.

CLUBS.

COLLEGES AND SCHOOLS.

COURTS OF JUSTICE.

CIVIL, CRIMINAL, AND ECCLESIASTICAL COURTS.

COUNTY COURTS.

POLICE COURTS.

EXCHANGES AND MARKETS.

FOREIGN EMBASSIES AND CONSULATES.

GOVERNMENT AND LAW OFFICES, ETC.

HOSPITALS.

HOTELS.

INSURANCE OFFICES.

The letters after the name of an Office signify respectively (F) Fire, (L) Life, (M) Marine, (A) Accident, (G) Guarantee, (B) Boiler, (P) Plate Glass.

MISCELLANEOUS.

PICTURE GALLERIES, MUSEUMS AND PUBLIC LIBRARIES.

PRISONS AND REFORMATORIES.

REGISTRARS' (SUPERINTENDENT) OFFICES.

SOCIETIES.

SURVEYORS OF TAXES' OFFICES.

THEATRES, CONCERT AND MUSIC HALLS, &C.

9-in. 4-in. sht. sht. mar.

Tussaud's Exhibn. Marylebone road W . . . 14 43...L 17
Variety Theatre, Pitfield-st. Hoxton N . . . 16 44...K 23
Vaudeville Theatre, Strand WC 15 43...M 20
Winchester Music Hall, Southwark Bridge-road SE 24 43...N 22

VESTRY HALLS.

Bermondsey, Spa-rd. SE . 24 42...O 24
Bromley, Bow-rd E . . 18 44...K 29
Camberwell, Peckham-rd. SE 32 48...R 23
Chelsea, King's-road SW . 21 42...P 16
Hackney, Mare-street E . 9 49...H 26
HamletofMile-end,Bancft-rdE 18 44...K 27
Lambeth,Kennington-gr'n. SE 23 48...P 21
Paddington, Harrow-road W 25 42...L 15
Rotherhithe,82 Paradise-st SE 25 44...O 25
St.Clement Danes,10 Clement's Inn-passage, Strand WC 15 43...M 20
St. Geo., Han-sq. Mount-st W 14 43...M 17
St. Geo. the Martyr,81 Boro-rd 24 43...O 22
St. ,, in the East, Cable-st E 17 44...M 25
St. James, Piccadilly W . 14 43...N 18
St. ,, & St.John, Rosoman-st 15 43...K 21
St. John, Hampstead, Haverstock-hill NW . 6 38...G 16
St. Leonard,Sh'ditch,Old-st EC 16 44...K 14

9-in. 4-in. sht. sht. mar.

St. Luke, City-rd N . . 17 43...K 22
St. Martin in the Fields WC 15 43...M 20
St.Mary Abbotts Kensington W 2[illegible] 42...N 14
St. Mary, Islington, Upper-st N 8 39...I 22
St. Marylebone, M'lebone-la W 14 43...L 18
St. Mary, Walworth-rd SE 24 48...P 22
St. Matthew, Bethnal-green E 17 44...K 25
St. Pancras, Pancras-rd NW 7 43...J 19
West Ham, Broadway, Stratford E . . . . 11 40...I 31
Westminster, Town Hall SW 23 43...O 19

WORKHOUSES.

Bermondsey Workhouse 24 44...O 24
Bethnal-green Workhouse, Bishop's-road E . . 9 44...J 26
Brentford Union — 46...R 3
Bromley Workhouse . 19 44...K 29
Camberwell Workhse, Havil street SE . . 32 48...R 23
Camberwell Workhse, Nazareth House SE . . 32 49...S 25
Chelsea Workhouse, Arthur-street SW . . 21 47...P 16
City Union Workhouse E . 18 44...K 28
Clerkenwell Workhse, Farringdon-road EC . . 15 43...K 21
FulhamWorkho.Ham'th-rd SW 28 47...P 12

9-in. 4-in. sht. sht. mar.

Greenwich Workhouse SE 27 49...P 31
HackneyWorkhse,Sidney-rd E 10 40...H 27
Holborn Workhse, 158, Gray's Inn-road EC . . 15 43...K 21
Islington Union Workhouse N 2 33...F 20
Kensington Workhse, Marloes-road SW . . . 21 42...O 14
Lambeth Workhse, Renfrew-road SE . . . 23 43...P 20
Lewisham Workhouse SE . — 49...U 29
Limehouse Workhouse E . 18 44...M 28
London Workhse.Homerton E 9 40...H 27
,, ,, Shadwell-rd N 2 39...F 20
Mile End Workhouse E . 18 44...K 27
Paddington Workhse, Harrow-road W . 13 42...K 14
Poplar Workhouse, High-st E 18 44...M 29
Richmond Union . . — 46...U 6
St. George's-in-the-East Workhouse E . . . 17 44...N 25
St.George's Workhse, Mount-street W . . 14 43...M 18
St. George's, Hanover-sq., Workhouse SW . 22 43...O 18
St.George's Workhse, Fulham-road SW . . 21 47...Q 15
St.George's Workh.Mint-st SE 24 43...N 22
St. Giles's & St. George's Workhouses, Endell-st. WC 15 43...L 20

9-in. 4-in. sht. sht. mar.

St. John's, Hampstead, Workhouse NW . . . 5 38...F 15
St. Luke's Workhse., Shepherdess walk N . 16 43...J 22
St. Mary's, Islington, Workhouse N . . . 7 39...I 21
St. Marylebone Workhouse, Northumberland-st. W 14 43...L 17
St.Olave's Workh.,Parish-st SE 24 44...N 24
St. ,, ,, Russell-st SE 24 44...N 24
St. ,, ,, Lower-rd SE 25 44...O 26
St.PancrasWorkh.King's-rd NW 7 39...I 19
St.Saviour's Workhse, Marlbro'-street SE . . . 24 43...N 22
Shoreditch Workh. Kingsland-road E . . . . 8 44...J 24
Stepney Workhse, St. Leonard-street E . . . 18 44...K 29
Wandsworth & Clapham Workhouse SW . . . 30 47...T 15
Westminster Workhouse, Poland-street W, and Marloes rd.W . . 14 43...M 19
West Ham Workhouse E . 11 40...G 31
Whitechapel Workhse, South grove E . . 18 44...K 28
Woolwich Union . . — 50...P 36

INDEX TO RAILWAY STATIONS.

ABBREVIATIONS:

B.	London Brighton & South Coast.
C. & D.	London Chatham & Dover.
Dist.	Metropolitan District.
G.E.	Great Eastern.
G.N.	Great Northern.
G.W.	Great Western.
M.Met.Metr.	Metropolitan.
Mid.	Midland.
N.L.	North London.
N.W.	London & North Western.
S.E.	South Eastern.
S.W.	London & South Western.
T. & S.	London Tilbury & Southend.

9-in. 4-in. sht. sht. mar.

Acton, Gt.W. & M. & N.L. — 42...M 8
Acton Green, Dist. . . — 41...O 8
Addiscombe-rd. Croydon S.E. — 57...D 24
Addison-rd.,Kensington N.W., S.W.,G.W.,B.Met.Dist. 20 42...O 12
Albert Docks, Gt.E. . — 45...N 34
Albert Docks, (Central) . — 45...M 35
Aldersgate-street, Met. 16 43...L 22
Aldgate, Met. . . . 16 44...L 24
,, High-st. Dist.&Met. 16 44...L 24
Alexandra-palace,Gt.N.&N.L. — 43...B 19
Anerley, B. . . . — 54...Z 25
Angel-rd. Gt.E. . . — 37...A 26
Arsenal (Woolwich) S.E. — 50...P 37
Baker street, Met. . 14 43...K 17
Balham, B. . . . — 53...V 17
Barking, T. & S., N.L. — 45...I 36
Barnes, S.W. . . . — 47...S 10
Barnsbury, N.L. . . 7 39...H 21
Battersea,G.W.,S.W.,B.,N.W. 30 47...R 16
Battersea-pk.,B. & C. & D. 22 48...Q 18
Bayswater, (Queen's-rd.) Dist. 13 42...M 14
Beckenham, C.& D., & S.E. — 54...Z 28
Beckton, Gt. E. . . — 45...M 35
Beddington, B . . . — 57...C 18
Bethnal-green Junc., Gt.E. 17 44...K 25
Bickley, C & D . . — 50...B 33
Bishopsgate, Gt.E. . . 16 44...K 24
,, Metr. . 16 43...L 23
Bishop's-road, Metr. . 13 42...L 15
Blackfriars, Dist. . 16 43...M 22
Blackfriars Bridge, C. & D. 16 43...M 22
Blackheath, S.E. . . 34 49...S 31
,, hill, C. & D. . 33 49...R 29
Blackwall Gt.E., & N.L. . 19 44...M 30
Borough-road, C. & D. . 24 43...O 22
Boston Road, Dist. . . — 41...O 3
Bow, N.L. . . . . 18 44...K 29
,, road., Gt.E. . . 18 44...K 28
Bowes Park . . . — 36...A 20
Brentford, S.W., Gt.W. . — 46...P 4
Bricklayers' Arms, S.E. . 24 49...P 24
Brixton, C.&D., B. . . 31 48...T 21
Broad-street GtN. N.L.& N.W. 16 43...L 23
Broadway, (Hammersmith) 28 42...O 11
Brockley, B. . . . 33 49...S 27
Brockley-lane, C.& D. . 33 49...S 17
Bromley, Kent, C. & D. . — 55...Z 32
,, S.E. . . . — 55...Z 32
,, Essex T. & S., & N. L. 19 40...K 30
Brondesbury,Edgw.-rd.&c.NL 4 38...H 13
Bruce-grove, Gt. E. . . — 36...B 24
Burdett-road, N.L. & T & S. 18 44...L 28
Camberwell New-rd.,C. & D. 32 48...R 22
Cambridge-heath, Gt. E. 17 44...J 25
Camden-rd., Mid. . . 7 39...H 9
Camden-town, N.L. . . 6 39...I 18
Canning-town, Gt. E. & N.L. 19 44...L 31
Cannon-street, S.E. . . 16 43...M 23
,, Dist. . 16 43...M 23
Canonbury, N.L. . . 8 39...H 22
Castle Hill&Ealing G.W.&M. — 41...L 3
Catford-bridge, S.E . . — 54...V 28
Chalk Farm, N.L. . . 6 39...I 17
Champion-hill, B. . . 32 49...T 24
Charing Cross, S.E. . . 15 43..M 20
,, ,, Dist. . 15 43...M 20
Charlton, S.E. . . . — 50...P 33
Chelsea, S.W.,G.W.,N.W.,B. 21 47...Q 14
Child's-h.or Cricklewood.Mid. — 38...G 12
Chislehurst, S.E. . . . — 55...Z 35

9-in. 4-in. sht. sht. mar.

Chiswick, S.W. . . . — 47...Q 7
ClaphamJunc.,S.W.,C.&D.,B. 30 47...S 16
Clapham & N. Stockwell, B., and C & D. . . . 31 48...S 19
Clapton, Gt. E. . . 3 40...F 25
Coborn-road, G.E. . . 18 44...J 28
Connaught-rd, (Vt.Docks)Gt.E— 45...M 34
Cricklewood or Child's-h.Mid. — 38...F 12
Crouch End, Gt. N. . . 2 39 ..D 20
,, hill, Mid., Gt.E . 2 39...E 20
Crystal Palace, B., . . — 54...Z 24
,, ,, HighLevel,C.&D.— 54...Y 24
Custom House, Gt. E. . — 45...M 33
Dalston Junction, N.L. . 8 40...H 24
Denmark-hill, B., C. & D. 32 48...S 23
Deptford, S.E., . . 26 49...Q 28
,, road, B., . . 25 44...O 26
Dockyard, (Woolwich) S.E. — 50...P 35
Dudding-h., Willesden, Mid. — 38...G 10
Dulwich, S.E., C. & D. . — 53...W 23
Ealing Broadway, G.W.,Dist. — 41...L 5
Ealing Common, G.W. . — 41...M 6
Earlsfield, S.W. . . — 52...V 4
Earl's-court, Dist. . . 21 47...P 14
East Croydon, S.E. . . — 57...E 23
East-end,Finchley,G.N.&N.L.— 35...C 16
East Ham, T. & S. . . — 45...I 35
Eden Park, S.E. . . — 58...C 28
Edgeware-rd. Brondesb. N.L. 4 38...H 13
,, Metr. . 13 42...L 16
Elephant and Castle, C. & D. 24 43...O 22
Elmers End, S.E. . . — 58...B 26
Eltham, S.E. . . . — 55...W 35
Euston, N.W. . . . 15 43...J 19
Farringdon-street, Met. . 16 43...L 51
Fenchurch-st., T. & S.& Gt.E. 16 44...M 24
Finchley, Gt.N., N.L. . — 45...A 14
,, road, N.L. . . 5 38...H 15
,, ,, Mid. . . 5 38...H 15
,, ,, Met. . . 5 38...A 15
Finsbury-park, G N.,N.L. 2 39...F 21
Forest Gate, Gt. E. . . — 45...H 32
Forest-hill, B. . . . — 54...W 26
Fulham & Putney-bri. Dist. 29 47...S 13
Fulwell, S.W. . . . — 51...W 11
Gallions, (N. Woolwich) G.E. — 45...N 37
Gipsy-hill, B. . . . — 53...Y 23
Gloucester-road, Dist. . 21 42...O 15
Gospel Oak, N.L. . . 6 39...G 18
Gower-street, Metr. . . 15 43...K 19
Gt. Ilford, Gt.E. . . — 45...G 36
Green-lanes, Gt. E. . . — 36...A 22
Greenwich, S.E. . . 26 49...Q 29
Grosvenor-road, C. & D., B. 22 48...P 18
Grove Park, S.E. . . — 55...X 32
Gunnersbury, S.W., N.L . — 46...P 7
Hackney, N.L. . . . 9 40...H 26
,, Downs-junct. Gt. E 9 40...H 25
Haggerston, N.L. . . 8 40...I 24
Hale End, Gt. E. . . — 37...A 30
Hammersmith, S.W. . 28 42...O 11
,, (Broadway)Met.Dis.28 42...O 11
Hammersmith, N.& S.W.J. — 42...O 9
Hampstead-heath, N.L. . 6 38...G 16
Hampton, S.W. . . . — 56...Z 1
Hampton Wick, S.W. . — 56...Z 4
Haringay Park, Mid. . 3 40...D 22
Harlesden, N.L. . . — 42...J 10
Harrow-rd, Mid. . . — 38...I 9
Haverstock-hill, Mid. . 6 39...G 17
Haydens-lane, S.W., & B. — 52...Y 14

9-in. 4-in. sht. sht. mar.

Holloway, Gt. N. . . 7 39...G 21
Homerton, N. L. . . 10 40...H 27
Hendon, Mid. . . . — 38...D 10
Herne-hill, S.W., & C. & D. — 48...U 22
Highgate, Gt.N. . . . 2 39...D 18
,, road, Mid. & Gt.E. 6 39...G 18
Hoe-st, Gt.E. . . . — 37...C 29
Honor Oak, C. & D. . — 49...U 25
Hornsey, Gt.N. . . . — 36...C 21
,, road, Mid. & G.E. 2 39...E 20
Isleworth & Spring-grove S.W.— 46...R 2
Islington, N.L. . . 8 39...H 21
Junction-rd., Mid., & G.E. 6 39...F 19
Kensal-gn. & Harlesden, N.L. 12 42...J 10
Kensington, High-st., Dist. 21 42...N 14
Kensington, Addison-road, N.W., G.W., S.W., & B. 20 42...O 12
Kent-house, Beckenham, C.D.— 58...Z 27
Kentish-town, Mid. . . 6 39...H 18
Kentish Town, N.L. . . 6 39...H 18
Kew Bridge, S.W. & N.L. — 46...P 6
Kew Gardens, S.W. . . — 46...R 6
Kilburn and Brondesbury, Met. 4 38...H 13
Kilburn, N.L., & N.W. . 5 38...I 14
Kingsbury and Neasdon, Met. — 38...G 9
King's Cross, Gt.N. . . 15 43...J 20
,, ,, Metr. . . 15 43...J 20
Kingston, S.W. . . . — 56...Z 5
Ladywell, S.E. . . . — 49...U 29
Latimer-rd., Metr. & G.W. 20 42...M 12
Lea-bridge, G.E. . . — 40...E 27
Lee, S.E. . . . . — 49...U 32
Leman-street, T.&S. G.E. 17 44...M 25
Lewisham Junction, S.E. 33 49...S 29
,, road, C. and D. 33 49...S 28
Leyton, Gt. E. . . . 11 40...G 30
Leytonstone, Gt.E. . . — 40...E 31
Limehouse, Gt. E. . . 18 44...M 28
Liverpool-street, Gt.E. & B. 16 43...L 23
London-bridge,S.E., and B. 24 43...N 25
,, fields, Gt.E. . 9 40...I 23
Lordship-lane, C. and D. — 54...W 25
Loudoun-rd NW . . . 5 38...I 15
Loughboro' Junction, C. & D. 32 48...S 22
,, park, B. . 31 48...S 21
LowerMerton,S.W.,and B. — 52...Z 13
,, Norwood, B. . . — 53...X 22
,, Sydenham, S.E. . — 54...Y 28
Ludgate-hill, C. & D. & S.W. 16 43...M 22
Manor-park, G.E. . . — 45...G 34
Manor-road, Gt.E . . — 45...M 36
Mansion-house Dt.,G.W.,N.W 16 43...M 22
Mark-lane, Dist. . . 16 43...M 23
Marlboro'-road, Metr. . 5 38...I 15
Maryland-point, Gt. E . 11 40...H 31
Maze-hill, S. E . . . 27 49...Q 31
Merton Abbey, S.W., and B. — 52...Z 15
Mildmay-park, N.L . . 8 39...H 23
Mill-hill park, Dist . . — 41...N 6
Mill-hill, G.N. . . . — 35...A 13
Mill-Hill, Mid. . . . — 35...A 9
Millwall-Docks, Gt. E. . 26 44...O 29
,, Junction, Gt. E. 19 44...M 29
Monument, Dist. . . 16 43...M 23
Moorgate-street, Metr. . 16 43...L 23
Morden, B. . . . . — 52...Z 14
Mortlake, S.W. . . . — 46...S 8
Muswell-hill, Gt.N. . . — 36...B 18
New Beckenham, S.E. . 22 54...Z 27
New Cross, B. . . . 33 49...R 27
,, ,, S. E. . . 33 49...R 28

9-in. 4-in. sht. sht. mar.

New Croydon, B. . . — 57...E 23
New Kingston, S.W . . — 56...Z 5
Norbiton, S.W. . . . — 56...Z 6
Norbury, B, . . . — 53...Z 20
North Dulwich, B. . . — 52...U 23
North Greenwich, Gt. E. 27 49...P 30
North Woolwich, Gt. E. — 45...N 36
Norwood-junc., B. . . — 57...B 24
Notting-hill, Metr. & G.W. 12 42...L 12
Notting-hill-gate, Dist. . 13 42...M 14
Nunhead, C.& D. . . 32 49...S 26
Old Ford, N.L. . . . 10 40...J 28
,, Kent-road, B. . . 25 49...Q 26
Osterley-park, Dist. . . — 46...Q 1
Paddington, Gt.W. . . 13 42...L 15
Palace-gate, Wood-gn. Gt.E. — 36...A 20
Park, Gt. E. . . . — 37...A 26
Parsons-green, Dist. . 22 47...R 13
Peckham, Queen's-road. B. 33 49...R 26
,, Rye, B., C. & D. 32 49...S 25
Penge Bridges B. . . — 54...Z 25
,, lane, C. & D . . — 04...Z 26
Plaistow, T. & S. . . — 45...J 32
Plaistow, New Bromley, S.E. — 55...Z 32
Plumstead, S.E. . . — 50...P 38
Pope-st, S.E. . . . — 55...W 36
Poplar, Gt.E. . . . 19 44...M 30
,, N.L. . . . 19 44...M 29
Portland-road, Metr. . 14 43...K 18
Praed-street, Dist. . . 13 42...L 15
Putney, S.W. . . . 29 47...T 12
Putney-bri. & Fulham, Dist. 29 47...S 13
Queen's-road, Battersea S.W. 31 48...R 18
,, ,, Peckham, B. 33 49...R 26
,, ,, Bayswater,Metr.13 42...M 14
,, park, N.W . . 12 42...J 13
Raynes-pk., S.W. . . — 52...Z 11
Rectory-road, Gt. E.. . 9 40...F 25
Richmond,S.W.,N.L.,Mt.,Dis.— 46...S 5
Rotherhithe, B. . . 25 44...N 26
Royal Arsenal, S.E. . — 50...P 37
Royal Oak, Metr. . . 13 42...L 14
St. Ann's-rd., Mid. . . 3 40...D 24
St. James's-park, Dist. . 23 43...O 19
St. James's-street, G.E. . — 37...C 27
St. John's, S.E. . . 33 49...S 29
St. John's-wood-road, Metr. 13 42...J 16
St. Margaret's, S.W. . — 46...U 3
St. Pancras, Mid. & Gt. E. 15 43...J 20
Selhurst, B. . . . — 57...B 23
Seven Sisters, Gt. E. . — 37...C 24
Shadwell, T. and S. & Gt. E. 17 44...M 26
,, B. . . . 17 44...M 26
Shaftesbury-road, S.W. . 28 42...O 10
Shepherd's-bush, Metr. . 20 42...N 11
,, ,, S.W. . 20 42...N 11
Shoreditch, N.L. . . 16 44...K 24
,, Gt. E. & B. . 17 44...K 24
Shortlands, C. & D. . , — 59...A 31
Sidcup, S.E . . . — 55...W 39
Silvertown, Gt. E. . . — 45...N 35
Sloane-square, Dist. . 22 43...O 17
Snow-hill, C. and D. . 16 43...L 22
South Acton, N.L. . . — 41...N 7
South Bermondsey, B. . 25 49...P 26
South Croydon, B. . . — 57...F 22
SouthDock(E.&W.India)G.E. 27 44...N 29
South Ealing, Dist. . . — 41...N 4
South Kensington, Dist . 21 42...O 16
SouthTottenham, Mid., Gt.E.— 37...C 24
Spa-road, S.E. . . . 25 44...O 25

INDEX

TO

PIERS, WHARVES, DOCKS, &c.

INDEX

TO

STREETS, ROADS, SQUARES, &c.

9-in. 4-in. sht. sht. mar.

Blackwall-lane E 27 44... O 31
,, basin E 18 44... N 29
Blagrove-rd., Notting-hill W 12 42... L 13
Blair-street E 19 44... M 30
Blakes road SE 24 49... Q 24
Blandford-square NW 14 42... K 16
Blechynden-street W 20 42... M 12
Blenheim-crescent W 20 42... M 12
,, place NW 5 42... J 15
,, road NW 5 42... J 15
,, ,, N 2 39... F 20
,, ter. S.Jn's.-wd. NW 5 42... J 15
Blessington-rd., Lee SE 34 49... T 30
Blind Lane NW — 35... B 12
Blind-lane, Plashet — 45... J 34
,, ,, Chapel End — 3... A 29
Blisset-st., Greenwich SE 34 49... R 29
Bloemfontein-rd. W — 42... M 10
Blondell-street SW 30 48... R 21
Bloomfield-rd. Bow E 18 44... L 28
Bloomfield-rd., Paddington W 13 42... K 15
,, ,, W 20 42... M 11
,, ,, Woolwich — 50... Q 37
,, st. Dalston E 9 40... I 24
,, st. London-wall EC 16 43... L 23
Bloomsbury-st. WC 15 43... L 20
,, square WC 15 43... L 20
,, place WC 15 43... L 20
Bloompark-road SW 28 47... Q 13
Blundell-st. Caledonian-rd. N 7 39... H 20
Blurton-road E 9 40... G 26
Blythe-lane, W 20 42... O 12
Blythe-road E 11 40... I 30
Boar's Head-court, EC 15 43... M 21
Boleyn-road N 8 40... H 24
,, ,, — 45... I 33
Bolingbroke-road SW — 47... T 16
Bolingbroke-rd, W 20 42... N 12
Bollobridge-rd, Acton — 41... N 7
Bolsover-st Regent's-park W 14 43... K 18
Bolt-court EC 15 43... M 21
Boltons (The) Brompton SW 21 47... P 15
Bolton-gardens SW 21 47... P 14
,, road NW 5 38... I 14
,, ,, Notting-hill W 20 42... M 13
,, street, Piccadilly W 14 43... N 18
Bonchurch-road W 12 42... L 12
Bond-street, Vauxhall SW 23 48... Q 20
Bonner's-road Victoria Park E 17 44... J 26
,, street ,, ,, E 17 44... J 26
Bookham-street, Hoxton N 16 43... J 23
Border-road SE — 54... Y 25
Borough High-street SE 24 43... N 23
,, market SE 24 43... N 23
,, road SE 24 43... O 22
Borthwick-road E 11 40... G 31
Boscombe-road W 20 42... N 10
Bostall-hill, Bostall-heath — 50... Q 40
Boston-lane, Hanwell — 41... N 2
Boston-street, Hackney-rd. E 17 44... J 25
Bosworth-rd W 12 42... K 13
Botolph-lane EC 16 43... M 23
Boundary-road, St.Jn's.Wd. NW 5 38... I 15
,, ,, Walthamstow — 40... D 28
Boundaries-road, SW — 53... V 17
Bounds Green-lane N — 36... A 20
Bouverie-road N. 3 39... F 23
Bouverie street, Fleet-street EC 15 43... M 21
Bow Common-lane E 18 44... L 28
,, Cemetery, E 18 44... K 24
,, lane, Cheapside EC 16 43... M 22
,, ,, Poplar E 19 44... M 29
,, road E 18 44... K 23
,, street, Long Acre WC 15 43... M 20
Bowes-rd. N — 36... A 10
Bowling-green-lane, Clerkwl EC 15 43... K 21
Boyson-road, Walworth SE 24 48... Q 23
Brackenbury-road W 20 42... O 11
Brackley-rd. — 54... Z 28
Brady street E 17 44... L 25
Bramah-road SW 31 48... R 21
Bramley Hall, Croydon — 57... F 22
Bramley-road W 20 42... M 12
Brandon-road, York-road N 7 39... I 20
,, ,, Brixton SW — 48... U 20
,, street SE 24 48... P 22
Brandram-road SE 34 49... T 31
Branksome-road SW 31 48... T 20
Brassey-square SW 30 47... S 17
Brayard-road, SE 32 49... S 25
Bread-street, Cheapside EC 16 43... M 20
Breakspear-road SE 33 49... S 28
Bream's-buildings EC 15 43... L 22
Brecknock-road, Holloway N 7 39... G 19
Brent Green NW — 35... C 12
,, street NW — 35... C 12
Brewer-street, Golden sq. W 15 43... M 19
Brewery-road N 7 39... H 20
Brewster-rd. N — 40... E 29
Brick-lane, E 17 44... L 24
Bride-court EC 16 43... M 21
,, lane EC 16 43... M 21
Bridge-avenue W 28 47... P 11
Bridge-street N 7 39... H 21
Bridge-street, Greenwich SE 27 49... Q 29
,, ,, Mile-end E 18 44... K 27
,, ,, Westminster SW 23 43... N 20
,, rd, Hammersmith W 28 47... P 11
,, ,, Hampton — 56... Z 1
,, ,, Stratford E 11 40... I 30
,, ,, Limehouse E 18 44... N 28
,, ,, SW 22 48... P 17
,, lane NW — 35... C 13
Bridgewater-square EC 16 43... L 22
Bridport-place, Hoxton N 8 43... J 23
Brighton-road N 8 40... G 24
Brighton-road, Croydon — 57... G 22
,, ,, Surbiton — 56... Z 4
Brigstock-rd. Croydon — 57... B 21
Brill-terr, Somers-town NW 7 43... J 19
Brisbane-street, SE 32 48... R 23
Britannia-row, Essex-road N 8 39... I 22

9-in. 4-in. sht. sht. mar.

Britannia-road, Fulham SW. 21 47... Q 14
Britannia-st N 16 43... J 23
Britannia-st. King's Cross 15 43... J 20
British-street, Bow-road E 18 44... K 28
Brixton-hill SW — 53... V 20
,, rise SW 31 48... T 20
,, road SW 31 48... R 21
Broad-green, Croydon — 57... D 21
Broad-lane — 37... C 25
Broad Sanctuary SW 23 43... N 19
,, street Golden-sq. W 14 43... M 19
,, street, Bloomsbury WC 15 43... L 20
,, ,, Lambeth SE 23 48... P 20
,, ,, Ratcliffe E 17 44... N 25
Broad-st. Teddington — 51... X 1
Broadhurst-gardens, NW 5 38... H 14
Broadwall, SE 15 43... M 21
Broadway, Barking — 45... J 37
,, Deptford SE 33 49... R 28
,, Ealing — 41... L 5
,, Hammersmith W 28 42... O 11
,, Lower Tooting SW — 52... Y 16
,, Ludgate-hill EC 16 43... M 22
,, London-fields, E 9 40... I 25
,, Westminster SW 23 43... O 19
,, Stratford E 11 40... I 30
Brockley-road SE 33 49... S 27
,, hill SE — 54... V 27
,, park SE — 54... V 27
,, road SE — 54... V 27
,, view SE — 54... V 27
,, Villas, SE 33 49... S 28
Brockwell-hall-park SE — 48... U 21
Brodrick-road SW — 52... W 16
Broke-road, Dalston E 9 40... I 25
Bromley-hill — 54... Z 31
,, road SE — 54... W 29
,, ,, Beckenham — 58... Z 29
,, — 55... W 32
,, street, Stepney E 18 44... M 27
Brompton-crescent SW 21 42... O 16
,, square SW 21 42... O 16
,, road SW 22 42... O 16
Brondesbury-road, Kilb'n NW 5 38... I 14
Brondesbury-park NW 4 38... I 12
,, villas NW 5 38... I 14
Brook-green W 20 42... O 11
Brook-street W 14 43... M 18
,, ,, Commercial-rd. E 17 44... M 26
,, ,, Kenning'n-rd. SE 23 43... O 21
,, ,, Holborn EC 15 43... L 21
,, green-road W 28 42... O 11
Brooke rd. E 9 40... F 25
Brookfield-rd. Hack.-wk. E. 10 40... H 27
Brooksby-st N 7 39... I 21
Brookville-road SW 28 47... Q 13
Broom-road — 51... X 3
Broomfield-road SW 31 48... S 19
Brougham-road, Dalston E 9 40... I 25
Broughton-road N 8 39... G 23
Broughton-street SW 31 48... R 17
Brownlow-road, Dalston E 9 40... I 25
,, ,, Wood-gn. N — 36... A 20
,, st., Holborn WC 15 43... L 21
Brownswood-park N 3 39... F 22
Brownswood-park-road, N 3 39... F 22
Bruce-grove — 37... A 24
,, road, Bromley E 18 44... K 29
Brunel-road 13 42... L 15
Brunswick-gardens W 21 42... N 14
,, road, Bromley E 19 44... L 30
,, square WC 15 43... K 20
,, ,, SE 32 48... R 23
,, street, Hackney-rd. E 9 44... J 24
,, ,, Blackwall E 19 44... M 30
,, ,, SE 15 43... N 21
Brushfield-st, Bishopsgate E 16 44... L 24
Bruton-street W 14 43... M 18
Bryans-lane, SW 30 47... R 4
Bryanston-square W 14 43... L 17
Bryantwood-road N 7 39... G 21
Buck-lane — 37... C 30
Buck-lane NW — 35... C 8
Buckingham Palace SW 22 43... N 18
,, ,, road SW 22 43... O 18
,, road, Kingsland N 8 39... H 23
,, street, Islington N 7 43... J 20
,, ,, WC 15 43... M 20
Buckland-cres. NW 5 38... H 16
,, street, Hoxton N 16 43... J 23
Bucklersbury EC 16 43... M 23
Budge-row EC 16 43... M 23
Bulfern-street SW 30 47... R 16
Bull and Mouth St. EC 16 43... L 22
Bunhill-row EC 16 43... K 23
Bunns Lane, Mill Hill — 35... A 10
Burcham-st. E 18 44... M 29
Burchell-road — 40... E 29
Burdett-road, Bow E. 18 44... K 27
Burghley-road NW 6 39... G 18
Burleigh-street WC 15 43... M 20
Burlington-arcade W 14 43... M 18
,, gardens W 14 43... M 18
,, road SW 29 47... S 20
Burney-street, Greenwich SE 27 49... Q 30
Burnt Ash Hill — 53... V 32
,, ,, — 55... X 32
Burnt-ash-lane SE — 49... U 31
Burntwood-lane SW — 52... W 15
Burrage-rd. Woolwich — 50... P 37
Burroughs-lane NW — 35... C 10
,, (The) NW — 35... C 11
Burton-crescent WC 15 43... K 20
,, road SW 31 48... R 21
Bury-place, Oxford-st. WC 15 43... L 20
,, street SW 14 43... N 19
Bury-street, St. Mary-axe EC 16 44... M 24
Bush-lane EC 16 43... M 23
Bushey-hill-road SE 32 49... R 24
,, park-rd Teddington — 56... Y 3
Bushy House — 56... Y 1
Butchers-lane NW — 35... C 11

9-in. 4-in. sht. sht. mar.

Butler-street SW 30 47... R 16
Buttesland-street N 16 43... K 23
Buxton-rd. Stratford E 11 40... H 31
,, street E 17 44... K 24
Byrne-road SW — 53... W 18

C

Cable-street, E 17 44... M 25
Cadogan-place, Chelsea, SW 22 43... O 17
,, street SW 22 43... O 16
,, square SW 22 43... O 17
Cæsar's Camp — 52... Y 10
Cage lane, Plumstead — 50... P 38
Caird-st. W 12 42... K 13
Calderon-rd. E 11 40... G 30
Cale street SW 21 47... P 16
Caledonian-rd., N 7 39... H 20
Calthorpe-st. Gray's-inn-rd WC 15 43... K 21
Calverley-road N 2 39... E 19
Cameroon-rd. E 11 40... H 31
Camberwell-green SE 31 48... R 23
,, grove SE 32 48... R 23
,, New-road SE 23 48... Q 21
,, road SE 24 48... Q 22
Cambrian-road SE 32 48... S 22
Cambridge Circus E 17 44... J 25
,, square W 13 42... L 16
,, street, Piml. SW. 22 48... P 18
,, ,, W 14 42... M 16
,, ,, NW 7 43... J 19
,, road E 17 44... K 26
,, ,, Kingston — 56... Z 6
,, ,, SW 30 47... R 16
,, ,, Kilb. NW 5 42... J 14
,, ,, SW — 52... Z 10
,, ,, Battersea SW 34 48... R 17
,, ,, Teddington — 51... X 2
,, ,, New Bromley — 55... Z 32
,, gardens W 12 42... L 12
Camden-road NW & N 7 39... H 19
,, street NW 6 39... I 18
,, grove SE 32 48... R 24
,, ,, south SE 24 49... Q 24
,, square NW 7 39... H 19
,, crescent NW 7 39... H 19
Camilla-road SE 24 49... P 25
Camelia street SW 31 48... R 19
Camomile-street EC 16 44... L 24
Campbell-road, Bow E 18 44... K 29
,, ,, N 2 39... F 21
Campden-hill-road W 20 42... N 13
,, House-road W 21 42... N 14
,, Hill New-road W 21 42... N 14
,, street W 13 42... N 14
Campsbourne-road N. — 36... B 20
Canal-road, Kingsland-rd. N 8 44... J 24
,, ,, Mile End E 18 44... K 27
Cann Hall-road E 11 40... G 31
Canning-road N 8 39... F 22
Cannon-street EC 16 43... M 22
,, street-road E. 17 44... M 25
,, hill NW 5 38... G 14
Canonbury-park N 8 39... H 22
,, road N 8 39... I 22
,, grove N 8 39... I 22
,, square N 8 39... I 22
Cantelowes-rd. Camden-rd NW 7 39... H 19
Canterbury-road, Kingsl. N 8 6... H 24
,, ,, SW 31 48... S 21
,, ,, Kilburn NW 12 42... J 13
,, ,, NW 13 42... J 15
,, ,, Old Kent-rd SE 25 49... Q 26
,, grove SE — 53... X 21
Canton-street E. 18 44... M 28
Cantrell-road E 18 44... L 28
Capel-court EC 16 43... M 23
,, road, Forest gate — 45... G 33
Capworth-street — 40... E 29
Carden-road SE 32 49... T 25
Cardington-st. Hamp.-rd. NW 14 43... K 19
Cardoza-road NW 7 39... G 20
Carey-lane EC 16 43... L 22
Carey-street, Linc.-inn WC 15 43... L 21
Carlisle-street SW 22 43... O 18
,, ,, NW 13 42... K 16
Carlton-hill, Edg.-rd. NW. 5 42... J 15
,, House-terrace SW. 15 43... N 19
,, road, Holloway N. 7 39... G 19
,, ,, Hav.-hill NW 6 39... H 18
,, ,, Maida-vale NW 13 42... J 14
,, ,, Putney SW — 47... T 12
,, ,, Mile-end E. 17 44... K 26
,, square, Mile-end E 17 44... K 26
Carlyle-square, Chelsea SW 21 47... P 16
Carnaby-street W 14 43... M 19
Caroline-st., Bedford-sq. WC 15 43... L 19
Carpenters road E 11 40... I 30
Carrol-road NW 6 39... G 18
Carter-lane EC 16 43... M 22
Carthusian-st. EC 16 43... L 22
Cassland-road, Hackney E 9 40... I 26
Cassella-road SE 33 49... R 27
Castellaine-rd, W 13 42... K 14
Casterton-street E 9 40... H 25
Castlebar-rd., Castlebar-hill — 41... L 4
Castle-road, Ken.-town NW 6 39... H 18
,, street, Drury-lane WC 15 43... M 20
,, ,, Oxford-mkt. W 14 43... L 19
,, ,, Falcon-sq. EC 16 43... L 22
,, ,, Up. Thames-st. EC 16 43... M 22
,, ,, Leicester-sq. WC 15 43... M 19
,, ,, Holborn EC 15 43... L 21
,, street SW 30 47... R 16
Castletown-road W 28 47... P 12
Castlewood-rd N 3 40... D 25
Catford-hill-rd. SE — 54... W 28
Cathcart-road SW 21 47... P 15
,, hill N 7 39... F 19
,, street NW 6 39... H 18
Catherine-street, Strand WC 15 43... M 20
,, ,, Islington. N 7 43... J 21
Cator-street SE 24 49... Q 24

9-in. 4-in. sht. sht. mar.

Cattle Market N 7 39... H 20
Cavendish-rd. St. Jn's-wd. NW 13 42... J 16
,, ,, Kentish.-tn. NW 6 39... H 18
,, ,, NW 4 38... I 12
,, ,, Clapham-pk. SW — 48... U 18
,, ,, Tooting SW — 52... Z 15
,, square W 14 43... L 18
,, street, Hoxton N 16 43... J 23
Caversham-road NW 6 39... H 18
Cawley-road E 10 40... I 27
Caxton-road W 20 42... N 11
,, ,, Wood Green N — 36... A 21
,, street E 18 44... J 28
,, ,, SW. 23 43... O 19
Cazenove-road 3 40... E 25
,, Park-road N 2 39... D 20
Cecil-street WC 15 43... M 20
Cedars-road SW 31 48... S 18
,, ,, E 11 40... H 31
Cemetery-rd., Norwood SE — 53... X 22
Central-street, St.Luke's EC 16 43... K 22
,, Hill SW — 53... Y 23
Chadwell-street EC 15 43... J 21
Chadwick-road SE 32 49... S 24
Chaldon road SW 28 47... Q 12
Chalgrove-road E 9 40... H 26
Chalk-farm-road NW 6 39... I 18
Challoner-st SW 28 47... P 13
Champion-hill SE 32 48... S 23
Champion-park SW 32 48... S 23
Chancery-lane WC 15 43... L 21
Chancellor-road SW 28 47... P 11
Chandos-street WC 15 43... M 20
,, ,, W 14 43... L 18
,, road, Stratford E 11 40... H 30
Change-alley EC 16 43... M 23
Chant-square E 11 40... I 31
Chapel-road SW — 53... X 22
,, street, Belg.-sq. SW 22 43... O 17
,, ,, Edg.-rd. NW. 13 42... L 16
,, ,, Pentonville N 7 43... J 21
,, ,, Sth Audley-st. W 14 43... M 17
,, ,, St. Pancras NW 15 43... J 19
,, ,, Stratford E 11 40... I 30
,, house-street E 26 49... P 29
Chaplin-road NW — 38... H 10
Chapter-street, Pimlico SW 23 48... P 19
Charford-road E 11 40... G 31
Charing-cross SW 15 43... M 19
Charles-sq., Hoxton N 16 43... K 23
Charles-street, Berk.-sq. W 14 43... M 18
,, ,, Grosvenor-sq. W 14 43... M 18
,, ,, Hatton-gar. EC 15 43... L 21
,, ,, St. James'-sq. SW 15 43... M 19
,, ,, Parliament-st. SW 23 43... N 19
,, ,, Stepney E 17 44... L 26
,, ,, Northam.-sq. EC 16 43... K 22
,, ,, City-road EC 16 43... K 22
Charlmont-road SW — 52... Y 16
Charlotte-st, Bedford-sq. WC 15 43... L 19
,, ,, Blackfriars SE 24 43... N 22
,, ,, Isling. N 7 43... J 20
,, ,, Fitz.-sq. W 14 43... L 19
Charlton-rd. SE 34 49... R 31
Charlton-st., Somers-town NW 15 43... J 19
,, ,, Marylebone W 14 43... L 18
,, ,, Euston-rd. NW 15 43... J 19
Charlville-road W 28 47... P 13
Charlwood-street SW 32 48... P 18
Charlwood-road SW 29 47... S 11
Charrington-st., Oakl.-sq. NW 7 39... J 19
Charterhouse-street EC 16 43... L 21
,, square EC 16 43... L 22
Chatham-place E 9 40... H 26
Chatham-rd. Wand. wth Com. — 47... U 16
Chatsworth-rd., Stratford E 11 40... H 31
,, ,, E 9 40... G 26
,, ,, SE — 53... W 22
Chatterton-road N 8 39... F 22
Chaucer-road SE — 48... U 21
Cheapside EC 16 43... M 22
Chelsea-bridge SW 22 48... Q 18
,, hospital SW 22 48... P 17
,, Embankment SW. 22 47... Q 16
Chelsham-road SW 31 48... S 19
Chenies-street, Tott.-ct-rd WC 15 43... L 19
Chepstow place W 13 42... M 14
,, villas, Nott'g-hill W 20 42... M 13
Cherry-garden-pier SE 25 44... N 25
Cherry-orchard-rd. Croydon — 57... D 23
Chesham road N 8 40... F 24
,, place SW 22 43... O 17
,, street, Belgravia SW 22 43... O 17
Chesson-road SW 28 47... P 13
Chester rd. Highgate N 2 39... F 18
,, street Greenwich SE 27 49... P 31
,, square, Pimlico SW 22 43... O 18
,, st., Grosvenor-pl. SW 22 43... O 18
,, terrace NW 14 43... J 18
Chesterfield-street W 14 43... M 18
Chestnut-walk — 37... C 30
,, road — 37... B 24
Chetwynd-road NW 6 39... F 18
Cheyne-walk, Chelsea SW 21 47... Q 16
Chichester-road NW 5 42... J 14
,, ,, Croydon — 57... E 23
Chilton-st. E 17 44... K 24
Chingford-road — 37... A 29
,, lane — 37... A 30
Chippenham-road W 13 42... K 14
Chislehurst-rd. Sidcup — 55... Y 39
Chiswell-street EC 16 43... L 23
Chiswick high-rd. — 41... O 7
,, Mall W — 47... P 9
,, lane W — 47... P 9
Chivalry-road SW 30 47... T 16
Chobham-road, East, E 11 40... H 30
Cholmeley-park N 2 39... E 18
Choumert-road SE 32 49... S 24
,, grove SE 32 49... S 24
Chrisp-street, Poplar E 18 44... L 29
Christ's-st., Poplar E 18 44... L 29

9-in.4-in. sht.sht.mar.

Christchurch-road SE . — 53... V 20
,, ,, NW . 5 38... F 15
,, ,, N . 2 39... D 20
Christian-street Com'l.-rd. E 17 44...M 25
Christie-road E . . . 10 40... I 27
Chryssell road, Brixton SW 23 48... Q 21
Chumleigh-street SE . 24 48... G 18
Church-end, Hendon NW . — 35... B 11
,, ,, Finchley N . — 35... A 13
Church-hill . . . — 37... C 29
Church-lane, Leyton . — 40... E 28
,, ,, Tooting SW . — 53... Y 17
,, ,, NW . . — 38... D 8
,, ,, Hendon NW . — 35... B 11
Church-lane, Finchley N . — 35... B 16
Church-ln. Kensington, W 13 42...M 14
Church Manor Way, Plumstead— 50... O 39
,, road, De Beauv.-tn. N 8 39... I 23
,, ,, Stoke Newington N 9 40... G 24
,, ,, Brixton SW . — 48... U 20
,, ,, Low Leyton . — 40... F 29
,, ,, Tulse-hill SE . — 53...W 21
,, ,, Upper Norwood SE — 53... Z 23
,, ,, Richmond . — 46... S 5
,, ,, Sydenham SE. — 54...W 26
,, , Tottenham . — 37... A 24
,, ,, Teddington . — 51... X 1
,, ,, Stoke Newington N 9 40... F 24
,, ,, Walthamstow — 37... C 29
,, ,, Homerton E . 10 40... H 27
,, ,, Willesden, NW — 38... H 9
,, rd, Upper Edmonton — 37... A 15
,, row, Bethnal-green E 17 44... K 21
,, ,, Hampstead NW 5 38... G 25
,, ,, Limehouse, E 18 44...M 16
,, street, NW . . 13 42... K 18
,, ,, Chelsea, SW 21 47... Q 24
,, ,, Clapham-rd. SE 23 48... Q 26
,, ,, Camberwell SE 32 48... R 23
,, ,, Croydon . — 57... E 22
,, ,, Cubitt-town E 27 49... P 31
,, ,, Deptford SE 26 49... Q 28
,, ,, Greenwich SE 27 49... Q 30
,, ,, Isleworth . — 46... R 3
,, ,, Kensington, W 21 42... N 14
,, ,, Rotherhithe, SE 25 44... N 26
,, ,, StokeNewington, N 3 38... F 23
,, ,, Spitalfields E . 17 44... L 24
,, ,, Soho, WC . 15 43... M 19
,, ,, Twickenham . — 51... V 2
,, ,, West Ham E . 11 44... J 31
,, ,, Woolwich . — 50... O 35
Churchfield-road, Ealing . — 41...M 4
Churchill-road, Homerton E 9 40... H 26
,, ,, Dartmouth-park NW . . . 6 39... G 18
Churton-street SW . . 22 48... P 19
Cintra-park SE . . . — 54... Z 24
Circus-road, Hav'stock-hill NW 6 39... G 17
,, ,, St. John's-wood NW 13 42... J 15
Cirencester-st., Westb-pk. W 13 42... L 14
Citizen-road, Holloway N . 7 39... G 21
City-road EC . . . 16 43... K 22
City-garden-row N . . 16 43... J 22
Clanricarde-gardens W . 13 42...M 14
Clapham-road SW . . 23 48... Q 21
,, common SW . 31 48... T 18
,, park-road SW . 31 48... T 19
Clapton-square E . . 9 40... G 26
Clare-market WC . . 15 43...M 20
Claremont-rd, Surbiton . — 56... Z 4
,, ,, Forest-hill — 45... H 32
,, square N . . 15 43... J 21
Clarence-gardens NW . 14 43... K 18
,, road, Clapton E . 9 40... G 26
,, ,, Kentish-town NW 6 39... I 18
,, ,, Wood-green N — 36... A 20
,, ,, Clapham SW — 48... U 19
,, ,, Teddington . — 56... Y 2
,, ,, Wimbledon, SW — 52... Y 14
,, street, Islington N 8 43... J 22
,, ,, Kingston . — 56... Z 4
Clarendon-square NW . 15 43... J 19
,, place W . . 13 42...M 16
,, street, Pimlico SW 22 48... P 18
,, road W . . 13 42... K 14
,, ,, W . . 21 42... O 14
,, ,, Uxbridge-rd. W 20 42...M 12
,, ,, Hornsey N . — 36... B 21
,, ,, Walthamstow — 40... D 29
,, ,, Lewisham SE 34 49... T 30
Clarges-street, Piccadilly W 14 43...M 18
Clarissa-street, Haggerston E 9 40... I 24
Clark-street E . . . 17 44... L 26
Claude-road SE . . . 32 49... S 25
Claverton-street, Pimlico SW 22 48... P 19
Clay-la, South Norwood . — 58... A 26
Clay-street . . . . — 37... B 28
Clayton-st., Caledonian-rd., N 7 39... I 20
,, road SE . . 32 49... R 25
Clements-court, Milk-st, EC 16 43... L 22
Clement's-inn WC . . 15 43...M 21
,, lane EC . . 16 43...M 23
Clephane-road N . . 8 39... H 23
Clerkenwell-green EC . 16 43... K 21
,, road EC . . 16 43... K 22
,, close EC . . 16 43... K 21
Cleve-rd. NW . . . 5 38...H 14
Cleveland-gardens W . 13 42... L 15
Cleveland-rd., De Beauv.-tn. N 8 39... I 23
,, ,, Castlebar-hill — 41... K 3
,, st. Fitzroy-sq. W 14 43... L 18
,, ,, Mile-end-road E 17 44... L 26
,, square W . . 13 42...M 15
,, row SW . . 22 43... N 19
Clifden-road E . . . 9 40... G 26
Clifford-street, Old Bond-st. W 14 43...M 18
Clifton-hill, St. John's-wd., NW 5 38... I 15
,, road SE . . 33 49... R 26
,, ,, Paddington W 13 42... K 15
,, ,, South Norwood — 57... B 23
,, ,, NW. . . 7 39... H 19
Clifton-villas NW . . 7 39... H 19
,, street, Finsb.-sq. EC 16 43... L 23
,, ,, Wands.-rd. SW 31 48... R 19
Clinger-street N . . 8 43... J 23
Clinton rd., Mile-end-road E 18 44... K 27
Clipstone-street W . . 14 43... L 18
Clissold-rd. Stoke New'ton N 8 39... F 23
Cloak lane EC . . . 16 43...M 23
Cloudesley-road N . . 7 39... I 21
,, square N . . 7 39... I 21
,, street N . . 7 39... J 21
Clyde-road, West-green . — 36... B 23
,, street, Redcliffe-gard'sW 21 47... Q 15
Coal-oak-lane NW . . . — 38... D 9
Cobbett's-lane SE . . 25 49... P 26
Cobbold-road W . . . — 42...
Cobden-road E . . . 11 40... F 31
Coborn-road, Bow-road E. 18 44... K 28
Coburg-road, Old Kent-road SE 24 49... Q 24
Coburg-road, Teddington — 51... X 1
Cockspur-street SW . . 15 43...M 19
Codrington-hill SE . . — 54... V 27
Colchester road . . . — 40... D 28
Coldbath-square EC . . 15 43... K 21
Coldharbour-lane SW & SE 32 48... S 22
Colebrook-row, Islington N 8 43... J 22
Colegrave-road, E . . 11 40... H 30
Coleherne-rd., W. Bromp. SW 21 47... P 14
Coleman-road, SE . . 24 48... Q 23
Coleman-st., New-north-rd. N 8 39... I 22
,, ,, Gresham-st. EC 16 43... L 23
Coleraine-road SE . . 27 50... Q 31
Colerton-street SW . . 30 47... R 16
College-hill, EC . . . 16 43...M 22
,, place, N . . . 7 39... I 19
,, road Dulwich SE . — 53... V 23
,, street, Fulham-rd. SW 21 47... P 16
,, street, Homerton E 9 40... H 26
,, street, Islington, N 8 39... I 21
,, villas-rd, NW . . 5 38... H 15
Collier-street, Pentonville N 15 43... J 20
Colliers-wat-la. NThornton-hth— 57... B 21
Collin Deep-lane NW . . — 35... B 9
Collingham-rd. Sth. Kens. SW 21 42... O 14
,, place SW. . 21 47... O 14
Collingwood-street, E . 17 44... K 25
Colney-Hatch-lane N. . — 36... A 18
Columbia-market E . . 17 44... K 24
,, road, Hackney-rd. E 17 44... K 24
Colverstone-crescent E . 9 40... H 24
Colville-road, Notting-hill W 12 42... L 13
Combe-rd, Kingston . — 56... Z 6
Combermere-road SW . 31 48... S 20
Comeragh-road W . . 28 47... P 12
Commerce-rd. Wood-green N — 36... A 20
Commercial-road E . . 17 44... L 25
,, ,, Pimlico SW 22 48... P 18
,, ,, Peckham SE 25 49... Q 25
,, ,, SE . . 15 43... N 21
,, street E . . 16 44... L 24
,, ,, Deptford SE 26 44... O 27
Common-lane, Higham-hill — 37... A 27
Compton-road, Canonbury N 8 39... H 22
Compton-street, Goswell-rd. EC 16 43... K 22
Conderton-road SE . . 32 48... S 22
Conduit-street, Regent-st W. 14 43... M 18
Coningham-road W . . 20 42... N 10
Connaught-place W . . 14 43...M 17
Connaught-square W . 14 42...M 16
Connaught-street W . . 14 43... L 17
Cooks-road SE . . . 24 48... Q 22
Coombe-lane . . . — 52... Z 10
Coombe-road, Croydon . — 57... F 22
,, street . . . — 57... F 23
,, wood . . . — 52... Z 8
Coomber-rd, SW . . . 28 47... Q 13
Copeland-road SE . . 32 49... S 25
Copenhagen-street N . 7 39... I 20
Coperscope-road . . . — 54... Z 28
Copleston-road SE . . 32 49... S 24
Copper-mill-lane . . — 40... D 27
Copse-hill . . . . — 52... Z 10
Copthall-court EC . . 16 43... L 23
Corbyn-street N . . . 2 39... E 20
Corfield-street E . . 17 44... K 25
Cornhill EC . . . 16 43...M 23
Cornwall-gard, Sth. Kens. SW 21 43... O 15
,, road SE . . 15 43... N 21
,, ,, Notting-hill W 12 42... L 13
,, ,, Brixton SW. — 48... U 20
,, street St. Geo. East 17 44...M 25
Cornwall-street, Fulham SW 21 47... Q 14
Cornwallis-rd. N . . . 2 39... F 20
Corporation-row Clerken'll EC 16 43... K 21
Cotleigh-rd, NW . . 5 38... I 14
Cottenham-road N . . 2 39... F 20
Countess-road NW . . 6 39... G 19
Court-rd, Eltham . . — 55... V 35
Court-road SE . . . — 53...W 22
,, hill-road SE . . — 49... T 29
Courtfield-gardens SW . 21 42... O 14
,, rd., Kensington SW 21 42... O 15
Courthope-road NW . . 6 39... G 17
Courtney-road Holloway N 7 39... G 21
Coutts-road, Burdett-road E 18 44... L 27
Coventry-street W & WC . 15 43...M 19
Cow-cross-st., St. John-st. EC 16 43... L 22
Cowley-road, Brixton SW . 31 48... R 21
Cowper-road N . . . 8 40... G 23
Crampton-street SE . . 24 48... P 22
Cranbourne-street WC . 15 43...M 19
Crane-court, Fleet-st. EC . 15 43...M 21
Cranham-road SE . . 25 49... P 25
Cranley-gardens SW . . 21 47... P 15
,, place SW . . 21 47... P 15
Cranmer-road, Brixton SW 23 48... Q 21
Craven-hill, Bayswater W 13 42...M 15
Craven-hill-gardens W . 13 42...M 15
,, road, W . . 13 42...M 15
,, street, Strand WC . 15 43...M 20
Crawford-street, Marylebn. W 14 42... L 16
Crayford-road N. . . 7 39... G 20

9-in.4-in. sht.sht.mar.

Creechurch-lane, EC . . 16 44...M 24
Creed-lane, St. Paul's EC . 16 43...M 22
Creek-road, Deptford SE . 26 49... Q 29
Crescent-road SW . . 31 48... T 9
,, ,, Kingston . — 56... Y 6
,, ,, South Norwood — 58... A 24
,, ,, Woolwich . — 50... P 36
,, lane SW . . . — 48... T 19
,, wood-road SE . — 54... X 24
Cricketfield-road E . . 9 40... G 25
Cripplegate-bldngs. Fore-st. EC 16 43... L 22
Crofton-road SE . . . 32 49... R 24
Crogsland-road NW . . 6 39... H 17
Croham-rd, Croydon . — 57... F 23
Cromer-st., Gray's Inn-rd. WC 15 43... K 20
Cromwell-road, Kens'ton SW 21 42... O 14
,, ,, Teddington — 56... Y 2
,, ,, Up. Holloway N 2 39... F 19
Crondall-st, Hoxton, E . 16 43... J 23
Croom's-hill, reenwich SE 34 49... S 30
Cropley-street, New-nth-rd. N 16 43... J 23
Crosby-square, Bishopsgate EC 16 43...M 23
Crosier-street, Lambeth SE 23 43... O 20
Cross-lane. New Eltham . — 55...W 36
,, street, Islington N . 8 39... I 22
,, ,, Hatton-gar. EC 15 43... L 21
Crouch-hill N . . . 2 39... E 20
Crouch-end-hill, N . . 2 39... D 20
Crowndale-rd. St. Pancras NW 6 43... J 19
Crownfield-road E . . 11 40... G 31
Crown-street, Soho WC . 15 43... L 19
,, hill SE . . . — 53... Y 22
,, lane SW . . . — 53... Y 21
Crown-office-row, Temple EC 15 43...M 21
Crown-road W . . . 28 47... Q 12
,, ,, Twickenham . — 46... T 3
Croxted-lane SE . . . — 53... V 22
,, road SE. . . — 53...W 23
Croydon-road SE . . . — 54... Z 26
,, ,, . . . — 58... A 27
Crutched Friars EC . . 16 44...M 24
Crystal Palace-road SE . 32 49... T 24
,, ,, park-road SE — 54... Y 15
Culford-road N . . . 8 39... I 23
Culloden-street E . . 19 44...M 30
Cullum-st, EC . . . 16 43...M 23
Culmore-road SE . . 33 49... R 26
Culvert-road SE . . . 30 48... R 17
Culvert-rd, SW . . . 30 48... R 17
Cumberland-st., Caled'n.-rd. N 7 39... I 20
,, market NW . . 14 43... J 18
,, street, Pimlico SW 22 48... P 18
,, terrace NW . . 14 43... J 18
Cumming-street N . . 15 43... J 20
Cursitor-street, Chancery-l. EC 15 43... L 21
Curtain-road, Shoreditch EC 16 44... K 24
Curzon-street, May Fair W 14 43... N 18
Cutthrough-lane SW . . — 47... U 12
,, road E . . 11 40... G 30
Cyprus-street, E . . 9 40... G 24

D

Dacre-road SE . . . — 54...W 26
,, park, Lee SE . 34 49... T 31
,, street, Lee SE . — ... T 31
Dagmar-road E . . . 10 40... H 27
Dalberg road SW . . 31 48... T 21
Dale-road NW . . . 6 39... G 17
Dalling-road W . . . 20 42... O 10
Dalmain-road . . . — 54... V 16
Dalmeny-road, N . . 7 39... G 19
Dalston-lane, Hackney E . 9 40... H 24
Dalyell-road SW . . 31 48... S 20
Dame-st, N . . . 8 43... J 12
Danby-street SE . . 32 49... S 24
Danes-inn, Strand WC . 15 43...M 21
Daniel-road SE . . . 32 49... S 25
Dante-road SE . . . 24 43... O 22
Darley-road SW . . . — 47... U 16
Darnley-road, Hackney E 9 40... H 26
Dartmouth-park, SE . . — 54...W 26
Dartmouth-park avenue NW 6 39... F 18
Dartmouth-park-road NW 6 39... F 18
,, ,, hill N . 6 39... F 18
,, road, Forest-hill SE — 54...W 26
,, row, Blackhth. SE 34 49... R 30
Darvill-road N . . . 9 40... F 24
Darwin-st., Great Dover-st. SE 24 43... O 23
Davies-st., Berkeley-square W 14 43...M 18
Davisville-road W . . 20 42... N 10
Dawes-road SW . . . 28 47... Q 13
Dawson-place, Bayswater W 13 42...M 14
Day's-lane, New Eltham . — 55... V 38
Deacon-street SE . . 24 43... O 22
Dead-meat-market EC . 16 43... L 22
Dean-street, Soho W . . 15 43... L 19
,, ,, EC . . 15 43... L 21
Dean's-court, St. Paul's EC 16 43...M 22
Dean's-yard, Westminster SW 23 43... O 19
De Beauvoir-crescent N . 8 39... I 23
,, road N . . 8 39... I 23
,, square N . 8 40... I 24
De Burgh-road . . . — 52... Z 14
De Crespigny-park SE . 32 48... S 23
Dee-street E . . . 19 44...M 30
Defoe-road SW . . . — 52... X 16
Delaford-road SW . . 28 47... Q 3
Delaford-rd, SE . . . 25 49... P 25
Delamere-road W . . 13 42... L 14
Delancey-st., Regent's-pk. NW 6 39... I 18
Delorme-road SW . . 28 47... Q 12
Dempsey-st., Stepney E . 17 44... L 26
Denbigh-street SW . . 22 48... P 19
Denman-road SE . . . 32 49... R 24
Denman-street, W . . 15 43...M 19
Denmark-hill SE . . 32 48... S 23
,, ,, Wimbledon . — 52... Z 12
,, road NW . . . 12 42... J 13
,, ,, Camberwell SE 12 48... R 22
,, street, St. Giles WC 15 43... L 19

9-in.4-in. sht.sht.mar.

Dennett-rd, Croydon . — 57... D 21
Dennett's-road SE . . 33 49... R 26
Dennington-rd, NW . . 5 38... H 14
Deptford-green SE . . 26 49... Q 28
Deptford-bridge SE . . 33 49... R 28
Deptford-lower-road SE . 26 49... P 27
Derby-road . . . — 36... C 22
Derby-rd, East Sheen . — 46... S 7
Derbyshire-st, Bethnal-green E 17 44... K 25
De Vere gardens W . . 21 42... N 15
Devonport rd, W . . 20 42... N 2
,, street E . . 17 44...M 26
Devon's-road, Bromley E . 18 44... K 29
Devonshire-road, Hackney E 9 40... I 26
,, ,, Balham SW — 53... V 18
,, ,, Tooting . — 52... Z 16
,, ,, Forest-h. SE — 54...W 26
,, ,, Holloway N 7 39... F 20
,, ,, S. Lamb'th SW 31 48... R 19
,, ,, SE . . 33 49... R 29
,, ,, Chiswick . — 47... P 9
,, st., Portland-pl. W 14 43... L 18
Devonshire-rd. Mile-end E 17 44... K 26
,, ,, Queen's-sq. WC 15 43... L 20
,, square E . 16 44... L 24
,, place W. . 14 43... K 18
Dickens-street SW . . 31 48... R 18
Dieppe-street W . . 28 47... P 13
Dilke-street SW . . 22 47... Q 17
Dinevor-road N . . . 8 40... F 24
Dingwall-rd, Croydon . — 57... D 22
Dirthouse-wood N . . — 36... C 17
Disraeli-road SW . . 29 47... T 12
Ditton-rd, Surbiton . . — 56... Z 5
Dockhead SE . . . 25 44... N 24
Dock-rd. Albert Docks . — 45...M 35
Dock-st., Commercial-rd. E 17 44...M 25
Dockyard-rails, Woolwich — 50... O 35
Dod-street E . . . 18 44...M 28
Doddington-grove SE . 24 48... P 22
Dollis-hill-lane NW . . — 38... F 10
Dollis-hill NW . . . — 38... F 10
Dorchester-street, Hoxton N 8 43... J 13
Dorinda-street, N . . 8 39... H 23
Dorset-square W . . 14 43... K 17
,, ,, S Lambeth SW 23 48... Q 20
,, ,, Baker-street W 14 43... L 17
,, ,, Fleet-street EC 15 43...M 21
Doughty-street WC . . 15 43... K 20
Douglas-road, Canonbury N 8 39... H 22
,, street, SE . . 33 49... R 28
Dover-street, Piccadilly W 14 43...M 18
Dowgate hill EC . . 16 43...M 23
Down-street, Piccadilly W 22 43... N 18
Down-lane . . . . — 37... B 25
Downham-road N . . 8 39... I 23
Downing-street, Whitehall SW 23 43... N 20
Downs-park-road E . . 9 40... G 25
,, ,, crescent E . 9 40... G 25
,, road E . . . 9 40... G 25
Downshire-hill NW . . 5 38... G 16
Dragon-road SE. . . 24 48... Q 23
Drakefield-rd. Nunhead SE 33 49... S 26
Drayton-green la ne . . — 41... ... 3
,, ,, road . . — 41...M 3
,, Park, Holloway-rd. N 8 39... G 21
Drayton-road . . . — 40... E 30
,, grove SW . . 21 47... P 15
Driffield-road E . . 10 44... J 27
Droop-street, Kens-gn, W 12 42... K 12
Drummond-rd, Rotherhithe SE 25 44... O 25
,, cres., Euston-sq. NW 15 43... J 19
,, street NW . . 14 43... K 19
Drury-lane WC . . . 15 43... L 20
Duckett-street E . . 18 44... L 27
Dudley-street, St. Giles's WC 15 43... M 19
Duffield-street SW . . 30 47... S 16
Duke-street, Oxford-street W 14 43... L 17
Duke-street, Bloomsbury, WC 15 43... L 20
,, ,, London-bridge SE 16 43... N 23
,, ,, Adelphi, WC . 15 43...M 20
,, ,, Aldgate EC . 16 44...M 24
,, ,, Grosvenor-sq W 14 43...M 17
,, ,, Smithfield EC 16 43... L 22
,, ,, St. James's SW 14 43...M 19
,, ,, SE . . . 15 43... N 21
,, Terrace, Haverstock-h. NW 6 39... H 17
Dulwich-court-road SE . — 54... V 24
,, common-lane SE. — 54... V 24
Duncan-ter, N . . . 16 43... J 21
Duncannon-street WC . 15 43...M 20
Duncombe-road N . . 2 39... E 19
,, hill SE . . — 54... V 27
Dunloe-street E. . . 9 44... J 24
Dunluce-road, Clapton E. 9 40... G 26
Dunston-st., Haggerston E 8 40... I 24
,, rd., Kingsland-rd. E 8 40... I 24
Duppas-hill-rd, Croydon . — 57... F 21
Durham-road N . . . 2 39... F 21
,, hill-lane SE . . — 54... Y 31
Durnford-road NW . . 6 39... H 17
Dynham-rd, NW . . 5 38... H 14
Dysons-lane . . . — 37... A 26

E

Eagle-st, WC . . . 15 43... L 20
Eagle Wharf-rd., New Nth. rd. N 8 43... J 23
Ealing-green . . . — 41...M 4
,, road, Brentford . — 46... P 5
Eardley-crescent SW. . 21 47... P 14
Earl's Court-road SW & W. 21 42... O 14
,, ,, sq. W. Bromptons W 21 47... P 14
,, ,, gardens WC . 21 42... O 14
,, street, Soho WC . 15 43...M 19
,, ,, Finsbury, EC . 16 43... L 23
,, ,, Edgware-road NW 13 42... L 16
,, ,, SW . . . 23 43... O 19
East End, Finchley N . — 35... B 16
,, Harding-street EC . 15 43... L 21
,, Ham, Manor-ln . — 45... J 35
,, hill, Wandsworth SW — 47... T 14

9-in. 4-in. sht. sht. mar.

East heath-road NW . . 5 38... F 16
,, India Avenue EC . 16 43... M 23
,, road, City-road N . 16 43... K 23
,, st, Barking . . — 45... J 37
,, street, Greenwich SE 27 49... Q 30
,, ,, Walworth SE . 24 48... P 23
,, ,, Lambeth-walk SE 23 43... O 21
,, st, Marylebone, W . 14 43... L 17
,, Ferry-road E . . 27 44... O 29
,, India Docks E . . 19 44... M 30
,, India Docks-road E . 18 44... M 28
,, ,, ,, wall-road E 19 44... M 30
,, Smithfield E . . 17 44... M 25
Eastbourne-terrace W . 13 42... L 15
Eastcheap EC . . . 16 43... M 23
Eastdown-park SE . . 34 49... T 30
Eastern-road E . . 11 40... I 31
Eastfield-street, E . 18 44... L 27
Eaton-place, Pimlico SW . 22 43... O 17
,, square SW . SW . 22 43... O 17
Eaton-rise, Castlebar-hill . — 41... L 4
Ebury-street, Pimlico SW 22 43... O 18
,, square SW . . 22 48... P 18
Eccles-rd, SW . . . 30 47... T 16
Ecclesbourne-rd., N.-Nth.-rd. 8 39... I 22
Eccleston-square SW . . 22 48... P 18
,, street SW . . 22 43... O 17
Edbrook-road W . . 13 42... K 14
Eden-grove, Holloway N . 7 39... H 21
,, road . . . — 35... C 29
,, road SE . . . — 53... Y 22
,, street, Kingston . — 56... Z 4
Edgware-road W and NW . 13 42... L 16
Edinburgh-road W . . 12 42... K 12
Edith-grove, SW . . 21 47... Q 15
Edith-road, SW . . . 28 47... P 12
,, ,, Hatcham SE . 33 49... S 26
Edmund-st., Camberwell SE 24 48... Q 23
Edward-street, Deptford SE 26 49... Q 28
,, ,, Wenlock-rd. N 16 43... J 22
Edward-square, N . . 7 43... J 21
Edwardes-square, Kens. W 20 42... O 13
Effra-road, Brixton SW . 31 48... T 21
,, ,, Wimbledon, SW — 52... Y 4
,, parade, Brixton SW . — 48... U 21
Egerton-road, Greenwich SE 33 49... R 29
,, ,, N . . 3 40... D 24
Eglinton-road, Bow E . 18 44... J 28
,, ,, Woolwich — 50... Q 36
Eland-road SW . . . 30 48... S 17
Elder-lane SE . . . — 53... X 21
Elderfield-rd., Up'r Clapton E 9 40... G 26
Eldon-street, Finsbury EC 16 43... L 23
,, road W . . . 21 42... O 14
,, road NW . . . 5 38... G 16
Eleanor-road, E . . . 9 40... I 25
Elephant and Castle SE . 24 43... O 22
Elfin-street SE . . . 24 48... Q 22
Elgin-crescent NW . . 20 42... M 12
Elgin-road W . . . 13 42... K 14
Eliot-park, Blackheath SE 34 49... S 30
Elizabeth-terrace, Islington N 7 43... J 21
,, street Eaton-sq. SW 22 43... O 18
Ellerdale-road NW . . 5 38... G 15
,, ,, SE . . 33 49... T 29
Ellerslie-road W . . 20 42... M 11
Ellesmere-road, Old Ford E 18 44... J 27
Ellingford-road, E . . 9 40... I 26
Ellington-street N . . 7 39... H 21
Elliot-bank, Forest-hill SE — 54... W 25
Elliott-road SW . . . 31 48... R 21
Ellison-road SW . . . — 53... Z 19
Ellsworthy-road NW . . 6 38... I 16
Elm-court, Temple EC . 15 43... M 21
,, park, SW . . . — 48... U 10
,, park-gardens SW . 21 47... P 15
,, ,, road SW . 21 47... P 15
,, road, Camden-town N 7 39... I 19
,, ,, Sidcup . . — 55... Y 39
Elmers-end-road . . — 58... B 27
Elmore-street, Essex-road N 8 39... I 23
Elsley-road SW . . . 30 48... S 17
Elstead-street, Walworth SE 24 48... P 23
Eltham-rd, SE . . . — 49... T 31
Elthorne-road, N . . 2 39... E 19
Elvaston-place SW . . 21 42... O 15
Ely-place, Holborn EC . 15 43... L 21
Emerson-street SE . . 16 43... N 22
Emmett-street, Limehouse E 18 44... M 28
Emperor's-gate SW . . 21 42... O 15
Enbrook-st, Kens-gardens, W 12 42... K 13
Endell-street, Long-acre WC 15 43... L 20
Endlesham-road SW . . — 52... V 17
Endsleigh-gardens, NW . 15 43... K 19
Endymion-rd, N . . . 3 39... D 22
Enfield-rd, N . . . 8 40... I 24
England-lane NW . . 6 39... H 17
Englefield-road N . . 8 39... I 23
Ennismore-gardens SW . 21 42... O 16
Epirus-road, SW . . 28 47... Q 13
Epsom rd, Croydon . . — 57... E 21
Erlanger-rd. Hatcham SE 33 49... R 24
Ernest-street, Regent's-pk. NW 14 43... K 18
Erpingham-rd. SW . . 29 47... S 11
Essex-street, Strand WC . 15 43... M 21
,, ,, N . . . 8 43... J 22
,, rd, Islington N . 8 39... I 22
Estcourt-road SW . . 28 47... Q 13
Estelle-road NW . . . 6 39... G 17
Esther-road . . . — 40... D 31
Ethelbridge-rd, N . . 12 42... K 12
Ethelburga-street SW . 30 47... R 16
Eton-avenue, NW . . 5 39... H 16
Eton-place, Primrose-hill NW 6 38... I 16
,, road NW . . . 6 39... H 17
,, College-road NW . 5 38... H 16
Ettrick-street E . . 19 44... L 30
Eustace-road SW . . 28 47... Q 13
Euston-square NW . . 15 43... K 19
Euston-road NW . . . 15 43... K 19
Euston-street NW . . 15 43... K 19
Evelina-road SE . . 33 49... S 26

Evelyn-street SE . . 26 49... Q 28
Evering-road E & N . . 9 40... F 25
Everington-street SW . 28 13... Q 12
Eversholt-st, NW . . 6 43... J 19
Evershot-road . . . 2 39... E 21
Eversleigh-road SW . . 30 48... S 17
Ewart-grove N . . . — 36... A 21
Ewart-road, Forest-hill SE — 54... V 26
Ewell-rd, Surbiton . . — 56... Z 5
Exchange-buildings, EC . 16 43... M 23
Exeter-street, Strand WC 15 43... M 20
Exhibition-road SW . . 21 42... O 16
Exmouth-st., Clerkenwell WC 15 43... K 21
,, ,, Stepney E . 17 44... L 26

F

Fair-street, Horsleydown SE 24 44... N 24
Fairfax-rd, St.John's-wd NW 5 38... I 15
,, ,, Teddington — 56... Y 2
Fairfield-road, Bow E . 18 44... J 28
,, ,, Croydon . — 57... E 23
Fairfoot-road E . . . 18 44... K 28
Fairholme-road W . . 28 47... P 13
Fairlop-road . . . — 40... E 31
Fairmead-rd, N . . . 7 39... F 20
Falcon-square EC . . 16 43... L 22
Falcon-rd SW . . . 30 47... S 16
Falkland-road NW . . 6 39... G 19
Fallow-corner N . . . — 35... A 15
Falmouth-road SE . . 24 43... O 22
Fann-street, EC . . . 16 43... K 22
Fanshaw-st., Pitfield-st NW 16 43... J 13
Faraday-street, Walworth SE 24 48... P 23
Farleigh-road N . . . 9 40... G 24
Farm-street, Berkeley-sq. W 14 43... M 18
Farmers-rd, Kennington-pk. SE 23 48... Q 21
Farquhar-road SE . . — 54... Y 24
Farrant-st, Kens. Gn. W . 12 42... K 13
Farringdon-road EC . . 16 43... K 21
,, street EC . . 16 43... L 21
Fassett square E . . 9 40... H 25
Featherstone-st., City-rd. EC 16 43... K 23
,, buildings WC 15 43... L 20
Felix-street, Hackney-rd. E 17 44... J 25
Fell-st, Wood-st, EC . . 16 43... L 22
Fellows-rd., Haverstock-h. NW 6 38... H 16
,, st. Kingsland-road E 9 40... J 24
Felton-st., Hyde-rd. Hoxton N 8 39... I 23
Fenchurch-avenue, EC . 16 43... M 23
Fenchurch-street EC . . 16 43... M 23
Fenham-rd. SE . . . 32 49... R 25
Fentiman-rd., S. Lambeth SW 23 48... Q 20
Ferdinand-st., Chalk-fm-rd. NW 6 39... H 18
Ferncliffe-rd, E . . . 9 40... G 25
Ferndale-road SW . . 31 48... T 20
Fernhead-road W . . 12 42... K 13
Fernlea-road SW . . — 53... V 18
Ferntower-road N . . 8 39... G 23
Ferron-road E . . . 9 40... G 25
Ferry-lane . . . . — 37... C 26
Fetter-lane, EC . . . 15 43... L 21
Field-road W . . . 28 47... P 12
Fifth-avenue W . . . 12 42... K 12
Fifth-cross-rd, Twickenham — 51... V 1
Fig-tree-court, Temple EC 15 43... M 21
Filmer-road SW . . . 28 47... Q 13
Finborough-road SW . . 21 47... P 14
Finch-lane EC . . . 16 43... M 23
Finchley-lane NW . . — 35... B 19
,, road SE . . . 24 48... Q 22
,, ,, NW . . 5 38... H 15
Findhorn-street E . . 19 44... L 30
Finsbury-avenue EC . . 16 43... L 23
,, circus EC . . 16 43... L 23
,, pavement EC . 16 43... L 23
,, park N . . . 2 39... E 21
,, ,, road N . . 3 39... F 22
,, square EC . . 16 43... L 23
,, street EC . . 16 43... L 23
First-avenue W . . . 12 42... K 13
Fish-street-hill EC . . 16 43... M 23
Fisher-st, Barking . . — 45... J 37
Fitzjohn's-avenue NW . 5 38... H 15
Fitzroy-square W . . 14 43... K 18
,, road NW . . . 6 39... H 17
Fitzroy-park N . . . 1 39... E 17
Flaxman-road, Camberwell SE 32 48... S 22
Fleet-lane, EC . . . 16 43... L 22
,, street EC . . . 15 43... M 21
,, road, Hampstead NW 6 38... G 16
Flint-street, Walworth SE 24 48... P 23
Flodden-road, Camberwell SE 32 48... R 22
Flood-street, Chelsea SW . 22 47... P 16
Florence-road, Lewisham SE 33 49... R 28
,, ,, Wimbledon, SW — 52... Y 4
,, ,, Stroud-green, N 2 39... E 21
Flower-lane, Mill-hill . — 35... A 10
Foley-street, Marylebone W 14 43... L 18
Folly-lane . . . . — 37... A 28
Fonthill-road N . . . 2 39... E 21
Foots-cray-rd, Eltham . — 55... W 37
Fopstone-road SW . . 21 47... O 14
Ford-street, Old Ford E . 10 44... J 27
Ford-road ,, ,, E . . 10 44... J 27
Fore-street, Cripplegate EC 16 43... L 23
Forest-road, Dalston E . 9 40... H 24
,, ,, Leytonstone E . — 40... E 30
,, hill-road SE . . — 49... U 25
,, lane E . . . 11 40... H 31
Formosa-street, Maida-hill W 13 42... K 14
Forston-street, Hoxton N . 16 43... J 22
Fort-road, Bermondsey SE 25 49... P 24
Fortess-road NW . . . 6 39... G 18
Fortis-green NW . . . — 36... B 17
Fortune-green NW . . 5 38... G 14
,, lane NW . . 5 38... G 14
Foster-lane, Cheapside EC 16 43... L 22
Foulden-road Amherst-rd. E 9 40... G 24
Fountain Court Temple EC 15 43... M 21
,, road SW . . . — 52... X 15
Fountayne-road E . . 3 40... F 25

Fountayne road SW . . — 53... M 8
Fourth-avenue W . . 12 42... K 22
Fourth-cross-road, Twickenham — 51... V 1
Foxberry-road SE . . 33 49... T 27
Foxgrove-road SE . . — 54... Z 29
Foxley-rd, Camber. New-rd. SE 23 48... Q 21
Frampton-park-road E . 9 40... I 26
Francis-rd, Leyton . . — 40... F 30
Francis-st, Woolwich . — 50... P 35
Francis-st., Westminster SW 22 43... O 19
,, ,, Tott.-ct.-rd. WC 15 43... K 19
Frederick-st., Caledonia-rd. N 7 39... I 20
,, ,, Gray's Inn-rd. WC 15 43... K 20
Freegrove-road N . . 7 39... G 20
Freeling-street N . . 7 39... I 20
Freke-road SW . . . 30 48... S 17
Frere-street SW . . . 30 47... R 16
Friar-street, Blackfriars-rd. SE 24 43... N 22
Friary-court SW . . . 22 43... N 19
Friday-street, Cheapside EC 16 43... M 22
Friern-road SE . . . — 54... V 24
Frith-lane, Finchley . . — 35... A 13
Frith-road, E . . . 11 40... G 30
Frith-street, Soho-square W 15 43... M 19
Frithville-gardens W . 20 42... M 11
Frognall-road, Hampstead NW 5 38... G 15
Fulham-road, SW . . . 21 42... O 15
Fulham-palace-road SW . 28 47... Q 12
,, park SW . . . 30 47... R 14
Fuller-street, Bethnal-green E 17 44... K 25
Fulwell-road, Teddington — 51... X 1
Furnival's-inn EC . . 15 43... L 21

G

Gainsboro'-road E . . 10 40... H 28
,, ,, Leyton . — 40... E 31
Gainsford-st., Kentish-tn NW 6 39... H 19
,, ,, Horsley-down. SE 25 44... N 24
,, ,, Islington N . 7 39... I 21
Galley-wall-road SE . . 25 49... P 25
Galton-st, Kens. Gn. W . 12 42... K 12
Garden-court EC . . . 15 43... M 21
Gardener's-lane, Putney SW 29 47... S 12
Garford-street, Limehouse E 18 44... M 28
Garlick-hill, EC . . . 16 43... M 22
Garnault-place, EC . . 15 43... K 21
Garratt SW . . . . — 52... W 15
,, lane SW . . . — 52... W 14
Garrick-street, Covent-gar. WC 15 43... M 20
Garway-road W . . . 13 42... M 14
Gascony-avenue NW . . 5 38... I 14
Gascoyne-rd., Victoria-park E 10 40... I 27
Gaselee-st, Blackwall, E . 19 44... M 30
Gate-street WC . . . 15 43... L 20
Gauden-road SW . . . 31 48... S 19
Gayford-road W . . . — 42... N 9
Gayhurst-road, Hackney E 9 40... I 25
Gayton-road NW . . . 5 38... G 15
,, crescent NW . . 5 38... G 15
Gee-street, Somers-town NW 15 43... J 19
,, ,, Goswell-road EC 16 43... K 22
George-st, Croydon . . — 57... E 22
George-yard, Lombard-st. EC 16 43... M 23
George's-road, Holloway N 7 39... H 20
,, street, Baker-street W 14 43... L 17
,, ,, Hanover-sq. W 14 43... M 18
,, ,, Camberwell SE 24 48... Q 23
,, ,, Mansion-ho, EC 16 43... M 23
,, ,, Richmond . — 46... T 4
,, ,, Woolwich . — 50... O 35
,, st., Hampstead-rd NW 14 43... K 19
Georgiana-street NW . . 6 43... I 19
Geraldine-road . . . — 47... U 15
Gerrard-street, Islington N 8 43... J 22
,, ,, Soho, W . 15 43... N 19
Gibbon-rd . . . . 33 49... R 26
Gibson-square, Islington N 7 39... I 21
Gibson's-hill SE . . . — 53... Z 21
Gideon-road SW . . . 30 48... S 17
Gifford-st., Caledonian-rd. N 7 39... I 20
Gilbert-road, NW . . 13 42... J 15
Gillespie-road N . . 8 39... F 22
Gillies-street, Kentish-tn. NW 6 39... H 18
Gillingham-st., Pimlico SW 22 43... O 18
Gilmore-road SE . . 34 49... T 30
Gilston-road, Brompton SW 21 47... P 15
Giltspur-street EC . . 16 43... L 22
Gipsy-hill SE . . . — 53... Y 23
,, lane, Upton . . — 45... H 33
,, road SE . . . — 53... X 22
,, house-road SE . — 53... Y 23
,, lane SE . . . — 54... Y 30
Girand-st, Poplar, E . 18 44... M 29
Girdlers-road W . . 28 42... O 12
Girdlestone-road N . . 2 39... F 19
Gladstone-avenue N . . — 36... A 22
Gladstone-road . . . — 52... Z 13
,, terrace SW . 31 48... R 18
Glamis-road E . . . 17 44... M 26
Glasshouse-st., Regent-st. W 14 43... M 19
Gledhow-gardens SW . 21 47... P 15
Glenarm-road E . . . 9 40... G 25
Glengall-road, Millwall E 27 44... O 29
,, ,, Old Kent-rd. SE 25 49... Q 24
Glentham-rd, Barnes, SW . 28 47... P 10
Glenthorne road W . . 28 42... O 11
Globe-road, Bethnal-green E 17 44... K 26
,, street SE . . . 24 43... O 23
Gloucester-cres. Reg.-pk. NW 6 39... I 18
,, crescent W . . 13 42... L 14
,, place W . . . 13 43... L 17
,, road, Kensington SW 21 42... O 15
,, ,, Peckham SE 24 49... Q 23
,, ,, Holloway N 7 39... F 20
,, ,, Hackney E . 10 40... H 27
,, ,, Regent's-pk. NW 6 39... I 17
,, street, Portman-sq. W 14 43... L 17
,, ,, Clerkenwell EC 16 43... K 21
,, ,, Pimlico SW 22 48... P 18
,, ,, Queen's-sq. WC 15 43... L 20
,, square W . . . 13 42... L 16
,, terrace, Reg.-pk. NW 6 43... J 18

Gloucester-terr., Westb.pk. W 13 42... L 15
Glyn rd, E . . . . 10 40... G 27
Glyndon-rd, Woolwich . — 50... P 37
Godliman-st, EC . . . 16 43... M 22
Godolphin-road W . . 20 42... N 11
Golborne-road W . . 12 42... L 12
Golden-lane, Old-street EC 16 43... K 22
,, square, Regent-st. W 14 43... M 19
Goldhawke-road W . . 20 42... N 11
Goldhurst-road NW . . 5 38... I 15
Goldington-crescent NW . 7 43... J 19
,, street NW. . 7 43... J 19
Goldney-rd, W . . . 13 42... K 14
Goldsmith-road . . . — 40... E 29
,, row E . . . 9 43... J 25
,, street, EC . . 16 43... L 22
Goldworth-road . . . — 40... D 31
Gomm-road, Deptford SE 25 44... O 26
Goodge-st., Tott.-Court-rd. W 15 43... L 19
Goodinge-road, N . . 7 39... H 20
Goodrich-road SE . . — 49... U 24
Goose-green SE . . . 32 49... T 24
Gopsall-street, Hoxton N . 8 43... J 23
Gordon-house-rd, NW . 6 38... G 18
Gordon-road N . . . 8 40... G 24
,, ,, Peckham SE . 32 49... S 25
,, ,, West Ealing — 41... L 4
,, square WC . . 15 43... K 19
,, street WC . . 15 43... K 19
Gore-road E . . . . 9 40... I 26
Goring-street, London-fields E 9 40... I 25
Gospel-oak-crescent, NW . 6 39... G 17
Gossett-street, Bethnal-gr. E 17 44... K 25
Goswell-road EC . . 16 43... K 22
Gough-st., Gray's Inn-rd. WC 15 43... K 21
,, square EC . . 15 43... L 21
Goulston-street, Whitecha'l E 17 44... L 24
Goulton-road, E . . . 9 40... G 26
Gower-street WC . . . 15 43... K 19
Gowrie-road SW. . . 30 48... S 17
Gracechurch-street EC . 16 43... M 23
Grafton-road E . . . 17 44... K 27
,, ,, Holloway N 7 39... F 20
,, st., Fitzroy-sq. WC 14 43... K 19
,, st., Soho WC . 15 43... M 19
,, ,, E . . . 18 44... K 27
,, ,, Albemarle-st. W 14 43... M 18
,, ,, Kentish Town NW 6 39... H 18
Graham-road, Dalston E . 9 40... H 25
,, ,, Wimbledon — 52... Z 13
,, street, City-rd, N . 16 43... J 22
Granby-st., Hampstead-rd. NW 14 43... J 18
Grand Junction-road W . 13 42... L 16
Grange (The). SE . . 24 44... O 24
,, ,, Ealing . — 41... M 5
Grange-road, Canonbury N 8 39... H 22
,, ,, Stoke Newington N 8 39... G 23
,, road Bermondsey SE 25 44... O 24
,, ,, Leyton . — 40... E 29
,, ,, Plaistow . — 45... K 31
,, ,, Thornton-hth — 57... A 28
Grange-park-road . . — 40... E 29
,, walk, SE . . . 24 44... O 24
,, street, Hoxton N . 8 43... J 23
Grant-road SW . . . 30 47... S 16
Granville-square WC . 15 43... K 21
,, place W . . . 14 43... M 17
,, park SE . . . 34 49... S 30
,, road SW . . . — 47... U 13
,, ,, Child's-hill NW — 38... F 13
,, ,, Hornsey N . 2 39... E 20
,, ,, Walthamstow — 40... D 29
,, ,, N . . . 2 39... F 20
Grave-lane, Southwark SE 24 43... N 22
Gravel-pit-lane, Eltham . — 50... U 37
Gravel-pit-wood . . — 36... C 17
Grayling-road N . . . 2 39... F 23
Gray's-Inn WC . . . 15 43... L 21
Gray's-Inn-road WC . . 15 43... L 21
Grayshott-road SW . . 30 48... S 17
Great Alie-street E . . 17 44... M 24
Great Bell-alley EC . . 16 43... L 23
,, Cambridge-st., Hack'y. E 9 44... J 24
,, Castle-st, W . . 14 43... L 18
,, Chart-st, N . . 16 43... K 23
,, Chapel-st., Westm'r. SW 23 43... O 19
,, College-street NW . 6 39... I 19
,, ,, ,, Westm'r. SW 23 43... O 20
,, Coram-street WC . 15 43... K 20
,, Cumberland-pl. W . 14 43... L 17
,, Dover-street SE . 24 43... O 23
,, Earl-st, WC . . 15 43... M 19
,, Eastern-square E . 17 44... L 25
,, ,, street EC . 16 43... K 23
,, George-street SW . 23 43... N 19
,, Guildford-street EC . 16 43... N 22
,, Hermitage-st, E . 25 44... N 25
,, James-st, WC . . 15 43... L 20
,, ,, ,, N . . 16 43... J 23
,, Marlboro'-street W . 14 43... M 19
,, Marylebone-street W 14 43... L 18
,, New-st, EC . . 15 43... L 21
,, Newport-st, WC . 15 43... M 19
,, Ormond-street WC . 15 43... L 20
,, Percy-st, WC . . 15 43... J 21
,, Peter-street SW . 23 43... O 19
,, Portland-street W . 14 43... L 18
,, Prescott-street E . 17 44... M 24
,, Pulteney street W . 15 43... M 19
,, Queen-street WC . 15 43... L 20
,, Russell-street WC . 15 43... L 09
,, Saffron-hill EC . . 15 43... L 11
,, St. Andrews-st, WC . 15 43... M 20
,, St. Thomas Apostle, EC 16 43... M 22
,, St. Helen's, Bishopgt. EC 15 43... M 23
,, Scotland-yard, SW . 15 43... N 20
,, Smith-st., Westm'r. SW 23 43... O 19
,, Stanhope-street W . 14 43... N 17
,, Suffolk-street SE . 24 43... N 22
,, Sutton-st. Goswell-rd. EC 16 43... K 22
,, Titchfield-street W . 14 43... L 18
,, Tower-hill EC . . 16 44... M 24

9-in. 4-in. sht. sht.mar.

Great Tower-street EC . 16 43...M 24
,, Western-road W . 12 42...L 13
,, Wild-street WC . 15 43...L 20
,, Winchester-street EC 16 43...L 23
,, Windmill-street W . 15 43...M 19
Greek-street, Soho-sq. W . 15 43...M 19
Green (The), Hampton . — 56...Z 1
,, ,, Mortlake . — 46...S 8
,, ,, West Wickham — 58...D 29
Green-lane, Finchley N . — 35...B 15
,, ,, N . . . 8 39...G 23
,, lanes, Wood-green N — 36...O 22
,, ,, Bowes-park — 36...A 21
,, park SW . . 22 43...N 18
,, street, Bethnal-gr. E 17 44...K 26
,, ,, WC 15 43...M 19
,, ,, Park-lane W . 14 43...M 7
,, ,, Plaistow — 45...J 33
Greenfield-st., Commer.-rd. E 17 44...L 25
Greengate st, Plaistow — 45...K 33
Greenhill-grove, Little Ilford — 45...H 35
Greenhill-road NW . 5 38...G 15
Greenland Dock SE . 26 44...O 27
Green-side, Richmond . — 46...T 4
Greenwich-park SE . 34 49...R 30
,, road SE . 33 49...R 29
Greenwood-road, Dalston E 9 40...H 25
Greffield-rd, Acton . — 41...M 6
Grenville-place SW . 21 42...O 15
Gresham-ho, Old-broad-st, EC 16 43...L 23
, street, EC . 16 43...L 22
,, road, Brixton SW 31 48...S 21
Greville-road NW . 5 38...I 14
Greville-place NW . 5 42...J 14
Greyhound-lane SW . — 53...Z 19
,, ,, W . 28 47...Q 12
Griffith-road . . — 52...Z 13
Griffin-rd, Woolwich . — 50...P 38
Grocers-hall-court, EC 16 43...M 23
Groombridge-road E . 10 40...I 27
Grosvenor-crescent SW . 22 43...N 17
,, gardens SW . 22 43...O 18
,, gate, Hyde-park W 14 43...M 17
,, park, Camberwell SE 24 48...Q 22
,, place, Hyde-pk. SW 22 43...N 18
,, road, Pimlico SW 22 48...P 18
,, road, Highbury N 8 39...H 22
,, square W . 14 43...M 17
,, st., Camberwell SE 24 48...Q 22
,, ,, Grosvenor-sq. W 14 43...M 18
,, ,, Stepney E . 18 44...M 27
,, hill . . . — 52...Y 12
,, park-road . — 40...D 29
Grove (the) Stratford E . 11 40...H 31
,, ,, Spring-grove — 46...R 1
,, ,, Hammersm. W 20 42...O 11
,, ,, Wandsworth SW — 47...U 14
Grove-lane, Hackney E . 9 40...H 25
,, ,, Camberwell SE 32 48...R 23
,, ,, Kingston . — 56...Z 5
,, ,, Stamford-hill N 2 40...E 24
,, Green-lane E . — 40...F 31
,, road, N . . 2 39...F 20
,, ,, St.John's wood NW 13 42...K 16
,, ,, Balham SW . — 53...V 18
,, ,, Brixton SW . 31 48...R 21
,, ,, Clapham-junc. SW 30 47...S 16
,, ,, Dartmouth-pk. 6 39...F 18
,, ,, Dulwich SE . 32 49...T 23
,, ,, Ealing . . — 41...M 5
,, ,, Kingston . — 56...Z 4
,, ,, Stamford-hill N 3 40...E 24
,, ,, Victoria-park E 10 44...J 27
,, ,, Walthamstow — 40...D 30
,, end-rd.St.Jn's.-wd.NW 13 42...J 15
,, hill-road, SE . 32 49...S 24
,, park-road SE . 32 49...S 24
,, st., Commercial-rd E 17 44...M 25
,, street, Deptford, SE 26 49...P 27
,, vale, Dulwich SE . 32 49...T 23
Grundy-street E . 18 44...M 29
Guildford-road SW . 31 48...R 20
,, ,, Greenwich SE 33 49...R 29
,, ,, Poplar E . 18 44...L 29
,, st., Gray's I.-rd. WC 15 43...K 20
,, ,, Southwark SE 24 43...N 22
Guildhall-chambers EC . 16 43...L 23
Gun-lane, Limehouse E . 18 44...M 28
Gunnersbury-la, Acton . — 41...N 7
Gunter-grove, Fulham SW 21 47...Q 15
Gunterstone-road SW . 28 47...P 12
Gurney-road, Stratford E 11 40...H 31
,, street SE . 24 43...O 22
Gutter-lane, Cheapside EC 16 43...L 22
Gwenow-road SW . 28 47...P 12

H

Haberdasher-st, N . . 16 44...J 23
Hackford-road SW . 31 48...R 21
Hackney-downs E . 9 40...G 25
,, road E . 17 44...J 25
,, wick E . 10 40...H 27
Haddo-street, Greenwich SE 27 49...Q 29
Hagger-lane . . — 37...B 30
Haggerston-road E . 9 44...J 24
Hainault-road E . . — 40...E 30
Haines-street, SW . 22 48...Q 19
Haldane-road SW . 28 47...Q 13
Hale-street, Poplar E . 18 44...M 29
Halfmoon-lane SE . — 48...U 22
,, street, Piccadilly W 14 43...N 18
Haling-pk-rd, Croydon . — 57...G 21
Halkin-street, Belg. sq. SW 22 43...N 17
Hall-lane NW . . — 35...A 10
,, road NW . . 13 42...K 15
,, ,, N . . . — 39...D 20
,, street, City-rd, N . 16 43...J 22
Halliford-street, Islington N 8 39...I 23
Hallville-street E . 19 44...M 31
Halton-road, Canonbury N 8 39...I 22
Ham-fields . . . — 51...W 3

Ham-road, Kingston . — 56...Z 4
Ham Frith-road E . 11 45...H 32
Hamilton-place, Piccadilly W 22 43...N 18
,, road SE . — 53...X 23
,, ,, Highbury, N 8 39...G 22
,, ,, Ealing . — 46...L 5
,, ,, Brentford . — 46...P 4
,, st., Camden-tn. NW 6 39...I 18
,, ter., Edge.-rd. NW 13 42...J 15
Hamlet-road SE . — 54...Z 24
Hammersmith-bridge SW. 28 47...P 11
,, road SW . 28 42...O 12
Hammond-st., Kentish-tn. NW 6 39...H 19
Hampden-road, Musl-hill N — 36...A 18
,, st., St. Pancras NW 15 43...J 19
Hampstead-heath NW . 5 38...F 15
,, lane NW . 1 38...E 16
,, road NW . 14 43...K 19
,, Hill-gar. NW 5 38...G 16
Hampton-bridge . . — 56...Z 1
,, road, Teddington — 51...X 1
,, ,, Twickenham — 51...W 1
Hamsell-st, EC . . 16 43...L 22
Hanbury-road N . . — 36...O 21
,, street E . 17 44...L 25
Handley road E . . 9 40...I 26
Hangers-lane . . — 41...K 6
Hanley-road N . . 2 36...E 20
Hancock-road E . . 19 44...K 29
Hanover-square W . 14 43...M 18
,, st., Haverstock-h. NW 6 39...G 17
,, st., Hanover-sq. W 14 43...M 18
,, st., Islington N . 16 43...J 22
,, ter., Regent's-pk. NW 14 42...K 16
Hans-place, Sloane-street SW 22 43...O 17
Harder-road SE . . 32 49...R 25
Harding-street E . . 17 44...M 26
Hardy-road SE . . 27 50...Q 32
Harefield-rd, SE . . 33 49...S 28
Hare-street, Bethnal-green E 17 44...K 24
Harewood-square NW . 14 42...K 16
Harford-street E . . 18 44...L 27
Hargrave-park-road N . 2 39...F 18
,, road N . 2 39...F 19
Haringay-park N . . 2 39...D 20
Harivar-st., Hackney-road E 16 44...J 24
Harlesden-green NW . — 42...J 10
Harleyford-road, Vauxhall SE 23 48...P 20
Harley-rd., St.John's-wd. NW 5 38...I 16
,, st., Cavendish-sq. W 14 43...L 18
,, ,, Bow-road E . 18 44...K 28
Harman-st., Kingsland-rd. N 16 44...J 24
Harmwood-street NW . 6 39...H 18
Harold-rd, Plaistow . — 45...J 33
Haroldstone-road SW . 21 42...O 14
Harp-lane EC . . 16 43...M 23
Harper-road . . . 24 43...O 22
Harrington-rd, Kensington SW 21 42...O 15
Harrison-st., Gray's Inn-rd. WC 15 43...K 20
Harrow-green E . . 11 40...G 31
,, lane, E . . 11 40...F 31
,, road W . . 13 42...K 17
Harrogate-rd., Victoria-pk. E 10 40...I 24
Hartham-rd, N . . 7 39...G 20
Hart-street, Bloomsbury WC 15 43...L 20
,, ,, WC . . 15 43...M 20
Hartfield-road . . — 52...Z 13
Hartington-road SW . 23 48...Q 20
Hartley-street E . . 17 44...J 26
Harvist-road N . . 7 39...G 21
Harwood-road, Fulham SW 21 47...Q 14
Haslemere-rd. . . — 39...D 20
Hassard-st, E . . 17 44...J 24
Hassett-road E . . 10 40...H 27
Hastings street WC . 15 43...K 20
Hatcham-park-road SE 33 49...R 27
,, rd., Old Kent-rd. SE 25 49...Q 26
Hatfield-street SE . 15 43...M 21
Hatherley-rd, Sidcup . — 55...X 39
Hatton-garden EC . 15 43...L 21
,, wall EC . 15 43...K 21
Havelock-terrace SW . 31 48...R 18
,, st., Caledonian-rd. N 7 39...I 20
Haven-green, Ealing . — 41...L 5
Haverstock-hill NW . 6 39...H 17
,, terrace, NW . 6 39...H 16
,, grove NW . 6 39...H 17
,, road NW . 6 39...G 17
Havil-street SE . . 32 48...R 23
Hawks-road . . . — 56...Z 5
Hawkesley-road N . 8 39...F 23
Hawkstone-rd., Dept.L.rd. SE 26 49...P 26
Hawley-crescent NW . 6 39...I 18
,, road NW . 6 39...I 18
Hawthorne-grove SE . — 54...Z 25
Hay-lane NW . . — 35...B 8
Haydon-square E . 17 44...M 24
Haydon's-lane . . — 52...Y 14
Haydon's-road . . — 52...Z 4
Haymarket SW . . 15 43...M 19
Hayne-street E . . 16 43...L 22
Hayter-road SW . — 48...T 20
Hazelrigge-road SW . 31 48...T 19
Hazelville-road N . 2 39...E 19
Hazelwood-crescent W . 12 42...K 13
Heath-road SW . . 31 48...S 18
,, ,, Thornton-hth — 57...A 22
,, ,, Twickenham — 51...V 2
,, street NW . 5 38...F 15
,, ,, Barking . — 45...J 37
Heathland-rd, N . . 3 39...E 23
Heaton-road, Peckham SE 32 49...S 25
Heber-road SE . . — 49...U 24
Hemingford-road Islington N 7 39...I 21
Hemmings-row, WC . 15 43...M 19
Hemstall-road NW . 5 38...H 14
Hemsworth-street, Hoxton N 8 43...J 23
Hendon-lane NW . — 35...B 13
,, road NW . — 38...D 13
Henniker-road, Stratford E 11 40...H 30
Henrietta-st., Cavendish-sq. W 14 43...L 18
,, ,, Covent-gard. WC 15 43...M 20

Henry-street, Pentonville N 15 43...J 21
,, ,, Regent's-pk. NW 5 42...J 16
Henshaw-street SE . 24 43...O 23
Hensloe-road SE . . — 49...U 25
Henson-street, Bishopsgate EC 16 43...L 23
Herbert-rd, Woolwich . — 50...Q 36
,, ,, Grove-pk . — 55...X 33
,, st., New North-rd. N 16 43...J 23
Hercules-bldngs, Lambeth SE 23 43...O 21
,, passage EC . 16 43...M 23
Hereford-gardens, W . 14 43...M 17
Hereford-road, Westb.-pk. W 13 42...L 14
,, square SW . 21 47...P 15
Hermes-street, Pentonville N 15 43...J 21
Hermit-road E . . 19 44...L 31
Hermitage-road N . 2 39...D 22
Herne-hill-road SE . 32 48...S 22
Herries-street, Kilburn W 12 42...J 13
Hertford-street, May Fair W 22 43...N 18
,, road, De Beau.-tn. N 8 40...I 24
Hertslet-road N . 7 39...G 20
Hewlett-road, Old Ford E. 10 44...J 27
High-cross-lane . . — 37...B 24
,, Holborn, WC . 15 43...L 20
,, street, Acton . — 41...M 7
,, ,, Battersea . 30 47...R 16
,, ,, Beckenham . — 58...Z 28
,, ,, Brentford . — 46...Q 4
,, ,, Bow E . 19 44...J 29
,, ,, Camden-tn. NW 6 39...I 18
,, ,, Clapham SW 31 48...S 19
,, ,, Croydon . — 57...E 22
,, ,, Deptford SE 26 49...Q 28
,, ,, Dulwich SE — 48...U 23
,, ,, Ealing . — 41...M 4
,, ,, Fulham SW 29 47...R 12
,, ,, Great Ilford — 45...G 36
,, ,, Hampstead NW 5 38...G 15
,, ,, Hampton Wick . — 56...Z 4
,, ,, Homerton E 9 40...H 26
,, ,, Highgate N 2 39...E 18
,, ,, Islington N 15 43...J 21
,, ,, Kew-bridge . — 46...P 6
,, ,, Kingsland, N 8 40...H 24
,, ,, Kingston . — 56...Z 4
,, ,, Lambeth SE 23 43...O 20
,, ,, Lewisham, SE 34 49...T 29
,, ,, Leyton . — 40...D 29
,, ,, Lower Tooting SW — 42...X 16
,, ,, ,, Norwood, SE — 43...X 22
,, ,, ,, Merton . — 42...Z 14
,, ,, Marylebone W 14 43...L 17
,, ,, Mortlake . — 46...S 8
,, ,, Notting-hill W 20 42...M 13
,, ,, Peckham SE 32 49...R 24
,, ,, Plaistow . — 45...J 32
,, ,, Plumstead E . — 50...P 38
,, ,, Poplar E . 18 44...M 29
,, ,, Portland Town NW 13 42...J 16
,, ,, Putney SW 29 47...T 12
,, ,, St. Giles's WC 15 43...L 19
,, ,, Shadwell E 17 44...M 26
,, ,, South Norwood — 58...A 24
,, ,, Stoke Newgtn. N 9 40...F 24
,, ,, Stratford E 11 40...I 30
,, ,, Teddington . — 51...X 2
,, ,, Thames Ditton . — 56...Z 2
,, ,, Tottenham . — 37...A 24
,, ,, Upr. Sydenham SE — 54...X 25
,, ,, Vauxhall, SE 23 48...P 20
,, ,, Wandsworth SW — 47...T 14
,, ,, Wapping E 25 44...N 25
,, ,, West Wickham — 58...E 29
,, ,, Whitechapel E 17 44...L 24
,, ,, Wimbledon . — 52...Y 12
,, ,, Woolwich . — 50...O 36
Highbury-crescent N . 8 39...H 21
,, grange N . 8 39...G 22
,, grove N . 8 39...H 22
,, hill N . . 8 39...G 22
,, New-park N . 8 39...G 22
,, park, N . 8 39...G 22
,, place N . 8 39...H 22
,, quadrant N . 8 39...F 22
,, station-road N . 7 39...H 21
,, terrace N . 8 39...G 22
,, vale N . . 8 39...F 22
Highgate-Archway N . 2 39...E 19
,, hill N . . 2 39...E 18
,, rise N . . 2 39...F 17
,, road NW . 6 39...G 18
Highfield-road NW . — 38...G 13
Hildyard-road SW . 21 47...Q 14
Hilgrove-road NW . 5 38...I 15
Hilldrop-crescent N . 7 39...H 19
,, street N . 7 39...H 19
Hillfield-rd, NW . . 4 38...G 13
Hillmartin-rd., Holloway N 7 39...H 20
Hill-rise, Richmond . — 46...U 5
Hill-road, St. John's-wood NW 13 42...J 15
,, street, Berkeley-square W 14 43...M 18
,, ,, Knightsbridge SW 22 42...N 16
,, ,, Walworth-rd. SE 24 48...Q 22
,, ,, Clapton-com. E 3 40...E 25
,, ,, Peckham SE 25 49...R 24
,, ,, Richmond . — 46...T 4
,, ,, Woolwich . — 50...P 35
Himley-road SW . — 52...Y 16
Hind-court, Fleet-st, EC 15 43...M 21
Hindman's-road SE . — 49...U 24
Hindon-street, Pimlico SW 22 43...O 18
Hither-green Lane, SE . — 54...V 30
Hoe-street . . . — 37...C 29
Holborn WC . . 15 43...L 21
,, viaduct EC . 16 43...L 21
,, circus EC . 15 43...L 21
Holbrook-lane, Chiselhurst — 55...Z 37
Holden-street SW . 30 48...S 17
Holford-road NW . 28 47...Q 13
,, road NW . 5 38...F 15
,, square WC . 15 43...J 21
Holland-park W . 20 42...N 13

Holland road W . 20 42...N 12
,, ,, Brixton SW . 32 48...S 22
,, ,, Hornsey N . 2 39...E 20
,, street, Kensington W 21 42...N 14
,, ,, SE . . 16 43...N 22
,, Villas-road W . 20 42...N 12
Holles-street W . . 14 43...L 18
Hollingsworth-st. N . 7 39...H 21
Holloway-road E . 11 40...G 31
,, road N . 7 39...G 21
Hollydale-road SE . 33 49...S 26
Hollywood-road, Bromp. SW 21 47...P 15
Holly-park, N . . 2 39...E 20
Holly-street, Dalston E 9 40...H 24
Holmesdale-rd, South Norwood — 57...B 23
Holmsdale-rd, Teddington — 56...Y 3
Holywell-lane, Shoreditch EC 16 44...K 24
,, street WC . 15 43...M 21
Holyoake-road SE . 23 43...O 21
Homer-road, Hackney E . 10 40...H 27
Home-rd, SW . . 30 47...R 16
Homerton-row E . 9 40...H 26
Homestead-road SW. 28 47...Q 13
Honor Oak-rise SE . — 49...U 28
Hoop-lane NW . . 1 38...D 14
Horace-street SW . 23 48...Q 20
Horn-lane, Acton . — 41...M 7
Horn-park-lane, Eltham . — 50...U 32
Hornsey-lane N . 2 39...E 19
,, park N. . — 36...B 21
,, rise N . . 2 39...E 20
,, road N . . 7 39...G 21
Horseferry-road SW . 23 43...O 19
Horton-road E . . 9 40...H 25
Hosier lane, EC . 16 43...L 22
Hotham-st, E . . 11 44...J 31
Houndsditch EC . 16 44...L 24
Howard-road N . . 8 39...G 23
,, ,, Plaistow — 45...K 32
,, street WC . 15 43...M 21
Howard's-lane SW . — 47...T 14
Howes-st, E . . 8 44...J 24
Howland-street W . 14 43...L 19
Hoxton-street N . 8 44...J 24
Hoxton-square N . 16 43...K 23
Hubert-road . . — 52...Z 14
Huddlestone-road N . 7 39...G 19
Huggin-lane EC . 16 43...L 22
Humber-road SE . 27 49...Q 31
Hungerford-road NW . 7 39...H 20
Hunter-street WC . 15 43...K 20
Huntingdon-st., Islington N 7 39...I 20
,, ,, N . 16 44...J 24
Huntley-st, WC . 15 43...K 19
Hurley-road SE . 23 48...P 21
Hurlingham-road SW . 29 47...S 13
Huxley-st, Ken.gardens, W 12 42...K 12
Hyde-lane NW . . — 35...C 9
,, ,, SW . . 30 47...R 16
,, park W . . 13 42...M 16
,, ,, corner W . 22 43...N 17
,, ,, gardens W 13 42...M 16
,, ,, gate, W . 21 42...N 15
,, ,, place W . 13 42...M 16
,, ,, square W . 13 42...M 16
,, ,, street W . 13 42...M 16
,, road, Hoxton N . 8 43...J 23
,, ,, Battersea SW 30 47...R 16
,, (The) NW . . — 35...C 9
,, vale SE . 34 49...R 30
Hyson-road SE . 25 49...P 25

I

Ida-street E . . 19 44...M 29
Idmiston-road E . 11 40...H 31
Idol-lane EC . . 16 43...M 23
Iffley-road, W . . 28 42...O 11
Ifield-road SW . 21 47...P 14
Ilbert-st, Kens-gardens, W 12 42...K 12
Ingestre-road NW . 6 39...G 18
Inglemere-road SE . — 54...X 26
Ingrave-street SW . 30 47...S 15
Inkerman-rd., Camden-t. NW 6 39...H 18
Inner-park-road SW . — 52...V 12
,, temple-lane EC . 15 43...M 21
Inverness-terrace W . 13 42...M 14
Inville-road, Walworth SE 24 48...P 23
Ironmill-road SW . — 47...U 14
Ironmonger-lane EC . 16 43...M 23
Ironmonger-row, Old-street EC 16 43...K 22
Isledon-road, Holloway N . 7 39...F 21
Isleworth-ait . . — 46...S 3
Islington-green N . 8 43...J 22
Islip-street, Kentish-town NW 6 39...H 19
Iverson-road NW . 4 38...H 13
Ivy-lane, Hoxton N . 16 43...J 23
Ivy lane, Newgate-street, EC 16 43...L 22
Ivydale-rd. Nunhead SE . 33 49...S 26
,, ,, EC . . 16 43...L 22

J

Jackson-road, Holloway N 7 39...G 21
,, lane, N . 2 39...D 18
Jamaica-road, Bermondsey SE 25 44...O 25
,, st., Commercial-rd. E 17 44...L 26
James-lane E . . — 40...E 30
,, st., Covent-garden WC 15 43...M 20
,, ,, Adelphi, WC 15 43...M 20
,, ,, Haymarket SW 15 43...M 19
,, ,, Mile-end E 17 44...K 26
,, ,, SW . . 22 43...O 18
Jardin-street SE . 24 48...Q 23
Jasmine-grove SE . — 54...Z 25
Jeffreys-road, Stockwell SW 31 48...R 19
,, street, Camden-tn. NW 6 39...I 18
Jenner-road, N . . 9 40...F 25
Jenning-road SE . — 39...U 24
Jermyn-street SW . 14 43...M 19
Jewin-street, Aldersgate-st. EC 16 43...L 22
Jewry-street, Aldgate EC. 16 43...M 24

9-in. 4-in. sht. sht. mar.

Mansfield-place NW . . 6 39... H 18
,, road, Hav.-hill NW 6 39... G 17
,, st., Kingsland-rd. E 8 44... J 24
Mansford-st, Hackney-rd E 17 44... K 25
Mantua-st, SW . . 30 47... S 16
Mansion House-st EC . 16 43... M 23
Mape-street, Bethnal-green E 17 44... K 25
Maple-road SE . . — 54... Z 25
,, ,, Surbiton . — 56... Z 4
Maplin-street E . 18 44... K 28
Marchmont-street SW 15 43... K 20
Mare-street, Hackney E . 9 40... I 26
Maresfield-gardens NW 5 39... H 15
Margaret-street, Hackney E 9 40... H 26
,, ,, Langham-pl. W 14 43... L 18
,, ,, WC . 15 43... K 21
Margarey-pk-rd, Upton . — 45... H 32
Margravine-rd W . 28 47... P 12
Maria-st. Kingsland-road E 16 44... J 24
Marigold-st., Rotherhithe SE 25 44... O 25
Mark-lane, Fenchurch-st. EC 16 44... M 24
,, house-road . — 40... E 28
Market-road, Barnsbury N 7 39... H 20
,, st., Caledonian-road N 7 39... H 20
,, ,, Edgeware-road W 13 42... L 16
,, ,, East Ham . — 45... J 35
Markfield-road . . — 37... C 25
Markham-square SW . 22 47... P 16
Marlborough-place, NW . 5 42... J 15
,, road, Chelsea SW 22 42... O 29
,, ,, Dalston E 9 40... I 25
,, ,, N . 2 39... F 19
,, ,, NW . 5 42... J 15
,, ,, Tooting SW — 52... Z 15
,, hill, St. J's-w. NW 5 42... J 15
,, square SW . 21 47... P 16
Marloes-road, Kensington W 21 42... O 14
Marlow-rd, Sth Norwood . — 58... A 25
Marmion-road SW . 30 48... S 17
Marne-st, Kens.-gardens W 12 42... J 12
Marner-street, Bromley E 19 44... K 29
Maroon-street E . 18 44... L 27
Marquess-road, Canonbury N 8 39... H 23
Marquis road NW . 7 39... H 19
Marr-road . . . — 40... D 22
Marriot-road N . . 2 39... E 18
Marsh Gate-lane E . 11 44... J 29
,, ,, road, Richmond — 46... T 5
,, lane E. Greenwich SE 37 49... P 31
,, ,, ,, . . — 37... H 28
,, road, Homerton E 10 40... H 28
Marsham-st., Westminster SW 23 43... O 10
Marshfield-gardens . 5 38... H 15
Marsland-road, SE . 24 48... P 22
Martineau-road N . 8 39... G 21
Martin-street, Stratford E 11 40... I 30
Mary-st., Kingsland-road N 8 44... J 24
Marylands-road, Maida-vale W 13 42... K 14
,, ,, Stratford E 11 40... H 30
Maryland Point E . 11 40... H 31
Marylebone-lane W . 14 43... L 18
,, road NW . 14 43... K 17
Masboro'-road W . 20 42... O 12
Matilda-street, Islington N 7 40... I 21
Matlock-la, Ealing . — 41... M 4
Matthias-rd, N . . 8 39... G 23
Maude-grove, Fulham SW 28 47... Q 15
Maury-rd N . . 9 40... F 25
May-street W . . 28 47... P 13
May-grove-road NW . 4 38... H 13
Mayall-road SE . . 31 48... T 21
Mayers-lane E . . — 45... E 30
Mayes-road, Wood-green N — 36... A 21
Mayfield-road, Dalston E . 9 40... I 24
Maygrove-road NW . 4 38... H 13
Maynard-street N . — 35... C 19
Mayow-road SE . . — 54... X 26
Mayton-st. N . . 7 39... F 20
Maze-pond SE . . 24 43... N 23
Meadow-road SW . 23 48... Q 20
Mecklenburgh-street WC . 15 43... K 20
,, square WC . 15 43... K 20
Medburn-street NW . 7 43... J 19
Median-road E . . 9 40... G 26
Medland-st, Limehouse E . 18 44... M 27
Medway-road E . . 18 44... J 27
Melbury-rd . . 28 42... O 13
Melford-road SE . — 54... V 25
Mellison-road . . — 52... Y 16
Melrose-road SW . — 47... U 13
Mentmore-terrace E . 9 40... I 25
Mercers-rd N . . 7 39... F 19
Meredith-st., Clerkenwell EC 16 43... K 21
Merrington-road SW 21 47... P 14
Merton-road . . — 52... Z 15
Merton-road NW . 6 38... I 16
Merton-lane . . — 52... Z 16
,, ,, Highgate N . 1 38... E 17
Messina-avenue NW . 5 38... I 14
Methley-street SE . 23 48... P 21
Meynell-road E . . 10 40... I 27
Meyrick-road SW . 30 47... S 15
Middlesex-st., Whitechl. E 16 44... L 24
,, ,, NW . 15 43... J 19
Middleton-road, Dalston E 9 40... I 24
Middleton-road, Hornsey N — 36... B 20
,, ,, N . 7 39... G 19
,, square EC . 15 43... J 21
Middle-lane N . . — 36... C 20
,, Temple-lane EC . 15 43... M 21
Midland Railway-depot NW 7 39... I 19
Mildmay-road N . 8 39... H 23
,, grove N . 8 39... H 23
,, park N . 8 39... H 23
,, street N . 8 39... H 23
Mile-end-road E . 7 44... L 26
Miles-street, S. Lambeth SW 23 48... Q 20
Milford-lane, Strand WC . 15 43... M 21
,, street SW . 31 48... S 18
Milk-street, Cheapside EC 16 43... L 22
Milkwood-road SE . 32 44... T 22
Mill-lane NW . . 4 38... G 13
Mill-lane SE . . 33 49... R 28
,, ,, Woolwich . — 50... P 36
Millars-rd E . . 11 40... G 30
Millbank SW . . 23 48... P 19
,, street SW . 23 43... O 20
Millbrook-road SW . 31 48... S 21
Millfield-lane N. . 1 39... F 17
Millwall-docks E . 26 44... O 29
Milman-road, Chelsea SW 21 47... Q 15
,, st., Guildford-st. WC 15 43... K 20
Milner-square, Liverpl.-rd. N 8 39... I 21
,, terrace, Brompton SW 22 42... O 16
Milson-road W . . 28 42... O 12
Milton-road N . . 8 39... G 23
,, ,, Old Ford E . 10 44... J 28
,, ,, Brixton SE . — 48... U 21
,, ,, Muswl.-hill N . — 36... A 18
,, street, Dorset-sq. NW 14 43... K 17
,, ,, Fore-street EC 16 43... L 23
Milverton-street SE . 23 48... P 21
Mina-road, Old Kent-rd. SE 24 49... P 24
Mincing-lane Fenchurch-st. EC 16 43... M 23
Minerva-st., Hackney-rd. E 17 44... J 25
Minories E . . 16 44... M 24
Mint-street, Borough SE . 24 43... N 22
Mintern-street, Hoxton N 16 43... J 23
Mitcham-rd, Croydon . — 57... C 19
Mitcham-road . . — 52... Z 17
,, ,, Lower Tooting — 52... Y 17
Mitre-court EC . . 15 43... M 21
,, ,, Milk-st EC . 16 43... L 22
,, street EC . . 16 44... M 24
Moffatt-rd, Thornton-hth — 57... A 22
Moncrieff-road SE . 32 49... R 25
Monier-road E . . 10 40... I 28
Monkwell-street EC . 16 43... L 22
Monnow-road SE . 25 49... P 25
Montague-road, Hackney E 9 40... H 24
,, ,, Merton . — 52... Z 14
,, ,, Twickenham — 46... T 5
,, place, Russell-sq. WC 15 43... L 19
,, place W . . 14 43... L 17
,, square W . 14 43... L 17
,, street W . 14 43... L 17
,, st., Russell-sq., WC 15 43... L 20
Montem-road SE . — 54... V 17
Montpelier-road, Peckham SE 32 49... R 25
,, ,, NW . 7 39... G 19
,, pla, Blackheath SE 34 49... S 31
,, sq., Brompton SW 22 43... N 16
,, st., ,, SW 22 42... O 16
Moor-lane (Fore-street) EC 16 43... L 23
Moore-park-road SW . 21 47... Q 14
Moorfields EC . . 16 43... L 23
Moorgate-street EC . 16 43... L 23
Moray-road N . . 2 39... E 21
Morden-road . . — 52... Z 14
Moreland-street N . 2 39... E 21
Moreton-st., Vauxh.-bg. SW 23 48... P 19
Morland-rd, Croydon . — 57... D 23
Morley-road SE . . 34 49... T 29
Morning-lane, Hackney E 9 40... H 26
Mornington-crescent NW . 6 43... J 18
,, road NW . 6 43... J 18
,, ,, E . 18 44... K 28
Morpeth-road, Victoria-park E 9 44... J 26
,, street, Bethnal-gn. E 17 44... K 26
Morris-road, Bromley E . 18 44... L 29
Mortham-street E . 11 44... J 31
Mortimer-road N . 8 40... I 24
,, ,, Kilburn NW 5 39... I 14
,, st., Langham-pl. W 14 43... L 18
Mortlake-rd, Richmond . — 46... S 5
,, ,, Kew . — 46... Q 6
Morton-road, Islington N. 8 39... I 22
Moscow-rd, Bayswater W 13 42... M 14
Moss-hall-lane, Finchley . — ... A 15
Mosslea-road, SE . — 54... Z 26
Mostyn-road, Bow E . 18 44... J 28
,, ,, Brixton SW . 31 48... R 21
Mottingham-lane . — 55... V 33
Mount-avenue, Castlebar-hill — 41... K 4
Mount Nod-rd. SW . — 53... W 20
Mount-street W . . 14 43... M 17
Mount-pk-rd, Castlebar-hill — 41... L 5
,, Pleasant WC . 15 43... K 21
,, ,, road N. . 2 39... E 20
,, ,, lane . — 36... B 23
,, ,, road . — 36... B 24
,, view-rd . . 2 39... D 20
Mountford-road E . 9 40... H 25
Mozart-street W . . 12 42... K 13
Mulgrave-road SW . 28 47... Q 13
Mulkern-road . . 2 39... E 19
Munster-square NW . 14 43... K 18
,, lane SW . 28 47... Q 12
,, road SW . 29 47... R 13
Murray-st., Camden-town NW 7 39... I 19
,, ,, Hoxton N . 16 43... J 23
Museum-street WC . 15 43... L 20
Muswell-hill N . . — 36... B 18
Muswell-road, Hornsey N . — 36... B 20
Matrix-road NW . 5 38... I 14
Mycenas-road SE . — 50... Q 32
Myddleton-st EC . 15 43... K 21
Myrtle-road, Acton . — 41... M 8
Myrtle-street, Dalston N . 9 40... I 24
,, ,, Hoxton N . 16 43... J 23

N

Nailour-st., Caledonian-rd. N 7 39... H 20
Napier-street, Hoxton N . 16 43... J 22
,, road NW . . 12 42... J 21
Narrow-street, Limehouse E 18 44... M 27
Nasmyth-street W . 20 42... O 10
Nassington-rd NW . 6 39... G 17
Natal-road SW . . — 53... Y 19
Navarino-road, Dalston E 9 40... H 25
Naylor-rd., Peckham SE . 25 49... Q 25
Neal-street, Long Acre WC 15 43... M 20
Neate-st., Old Kent-rd. SE 24 49... Q 24
Neckinger-road SE . . 25 44... O 24
Neeld-road NW . . 12 42... J 13
Nelson-square, Blackfriars SE 24 43... N 22
,, st. Long-l. Bermond. SE 24 43... N 23
Nesbit-street E . . 10 40... H 27
Nether-street N . . — 35... A 14
Netherhill-road NW . . 5 38... G 15
Netherwood-rd., Edg.-rd. NW 4 38... H 13
,, ,, Uxbrg.-rd. W 20 42... N 12
Nevern-road SW . . 21 47... P 14
Nevill-road N . . 8 40... F 24
New Basinghall-st EC . 16 43... L 23
,, Bond-street W . 14 43... M 18
,, Bridge-street EC . 16 43... M 21
,, Broad-street EC . 16 43... L 23
,, Cavendish-street W . 14 43... L 18
,, Church-road SE . 24 48... Q 23
,, ,, street SE . 25 44... O 25
,, Compton-st., Soho WC 15 43... M 19
,, court EC . . 15 43... M 21
,, Cross-road SE . 33 49... R 26
,, Cut SE . . 23 43... N 21
,, Gravel-lane E . 17 44... M 26
,, Inn WC . . 15 43... M 20
,, Ivy-street, Hoxton N 8 43... J 23
,, Kent-road SE . 24 43... O 22
,, King-street, Deptford SE 26 49... Q 28
,, North-road N . 8 43... J 23
,, Oxford-street WC . 15 43... L 20
,, Palace-yard, Westm. SW 23 43... N 20
,, park-road SW . — 53... V 19
,, road, SW . . 31 48... R 19
,, ,, Millwall SE . 27 44... N 30
,, ,, Whitechapel E 17 44... L 25
,, square WC . . 15 43... L 21
,, street, Horselydown SE 24 44... N 24
,, ,, Kennington SE 24 48... P 21
,, ,, square EC . 15 43... L 21
,, West-end, Finchley NW 5 38... G 14
Newborn-st, Plaistow . — 45... L 32
Newcastle-street, Strand WC 15 43... M 20
Newcomen-street, Borough SE 24 43... N 23
Newgate-street EC . 16 43... L 22
Newington-causeway SE . 24 43... O 22
,, butts SE . . 24 43... O 22
,, green N . . 8 39... G 23
,, green-road N 8 39... H 23
,, park N . . 8 39... F 23
Newlands SE . . — 39... T 26
,, road N . . — 36... B 20
Newman-street, Oxford-st. W 15 43... L 19
,, ,, SW . 30 47... S 16
Newport-market WC . 15 43... M 19
Newton-street, Holborn WC 15 43... L 20
,, ,, Hoxton N . 8 43... J 23
Nichol-sq., Hackney-road E 17 44... J 24
Nicholl-sq EC . . 16 43... L 22
Nicholas-street, Hoxton N 16 43... J 23
,, lane EC . . 16 43... M 23
Nightingale-lane, Wapping E 17 44... M 25
,, ,, Greenw. SE 34 49... R 30
,, ,, SW . . — 48... U 17
,, road E . . 9 40... G 25
,, ,, Wood-grn. N — 36... A 20
Nine Elms SW . . 23 48... Q 19
Noble-street EC . . 16 43... L 22
Noble-street, Goswell-rd EC 16 43... K 22
Norbury-hill SE . . — 53... Z 21
Norfolk-crescent W . 14 42... L 16
,, rd. St. John's-wd.-rd. NW 5 38... I 15
,, ,, Dalston E . 9 40... H 25
,, ,, Ball's-pond N 8 39... H 23
,, ,, Tooting SW — 52... Z 16
,, square W . . 13 42... L 16
,, street, Strand WC . 15 43... M 21
Norland-road W . 20 42... N 12
,, square W . 20 42... N 12
Norman-road, Old Ford E 18 44... J 27
,, ,, SE . 26 49... Q 29
North Audley-st., Oxford-st. W 14 43... M 17
,, bank, Regent's-pk. NW 13 42... K 16
,, end NW . . 1 38... E 15
,, ,, Croydon . — 57... E 22
,, ,, road SW . 28 47... Q 13
,, ,, ,, NW . 1 39... F 15
,, grove, Highgate N . 1 39... E 18
,, hill N . . 1 39... D 17
,, Pole-road W . 12 42... L 11
,, road SW . . 31 48... T 19
,, ,, N . . 7 39... H 20
,, row, Park-lane W 24 43... M 17
,, street, Barking . — 45... I 37
,, street, Cambridge-h. E 9 44... J 26
,, ,, Clapham SW . 31 48... S 18
,, ,, Edgeware-rd. NW 13 42... K 16
,, ,, Isleworth . — 46... R 3
,, ,, Marylebone W . 14 43... L 17
,, ,, Poplar E . 18 44... M 29
,, ,, Wandsworth SW 30 47... T 14
,, ,, Walworth SE 24 48... P 23
Northampton-rd. Clerken. EC 15 43... K 21
Northcote-road SW . 30 47... T 16
Northcote-rd, Croydon . — 57... C 23
Northfield-lane, Ealing . — 41... N 3
Northumberland-avenue SW 15 43... N 20
,, park-rd . . — 37... A 25
,, place W . 13 42... L 14
,, street WC . 15 43... M 20
,, st., Essex-rd. N 8 39... I 22
,, ,, EC . 16 43... K 22
,, park N . . 8 39... H 23
,, sq., Goswell-rd. EC 16 43... K 22
Northport-street, Hoxton N 8 43... J 23
Northwold rd, Upper Clapton E 3 40... F 25
North Warple-way SW . 30 47... T 14
,, wharf-rd W . . 13 42... L 15
Norton Folgate E . 16 44... L 24
Norwood-lane SE . — 53... V 21
Norwood Reservoir . — 58... Z 24
Notting-hill W . . 12 42... M 14
,, square W . 20 42... N 13
Nunhead-green SE . . 33 49... S 25
Nunhead-grove SE . . 33 49... S 26
,, lane SE . . 32 49... T 25
,, Cemetery SE . 33 49... T 26
Nutbourne-st, Kens-grn W 12 42... J 12

O

Oak-hill NW . . . 5 38... G 15
Oak-village NW . . 6 39... G 17
Oakden-street SE . . 23 43... O 21
Oakfield-road E . . 9 40... I 25
,, ,, Anerley SE . — 54... Z 25
,, ,, Croydon . — 57... D 22
Oakington-road W . 13 42... K 14
Oakley-cres, City-rd N . 16 43... J 22
Oakley-road N . . 8 39... I 23
,, ,, W . . 20 42... O 11
,, street, Chelsea SW . 21 47... P 16
,, ,, SE . . 23 43... O 21
,, sqre., Bedfd.-nw.-tn. NW 7 43... J 19
Ockenden-road, Ball's-pd. N 8 39... H 23
Odell-street SE . . 24 49... P 24
Offord-road, Barnsbury N 7 39... I 21
,, street ,, N 7 39... I 21
Oglander-road SE . 32 49... T 24
Old Bailey EC . . 16 43... L 22
,, Bethnal-green-road E 17 44... K 25
,, Bond-street W . 14 43... M 18
,, Broad-street EC . 16 43... L 23
,, Brompton SW . 21 42... O 16
,, ,, road SW . 21 47... P 15
,, Burlington-street W . 14 43... M 18
,, Cavendish-st W . 14 43... L 18
,, Change, Cheapside EC 16 43... M 22
,, Compton-street, Soho W 14 43... M 19
,, Dover-rd, Shooters-hill — 50... S 37
,, Fish-street EC . 16 43... M 22
,, Ford-road E . . 10 44... J 28
,, Gravel-lane E . 17 44... M 25
,, Jewry EC . . 16 43... M 23
,, Kent-road SE . 24 48... P 23
,, Montague-st E . 17 44... L 24
,, Nichol-street, Shordch. E 16 44... K 24
,, Oak-lane, Acton W . — 42... L 9
,, Palace-yard, Westr. SW 23 43... O 20
,, Pye-street SW . . 23 43... O 19
,, road SE . . — 50... R 32
,, square, Lincoln's Inn WC 15 43... L 21
,, street EC . . 16 43... K 23
,, Town, Croydon . — 57... E 21
,, Woolwich-road SE . 27 59... Q 30
Olders-hill N . . — 35... A 13
Oldfield-road N . . 8 40... F 24
,, ,, SE . 25 49... P 26
Oldridge-road SW . — 52... V 17
Olga-street E . . 18 44... J 27
Oliphant-st, Kensal-gn W . 12 42... J 12
Oliver-road SE . . 32 49... R 25
Onslow-square, Bromp. SW 21 47... P 15
,, gardens SW . 21 47... P 15
,, crescent SW . 21 42... O 15
,, road, Twickenham — 46... T 5
Opera Arcade, Pall Mall SW 15 43... M 19
Opidians-road NW . 6 39... I 17
Orange-street, Bethnal-grn. E 17 44... K 24
,, ,, Southwk.-b.-rd. SE 24 43... N 22
,, ,, WC . 15 43... M 19
Orb-street SE . . 24 48... P 23
Orbell-street SW . . 30 47... R 16
Orchard-rd. E . . 19 44... M 30
Orchard-street, Oxford-st. W 14 43... L 17
,, ,, Blackwall E 19 44... M 31
Ordell-road E . . 18 44... J 28
Ordnance-road NW . 5 38... I 16
Orford-rd, Twickenham . — 51... W 2
Oriel-road E . . 10 40... H 27
Oriental-street E . 18 44... M 28
Orleans-rd, Twickenham . — 46... U 3
Orme-square W . . 13 42... M 14
Ormond-road N . . 2 39... E 20
Ormsby-st E . . 8 44... J 24
Ormside-street SE . 25 49... Q 26
Ormsley-st. Kingsland-rd E 25 49... J 14
Ornan-road NW . . 5 38... G 16
Osborne-road N . . 2 40... E 21
,, ,, Hornsey N . — 37... C 21
,, street, Whitechapel E 17 44... L 24
,, terrace, Claphm.-rd. SW 23 48... Q 20
Oseney-cres., Cam-nw-twn NW 7 39... H 19
Osnaburgh-street, Reg.-pk. NW 14 43... K 18
,, terrace NW . 14 43... K 18
Ospringe-road NW . 6 39... G 19
Ossian-rd N . . 2 39... D 20
Ossington-street W . 13 42... M 14
Ossulston-st., Somers-tn. NW 15 43... J 19
Osterley-park . . — 41... O 1
,, road . . — 46... Q 1
Outram-street, Caledn.-rd. N 7 39... I 20
Oval (The) E . . 17 44... J 25
Oval-road, Kennington SW 23 48... Q 20
,, ,, Regent's-pk. NW 6 39... I 18
Overbury-avenue, Beckenham — 58... A 29
Overhill-road SE . — 54... V 25
Overstone-rd W . 28 42... O 11
Overton-road SW . 31 48... S 21
Ovington-square, Bromp. SW — 42... O 16
Ox-Gate-lane NW . — 38... E 11
Oxenden-street SW . 15 43... M 19
Oxford-gardens, Notting-h. W 12 42... L 12
,, road, Halliford-st. NW 8 39... I 33
,, ,, Stepney E 17 42... L 26
,, ,, Kilburn-pk. NW 5 44... J 14
,, ,, Islington N . 8 39... I 23
,, ,, Putney SW . 29 47... T 12
,, square W . . 13 42... L 16
,, street W . . 14 43... L 18

P

Packington-st., Islington N 8 43... J 22
Paddensurick-rd W . 20 42... O 10
Paddington-green W . 13 42... L 16

9-in. 4-in.
sht. sht. mar.
Paddington-green-road, w 13 42... L 15
" road N . . 13 42... L 15
" street w . 14 43... L 17
Page-green-road — 37... C 25
Page-street NW . — 35... A 10
" " Westminster sw 23 43... O 19
Page's-lane N . . — 36... B 18
" walk, Bermondsey SE 24 43... O 23
Palace-gardens, Kensington w 13 42... N 14
" " Kentish-town — 56... Z 1
" " terrace w . 13 42... N 14
" gate w . . 21 42... N 15
" road, Sydenham SE — 54... Y 24
" square, Norwood SE — 54... Z 24
Palatine-road N. . 8 40... G 24
Palestine-place, Camb.-h'th. E 17 44... J 26
Palk-road sw . . 30 47... S 15
Pall Mall sw . . 15 43... N 19
" " East sw . 15 43... M 19
Palmerston-buildings EC . 16 43... L 23
" road, Wood-green N — 36... A 21
" " Hornsey N 2 39... F 21
" " Wimbledon — 52... Z 13
Palsgrave-place, Strand wc 15 43... M 21
Pancras-road NW . 15 43... J 19
" lane EC . 16 43... M 23
Panton-street sw . 15 43... M 19
Paradise-road, Richmond . — 46... T 4
Paradise-road sw . 31 48... R 20
" street . . 25 44... O 25
Paragon, Blackheath SE . 34 49... S 32
" New Kent-road SE 24 43... O 23
" road, Hackney E 9 40... H 26
Parchmore-rd. Thorton-hth — 57... A 22
Parfitt-road SE . . 25 45... P 25
Parish-lane SE . . — 54... Z 26
Park-crescent, Regent's-pk. NW 14 43... K 18
" " Stockwell sw 31 48... R 20
" gardens, Haverstock-hl NW 6 39... H 16
" grove sw . . 30 14... R 17
" hill, Clapham sw . 31 48... T 19
" " road, Croydon . — 57... E 23
" lane, Hyde-park w . 14 43... M 17
" " Stoke Newington N 8 39... G 23
" place, Greenwich SE 27 49... Q 30
" " Leyton . — 40... E 28
" road, Stratford E . 11 40... I 31
" " Haverstock-hill NW 6 39... H 17
" " NW . . 14 43... K 17
" " Alexandra-park N — 36... C 19
" " Battersea sw 22 47... Q 16
" " Hampton Wick . — 56... Z 3
" " Kilburn-park NW 5 42... J 14
" " Leyton . — 40... E 29
" " New Beckenham — 54... Z 28
" " New Bromley . — 55... Z 32
" " North, Acton . — 41... N 7
" " Teddington. . — 56... Y 2
" " Twickenham . — 46... T 5
" " Wimbledon . — 52... X 12
" " Wandsworth sw 30 47... T 15
" row, Greenwich SE . 27 49... Q 30
" square, Regent's-pk. 14 43... K 18
" street, Barnsbury N 7 39... I 21
" " Camden-town 6 39... I 18
" " Hyde-park w. 14 43... M 17
" " Southwark SE 16 43... N 22
" " Stoke Newingt. N 3 39... F 23
" terrace, Kilburn-park NW 13 42... J 14
" villas SE . . — 53... X 22
" village East, Reg's-pk. NW 6 43... J 18
" " West, " " NW 6 43... J 18
" Walk, Fulham-road sw 21 47... Q 15
Parker-street, Westminster sw 23 43... N 19
" " wc . 15 43... L 20
Parkfield-street, Islington N 7 43... J 21
Parkgate-house . . — 51... X 5
Parkholme-road E . 9 40... H 25
Parkhurst-road N . 7 39... G 20
Parkside sw . . — 52... W 11
Parliament-street sw . 23 43... N 20
Parma-crescent sw . — 47... T 16
Parnell-road E . . 10 44... J 28
Parsonage-walk SE . 24 43... O 22
Parson's-green sw . 29 47... R 13
" st., Hendon NW . — 35... B 12
Pasley-road SE . . 24 48... P 22
Paternoster-row, St. Paul's EC 16 43... M 22
" buildings EC . 16 43... L 22
" square EC . 16 43... L 22
Patshull-rd., Kentish-tn. NW 6 39... H 19
Paul-street, Finsbury EC . 16 43... K 23
" " West-ham E . 11 40... I 31
Paulett-road SE . . 32 48... R 22
Paultons-square sw . 21 47... Q 16
Pavilion-road, Brompton sw 22 43... O 17
Pawsons-pl, Sth. Norwood — 57... A 24
" road, Nth. Park — 57... B 22
Peach-st, Kensington-grn w 12 42... K 12
Peak-hill SE . . — 54... X 26
Pearson-st., Kingsland-rd. E 16 44... J 24
" " sw . . 30 47... S 16
Peckham-park-road SE . 25 49... Q 25
" road SE . . 32 48... R 23
" " Forest-hill SE — 54... V 26
" Rye-road SE . 32 49... T 25
" grove SE . . 24 48... Q 23
Pelham-st., Brompton sw 21 42... O 16
" crescent sw . 21 42... O 16
" road, Merton . — 52... Z 13
Pellatt-grove N . . — 36... A 21
" road SE . . — 49... U 24
Pelly-road . . . — 45... J 32
Pelton-rd., East Greenw. SE 27 49... P 31
Pemberton-road N . 2 39... F 19
Pembridge-gardens w . 13 42... M 14
" place w . 13 42... M 14
" square w . 13 42... M 14
Pembroke-rd., Kensington w 28 42... O 13
" " Kilburn-pk. NW 13 42... J 14
" " Walthamstow — 40... D 29
" street, Islington N 7 43... I 20

9in. 4-in.
sht. sht. mar.
Pembroke-square w . 21 42... O 14
Pembury-road E . . 9 40... H 25
Penarth-street SE . 25 49... Q 26
Penge-lane SE . . — 54... Y 26
" rd, South Norwood — 56... A 27
Penn-road N . . 7 39... G 24
" street, Hoxton N 8 43... J 25
Pennington-st., Lond.-docks E 17 44... M 28
Penny-fields, E . . 18 44... M 23
Penrose-st., Walworth-road SE 24 48... P 22
Penshurst-rd., Victoria-pk. E 10 40... I 20
Pentonville-road N . 15 43... J 21
Penton-place Pentonville wc 15 43... J 20
" " Newington SE 24 48... P 22
" street, Pentonville N 15 43... V 21
" " sw . 29 47... S 11
Penywern-rd., Earl's-ct. rd. sw 21 42... P 14
Pepler-road SE . . 25 49... Q 24
Pepys-road SE . . 33 49... R 25
Percival-st., Goswell-road EC 16 43... K 22
Percy-cross sw . . 28 47... R 13
" circus wc . . 15 43... J 21
" road, Kilburn-pk. NW 13 42... J 14
" " w . . 20 42... N 10
" " sw . . 29 47... R 13
" street, Tott.-ct.-road w 15 43... L 19
Perham-road w . . 28 47... P 13
Perry-hill SE . . — 54... W 27
" rise SE . . — 54... X 27
" vale SE . . — 54... W 26
Perth-road N . . 2 39... E 21
Peterboro'-court EC . 15 43... L 21
Petherton-road N . 8 39... G 23
Philip-lane . . . — 36... B 23
" road SE . . 32 49... S 25
" street, Kingsland-rd. N 8 44... J 24
" " sw . 31 48... S 18
Phillibrook-road E . — 40... E 31
Phillimore-gardens w . 20 42... N 13
Philpot-lane EC . . 16 43... M 23
" st., Commercial-rd. E 17 44... L 25
Phœnix-st., St. Pancras NW 15 43... J 19
" " wc . . 15 43... K 21
Piccadilly w . . 14 43... N 18
" circus w . 15 43... M 19
Pickett-st., Strand wc 15 43... M 21
Picton-street, Camberwell SE 32 48... R 23
Piggot-street, Limehouse E 18 44... M 28
Pilgrim-hill SE . . — 53... X 22
Pimlico-road sw . 22 48... P 17
Pitfield-street, Hoxton N . 16 43... K 23
Plaistow-road E . . 11 44... J 32
Plashet-lane, Upton . — 45... I 33
Platt-street NW . . 7 43... J 19
Pleydell-street wc . 15 43... M 21
Plimsoll-road N . . 3 39... F 22
Plough-rd., Deptford-lr.-rd. SE 26 44... O 27
" " sw . . 30 47... S 15
Plumstead-common-rd . — 50... Q 37
" rd. . . — 50... P 37
Point-hill SE . . 34 49... R 30
Poland-st., Oxford-st., w . 14 43... L 19
Polygon (The) NW . . 15 43... J 19
Pomeroy-st., New-cross-rd. SE 33 49... R 26
Pond-lane E . . . 9 40... G 26
" street, Hampstead NW 5 39... G 16
Pont-street, Belgravia sw 22 43... O 17
Poole-street, Hoxton N . 8 43... J 23
Pooles-park N . . 2 39... F 21
Pope's-grove, Twickenham — 51... V 2
" lane, Gunnersbury . — 41... N 5
" st, New Eltham . — 55... V 37
Popham-road, Islington N 8 39... I 22
Poplar Walk-road SE . 32 48... T 22
Porchester-road w . 13 42... L 14
" ter., Bayswater w 13 42... M 15
" gardens w . 13 42... M 14
Port-way, West Ham E . 11 44... I 31
Portinscale-road sw . — 47... T 12
Portland-avenue E . 3 40... E 24
" place, Marylebone w 14 43... L 18
" " North SE . 31 48... R 20
" st., Walworth SE 24 48... P 23
" rd., Notting-hill w 20 42... M 12
" " Sth. Norwood — 58... B 25
" terrace NW . 14 42... J 16
Portman-square w . 14 43... L 17
" st., Portman-sq. w 14 43... M 17
Portobello-rd., Notting-hill w 20 42... M 13
Portpool-lane wc . 15 43... L 21
Portsdown-rd., Maida-hill w 13 42... J 15
Portsmouth-rd, Surbiton . — 56... Z 4
Portugal-street wc . 15 43... L 21
Portway, Upton . . — 45... I 32
Poultry EC . . 16 43... M 23
Powell-road E . . 9 40... G 26
Powerscroft-road E . 9 40... G 26
Powis-gardens w . 12 42... L 13
" street, Woolwich . — 50... O 36
Pownal-road, Dalston E . 9 40... I 25
Poynders-road sw . — 48... U 18
Praed-street, Paddington w 13 42... L 16
Pratt-street, Camden-tn. NW 6 39... I 19
Pratts-lane NW . . 5 38... F 14
Prebend-st., Camden-tn. NW 7 39... I 19
" " New-north-rd. N 8 39... I 22
President-st., Goswell-rd. EC 16 43... K 22
Preston-new-road, Blackwall E 19 44... M 30
Primrose-hill NW . . 6 39... I 17
" " road NW . 6 39... I 17
" road . . — 40... E 29
" street EC . 16 43... L 23
Prince Arthur-road NW . 5 39... G 15
Prince of Wales-rd., Kent.-t. NW 6 39... H 18
" " Battersea sw 30 48... R 17
" " terrace w . 21 42... N 14
Prince's-gard., Kensington sw 21 42... O 16
" gate sw. . 21 42... N 16
" rd. Bermondsey SE 25 44... O 25
" " Lambeth SE 23 48... P 20
" " Teddington . — 51... X 1
" " Wimbled.-pk. sw — 52... V 12

9in. 4-in.
sht. sht. mar.
Prince's-sq., Bayswater w 13 42... M 14
" " Kennington SE 23 48... P 21
" " S.George's East E 17 44... M 25
" street, Bank EC . 16 43... M 23
" " Deptford SE 26 49... Q 28
" " Gt. George-st. sw 23 43... N 19
" " Rotherhithe SE 25 44... N 26
" " Hanover-sq w 14 43... M 18
" " Oxford-street w 14 43... L 18
Princess-rd, Croydon . — 57... C 22
" terrace NW . 6 39... I 17
" street NW . 13 42... K 16
Printing-house-sq EC . 16 43... M 22
Priory-road, Wandsw.-rd. sw 31 48... R 9
" " Kew . — 46... Q 6
" " Kilburn NW . 5 38... I 14
" " Muswell-hill N — 37... C 9
Pritchard-rd, Hackney-rd. E 17 44... J 25
Prospect-place, Camb.-heath E 17 44... J 26
" road . . — 40... D 28
" " Sydenham SE — 54... X 25
Provost-street, Hoxton N 16 43... J 23
" road NW . . 6 39... H 17
Prusom-street, Wapping E 25 44... N 26
Pudding-lane EC . . 16 43... M 23
Pulross-road sw . 31 48... S 20
Pulteney-street, Islington N 7 39... I 21
Pump-court, Temple EC . 15 43... M 21
Putney-bridge sw . . 29 47... S 12
" " road sw . 29 47... T 12
" heath sw . . — 47... U 10
" hill sw . . 29 47... T 12
" park-lane sw . — 47... T 10
" vale sw . . — 52... W 9
Pyrland-road N . . 8 39... H 23

Q

Quadrant-road N. . 8 39... I 22
Quaker-street, Spitalfields E 17 44... K 24
Quarter-mile-lane E . 10 40... G 29
Queenhithe EC . . 16 43... M 22
Queen Anne's-gate sw . 23 43... N 19
" " mansions sw 23 43... O 19
" " street w . 14 43... L 18
" Elizabeth-street SE 24 44... N 24
" " walk N . 3 39... E 23
" Margaret's-grove N 8 39... H 23
" Victoria-street EC . 16 43... M 22
" square, Bloomsbury wc 15 43... L 20
" street, Curzon-street w 14 43... N 18
" " Hammersmith w 28 47... P 11
" " Camden-town NW 6 39... I 19
" " Cheapside EC 16 43... M 22
Queen's cres., Haverstock-h. NW 6 39... H 17
" gate, Kensington sw 21 42... O 15
" " place, Kensingt sw 21 42... O 15
" " terrace sw . 21 42... O 15
" gardens, Bayswater w 13 42... M 15
" ride, Richmond-pk — 51... V 7
" road w . . 13 42... M 14
" " N . . 3 39... F 22
" " SE . . 25 40... O 24
" " Chelsea sw . 22 48... P 17
" " Clapham sw . 31 48... S 18
" " " sw . — 52... V 19
" " Croydon . — 57... C 22
" " Dalston E. . 9 40... I 24
" " Kingston . — 56... Z 6
" " Notting-hill w 20 42... N 12
" " Peckham SE . 32 49... R 25
" " Richmond Hill — 46... U 5
" " South Norwood — 58... A 25
" " St. John's-wood NW 5 38... I 16
" " Teddington . — 56... Y 1
" " Victoria-docks — 45... M 32
Queensborough-ter. w . 13 42... M 15
Queensbury-st N . . 8 39... I 22
Queensdown-rd E . . 9 40... G 25
Queensland-road, Highbury N 7 39... G 21
Quex-road, Kilburn NW . 5 38... I 14
Quilter-st., Hackney-rd. E 17 44... K 25

R

Race-course, South Norwood — 58... C 26
Rackham-street w . . 12 42... K 12
Racquet-court, Fleet-street EC 16 43... M 21
Radnor-place w . . 13 42... L 16
Rahere-street, Goswell-rd. 16 43... K 22
Railton-road SE . . 31 48... T 21
Ramsden-road sw . — 48... U 17
Randall's Market E . 19 44... M 29
Randell's-road, York-road N 7 39... I 20
Randolph-crescent w . 13 42... K 15
" st., Camden-tn. NW 7 39... I 19
Ranelagh-drive, Richmond — 46... T 3
" road, Pimlico sw 22 48... P 19
" square sw . 29 47... T 12
Rathbone-place, Oxford-st. w 15 43... L 19
" street E . 19 44... L 31
Rattray-rd sw . . 31 48... T 21
Raven-row E . . 17 44... L 25
Ravenna-road sw . 29 47... T 12
Ravensbourne-park SE . — 54... V 28
Ravenscroft-st., Hackney-rd. E 17 44... J 24
" rd., Beckenh. SE — 54... Z 26
Ravensdale-road N . 3 40... D 24
Ravensdon-street SE . 23 48... P 21
Ravenswood-road sw . — 53... V 18
Rawstorne-st, St. Jhn's-st-rd. EC 16 43... K 22
Raydon-st N . . 2 39... F 18
Rayment-rd., Bow E . 18 44... K 27
" street w . . 14 44... K 12
Raymond-buildgs. G's Inn wc 15 43... L 21
Raymouth-road SE . 25 49... P 26
Rectory-grove sw . 31 48... S 18
" road N . . 9 40... F 24
" " Beckenham SE — 54... Z 28
" square E . 18 44... L 27
Red-cross-street EC . 16 43... L 22
" " Southw'k-st. SE 24 43... N 22

9-in. 4in.
sht. sht. mar.
Red Lion-court EC . . 15 43... M 21
" " square wc . 15 43... L 20
" " street wc . 15 43... L 20
" " " Clerkenwell-g. EC 16 43... K 21
" " " Wandsworth sw — 47... T 14
Redcliffe-gardens sw . 21 47... P 14
" square sw . 21 47... P 14
Redesdale-street sw . 23 47... P 16
Redhill-street NW . 14 43... J 18
" NW . . . — 35... A 8
Redington-road NW . 5 38... G 15
Redman's-rd E . . 11 44... L 26
Redpost-la, Plashet . — 45... I 34
Reedworth-st SE . . 23 48... P 21
Reeves-road E . . 18 44... K 29
Regency-st., Westminster sw 23 43... O 19
Regency-sq SE . . 23 48... P 21
Regent-circus w . . 14 43... L 18
" park NW . . 13 43... J 17
" park-road NW . 6 39... I 17
" quadrant w . 15 43... M 19
" road, Dalston E . 9 44... J 25
" square wc . 15 43... K 20
" street w . . 14 43... L 18
" " Lambeth-walk SE 23 48... P 21
Regent's-canal-docks E. . 18 44... M 27
Regina-road N . . 2 39... E 21
Reighton-rd E . . 3 40... F 25
Rendlesham-road E . 9 40... G 25
Renfrew-road SE . . 23 48... P 21
Renters-lane NW . . — 38... E 12
Reporton-road sw . 28 47... Q 13
Retreat-place, Hackney E 9 40... H 26
Reverdy-road SE . . 25 49... P 24
Reyner-road sw . . — 47... T 12
Rheidol-terrace, Islington N 8 43... J 22
Rhodeswell-road E . 18 44... L 27
Rhyl-street NW. . 6 39... H 17
Richard-street, Islington N 7 43... J 21
Richmond-bridge . — 46... T 4
" gate . . — 46... U 5
" green . . — 46... T 4
" park sw . . — 52... V 8
" " road . . — 56... Z 5
" road . . — 56... Z 5
" road, Dalston E . 8 40... I 24
" " Islington N 7 39... I 21
" " w . . 20 42... N 21
" " Twickenham — 46... U 3
" " Kew . . — 46... R 5
" " Isleworth . — 46... T 3
" crescent N . . 7 39... I 21
" gardens w . . 20 42... N 12
" ter., Whitehall sw 23 43... N 20
" road, Bayswater w 13 42... L 14
" " sw . . 21 47... P 14
" E, Kensington . 20 42... N 12
" st., Edgew.-rd. NW 13 42... K 16
Ridgway, Wimbledon . — 52... Z 11
" pl., . . — 52... Y 12
Ridley-road, Dalston N . 9 40... H 24
Ringford-road sw . — 47... U 13
Risinghill-st. N. . 15 43... J 21
River-street, Islington N . 7 39... I 20
" " EC. . 15 43... J 21
" court-road w . 28 47... P 10
Riversdale-road N . 8 39... F 22
Rivington-st EC . . 16 43... K 23
Roan-street, Greenwich SE 27 49... Q 29
Robert-st., King's-rd. Chels. sw 21 47... P 16
" " Adelphi wc . 15 43... M 20
Robertson-street sw . 31 48... S 18
Robin-hood-lane E . 19 44... M 30
" " " Kingst.-vale sw — 52... X 8
" " road. . — 52... X 9
Rochester-rd., Camd.-tn. NW 6 39... H 18
" row, Westm. sw 22 43... O 19
" sq., Camden-tn. NW 7 39... I 19
Rock-avenue sw . . 28 47... Q 13
" hill, Sydenham SE . — 54... X 24
Rockingham-street, Boro' SE 24 43... O 22
Rockley-road w . . 20 42... N 12
Rockmead-road E . . 10 40... I 27
Roderick-road NW . 6 39... G 17
Rodney-place SE . . 24 43... O 22
" road, New Kent-rd. SE 24 48... P 23
" street, Pentonville N 15 43... J 21
Rodwell-road SE . . — 49... U 24
Roe-green NW . . — 35... C 8
Roehampton-lane sw . — 47... T 10
Rokeby-road SE . . 33 49... S 28
Rokery-street E . . 11 44... J 31
Roll's-road, Bermondsey SE 25 49... P 24
Rolls-buildings EC . 15 43... L 21
" yard wc . . 15 43... L 21
Rolt-street, Deptford SE . 26 49... Q 27
Roman-road N . . 7 39... H 27
" " Old Ford E . 10 44... J 28
Romford-road E . . 11 40... I 31
" " . . — 45... H 33
Romney-st., Westminster sw 23 43... O 19
Rona-road NW . . 6 39... G 18
Rood-lane EC . . 16 43... M 23
Rookwood-rd E . . 3 40... D 25
Ropemaker-st., Finsbury EC 16 43... L 23
Roscoe-street E . . 19 44... M 31
Rosebank-road, Old Ford E 18 44... J 28
" " Hanwell . — 41... N 2
Roseberry-pl., Dalston E . 9 40... H 24
Rosehill-road sw . . — 47... U 14
Rosemary-road, Peckham SE 25 49... Q 24
Rosemount-rd, Acton . — 41... M 7
Rosendale-road SE . — 53... X 22
Rosher-road E . . 11 40... I 30
Rosherville-road sw . 28 47... Q 13
Rosoman-st., Clerkenwell EC 15 43... K 21
Rosslyn-street, Hampstd NW 5 38... G 16
" terrace, Twickenham — 46... U 7
Ross-rd, South Norwood . — 57... A 23
Rotherfield-street, N . 8 39... I 22
Rotherhithe New-road SE 25 49... P 22
" street SE . 25 44... N 26

9in. 4-in. sht. sht. mar.

Rouel-road, SE . . . 25 44... O 24
Rounton-road E . . 18 44... K 29
,, road SW . . — 53... V 20
Roupell-st SE . . . 23 43... N 21
Royal-avenue SW . . 22 48... P 17
,, Bot.-gard., Reg't's-pk. NW 14 43... K 17
,, circus, Greenwich SE 34 49... R 30
,, crescent, Notting-h. W 20 42... N 12
,, Exchange-avenue EC 16 43... M 23
,, hill SE . . . 34 49... R 30
,, Mint-street E . . 17 44... M 24
,, road, Kennington-pk SW 24 48... Q 21
,, Victualling-yard SE 26 49... P 28
Royston-street, E . . 17 44... J 26
Rozel-road SW . . . 31 48... S 18
Rudolph-road NW . . 13 42... K 14
Rugon-rd. Fulham SW . 30 47... R 14
Rupert-st., Goodman's-fields E 17 44... M 24
,, ,, W . . . 15 43... M 19
Rushmore-road E . . 9 40... G 26
Rushton-street, Hoxton N 8 43... J 23
Rush-hill-road SW . . 30 48... S 17
Russell-square WC . . 15 43... L 20
,, street, Drury-lane WC 15 43... M 20
,, road W . . . 20 42... O 12
,, ,, Wimbledon . — 52... Z 13
,, ,, Lea-bridge-road — 40... D 29
,, ,, Bowes-pk . — ... A 20
Russia-lane, Bethnal-green E 17 44... J 26
Rust-sq. SE . . . 24 48... Q 22
Rutland-gate SW . . 21 42... N 16
,, road, Victoria-pk. E 9 40... I 26
,, st., Hampst.-rd. NW 14 43... J 18
,, ,, Whitechapel E 17 44... L 25
Ryde-vale-road SW . . — 53... W 18
Rye-lane, Peckham SE . 32 49... S 25
Ryllett-rd W . . . — 42... N 10
Rylston-road SW . . 28 47... Q 17

S

Sabine-road SW . . . 30 48... S 17
Sackville-street W . . 14 43... M 19
Salcott-road SW . . — 47... T 16
Salisbury-court EC . . 15 43... M 21
,, road E . . 9 40... H 25
,, street WC . . 15 43... M 20
,, ,, Hoxton N 8 43... J 23
,, ,, Lisson-gr. NW 13 42... K 16
,, square, Fleet-st. EC 15 43... M 21
Salmon-lane, Limehouse E 18 44... M 27
Salters-hill SE . . . — 53... Y 22
Samuel-st, Woolwich . — 50... P 35
Sancroft-st SE . . . 23 48... P 21
Sandall-road NW . . 7 39... H 19
Sandbourne-road SE . . 33 49... S 27
Sandbrook-rd N . . . 8 39... F 23
Sandell-street E . . 11 44... J 31
Sandringham-road E . 9 40... H 25
Sands-end-lane SW . . 30 47... R 14
Sandy-hill rd., Woolwich . — 50... P 32
,, lane, Kew . . — 46... R 6
,, ,, Teddington . — 56... Y 2
Sardinia-st WC . . . 15 43... L 10
Saunders-lane NW . . — 35... A 12
Savernake-road NW . . 6 39... G 17
Saville-row W . . . 14 43... M 18
Savona-street SW . . 22 48... Q 18
Savoy-street WC . . 15 43... M 20
Saxon-road, Old Ford E . 18 44... J 28
,, ,, Selhurst . — 57... B 23
Scarsdale-road SE . . 24 48... Q 23
,, villas W . . 21 42... O 14
Scawfell-st., Hackney-rd. E 17 44... J 24
Scotland-yard SW . . 15 43... N 20
Scrutton-st, EC . . . 16 43... K 23
Scylla-road SE . . . 32 49... S 25
Seabright-st., Bethnal-green E 17 44... K 25
Seamore-place W . . 14 43... N 17
Sebert-rd, Forest-gt . . — 45... H 33
Seckford-street, Clerkenw. EC 16 43... K 21
Second-avenue E . . 11 40... G 31
,, ,, W. . . 12 42... K 13
,, Cross-rd. Twickenham — 51... V 1
Seething-lane EC . . 16 44 M 24
Sefton-street SW . . 29 47... S 11
Selhurst-rd, South Norwood — 57... B 23
Selincourt-road . . . — 52... Y 16
Sergeants' Inn EC . . 15 43... M 21
Serle-street WC . . . 15 43... L 21
Sermon-lane, Islington N 7 43... J 21
Seven-dials, WC . . . 15 43... M 20
,, sisters-road N . . 7 39... G 20
Seward-street, Goswell-rd. EC 16 43... K 22
Sewardstone-rd., Vict.-pk. E 17 44... J 26
Seymour-road SW . . — 47... U 13
,, street, Portm.-sq. W 14 43... L 17
,, ,, Euston-sq. NW 15 43... K 19
,, ,, Lewisham SE 33 49... R 28
,, place, Marylebone W 14 43... L 16
Shacklegate-rd, Teddington — 51... X 1
Shad Thames SE . . 25 44... N 24
Shadwell-road N . . 2 39... F 20
Shaftesbury-street, Hoxton N 16 43... J 23
,, road W . . 28 42... O 10
,, ,, N . . 2 39... E 20
Shakespeare-road N . . 8 39... G 23
,, ,, SE . 32 48... T 22
,, ,, Brixton SE — 48... U 21
Shandy-st E . . . 18 44... L 27
Shardloes-road SE . . 33 49... R 27
Sheen-lane . . . . — 46... S 8
Sheepcote-road SW . . 30 47... R 16
,, lane SW . . 30 48... R 17
Sheffield-ter., Kensington W 21 42... N 14
Shelgate-road SW . . 30 47... T 16
Shellgrove-road N . . 8 40... G 24
Shellwood-road SW . . 30 48... S 17
Shelton-street, Drury-lane WC 15 43... L 20
Shenley-road SE . . 32 49... R 24
Shepherdess-walk, Hoxton N 16 43... J 22
Shepherd's-bush-road W . 20 42... N 11
Shepherd's-bush-green NW 20 42... N 11
,, lane SW . . 31 48... T 20
,, market W . 14 43... N 18
Shepperton-road N . . 8 39... I 22
Sherborne-lane EC . . 16 43... M 23
Sherbrook-road SW . . 28 47... Q 13
Sherriff-road NW . . 5 39... H 14
Sherrick-green NW . . — 38... G 10
Sherwood-street W . . 15 43... M 19
Shield-st SE . . . 23 48... Q 21
Shipley-street, E . . 19 44... M 31
Shire-hall-lane NW . . — 38... D 12
Shirland-road W . . 13 42... K 14
Shirley-church-rd, Shirley — 58... E 26
Shirley-rd, Croydon . — 58... E 25
Shirlock-road NW . . 6 39... G 17
Shoe-lane, Fleet-street EC 15 43... L 21
Shooters-hill-road SE . 34 49... R 31
Shoreditch High-street E 16 44... K 24
Shore-road, Hackney E . 9 40... I 26
Shortlands-rd, Beckenham — 58... A 29
Short-lane NW . . . — 35... A 15
Shrubland-road, Dalston E 9 40... I 25
,, ,, Lea-bridge-rd. — 40... D 29
,, grove E . . 9 40... I 24
Sibella-road SW . . 31 48... S 19
Sidmouth-st., G'y's-Inn-rd. WC 15 43... K 20
Sidner-rd., Stoke Newin. E 9 40... G 24
Sidney-road E . . . 10 40... H 27
,, st., Commercial-rd. E 17 44... L 26
,, square, E - - 17 44... L 26
Silchester-road W . . 20 42... N 12
Silgrave-rd W . . . 20 42.. N 11
Silk-st EC . . . 16 43... L 23
Silver-street, Falcon-square EC 16 43... L 22
Silver-st, Upper Edmonton — ... A 24
Silverthorne-road SW . 31 48... R 18
Silvester-road SE . . — 49... U 24
,, ,, E . . 9 40... H 26
Sinclair-road W . . . 20 42... O 12
Sise-lane EC. . . . 16 43... M 23
Sisters avenue SW . . 30 48... T 17
Sixth ,, W . . 12 42... K 12
Skidmore-street E . . 18 44... L 27
Skiers-street E . . . 11 44... J 31
Skinner-street, Clerkenwell EC 15 43... K 21
,, ,, EC . . 16 43... L 23
Sloane-street SW . . 22 43... O 17
,, square SW . . 22 43... O 17
Smallbury-green . . — 46... R 2
Smallwood-road SW . . — 52... X 15
Smith-sq., Westminster SW 23 43... O 20
Smith-street, Chelsea, SW 22 47... P 16
Smyrks-rd., Old Kent-rd. SE 24 49... P 24
Smyrna-road NW . . 5 38... I 14
Snakes-lane N . . . — 36... A 22
Snow-hill EC . . . 16 43... L 22
Snow's-fields, Bermondsey SE 24 43... N 23
oho-square W . . . 15 43... L 19
Somerfield-road N . . 3 39... F 22
Somerset-rd., Tottenham — 37... B 24
,, ,, Wimbledon — 52... X 12
,, ,, Teddington — 51... X 1
,, street WC . . 15 43... M 20
Somerville-road SE . . 33 49... R 26
Sommerford-grove N . 9 40... G 24
Sophia-rd E . . . — 40... E 29
South-end, Croydon . — 57... F 22
South-grove, Highgate N 2 39... E 18
,, ,, Mile End E . 18 44... K 28
,, place EC . . . 16 43... L 23
,, road SW . . . — 44... V 19
,, square WC . . 15 43... L 21
,, street, Barking . — 45... I 37
,, ,, Camberwell SE 32 49... R 24
,, ,, Finsbury EC 16 43... L 23
,, ,, Marylebone W 14 43... L 17
,, ,, Greenwich SE 34 49... R 29
,, ,, Isleworth . — 46... S 2
,, ,, New North-rd N 8 39... I 22
,, ,, Park-lane W 14 43... M 17
,, ,, Walworth SE 24 48... P 23
,, ,, Wandsworth SW — 47... U 14
,, Audley-street W . 14 43... M 17
,, Bank, Regent's-park NW 13 42... K 16
,, Molton-st., Oxford-st. W 14 43... M 18
,, Norwood-hill . . — 57... A 23
,, Lambeth Road SW 23 48... Q 20
,, Portland-rd, S.Norwood — 58... B 25
Southam-st W . . . 12 42... K 13
Southampton-buildings WC 15 43... L 21
,, road NW . 6 39... H 17
,, row WC . 15 43... L 20
,, st., Camberw. SE 24 48... Q 23
,, ,, Pentonville N 15 43... J 20
,, ,, Strand WC 15 43... M 20
,, ,, Holborn WC 15 43... L 20
South-boro'-road E . . 9 40... I 26
Southbridge-rd, Croydon . — 57... F 22
Southern-lane . . . — 54... X 28
Southerton-road W . . 28 42... O 11
Southey-road, Merton . — 52... Z 14
Southgate-road, De Beau Tw. N 8 39... I 23
,, ,, N . . 3 39... D 22
Southhill-park-gardens NW 6 38... G 16
,, ,, road NW . 6 38... G 16
,, ,, SW . 29 47... T 12
South-pk-rd SW . . . — 52... Z 13
Southside, Wimbledon . — 52... Y 11
Southville SW . . . 31 48... R 19
Southwark-bridge . . 16 43... M 22
Southwark-park-road SE . 25 44... O 25
,, bridge-rd. SE . 16 43... N 22
,, street SE . 16 43... N 22
Southwell-gardens SW . 21 42... O 15
Southwick-crescent W . 13 42... L 16
South-wharf-rd W . . 13 42... L 15
Southwold-rd E . . . 3 40... F 26
Southwood-lane N . . 2 39... D 18
Spa-road, Bermondsey SE 25 44... O 24
Spaniards-road NW . . 1 38... F 15
Sparsholt-road N . . 2 39... E 20
Speke-road, Lavender-hill SW 30 47... S 15
Speldhurst-road E . . 9 40... I 26
Spencer-park SW . . — 47... T 15
,, rd., Breck.-rd. NW 6 39... G 18
,, ,, Brixton SE . — 48... U 21
,, ,, Holloway N . 7 39... G 21
,, ,, Stoke Newing. N 8 39... G 23
,, ,, West-hill SW . — 47... U 13
,, street, Goswell-rd. EC 16 43... K 22
,, ,, Islington N 8 39... I 22
Spey-street E . . . 19 44... L 29
Spital-square E . . . 16 44... L 24
Spitalfields-market E . 16 44... L 24
Spratts-row N . . . — 36... C 23
Springdale-road N . . 8 39... G 23
Spring-gar., Charing Cross SW 15 43... N 19
,, hill E . . . 3 40... E 25
Springfield, Lower Clapton E 3 40... E 25
,, rd., St. John's-w. NW 5 38... I 15
Spurstowe-road, Hackney E 9 40... H 25
St. Alban's-pl., Haymarket SW 15 43... M 19
,, road NW . . 2 39... F 18
,, ,, Sth. Kensn. W 21 42... O 14
St. Andrew-street EC . 15 43... L 21
,, ,, SW . 31 48... R 18
,, hill EC . . 16 43... M 22
St. Ann's-hill, Wandsworth SW — 47... U 14
,, road W . . 20 42... M 12
,, ,, E. . . 18 44... L 28
,, ,, West-green N. — 36... C 23
St. Augustine's-road NW . 7 39... H 19
St. Bartholomew-road N . 7 39... G 20
St. Bride-street EC . . 15 43... L 21
St. Catherine's-rd., Nott.-h. W 20 42... M 12
St. Charles-square W . 12 42... L 12
St. Clement's-road W . 20 42... M 12
St. Donatt's-road SE . . 33 49... R 27
St. Dunstan's-road, E . 18 44... L 28
St. Dunstan's-hill EC. . 16 43... M 23
St. Edmund's-terrace NW . 6 38... I 16
St. Ervan's-rd W . . 12 42... K 13
St. George's-circus SE . 24 43... O 21
,, road, Reg.-pk. NW 6 39... I 17
,, ,, Leyton E 11 40... F 30
,, ,, Pimlico SW 22 48... P 18
,, ,, Southw. SE 23 43... O 21
,, ,, N. Kt.-rd. SE 24 49... Q 24
,, ,, Kilburn NW 5 38... I 14
,, ,, SE. . 24 48... Q 23
,, ,, Upton . — 45... I 33
,, square, Pimlico SW 23 48... P 19
,, street, Ratcliffe E 17 44... M 25
St. Germaine's place SE . — 50... S 32
St. Helen's-place EC . . 16 43... L 23
St. James's-lane N . . — 35... B 18
,, park SW . . 23 43... N 19
,, rd., Rotherhithe SE 25 49... P 25
,, ,, Croydon . — 57... D 23
,, ,, Holloway N. 7 39... H 20
,, ,, Brixton SW . 31 48... S 21
,, ,, Stratford E 11 40... H 32
,, ,, Victoria-pk. E 17 44... J 26
,, square SW . . 15 43... M 19
,, ,, Nott.-hill W 20 42... M 12
,, street, Pall Mall SW 14 43... N 19
,, ,, Islington N 8 43... J 22
,, ,, Walthamstow — 37... C 27
St. John-lane EC . . 16 43... L 22
St. John's-hill SW . . 30 47... T 15
,, street-road EC . 16 43... K 21
,, park SE . . 34 49... R 32
,, ,, N . . 2 39... F 19
,, road, Hoxton N 8 43... J 23
,, ,, Brixton SW 31 48... S 21
,, ,, Clapham SW 30 47... T 16
,, ,, Lewisham SE 33 49... R 28
,, ,, SW . . 29 47... T 12
,, ,, SE . . 33 49... S 28
,, lane SE . . 34 50... R 32
,, ,, Highgate N 2 39... E 19
,, sq., Clerkenwell EC 16 43... K 22
,, street, Islington N 8 43... J 22
,, ,, EC . . 16 43... L 22
,, wood-park NW . 5 38... I 16
,, ,, road NW . 13 42... K 16
,, ,, terrace NW 5 42... J 16
St. Katherine's Docks E . 17 44... M 24
St. Leonard's-st. Bromley E 19 44... K 29
St. Leonard's-rd, Bromley E 19 44... L 29
St. Luke's-rd W . . . 12 42... L 13
St. Margaret-st SW . . 23 43... O 20
,, rd, Twickenham — 46... U 3
,, Drive, Richmond — 46... T 3
St. Mark's-rd., Camberwell SE 23 48... Q 21
,, ,, W . . 12 42... L 12
,, ,, E . . 9 40... H 24
,, square NW . 6 39... I 7
,, st., Gdmn's-fds E 17 44... M 24
St. Martin's-lane WC . . 15 43... M 20
,, le-grand EC . 16 43... L 22
,, place WC . 15 43... M 20
,, street WC . 15 43... M 19
,, road SW. . 31 48... R 20
St. Mary Axe EC . . 16 43... M 23
St. Mary-at-hill EC . . 16 43... M 23
St. Mary's-terrace W. . 13 42... L 15
,, road, Canonbury N 8 39... H 22
,, ,, Hatcham SE 33 49... R 26
,, ,, Hornsey N. — 36... C 20
,, ,, SW . . — 52... Y 12
,, ,, W . . 12 42... L 13
St. Michael's road SW . 31 48... R 20
St. Mildred's-court EC . 16 43... M 23
St. Nicholas-road, Balham SW — 53... W 17
St. Paul's-churchyard EC . 16 43... M 22
,, crescent NW . 7 39... I 19
,, road, Camd.-tn. NW 7 39... I 19
,, ,, Canonbury N 8 39... H 22
,, ,, Bow E . 18 44... L 28
,, ,, Tottenham 37 25... A 25
,, ,, Thornton-h.th — 57... A 22
,, ,, SE . . 24 48... P 22
St. Paul's-street, N. Nth.-rd. N 8 43... J 22
St. Petersburgh-place W . 13 42... M 14
St. Peter's-square W . . — 42... O 10
,, road Mile-end E 17 44... K 26
,, street, Islington N 8 43... J 22
,, ,, Hackney-rd. E 17 44... J 25
,, road SE . . 33 49... S 28
,, ,, N . . 7 39... G 20
St. Philip-road E . . 9 40... H 25
St. Saviour's-rd, Croydon — 57... C 22
St. Stephen's-road, O. Ford E 10 44... J 28
,, ,, W . . 13 42... L 14
,, ,, Castlebar-hl — 41... L 4
,, square W . 13 42... L 14
,, ,, SE . 24 43... O 23
,, avenue W . 20 42... N 11
St. Swithin's-lane EC . 16 43... M 23
St. Thomas'-road, Hack. E 9 40... I 26
,, ,, N . . 2 39... F 21
,, ,, E . . 18 44... L 28
,, Hospital SE . 23 43... O 20
,, square E . 9 40... I 26
,, street, Isling. N 8 43... J 22
,, ,, Boro' SE 24 43... N 23
Stable-yard, St. James's SW 22 43... N 18
Stafford-road, Old Ford E 18 44... J 28
,, ,, Hendon NW — 35... C 12
,, street, Old Bond-st. W 14 43... M 18
,, street W . . 14 42... L 16
,, terrace W . 21 42... N 14
Stag-lane SW . . . — 52... W 9
Staines-rd, Twickenham . — 51... V 1
Staining-lane EC . . 16 43... L 22
Stainsby-road E . . 18 44... M 28
Staithwaite-road SE . . 34 49... T 29
Stamford-hill N. . . 3 40... E 24
,, road . . . — 37... C 25
,, ,, De Beau.-tn. N 8 40... I 24
,, street . . 15 43... N 21
Stanbury-road SE . . 33 49... R 25
Stanfield-st., E . . 18 44... J 27
Stanford-road SW . . 21 47... Q 14
,, ,, W . . 21 42... O 14
Stangate, Lambeth SE . 23 43... N 20
Stanhope-street WC . . 15 43... M 20
,, ,, Hampsd.-rd. NW 14 43... K 18
,, ,, Hyde-park W 13 42... M 16
,, place W . . 14 42... M 16
Stanhope-gardens SW . 21 42... O 15
Stanley-gardens NW . . 6 38... H 16
,, road, Kingsland N 8 40... H 24
,, ,, Teddington — 51... X 1
,, crescent W . . 20 42... M 13
Stanmer-street SW . . 30 47... R 16
Stanmore-street N . . 7 39... I 20
Stanstead-road SE . . — 54... V 27
Staple-inn WC . . . 15 43... L 21
Star Corner SE . . . 24 43... O 23
Starch-green W . . . 20 42... N 10
,, ,, road W . . — 42... N 10
Station-parade, S.Ealing . — 41... N 4
Station-road W . . . 20 42... N 10
,, ,, SW . . 30 47... S 16
,, ,, Norwood SE . — 53... Y 22
,, ,, South Norwood — 57... A 24
,, street, Stratford E 11 40... I 30
Stationers'-hall-court EC . 16 43... M 22
Stebondale-street, E . . 27 49... P 30
Steel's-rd., Haverstock-h. NW 6 39... H 17
Stelman-street E . . . 9 40... G 25
Stephens-road, West Ham E 19 44... J 31
Stephenson-street E . . 19 44... L 31
Stepney-green E . . 17 44... L 26
,, Causeway E. . 17 44... M 27
,, High-st E . . 18 44... L 27
Sternhold-rd . . . — 53... W 19
Stewart-road E. . . 11 40... G 30
Stewarts-road SW . . 31 48... R 19
,, lane SW . . 31 48... R 18
Steyne (The), Acton . . — 41... M 7
Stibbington-st NW . . 15 43... J 19
Stock Orchard-crescent N 7 39... G 20
Stockmar-road, Hackney E 9 40... H 26
Stockwell-park-road SW . 31 48... R 20
,, road SW . . 31 48... S 20
,, green SW . . 31 48... S 20
Stoke Newington-road N . 8 40... G 24
Stone-buildings WC . . 15 43... L 21
,, cutter-street EC 15 43... L 21
Stonefield-street, Islington N 7 39... I 21
Stoney-street N . . . — 36... C 22
Store-st., Tottenh.-ct.-rd., WC 15 43... I 19
Storey-st., Caledonian-road N 7 39... I 20
Storks-rd SE . . . 25 44... O 25
Stormont-road SW . . 30 48... S 17
Stowe-road W . . . 20 42... N 10
Strafford-road W . . 21 42... O 14
Strand WC . . . . 15 43... M 20
Stratford-place, Camden-tn. NW 7 39... I 19
,, ,, Oxford-st., W 14 43... M 18
,, road E . . 11 44... J 30
Strathblane-rd SW . . 30 47... T 16
Stratton-street W . . 14 43... N 18
Streatham-hill SW . . — 53... W 20
,, place SW . . — 53... V 20
Strode-road NW . . . — 38... H 10
Stroud-green . . . — 58... D 25
Stroud-green-road N . 2 39... E 21
Studley-road SE . . 31 48... R 20
Stumps-hill SE . . . — 54... Y 29
Sturgeon-road SE . . 24 48... P 22
Sudbourne-road SW . . — 48... T 20
Suffolk-lane EC . . . 16 43... M 23
Suffolk-road, Dalston N . 9 40... J 25
,, st., Pall Mall SW 15 43... M 19
Sumatra-rd NW . . . 5 38... H 14
Summer-hill-road N . . — 36... C 23
Summers-lane N . . . — 35... A 16
Sumner-road SE . . 25 49... Q 24
,, ,, East Moulsey — 56... Z 1
,, street SE . . 15 43... N 22
Sun-st EC . . . . 16 43... L 23

9-in. 4-in. sht. sht. mar.

Sunny-side, Wimbledon — 52... Y 12
Sunny-side-road N 2 39... E 20
Surbiton-rd, Kingston — 56... Z 4
,, hill-rd — 56... Z 5
,, lane SW 30 47... R 16
,, ,, south SW 30 47... R 16
Surrey-commercial-docks SE 26 44... N 27
,, square, Old K't.-rd. SE 24 48... P 23
,, street, Strand WC 15 43... M 21
Sussex-gardens W 13 42... M 15
,, place, NW 14 43... K 17
,, ,, W 13 42... M 16
,, rd. Holloway N 7 39... F 20
,, ,, SW 31 48... T 21
,, ,, W 20 42... L 13
,, square, Hyde-park W 13 42... M 16
,, st., Pimlico SW 22 48... P 18
,, villas, Kensington W 21 42... O 15
Sutherland Avenue N 13 49... K 14
Sutherland-gardens W 13 42... K 14
,, place W 13 42... L 14
,, rd, Drayton-gns — 41... L 3
,, road, Old Ford E 18 44... J 28
,, ,, West-hill SW — 47... U 12
,, sq., Walworth SE 24 48... P 22
,, st., Pimlico SW 22 48... P 18
Sutton-lane — 46... P 7
Sutton street, East E 17 44... M 26
Swains-lane — 52... Z 16
,, ,, N 2 39... F 18
Swan-street SE 24 43... O 22
Swaton-road E 18 44... K 29
Swinbrook-road W 12 42... L 13
Swinton-st., Gray's-Inn-rd. WC 15 43... K 20
Sydenham-avenue SE — 54... Y 25
,, grove SE — 53... X 21
,, hill SE — 54... W 25
,, ,, road SE — 54... W 25
,, park SE — 54... X 26
,, rise SE — 54... W 25
,, road SE — 54... X 25
,, ,, Croydon — 57... D 22
Sydney-place SW 21 42... O 16
,, street SW 21 47... P 16
,, road N — 36... A 18
Syon-pk, Brentford — 46... Q 3

T

Tabard-street, Boro' SE 24 43... O 23
Tabernacle-st, Finsbury EC 16 43... K 23
,, square EC 16 43... K 23
Tachbrook-street SW. 22 48... P 19
Tadema-rd SW 21 47... Q 15
Tainworth-rd, Croydon — 57... E 22
Talbot-grove, Notting-h. W 20 42... L 12
,, road W 13 42... L 14
,, square W 13 42... L 15
Talfourd-road SE 32 49... R 24
Talgarth-rd, Hammersmith W 28 47... P 12
Tanners-hill SE 33 49... R 28
Tanner-st SE 25 44... N 24
,, ,, Barking — 45... I 35
Tatterdown-lane N — 36... A 17
Tattersall's, Hde.-pk.-cor. SW 22 43... N 17
Tavistock-place WC 15 43... K 20
,, road W 12 42... L 13
,, ,, Croydon — 57... D 22
,, square WC 15 43... K 19
,, street WC 15 43... L 19
,, ,, Cov.-gdn. WC 15 43... M 20
Taviton-street WC 15 43... K 19
Teddington-pk-rd — 51... X 2
Teesdale-street E 17 44... J 25
Telford-road SW — 53... V 19
Temperley-road SW — 53... V 17
Templar-rd E 9 40... H 26
Temple (The), Fleet-street EC 15 43... M 21
,, Fortune NW — 35... C 14
,, ,, lane NW 1 37... D 14
,, mills-lane E 10 40... G 29
,, lane EC 15 43... M 21
,, st, Hackney E 17 44... J 25
,, ,, Blackfriars EC 15 43... M 21
Tennyson-street SW 31 48... S 18
Tenter-street EC 16 43... L 23
Tenter-st., Goodman's-flds. E 17 44... M 24
Tenterden-street W 14 43... M 18
Terrace-road, Hackney E 9 40... I 26
Tesco-road SE 33 49... T 25
Testerton-street W 20 42... M 12
Tetcott-rd SW 21 47... Q 15
Teviot-street E 19 44... L 29
Tewkesbury-rd N 3 39... D 23
Thackeray-street SW 31 48... S 18
Thames-embankment SW 15 43... M 21
Thames-street, Greenwich SE 27 49... Q 29
,, Subway EC 16 44... M 24
Thanet-place, Strand WC 15 43... M 21
Thatchedhouse-lodge — 51... X 6
Thavies-inn EC 15 43... L 21
Thayer-street, Manch.-sq. W 14 43... L 17
Theberton-street, Islington N 7 39... I 21
The Avenue, Brixton SW 31 48... T 20
,, Chase SW 31 48... S 18
,, Lake-road — 52... Y 13
,, Mall, St. Jas.-pk. SW 23 43... N 19
,, Grove, Boltons SW 21 47... P 14
,, Glebe, Blackheath SE 34 49... S 31
,, Pavement SW 31 48... T 18
Theobald's-road WC 15 43... L 20
Thicket-road SE — 54... Z 25
Third Avenue W 12 42... K 13
Third-cross-rd, Twickenham — 51... V 1
Thistle-grove SW 21 47... P 15
Thomas-street, E 18 44... L 28
Thorburn-square SE 25 49... P 25
Thornbury-rd, Spring-grove — 46... Q 1
Thornfield-road W 20 42... N 11
Thornhill-square, Caled.-rd. N 7 39... I 21
,, crescent N 7 39... I 21
,, road N 7 39... I 21

Thornhill-road, Low Leyton SE — 40... F 29
Thornton-hill — 52... Z 12
,, road SW — 52... Z 12
,, road SW — 53... V 19
,, ,, Croydon — 57... C 20
Thorold-street E 17 44... K 24
Thorpdale-rd N 2 39... E 20
Thoydon-road E 18 44... J 27
Thrale-road — 53... Y 18
Threadneedle-street EC 16 43... M 23
Three-colt-lane E 17 44... K 25
Three-colt-street E 18 44... M 28
Three-cranes-lane EC 16 43... M 22
,, mills-lane E 19 44... K 29
Throgmorton-street EC 16 43... L 23
,, avenue EC 16 43... L 23
Thurleigh-road SW — 48... U 17
Thurlow-square SW 21 42... O 16
Thurlow-road, Hampstead NW 5 38... G 16
,, street, Walworth SE 24 48... P 23
,, park-road SE — 53... W 22
Thurston-street SE 33 49... S 29
Tibbett's-road E 18 44... K 29
Tidey-street E 18 44... L 29
Tilbury-road, Plaistow — 45... J 33
Tilekiln-lane, Bowes-pk — ... A 21
Tilney-street W 14 43... N 17
Tite-street SW 22 48... Q 17
Tokenhouse-yard EC 16 43... L 23
Tollington-park N 2 39... F 20
,, road N 7 39... G 20
Tolmers-square NW 14 43... K 19
Tomlins-grove E 18 44... K 29
Tonsley-place SW 30 47... T 14
Tooley-street SE 16 43... N 23
Tooting-bec-rd SW — 53... X 18
Tooting-common SW — 53... X 18
Torriano-avenue NW 7 39... H 19
Torrington-square WC 15 43... K 19
Tostin-street SE 25 49... Q 26
Tothill-st., Westminster SW 23 43... O 19
Tottenham-court-road W 14 43... K 19
,, High-cross — 37... B 24
,, park — 36... A 23
,, road, Kingsland N 8 39... H 23
,, street W 15 43... L 19
Totty-street, Old Ford E 18 44... J 27
Tournay-rd SW 28 47... Q 13
Tower (The) EC 16 44... M 24
,, Hamlet — 37... B 29
Tower Hamlets-rd, Forest-gt — 45... H 32
Tower Royal EC 16 43... M 23
Townsend-lane NW — 38... D 9
Townsend-road NW 5 38... I 16
Trafalgar-rd., Old Kent-rd. SE 25 49... Q 24
,, ,, Dalston E 9 40... I 24
,, ,, Greenwich SE 27 49... Q 30
,, square WC 15 43... M 19
,, ,, Stepney E 18 44... L 27
,, ,, Chelsea SW 21 47... P 16
,, st., Walworth-rd. SE 24 48... P 22
Tranquil-vale, Blackheath SE 24 49... S 31
Tranton-road SE 25 44... O 25
Traps-lane. — 52... Z 8
Trebovir-road SW 21 47... P 14
Tredegar-rd., Old Ford-rd. E 18 44... J 28
,, square, Bow-road E 18 44... K 28
Tredway-st E 17 44... J 25
Tregunter-road, Brompton SW 21 47... P 14
Tresillion-road SE 33 49... S 28
Trevelyan-road — 52... Y 16
Treverton-street W 12 42... K 12
Trevor-sq., Knightsbridge SW 22 42... N 16
Tricon-road SW 23 48... Q 20
Trinity-road SW — 52... V 16
,, ,, E 19 44... M 31
,, ,, SE — 53... V 21
,, square, Boro' SE 24 43... O 22
,, ,, Brixton SW 31 48... T 20
,, ,, Tower-hill EC 16 44... M 24
,, street, Gt.-Dover-st. SE 24 43... O 22
,, ,, Islington N 7 43... J 21
,, ,, Woolwich — 50... O 34
Trundleys-lane SE 26 49... P 27
Truro-road, Wood-green N — 36... A 20
Tudor-road, Hackney E 9 40... I 26
,, street, Blackfriars EC 15 43... M 21
Tufnell-park-road N 7 39... G 19
Tufton-st., Westminster SW 23 43... O 19
Tuilerie-st., Hackney-rd. E 17 44... J 25
Tulse-hill, Brixton SW — 53... V 21
Turin-street E 17 44... K 25
Turners-road, Bow E 18 44... L 28
,, ,, Lee SE 34 49... T 31
,, st., Whitechapel E 17 44... L 25
,, wood NW 1 38... D 15
Turnmill-street EC 15 43... L 21
Turnpike-lane — 36... B 21
Tustin-street, Hatcham SE 25 49... Q 26
Twickenham-rd, Isleworth — 46... R 2
,, ,, Teddington — 51... X 2
Twyford-street N 7 39... I 20
Tyers-street, Vauxhall SE 23 48... P 20
Tyneham-road SW 30 48... S 17
Type-street, Finsbury EC 16 43... L 23
Tyrrell-road SE 32 49... T 24
Tyrwhitt-road SE 33 49... S 28
Tysoe-street, Clerkenwell WC 15 43... K 21

U

Ufton-rd., De Beauvoir-tn. N 8 39... I 23
Ullin-street E 19 44... L 29
Underhill-road SE — 54... V 25
,, st NW 15 43... J 19
Union-court, O.Brd.-st EC 16 9... L 23
,, house-lane E 11 40... G 30
,, grove SW 31 48... R 19
,, road, Clapham SW 31 48... S 19
,, ,, Dulwich SE — 53... W 23
,, ,, Liverpool-road N 7 39... H 21
,, ,, N 7 39... G 19

Union road, Rotherhithe SE 25 44... O 25
,, ,, Southwark SE 24 43... O 22
,, ,, Leyton E 11 40... G 30
,, square, Islington N 8 43... J 22
,, street, Boro' SE 24 43... N 22
,, ,, Hackney-road E 16 44... K 24
,, ,, Lambeth SE 23 43... O 21
,, ,, Mayfair W 14 43... M 18
,, ,, Whitechapel E 17 44... L 25
,, ,, Woolwich — 50... O 36
University-street WC 15 43... K 19
Unwin-road SE 25 49... Q 24
Upcerne-rd SW 21 47... Q 15
Upland-road SE — 49... T 24
UpperAddiscombe-rd, Croydon — 57... E 23
,, Baker-st., Reg.-pk. NW 14 43... K 17
,, Barnsbury-street N 7 39... I 21
,, Bedford-pl., Rus.-sq. WC 15 43... K 19
,, Belgrave-street SW 22 43... O 18
,, Bridge-road, Barnes SW 28 47... Q 10
,, Brook-street, Gros.-sq. W 14 43... M 17
,, Clapton-road E 3 40... F 25
,, Dorset-street W 14 42... L 16
,, East Smithfield E 17 44... M 24
,, Elmers-end — 58... C 27
,, Fore-st, UpperEdmonton — ... A 25
,, George-st W 14 43... L 17
,, Gloucester-place NW 14 43... K 17
,, Grange-road SE 24 49... P 24
,, Grosvenor-street W 14 43... M 17
,, ,, gardens SW 22 43... O 18
,, Ground-st, SE 15 43... N 21
,, Hamilton-terrace NW 13 42... J 15
,, Ham-rd — 56... Y 4
,, hill, Richmond-hill — 46... T 4
,, Kennington-lane SE 23 48... P 20
,, Marylebone-street W 14 43... L 18
,, North-street, Poplar E 18 44... M 29
,, Park-road NW 6 39... H 17
,, ,, ,, SE 25 49... Q 25
,, ,, street, Barnsbury N 7 39... I 21
,, Richmond-road SW 29 47... S 10
,, Seymour-street W 14 43... M 17
,, St. John's-road SE — 50... R 32
,, St. Martin's-ln WC 15 43... M 20
,, street, Islington N 8 39... I 22
,, Thames-street EC 16 43... M 22
,, Tollington-road N 7 39... G 21
,, Tooting-park SW — 53... W 17
,, Tulse-hill SW — 53... V 20
,, White Cross-street EC 16 43... K 22
,, Wimpole-street W 14 43... L 18
,, Woburn-place WC 15 43... K 19
Upton-lane, Upton — 45... H 33
Urswick-road, Homerton E 9 40... H 26
Usher-road, Old Ford E 10 44... J 28
Usk-road, N.Wandsworth SW 30 47... T 15
Uverdale-rd SW 21 47... Q 15
Uxbridge-road W 13 42... M 14
,, ,, Ealing — 41... M 4

V

Vale of Health NW 1 38... F 15
Valentine-road, Hackney E 9 40... H 26
Vanbrugh-park SE 34 49... R 31
,, ,, road SE 27 50... Q 32
Vancouvers-rd SE — 54... W 27
Varna-road SW 28 47... Q 13
Varnell-road W 20 42... N 12
Vartry-rd N 3 39... D 23
Vassall-road, Brixton SW 31 48... R 21
Vauxhall-bridge 23 48... P 20
,, ,, road SW 23 48... P 19
,, st., SE 23 48... P 20
,, walk SE 23 48... P 20
Venue-street E 19 44... L 29
Vere-street, Oxford-street W 14 43... L 18
,, ,, WC 15 43... M 20
Vereker-rd. SW 28 47... P 13
Vernon-road, Bow E 18 44... J 28
Verulam-buildings WC 15 43... L 21
Vesta-road SE 33 49... S 27
Vestry-road SE 32 48... R 23
Vicarage-lane E 11 40... I 31
,, road E 11 40... I 31
,, ,, Waddon — 57... E 21
,, ,, ,, — 40... E 29
Vicar's-rd., Kentish Tn. NW 6 39... G 17
Victoria-bridge 22 48... Q 18
,, Docks E 19 44... N 32
,, Dock-road E 19 44... M 31
,, Embankment WC 15 43... M 20
,, grove, W 21 42... O 15
,, ,, Stoke Newgtn. N 8 40... G 24
,, park cemetery E 18 44... K 27
,, park-road E 9 40... I 26
,, ,, square E 17 44... K 26
,, road W 21 42... N 15
,, ,, Chelsea SW 22 48... Q 18
,, ,, Gipsy Hill SE — 53... Y 23
,, ,, Hendon NW — 35... C 12
,, ,, Holloway N 7 39... H 21
,, ,, Hornsey N 2 39... E 21
,, ,, Peckham SE 32 49... S 24
,, ,, Wimbldn.-pk. SW — 52... V 12
,, ,, Kensington W 21 42... O 15
,, ,, Kentish Town NW 6 39... H 18
,, ,, SW 31 48... S 18
,, ,, Hackney Wick E 10 40... H 28
,, ,, Kilburn NW 5 38... I 14
,, ,, Stoke.-New. 8 40... G 24
,, ,, Surbiton — 56... Z 4
,, street, Pimlico SW 22 43... O 18
Victory-street SE 33 49... R 28
Vigo-street, Regent-st. W 14 43... M 19
Villa-st. Walworth SE 24 48... P 23
Villiers-st. Strand WC 15 43... M 20
,, road NW 4 38... H 10
Vincent-square, Westmstr. SW 23 43... O 19
,, terrace, City-road N 16 43... J 22
Virginia-rd., Shoreditch E 17 44... K 24

Vivian-road, Old Ford E 18 44... J 27
Vorley-road N 2 39... F 19

W

Wadding-street SE 24 48... P 23
Waddington-street, Stratfd. E 11 40... H 30
Waddon-rd, Croydon — 57... E 21
Wadley-road E — 40... D 31
Wakefield-road 37 24... C 24
,, st, East Ham — 45... J 35
Wakehurst-road SW — 47... T 16
Walbrook EC 16 43... M 23
Walcot-square, Lambeth SE 23 43... O 21
Waldegrave-rd, Teddington — 51... X 2
Walford-road N 8 40... G 24
Wallace-rd. N 8 39... H 23
Wallend, East Ham — 45... J 36
Wallwood-street E 18 44... L 28
Walmer-road W. 20 42... L 12
,, ,, Woolwich — 50... P 37
Walpole-street SW 22 48... P 17
,, road SE 33 49... R 27
Waltersville-road N 2 39... E 20
Walterton-road W 12 42... K 13
Walton-street, Brompton SW 22 42... O 16
Walwood-road E — 40... E 30
Walworth-road SE 24 48... P 22
Wandle-road SW — 52... W 16
Wandsworth Bridge SW 30 47... S 14
,, ,, road SW 30 47... R 14
,, road SW 23 48... Q 19
,, common SW — 47... U 15
,, plain SW 30 47... T 14
Wanford-street SW 30 47... S 16
Wapping-wall E 17 44... N 26
Warden-road NW 6 39... H 18
Wardour-street, Oxford-st. W 15 43... L 19
Warham-rd, Croydon — 57... F 22
Warley-st E 17 44... K 26
Warlock-rd W 12 42... K 13
Warner-place, Hackney-rd. E 17 44... J 25
,, street, N 7 39... H 21
,, ,, Clerkenwell EC 15 43... K 21
,, road, Camberwell SE 32 48... R 32
Warple-way SW 29 47... T 14
Warren-street, Fitzroy-sq. W 14 43... K 18
,, ,, Pentonville N 7 43... J 21
Warrender-road N 7 39... G 19
Warriner-gardens SW 30 48... R 17
Warrington-crescent W 13 42... K 15
Warrior-street SE 24 48... Q 32
Warton-road E 11 44... J 30
Warwick-court, Holborn WC 15 43... L 21
,, gardens, Kens. SW 28 42... O 13
,, road, Clapton E 3 40... E 25
,, ,, W 28 47... P 13
,, ,, Kens. SW 21 47... P 14
,, ,, Maida-hill W 13 42... K 15
,, ,, Ealing — 41... M 5
,, ,, SouthNorwood — 58... A 25
,, square, Pimlico SW 22 48... P 18
,, ,, Newgate-st. EC 16 43... L 22
,, lane EC 16 43... L 22
,, street SW 22 48... P 18
Washington-sq, Kingston — 56... Z 6
Water-lane EC 16 43... M 23
,, ,, Brixton SW — 48... U 20
,, ,, Homerton E 9 40... H 26
,, ,, Stratford E 11 40... H 31
,, street WC 15 43... M 21
Waterford-road, Fulh. SW 21 47... Q 14
Watergate-st., Deptford SE 26 49... Q 28
Waterloo-bridge WC 15 43... M 20
,, place, Pall Mall SW 15 43... N 19
,, road SE 23 43... N 21
,, street, Camberll. SE 32 48... R 23
Watery-lane, Foots Cray — 55... Z 39
Watling-street, City EC 16 43... M 22
Watney-street, Commer.-rd. E 17 44... M 26
Wayland-avenue E 9 40... H 25
Webber-street SE 23 43... N 21
,, row SE 23 43... N 21
Weedington-road NW 6 39... H 18
Wegg-avenue, Acton — 41... M 6
Welbeck-street, Cavdsh.-sq. W 14 43... L 18
Well-road NW 5 39... F 15
,, street, Hackney E 9 40... I 22
,, ,, Jewin-st EC 16 43... L 22
Wellclose-square E 17 44... M 25
Wellesley-rd, Acton-green — 46... P 7
,, ,, Croydon — 57... D 22
,, ,, NW 6 39... H 17
Well Hall-la. Eltham — 50... U 35
Wellington-rd, St.J's.-wd. NW 13 42... J 16
,, ,, Bow E 18 44... K 28
,, ,, N 7 39... H 21
,, ,, N 9 40... G 24
,, ,, SW 31 48... S 20
,, ,, Teddington — 51... X 1
,, square SW 22 47... P 16
,, street, Strand WC 15 43... M 20
,, ,, Woolwich — 50... P 36
,, place, St.J's-wd. NW 13 42... J 16
Wells-road N 2 39... F 21
,, ,, Up. Sydenhm. SE — 54... X 25
,, street, Camberwell SE 24 48... Q 23
,, ,, Oxford-st. W 14 43... L 19
,, ,, StGeorge's-in-East E 17 44... M 25
Wenlock-road, City-road N 16 43... J 22
,, st., New N'th.-rd., N 16 43... J 22
Wennington-road E 18 44... J 27
Wentworth-street, E 17 44... L 24
Werrington-st., St.Pancras NW 7 43... J 19
Werter-rd, Putney SW — 47... T 2
West Ham Abbey-rd., E 11 44... J 31
,, Combe-park SE 27 49... Q 31
,, ,, road SE 27 49... Q 31
,, End-lane, Hampst'd. NW 5 39... G 14
,, road NW 5 39... G 14
,, Ferry-road, Millwall E 26 44... O 28
,, Green-road — 36... C 23